BARCODE IN BACK

CTICE

RISK

Social Work Practice with Men at Risk

Rich Furman

COLUMBIA UNIVERSITY PRESS  New York

Columbia University Press
Publishers Since 1893
New York   Chichester, West Sussex

Library of Congress Cataloging-in-Publication Data
Furman, Rich.
Social work practice with men at risk / Rich Furman.
p.   cm.
Includes bibliographical references and index.
ISBN 978-0-231-14380-6 (cloth : alk. paper) — ISBN 978-0-231-14381-3 (pbk. : alk. paper)
— ISBN 978-0-231-51298-5 (ebook)
1. Social work with men. 2. Men—Services for. 3. Men—Social conditions. I. Title.

HV1441.4.F87 2010
362.8—dc22
2009048026

References to Internet Web sites (URLs) were accurate at the time of writing.
Neither the author nor Columbia University Press is responsible for URLs
that may have expired or changed siince the manuscript was prepared.

To my friends—
the oars that steady the boat of self in an often stormy sea—
and my boys, Slick and Brownie,
for the warmth and comfort that made this easier.

Contents

Acknowledgments

The things that we're afraid of are gonna
show us what we're made of in the end.
—Blessed Union of Souls, Hey Leonardo

Aquí, no se rinde nadie.
—Augusto César Sandino

Throughout the years, many men have generously mentored me on what it means to be a social worker, a professor, and, most important, a man. I am grateful to them for their love, support, and kindness, and for caring enough to sometimes kick me in the rear. I have needed it all. Some of these wonderful men include Jerry Finn, Gary Delurey, Mark Whiteman, Kip Wyle, Aram Terzian, David Ishisaki, Tony Bruno, Bob Jackson, and Roger Roffman. Also many thanks to the friends with whom I have discussed some of the core concepts developed in this text, most notably Mark Sokol and Ben Gedalecia.

I am especially grateful to Lauren Dockett, social work editor at Columbia University Press. She understood my vision for this project from the beginning and pushed me throughout to make this the best book it could be. And, as always, my thanks go to my biggest cheerleader, my wonderful wife, Jill. You are, and will always be, my heart.

SOCIAL WORK PRACTICE
WITH MEN AT RISK

Introduction | ONE

This book is about men at risk. It is written by a man for both men and women. As with any practice text, my preferred theories, perspectives, and worldviews are deeply ingrained in the chapters. My professional and personal experiences have shaped the way I see men and what I see as possible for them. Additionally, one can never transcend the influence of one's gender, race, ethnicity, or class. These influences are especially important when discussing gender. As much as I have attempted to transcend my own history and prejudices in providing a balanced view of the strengths and weaknesses, needs and challenges of men, I am certain you will find many blind spots. I am also sure that at times your own gender biases will clash with mine. Disagreements and debates among social workers about important issues are healthy. We all must learn to accept the diversity of thought that exists within the profession (and in society) and to appreciate perspectives that differ from our own. Additionally, empirical research or current thinking from important theorists may challenge your gender biases. The cognitive dissonance that you may experience is an important part of the process of professional growth and development.

Since my frame of reference is important, and since many of the case examples are in part based upon my own social work practice, I think it is important for the reader to understand a bit about me in order to properly contextualize this book. This is only fair, because I view the reading of a practice book as a dialogue between author and reader. However, writing this section has been difficult. Men often find it difficult to know precisely how to express themselves. Some of our internalized expectations as men preclude the sharing of personal information, and certainly the sharing of information about our vulnerabilities. Yet, another aspect of my identity makes it easier for me to be open about who I am. I am a liberal Jewish man from California. Jewish men, even those of us who have been significantly assimilated into the dominant culture, tend to be more comfortable with expressing feelings than those who conform more fully to the hegemonic masculine ideal, a concept I will explore later. I am a 44-year-old heterosexual married man. I am the stepfather of two lovely children aged 12 and 16. I have been with the girls for so long that I often forget that I am not their biological father and usually feel like I am the "real dad." But I do understand the complex issues with which stepfathers must contend.

My close friends are eclectic and diverse. I have spent considerable time working in Latino communities, and I have worked and traveled throughout Latin America. I also was fortunate to have lived in San Francisco for many years and had the opportunity to understand the impact of homophobia on my relationships with other men. I was able to establish deep friendships with gay and bisexual men; this challenged my own notions of masculinity. In so doing, I was compelled to look at my own developing sense of self, and I have since attempted to expand my own notions of what it means to be a man. However, I also recognize the deep and profound effect that homophobia has had upon my understanding of masculine development; I still can hear myself thinking and even saying things that suggest a continued allegiance to certain masculine ideals. Homophobic messages are deeply ingrained in American life. Although society has become more tolerant of nondominant forms of sexuality and identity, childhood messages are often enduring. It is also important not to overestimate the degree of tolerance and acceptance of other ways of being male, as I will explore later.

Philosophically, I strongly support equal rights for men and women but am concerned at the lack of "space" within many feminist spaces for assertive heterosexual men like me. At times I have felt judged by groups of women for expressing myself emotionally and assertively. I have had to learn to balance an appreciation for how women have been affected and even oppressed by the emotions of men with the acceptance of my own very Jewish way of feeling and expressing. The intersections of gender, ethnicity, and power are rarely simple.

In part because of my own struggles with my father, friendships with other men have been extremely important to my growth and development. I have also been involved in men's groups and for years have worked at understanding my own sense of masculinity. My experiences as a man have been both typical and atypical. That I have had experiences and hold ideas that are both universal and idiosyncratic is probably true for all men. Understanding the cultural tendencies of any group must be balanced by each individual's experiences.

While this book is grounded in the empirical and theoretical literature, it is also an outgrowth of my understanding of what it means to be a man, what it means to be a man in social work, and what it means to provide social work services to men. In writing this book I have been forced to grapple with many paradoxes, which I will discuss throughout the book. For instance, how can I write about the risks of a supposedly privileged population? How can I incorporate the valuable analytic lenses of movements that at times have stood in bitter and diametric opposition to each other (for instance, feminism and certain branches of the men's movement)? What are the social and political ramifications of such a book? Most important, how can I challenge and demonstrate the costs of the hegemonic model of masculinity (a dominant model that is held up as the ideal yet one to which most men do not, and perhaps should not, measure up) while showing acceptance, support, and appreciation for men who embody many of these traits?

Grappling with these questions has been personally and professional valuable and serves as a parallel process for practicing social work with men. Those of you who will work with men in the early twenty-first century (and dare I say that will be nearly all social workers?) must also confront these and similar dilemmas. Each chapter includes exercises that I developed and that are informed by the theoretical and empirical knowledge discussed in the chapter, my social work practice with men, and my experience in teaching undergraduate and graduate social work. The exercises are designed to stimulate self-reflection, which I believe to be one of the most important skills that social workers can possess.

Why a Book on Men?

I firmly believe the profession of social work is ready to explore the problems and concerns of men in an open and critical manner. In May 2008 the University of Alabama School of Social Work hosted the first annual National Conference on Social Work with and for Men. This conference brought together dozens of social workers and social work scholars, as well as other practitioners and academics, to explore what we know about social work practice with men. The conference focused on encouraging dialogue about the strengths of men, as well as the normative developmental challenges that men face. Workshops delved into practitioners' experiences and challenges in providing services to this too-often-underserved population.

The notion of at-risk men may be troubling for some in the social work community (Kosberg 2002; Böhnisch 2008). Critics may cite statistics about income or other economic disparities that heavily favor men, such as women's wages averaging only 76.5 percent of men's in 2004 (DeNavas-Walt, Proctor, and Lee 2005). While both men and women experience workplace stress, women experience additional burdens because of the male-oriented culture of the workplace or disproportionate family responsibilities (Blechman and Brownell 1998; Lundberg and Frankenhaeuser 1999). Other authors may carefully explain the well-documented power differentials between men and women (Andersen 2007), clearly exhibited by the prevalence of men in power (Powell and Owen 2007) and by the number of women abused at the hands of men. According to Tjaden and Thoennes (2000), each year women report more than five million incidents of violence against them by their intimate partners. The Commonwealth Fund (1999) reports that, depending on the definition used, two to three million women per year are abused by their significant others. Women who have been victimized by men deserve protection; to ensure that women are empowered and safe, men and society must respond by changing the behaviors of men and the social structures that reinforce violence. Thus women experience many psychosocial stressors more frequently or more severely than men. Men have much to improve in their treatment of women, and in their understanding of and determination to change social structures and personal traits and habits that support oppression and discrimination. These structures must be dismantled and replaced. Further, as Faludi (1999) observed, how can we explore the disenfranchisement of men when the identity of their oppressor is not clear, and when they themselves have been identified as oppressors.

My purpose here is not to argue that men are somehow more at risk than women; the premise of this book is that, despite being more privileged than women, many men suffer deeply. Whatever the root causes of various psychosocial problems that men face, regardless of the degree to which men are implicated in the cause or perpetuation of their own pains, many men are hurting and are worthy of help. It is also clear that many problems that men experience lead them to the offices of social workers, many of whom are not fully prepared to help men resolve their dilemmas. Further, while many men have not experienced oppression, many have. Men of color, gay men, and men of diverse religions and cultural backgrounds have been historical targets of discrimination and have often been disadvantaged when attempting to interact with mainstream institutions. The American legacy of discrimination and racism toward African American men remains one of our most significant blemishes.

Kosberg (2005) notes that the stories of men have not been fully told in the social work or social science literature. Many theories and practices that have been critiqued as being irrelevant to the lives of women may be equally irrelevant to men; gender-neutral practices may ignore the needs of both populations. While numerous articles and books have addressed this problem as it pertains to women, few have done so for men. Cavanaugh and Cree (1996) note a near invisibility of men within the social work literature. The few books concerning men and social work are largely concerned about subgroups of men (Rasheed and Rasheed 1999) or have been written in the context of British social work (Pringle 1995). No current book has addressed social work with men in the North American context.

The paucity of scholarship about men from a social work perspective is troubling, and not without consequences. Sadly, men are often invisible in social development and social work programs designed for the poorest people in the world. In their landmark book on international development, Bannon and Correia (2006) show how men have been excluded from the majority of social development and international aid programs. The reasons for this are valid: women have been disempowered throughout the developing world and need support and programs to help them achieve gender equality. Yet excluding men from this process may have served only to make the most vulnerable, poorest, and most disenfranchised men feel more powerless and subsequently more likely to engage in reactive violence (Gomez Alcaraz and Garcia Suarez 2006). International social development specialists are beginning to realize that men must become full partners in the social development process. It is essential to help men understand the effects of their own disenfranchisement and how these experiences and their reactions sometimes have contributed to their committing violence against women, children, and themselves. This awareness does not excuse men's participation in oppressive and violent behavior; it deconstructs it for them, and it must become part of an ongoing process of change. This approach from international social development may have important implications for social work practice.

An analogous situation can be found in the literature on fathering. Some practitioners and scholars fear that the development of fathering programs will come at the expense of programs geared toward women, and that explorations of the benefits of fathering will be used to diminish the success of female-headed single-parent households (Doherty, Kouneski, and Erickson 1998). However, as Doherty, Kouneski, and Erickson contend, "Only an ecologically sensitive approach to parenting, which views the welfare of fathers, mothers, and children as intertwined and interdependent, can avoid a zero-sum approach to parenting in which fathers' gains become mothers' losses" (277).

Paradoxically, while men may be a privileged group in many sectors in society, as social work clients they are not. In his discussion of services for men who have been raped, Scarce (1997:9) explores many of the complex nuances of power and privilege:

> The more recent gendering of rape as an act of violence against women has occurred for a variety of reasons, not least of which is the fact that approximately 90% of rapes involve female victims. The bulk of political progress and organizational response to rape must be credited to feminist social movement activity since the 1960s, including the understanding that rape is an act of violence and power rather than sexual passion. But where do the 5–10% of rape victims who are male fall in this realm of women-centered knowledge and practice? Very often they may slip through the cracks of an already overburdened and underfunded social service network and a cultural that believes the rape of men to be a laughable impossibility.

Vulnerable men are often misunderstood or pathologized. Men who have a difficult time expressing their feelings are viewed as resistant. Men who express their anger vigorously are accused of being hostile or, worse, abusive. While many angry men are abusive, it is also true that anger serves as a mask for depression for many men (Cochran and Rabinowitz 2000). Men entering treatment are often seen as the generators of their problems and as perpetrators or outsiders. Because traditional male cultural norms make it difficult for many men to seek and receive help, the often not-so-subtle message that men are the problem, or are not wanted as clients, serves only to exacerbate matters. While some men are largely responsible for their pain and that of those around them, it is against the interests of the women and children in these men's lives for social work to engage in practices that make men less likely to seek services and to begin the process of change. Many men need help, and making services appealing, accessible, and effective for men is in everyone's best interest. Social work services that do not treat men with empathy, respect, and dignity may fail to prevent or resolve many of the most severe social problems that social workers are dedicated to ameliorating.

Organization of This Book

The chapters of this book explore various at-risk male populations: veterans, displaced workers, substance abusers, consumers of mental heath services, men with health problems, older men, and other groups. Each group is at risk not only because of the psychosocial dilemmas at the heart of their problems but also because men are often less likely than women to seek help (Baum 2004; Brindis et al. 2005; Spector 2006) and are more likely to underreport symptoms they are experiencing (Robertson and Fitzgerald 1992). Further, men do actually experience many psychosocial dilemmas (Courtenay 2003) and health problems (Arras, Ogletree, and Welshimer 2006) with greater frequency or intensity than do women. I will explore these problems in depth throughout this book but will touch on a few briefly here.

When we state that men are at risk, what do we mean? Greene (2007) notes that risk refers to critical life events that will increase the likelihood that an individual will experience future difficulties. Risks contribute to an increase in stress and a decline in one's capacity for coping. Ephross (2005) contends that people can be placed at risk by a variety of unmet needs and conditions, including discrimination, physical health concerns, personal histories, developmental crises, or acute syndromes. He stresses that what unites these populations is the need for intervention to prevent future harm, pain, or dysfunction. Dudley and Stone (2001:4) provide a simple and useful definition when they define "at risk" as "exposure to loss or harm; a hazard; danger and peril." Examples of how men meet these criteria are numerous. For instance, men are more likely to be victims of all violent crimes except sexual assault and rape (Bureau of Justice Statistics 2005a). The number of incarcerated men has reached epidemic proportions, with more than two million in state and federal prisons and local jails (Bureau of Justice Statistics 2005b). Returning veterans suffer from health and mental health problems with greater frequency and in greater numbers than previously thought (Hoff and Rosenheck 2000); the confluence of their mental health concerns, substance abuse, and trauma has predisposed male veterans to homelessness (Benda 2006) and work problems (Rosenheck, Frisman, and Sindelar 1995). Even problems that are typically associated with women impact men significantly. For instance, approximately 35 percent of people diagnosed with binge-eating disorders and 5 to 10 percent of those diagnosed with bulimia and anorexia are men (Spitzer et. al. 1993; Andersen 1995). Body image dysfunction and body dysmorphia disorder are also problems that afflict many men (Olivardia 2001; Pope et al. 1999). Most significantly, men die nearly seven years younger than women (Courtenay 2000).

Not only are many men at risk, but many also are not well served by the models and programs that are available to them. Most social work programs are not designed to meet the needs of men. Paradoxically, perhaps the same can be said about services for women. Many services do not consider gender to be an important factor in the design of services. Such "gender-neutral" services often split the difference and do not meet the treatment needs of either men or women. These generic services do not take into account the realities of men, nor are the practitioners who work within them trained to provide services to meet the specific needs of men.

Social programs that do not consider the specific needs of men as a cultural group are bound to fail. For instance, reproductive health programs that ignore the nature of male culture are often unsuccessful. Brindis and colleagues (2005) observed that young men often feel marginalized and discounted by many of these programs because they fail to reflect the developmental and cultural realities of these men. Such oversights are egregious in a profession devoted to culturally competent practice. Social workers know that the helping process must accommodate the cultural realities and values of client groups in order to be effective (Furman and Collins 2005; Furman and Negi 2007). For instance, social workers know that they should assess, and use as strengths, the spirituality and/or religious practices of their clients (Canda 1998). Spiritual practices often define culturally relevant healing practices and can be profound sources of psychosocial health (Gilligan and Furness 2006). For example, when working with traditional Asian men, it is important to understand that they may view the expression of strong emotions or personal problems as a lack of dignity or as a betrayal of the family (Nghe, Mahalik, and Lowe 2003).

Key Theories and Perspectives

I discuss a variety of theories and perspectives in this book, but four theories are integrated throughout: the strengths perspective, narrative therapy, existential theory, and cognitive behavior theory. Each offers social workers valuable tools when working with at-risk men.

Each theory can help enliven and enrich social work practice. Working from a strengths perspective helps social workers view the problems of men in context: while many men have numerous problems, they also have many strengths and capacities. Practicing from a strengths perspective can help practitioners keep in mind the important social work values of client self-determination and the worth and dignity of each individual, as well as the importance of viewing culture as a valuable resource. Practitioners who use a narrative approach show men how their lives are developing stories in which they have many choices and the power to change. Men are helped to see themselves as the protagonists in an unfolding drama with many potential plots and subplots. Helping men to see their choices and to develop a sense of control is also congruent with both traditional and nontraditional masculinities.

A basic understanding of the existential perspective helps social workers to avoid emphasizing problems at the expense of the core experiences that bind all human beings in their journey through life. Existentialism helps social workers focus on core human truths and the development of meaning. According to existential theory, helping people focus on developing meaningful and fulfilling lives will help alleviate many of the symptoms for which they enter treatment. Existential theory can be used to help deepen the helping relationship as both client and practitioner focus on a client's long-term dreams and aspirations.

Cognitive behavioral therapy (CBT) encompasses a variety of evidenced-based approaches that are congruent with how men view the process of change and growth (Beck and Emery 1985; Pucci 2005; Turner 2005). CBT approaches are user-friendly and hands-on, practical approaches that social workers can adapt to many situations (Dryden and DiGiuseppe 1990; Berlin 2001). While some types of CBT can seem a bit rigid and authoritarian (Payne 1991), many CBT approaches are highly humanistic, incorporate a person-in-environment perspective (Bernard and Joyce 1984; Ellis 1979; Goldstein 1981, 1984), and fit well with social work practice (Werner 1986). Even approaches that are not viewed as CBT may be used eclectically under the CBT umbrella (DiGiuseppe 1981). For instance, Werner (1986) effectively argues that existential theory and strengths-based approaches are largely cognitive in nature.

While I try to include each of these four theories in each chapter, I discuss CBT-oriented approaches more frequently than the others for several reasons: (1) CBT may be more developed than the other theories; (2) CBT is far more prescriptive and thus allows for easier discussion of "techniques"; (3) the literature on CBT is more extensive than the literature on other approaches, and many studies show it to be effective with a variety psychosocial problems

(Feske and Chambless 1995; Compas et al. 1998); (4) I was trained in rational emotive behavior therapy, one of the more prevalent CBT approaches; and (5) CBT approaches, when used in a constructive and humanistic manner can serve as an organizing or metatheory into which the other approaches may easily fit. What follows is a brief discussion of each approach; for an in-depth discussion, see chapter 5.

Cognitive Behavior Theories

In general, cognitive behavioral approaches focus on the relative importance of human thinking in the creation of emotion and behavior (Beck 1976; Meichenbaum 1977; Mahoney 1974; Ellis, Abrams, and Abrams 2009). Some approaches focus more on the importance of thinking (Beck 1995), while others see behavior and thinking as equally important. Regardless, CBT approaches differ from traditional psychotherapies, which tend to view historical and familial factors as central to well-being. Cognitive approaches focus on the here and now and on the beliefs, attitudes, perspectives, and day-to-day thoughts of an individual. Ellis (1997) and other cognitive therapists often quote the philosopher Epictetus, who contended that it was not events that disturbed people but the views they held of these events.

The strength of cognitive behavioral theories is that they are often evidence based (Dobson 2002), are easy to learn and implement (Corcoran 2006), and can be extremely empowering to men (Mooney 1998). Werner (1982) and Goldstein (1984) developed models of humanistic cognitive practice that have had lasting influence and are as useful today as they were when they were developed.

In his discussion of the relationship between humanism and cognitive therapy, H. D. Werner (1982:36) observes:

> Those therapies that stress the potentialities of cognitive control over dysfunctional emotional processes are in some respects the most humanistic means of personality change, usually being man-centered, creativity-oriented, and relevant to the maximum actualization of the human potential. . . . Humanism views man as a creature who, having acquired language and the ability to think both abstractly and creatively, largely determines his own behavior. Some of the sources of his conduct are his judgments, choices, and goals. His existence is shaped by his own human thoughts and the tendency of most human beings to strive for competence. He is not controlled by demons, uncontrolled drives, or divine powers.

Social workers must use theories congruent with the values systems of their clients. In her discussion of the importance of values to social work practice, Gordon (1965) observes the centrality of values to positive client outcomes. She notes that when the values of social work are not aligned with the needs of its clients, practice loses its purpose. Social workers who work with men must pay particular attention to the congruence of their own values and the values and needs of men. Throughout this book I explore the ways that male values and sensibilities differ from those of women. Social work is a profession in which the majority of professionals are women; at times value differences between female social workers and their male clients may affect practice. One way for social workers to align their practice with the needs of men is to adopt theories that are congruent with men's values and ways of viewing the world. Most CBT approaches stress the importance of client self-determination, the importance of individual freedom and dignity, and the capacity of people for growth and change. As I will show, these are values congruent with male-centered ways of thinking.

Since the late 1980s practitioners have often used CBT in a reductionistic and rather mechanical way. Rational emotive behavior therapy (REBT), a cognitive behavioral approach used frequently is this book, may at times appear to be overly rigid and dogmatic. Yet in working with men it is important to keep in the mind the deep roots of humanism that lie at the core of cognitive behavioral theories. By focusing on the individual's capacity to change, on helping men seek empowerment by developing new skills and resources, CBT can be an extremely valuable theory into which other approaches may fit nicely.

Strengths-Based Approaches

When working with men at risk, it is important to remember that all human beings possess considerable strengths. When working with clients with multiple problems, stressors, and dilemmas, it is easy and tempting to focus only on the severe presenting problems. This is natural; when we see men in pain, we want to help eliminate their troubles. Yet by maximizing men's strengths and capacities, men are often able to transcend their most pressing concerns. A man uses his strengths and capacities to ameliorate, overcome, and transcend his pains.

The maxim of teaching a man to fish instead of merely giving him fish is a metaphor for strengths-oriented work. Those who adopt such an approach help men to understand their goals and dreams and to develop the means of achieving those goals. In recent decades numerous social work scholars and practitioners have begun to recognize the importance of helping people maximize their internal and external sources. This approach has been termed the strengths perspective.

According to Saleebey (2002:3), "Practicing from a strengths orientation means that everything you do as a social worker (or therapist) will be predicated, in some way, on helping to discover and embellish, explore and exploit clients' strengths and resources in the service of assisting them to achieve their goals, realize their dreams, and shed the irons of their own inhibitions and misgivings."

The strengths perspective is not a theory with clearly defined interventions. Like existentialism, it is more of a stance that a social worker may adopt with clients and a perspective with a set of practice guidelines and values (see chapter 5). A strengths perspective is a commitment to help men recognize, explore, and develop the resources, skills, and abilities they already possess.

U.S. society in general, and its helping professions in particular, is not particularly strengths based. The medical model, which has been increasingly influential in social work since the 1980s, views the human condition in terms of pathology and problems. In this mechanistic model the role of the social worker is to identify the problem, determine its cause, and suggest the most evidenced-based solutions. While this model is not without its strengths, the psychosocial problems of human beings are usually complex and defy linear cause-and-effect explanations. Additionally, working in this manner can lead to the disempowerment of men and at times to an overreliance on symptom alleviation to the detriment of long-term growth and development. The goal of social work should not be merely to resolve the current crisis but to help men develop the means of resolving similar dilemmas in the future. Also, working from a strengths perspective encourages men not only to resolve problems but to achieve excellence, mastery, command, creativity, artistry, and community and self- actualization.

When working with men who may be at crisis points in their lives, seeing their strengths can often be difficult. They may be extremely shut down, resistant, and unwilling or unable to open up to and trust a stranger (even worse, a stranger that is a helping professional). They may seem irreparably broken and lost, angry and detached. In such cases, what strengths could they possibly possess? Becoming a strengths-based social worker demands developing a new set of observational and assessment skills. It requires learning to notice what people do well, what has worked for them in the past, and what did not work, as well as to see people's potential.

Human strengths are biological, psychological, and social. For instance, strengths in the social domain may include close relatives, friends, and other relationships. They may include colleagues at work and old friends with whom one does not often have consistent contact. Often men report few supportive relationships in their lives. It is important to help men mend fractured or broken relationships with people who may still care for them a great deal and who may be willing to provide them with help and support. Such an assessment is part of the process of mining for strengths and is an important part of working from a strengths perspective.

Existential Theory

The existential perspective is really several different approaches that have key aspects in common. Born out of the alienation of the industrial revolution and the period between the world wars, existential philosophy first became popular in Europe and spread to the North American therapeutic communities in the 1950s and 1960s, when humanistic psychology was popular. Humanistic therapists and social workers were attracted to existentialism's focus on the core issues of living, which people in many cultural contexts shared. Existentialism is a perspective that developed from and was articulated in literature, philosophy, and the humanities (see Camus 1942). Existential authors and thinkers saw the potential homogenizing effects of industrial life, where people became replaceable cogs in the machine of production. Early existential social workers and therapists eschewed the determinism of behaviorism and psychoanalysis, focusing on the importance of human will, freedom, and choice.

At its core, existential social work seeks to help people live more meaningful lives. It is concerned with helping clients face the key realities of human existence: death, the meaning of life, anxiety, isolation, responsibility, suffering. Existential practitioners posit that many symptoms that people exhibit are caused by their living unconscious and unexamined lives, proceeding according to the dictates of society, their parents' wishes, or other external forces. Existential social work helps men explore their deepest values, desires, and needs and pushes them to discover ways of developing their own mission and purpose. The existential perspective can help humanize and deepen practice for social workers who use other approaches. By drawing attention to the core problems of being, social workers who study existential thought and seek to apply its principles are compelled to deal with the deeper aspects of being human.

The existential approach has declined in popularity in social work circles since the 1960s and 1970s, when it was very important to social work practice (Krill 1969; Sinsheimer 1969; Swaine and Baird 1977; Weiss 1975). As social work practice has become increasingly influenced by evidence-based models and the medical model, humanistic and "softer" approaches have become less popular. However, integrating the existential perspective into social work practice with men can be an important balance to more symptom-focused therapies. For instance, short-term cognitive behavioral therapy is often used to help alleviate the symptoms of depression (Turnbull 1991). However, if a man is not helped to live a more authentic, meaningful life and to examine his purpose for being in the world, he may slip into hopelessness and despair.

Some social workers may struggle with existentialism's heavy emphasis on individuals' responsibility for their own beliefs, choices, and behavior. Some clinicians seem to have a difficult time separating responsibility from blame and recrimination. Indeed, this is a difficult task. One of the great merits of social work is its ability to empower people. It is easy to see that men who have been historically oppressed are not responsible for much of what they have learned about themselves (e.g., internalized racism and oppression). Each theory that I explore in this book offers different ways of helping people take responsibility for their life in the here and now. Existentialism focuses on helping people view the deeper truths of their lives and considers the ability to hold a vision of what is essential for oneself as the first step to self-determination. The existentialist social worker helps people focus on the moment, on the importance of the day, and on the importance of being aware of the forces that influence our thinking, feelings, and behavior. Self-blame and self-pity are viewed as examples of "bad faith," feelings that block us from living fully in each and every moment.

Narrative Therapy

Encouraging a man to discuss his life experiences can be a catalyst for change. Attentively embracing a person's stories leads to understanding the point of view of the storyteller. A man's stories reveal his personal history, where he has been, where he is now, and where he hopes to go. Through this personal history the storyteller develops a greater knowledge of himself, and the person who attentively listens to the stories develops a greater knowledge of the storyteller (Carlick and Biley 2004:310).

A newer approach developed in the 1970s and 1980s, narrative therapy, stresses how people construct their lives as stories (Gergen and Kaye 1992). Narrative therapy focuses on helping individuals and groups uncover the themes in their lives and on working collaboratively with clients to rewrite these stories. With roots in constructivist psychology, narrative psychology, and literary approaches to helping, narrative therapy is an approach that is highly congruent with social work practice with men at risk. White and Epston

(1990) stress the collaborative relationship between social worker and client. Morgan (2000) provides a nice summation of the perspective of narrative therapists: "Narrative therapy seeks to be a respectful, non-blaming approach to counseling and community work, which centers people as the experts in their own lives. It views problems as separate from people and assumes people have many skills, competencies, beliefs, values, commitments and abilities that will assist them to reduce the influence of problems in their lives."

The connections between the narrative approach and other social work theories and perspectives are important. For instance, cancer survivors who shared their stories at a national conference found that the experience instilled an increased sense of hope (one of Yalom's existential therapeutic factors) and produced powerful changes in their cognitions and behavior (Harper Chelf et al. 2000). Also, narrative work powerfully connects to existentialism through their common focus on the creation of meaning and the importance of helping people actively engage in the construction of their sense of meaning and mission in the therapeutic process.

Richert (2002:77) explores the commonalities of the two approaches, in particular how individuals construct their sense of self and identity. In fact, he argues that in most psychotherapeutic approaches, a key goal is to help individuals understand their own values, choose their goals, and develop behaviors that are life enhancing and self-directed. One goal of all these approaches is to help individuals be less captive of their internal drives or social pressures (for example, the pressure to abuse drugs). Richert observed that "a common theme across therapies . . . has been that one of the overarching objectives of treatment is to enable the client to behave more flexibly. While not all approaches to treatment have understood such an increase in flexibility as a function of client choice or will, the narrative and the humanistic/existential traditions have thought of treatment in this way."

The four theories that I discuss here and apply to practice with men at risk have many commonalities. In truth, many social workers practice eclectically (Parton 2000). As long as eclecticism means a conscious use of theory to meet the needs of the clients and not a haphazard approach that results from a lack of theoretical depth or sophistication, it may be of great value.

The Call to Work with Men

Social work has an ethical obligation to provide services to those who have been victims of the disintegration and transformation of social structures

(International Federation of Social Workers 2004). Many men have been significantly affected by globalization, postindustrialization, and other cultural and economic shifts in the social landscape (Kreuger 1997; Singha and House 1998). Working-class men with high school diplomas historically have had access to relatively high-paying jobs in the industrial sector. Their jobs provided them with the opportunity to live the classic American dream and to be good providers for their families. Many of these jobs no longer exist in the United States. Unable to support their families and achieve the self-affirmation of being able to do so, some men have turned to self-destructive and violent behaviors (Moore and Gillette 1990; Jacobson, LaLonde, and Sullivan 1993). Yet many men have overcome these obstacles. An important theme of this book is that men at risk often have amazing strengths and resiliencies, which they use to overcome life's challenges.

For instance, a former client of mine struggled with substance abuse until his wife, who was the primary breadwinner for many years, was injured at her factory job. Unable to kick his habit by himself, this 35-year-old Nicaraguan man was motivated by the prosocial aspects of machismo, which calls on Latino men to endure hardships for their family. He was able to reduce his drinking and drug use and maintain two jobs. He reported doing what "a man had to do" and that the long hours of working two jobs were just "something to be endured." Out of crisis and difficulty, he was able to reach deep within himself to overcome his personal and social limitations.

At times, however, many men are not able to overcome such obstacles. At these times social work has an ethical obligation to understand and serve this population. This is the purpose of this book: to provide social work students and social workers with an understanding of the knowledge, skills, and values that they must possess in order to provide social work services to men.

In each chapter you will find case examples based on the life experiences of real men that exemplify key points and issues the chapter explores. Some cases examine the work of a social worker and client. Other cases explore why a man was not able to find or receive help, did not have help available to him, did not know about social work services, or was not open to professional assistance. A sad reality is that many men will suffer pain and despair until their problems kill them. Until men become more receptive to professional help, and until social work becomes more receptive to men, this tragic reality will be true more often than is necessary.

The issues that these men have faced often are complex; indeed, some cases could easily have fit into several chapters. Following each case are questions to stimulate self-reflection or class discussion. If you are using the questions for in-class discussion, try to be as open and honest as possible when answering each question. Only through exploring our biases and limitations can we improve and change our practice. For you and your classmates to grow, you will need to be open to and accepting of each other's differences; do not judge each other's responses. Engage in critical dialogue with respect and dignity. Many issues that this book explores—identity, violence, and war, to name but three—evoke strong feelings for many of us. It is important to support your colleagues and their growth as professional social workers.

If you are reading this book for your professional development, please spend some time writing and reflecting about each case. The ability to critically reflect upon practice is one of the most important skills that a social worker can possess. The cases presented here have value to the degree to which they help you develop new understandings and possibilities for working with the male clients in your practice. I hope that the ideas contained in this book will expand your cognitive and behavioral repertoire when practicing with men, but it ultimately is up to you to integrate these ideas with your current conceptions of practice.

The first part of the book, "Understanding the Worlds of Men," explores the various factors that shape the lives of men. Each chapter focuses on key contextual, historical, and developmental factors that affect the lives of men. Taken together, the chapters form a biopsychosocial, holistic view of what it means to be a man.

Chapter 2 examines the relationship between globalization and the lives of men. Men in the United States greatly affect and are affected by the forces of globalization, migration, and transmigration. Social and economic events that transcend national boundaries influence the well-being of men in the United States and ultimately influence which men will wind up calling themselves "Americans."

Chapter 3 focuses on different conceptions of masculinity and development. I pay particular attention to the concept of hegemonic masculinity and explore the paradox of providing social work services to men. *Hegemonic masculinity* refers to the notion that society sanctions certain male behavior as preferred, based on key power arrangements within society (Connell 2000). That is, those in power, through various structural mechanisms (i.e., media, economic rewards, who is allowed positions of power and privilege) create incentives for men to behave in certain preferred or privileged ways. This chapter pays particular attention to how men of various backgrounds are trained to attain this ideal and the rejection and punishment they suffer when they fail. Chapter 3 also explores several influential models of adult development and the strengths and limitations of these approaches. Diverse populations of men often do not conform to some of these notions, and the chapter discusses how social workers can adapt these models in their work with men.

Chapter 4 focuses on the relationships of men. Social work as a profession has long made relationships one of its central concepts (Gordon 1965; Perlman 1979; Turner 1986), yet the relationships of men are often misunderstood. Common social discourse presents these relationships as nonexistent, detached, conflictual, and usually dysfunctional. Men are viewed as not possessing the requisite affective and communication skills that intimate and supportive relationships require. While many men do need to improve their relational skills and would benefit from having more numerous intimate relationships, many men have meaningful and healthy relationships. The chapter also discusses differences in relational styles and explores men's relationship strengths and issues.

Chapter 5 examines the four theories introduced above, including the relevance of each to social work practice with men, especially men at risk. The discussion includes the congruence of each theory with different aspects of masculinity and the use of each theory to help men maximize their strengths and minimize their deficits. Finally, the chapter presents a discussion of the help-seeking behaviors of men and general practice guidelines.

The chapters in the second part of the book, "Men at Risk: Problems and Solutions," focus on specific at-risk populations. Chapter 6 addresses men and violence, looking at men as both perpetrators and victims of violent crime. The section on sexual violence discusses men as perpetrators and victims of rape. While the vast majority of sexually violent acts are perpetrated by men against women, male-on-male rape may be underreported and presents serious health and psychosocial consequences. Gangs and prison-related violence highlight the complex social factors that influence the lives of men; the discussion of gang violence in this chapter demonstrates the extent to which many problems are global and transnational.

Chapter 7 considers men as workers at risk, exploring the central role that work plays in the lives of men. As the world of work has gone through enormous changes, many men find themselves displaced and uncertain about how to earn a living. The chapter also discusses some of the dangerous professions that men are engaged in. It concludes with a discussion of services to men in regard to issues of work.

Chapter 8 presents information about men who have served in the armed forces. Recent revelations about substandard care at military hospitals have highlighted the shortcomings of the military medical system for both active-duty personnel and veterans. New studies have provided long-needed information about the psychosocial impact of war on servicemen (and women); social workers are among the clinicians providing quality and empathic care to men returning from Iraq and Afghanistan. Additionally, the medical centers run by the U.S. Department of Veterans Affairs are important training and employment centers for social work students and social workers.

Chapter 9 discusses the health risks that men face. Men experience extremely high rates of heart disease, stroke, and some types of cancer. Men also fail to seek routine medical care as frequently as women and are less likely to seek medical treatment when they experience physical symptoms. This chapter explores how social workers can encourage habits that lead to improved health.

Chapter 10 looks at mental illness and mental health. Numerous misconceptions about the incidence and expression of mental illness affect the way social workers provide care to men. Historically, clinicians have regarded depression as a problem that men do not face. However, recent research has challenged this myth (Rochlen, McKelley, and Pituch 2006). Social workers need to help men understand that experiencing mental illness is not a sign of personal weaknesses, that mental illnesses are diseases in their own right. Helping men view the treatment of their mental illness as a sign of strength and personal empowerment will help them to be more receptive to social work services.

Chapter 11 takes up older men, perhaps one of the most underexplored and misunderstood populations. Older men are often viewed as being relatively privileged and in need of few social work resources. However, the reality is that older men often have profound biopsychosocial needs. Many older men experience debilitating health conditions, such as Alzheimer's, substance abuse, and depression. They often find themselves alone and without the careers that provided much of their sense of well-being.

Chapter 12 focuses on specific male populations and the history of some of the obstacles they have faced. For instance, Latinos constantly face questions about "where they are from," even though their families may have been Americans for far longer than many white Americans. The chapter begins with a discussion of culturally sensitive and culturally competent social work practice. It also explores some of the special needs and issues that surround different ethnic and cultural groups.

Chapter 13 addresses compulsive disorders and addictions. These include substance abuse and compulsive behavioral disorders, such as sexual addiction and compulsive gambling. In today's high-pressure world, compulsive behaviors and addictions have become increasingly common. An issue of particular importance is how well current treatment approaches fit the needs of men.

Chapter 14, the concluding chapter, is titled "What Is Right about Men?." This chapter discusses what men do well and details issues for social workers who work with men to consider.

Finally, I would like to say that many of the principles in this book are applicable to social work practice with women. For example, the discussion of group work with men explores Yalom's (1995) therapeutic factors. Understanding these principles also will help you in your group work practice with women. An important social work skill is to learn how to translate and apply knowledge from one situation to another.

EXERCISE 1

As social workers you sometimes face competing obligations. In your work with men (in all social work practice, really) you will face many ethical dilemmas, situations that offer ethical justifications for more than one course of action (Furman, Downey, and Jackson 2004). For instance, suppose you are a social worker in an inpatient substance abuse treatment program, providing therapy to men. The program is four weeks long, and you provide therapy to your clients twice a week. During your first session with your client, you find out that, in addition to having a substance abuse problem, he seems to hold views that you assess as being extremely sexist. For example, he reports anger toward his wife for working outside the home. He blames "those goddamn liberal feminists who want to destroy the American family" for her desire to work. He reports no incidents of physical abuse and says that he and his wife do not argue. He does report behavior that appears to be controlling and authoritarian. During your assessment you hear no overt connections between his substance abuse and his relationship with his wife.

Please answer the following questions:

1. Do you address the issue of his domineering, sexist attitudes?
2. If you do, how would you proceed?
3. If you do, how might your intercession affect the helping relationship?
4. How might your gender affect your handling of the situation?
5. Do you, as a social worker, have an ethical obligation to effect social change in this situation? If so, what would that be?
6. After reflecting upon all these issues, what are your treatment options?

Case Example

The two cases in this chapter are not related to a particular problem area, concern, or theme. These cases introduce the complexity of psychosocial strengths and concerns that men present.

George Casala is a 41-year-old Cuban American living in Miami. George's parents were born in Cuba and came to the United States shortly after the Cuban Revolution. George has been married for twenty-two years to Blanca. Blanca was born in Cuba, and her parents left Havana several years after Castro took over the island. George's father was a carpenter in Havana, and his mother worked in the home, caring for George and his six siblings. Both parents were kind, Catholic, and hard working; they had a sixth-grade education. Despite the senior Casala's lack of education, he opened a small furniture repair shop in Miami and soon began to sell furniture. Within several years his business grew and the family was firmly lower middle class. Over the years the business continued to grow. Although the Casalas were not rich, they were able to take annual family vacations and bought a house in an upper-middle-class neighborhood. In the estimation of George's father, the family had arrived. However, while growing up George felt self-conscious because of his parents' humble roots. He kept these feelings to himself; he learned that respect and dignity were more important than his judgments. He did vow to do "more" with his life than his parents had done.

George attended the University of Miami and graduated with a degree in business; he received his MBA two years later. George had dreamed of working his way up to CEO of a large company. His first job out of school was in marketing for a local technology firm. This was one of the few companies of this type in Miami at the time, and George was excited. While his father was proud of George, he had hoped that his son would help him run the family furniture store. But George saw the business as "small potatoes." During the first two years of his new career, George was well regarded and received two promotions. His future in the company looked bright. However, as the senior Casala's health had begun to fail, he pressured George to help. George soon quit his job and became vice president of the family business (his father was president). This was an extremely painful decision for George, yet he mostly kept his feelings to himself, not even sharing them with his wife. As a good Latino son, he knew what was expected of him and honored the wishes and needs of his father, putting his own aspirations aside. However, George was also deeply American, and suppressing his own desires caused him a great deal of anguish. George soon became impatient, well known for having a very short fuse.

George used his business skills to increase the efficiency of the family business and developed a sophisticated marketing plan that greatly increased sales and profits. However, the more successful the business became, the more he struggled with his own sense of identity and began to feel depressed. This was greatly exacerbated by problems that his 17-year-old daughter, Consuela, was having and that required George to engage the legal and child welfare systems.

George and his family recently sought social work services, and he is less than thrilled. Like many American men, George believes in solving his problems on his own and regards the need for outside help for "private problems" as a sign of personal failure. However, after months of prodding by his wife, George has admitted that he is unable to help Consuela on his own. Privately, George was afraid that the social worker who was seeing the Casalas for family therapy would tell him that Consuela's problems were his fault.

Consuela has been "misbehaving," in George's words, for two years. He sees her becoming increasingly defiant, oppositional, and difficult. George believed that the problem started when Consuela began spending time with one of her classmates, of whom George did not approve. Consuela missed curfews, "talked back," and let her grades slip.

One evening Consuela was supposed to be at the movies with her friend and was expected home at 10 p.m. However, she did not arrive until 2 a.m. when she pulled up in a car driven by a boy. George ran outside, screamed at the boy, and slapped Consuela across the face. The boy stepped out of the car to confront George, and the two began to push each other. Within seconds they were on the ground fighting. Consuela ran into the house and called 911. Consuela's friend hit George in the face several times and was able to free himself and leave. George returned to the house. Several minutes later the police showed up. When George answered the door, he told the police that everything was all right, that he had had a conflict with his daughter's boyfriend. The police asked to see Consuela, to make sure she was all right. George refused, stating that he would take care of his daughter, and that he did not need their help. The police told George that if he did not produce Consuela, they would arrest him. George then brought Consuela to the door. When the police asked her if everything was all right, Consuela said that her father had hit her. George was taken to the police station, booked, and released on bail several hours later. Three days later the judge stipulated that George was to attend family therapy with his wife and daughter at the local child protective services agency.

The following week George and his family went to the agency for therapy. The therapist assigned to the family was not well versed in culturally competent practice with Latinos men. She pushed George to immediately take ownership of his behavior, which she referred to as "abusive" in front of his family. George felt judged, ashamed, and furious. He wondered why the therapist did not speak to him about this matter in private. He became concerned that he would lose all authority in his home and that his daughter's acting out behavior would become even worse.

The worker was oblivious to George's feelings about his inability to control his daughter and the shame that that caused him as a Latino male. She quickly confronted him and insisted that he also attend group therapy for child abusers. George became very quiet, aware that the therapist would not be "on his side." He realized that he would have to find a way to comply with her demands to stay out of trouble but that therapy for him was going to be merely a form of punishment to endure.

STUDY QUESTIONS

1. If you were George's social worker, how would you proceed?
2. What skills would help you resolve work with George and his family?
3. In this case, what nonclinical interventions might be helpful?
4. How might the community or extended family be involved?
5. How might George be encouraged to use this situation to help him improve the quality of his and his family's life?

Case Example

Billy Felicita is a 48-year-old man going through a difficult life transition. Billy was recently divorced. Billy met his wife, Wynn, while he was teaching English in Vietnam. She was a lower-middle-class Vietnamese woman, nineteen years his junior. When they first started dating, Billy was skeptical about the long-term potential of this new relationship. He worried that the generational and cultural differences would ultimately get in the way. He also feared that perhaps Wynn was more interested in what marrying an American man represented than in Billy himself. Billy is introspective and insightful from therapy, attendance at men's groups, and a long history of attending recovery programs for marijuana addiction (he has been clean for many years). He realized that his doubts about his girlfriend's sincerity tied into his own insecurities, fears, and doubts. He grew up in a family with an alcoholic mother and had spent many years struggling with depression.

As their relationship developed, Billy became confident that Wynn's love was real. Within two years they were married and moved to the United States. For the first two years their relationship was good. They learned about each other, communicated well, shared a great deal of kindness and love, and enjoyed a good sex life. Wynn began to work in nail salon, a common career for Vietnamese women in the United States. During these first two years she seemed grateful for their relative material wealth. Billy bought a small three-bedroom house in a middle- to upper-middle-class neighborhood. They seemed wealthy to Wynn, and she felt a sense of security. Over time, however, she began to compare their lifestyle to their neighbors'. She began to see Billy's twenty-year-old pickup truck as an embarrassment. Billy, a successful housepainter, never cared much for material possessions. He began to worry about his wife's growing interest in what he regarded as American materialism. His position was that if Wynn wanted more material wealth, she should perhaps make more money. While culturally this was a difficult concept for her to accept, she began to grow accustomed to the idea. One day she came home and told Billy that she had heard about a nail salon that was for sale and wanted to buy it. Billy was glad that she was thinking entrepreneurially and suggested that they check out the business. Wynn stated that this was not necessary, that it was a good business, and that Billy should give her $30,000 in the morning to buy it. Billy told her that while business decisions in Vietnam were based upon trust and faith, in the United States it is necessary to investigate business opportunities carefully and methodically. Further, coming up with that much money would take time and mean dipping into their retirement account. Wynn was furious, claiming that Billy's refusal to support her was a betrayal. As Billy began to investigate the business, with the help of an attorney friend, he learned that it was less than profitable and in a bad location. When Billy presented Wynn with the information in a dispassionate manner, she cried and stated that this was proof that he did not care about her, and only cared about money.

Billy identifies this as the beginning of the end of their relationship. They began to fight a great deal and started to sleep in separate rooms. Within six months Wynn had moved in with a Vietnamese couple several miles away. Soon she began to talk about divorce. Billy was devastated. He saw his marriage as the beginning of his dream of having a family. Billy called a mutual friend of theirs, a Vietnamese woman who had known Wynn for many years, to see if she had any ideas about how to save their marriage. To Billy's chagrin, he learned that Wynn was dating at least two other men and that she may have been doing so for a long time. He began to feel depressed and withdrew, playing his guitar and working as little as possible. Within several months he had agreed to a divorce and financial terms.

When the divorce became final, Billy's back also was in very bad shape. For several years he had been experiencing back and shoulder problems. House painting was an especially strenuous career for someone with back pain; the stress of his divorce brought about a particularly painful episode. Billy felt as if his world was falling apart.

A year after the divorce Billy was able to sell his house and move into a small apartment in the back of a house. With such greatly reduced living costs, he was able to cut back significantly on his work hours. While this allowed him to experience less physical pain, the large amounts of free time proved to be a mixed blessing. He had more time to do many of the things he loved to do, like play the guitar and fish, but he struggled with depression and anxiety because he did not know how he would make a living in the future, and he was still grieving the loss of his marriage and the dream of having a family. He previously had taken medication for depression, which had helped. He did not want to take medication this time, however, as he felt that his emotions were directly related to the profound life changes he was experiencing, and he wanted to "face them head on."

Billy sought counseling from a clinical social worker trained in narrative therapy. During their phone consultation the social worker described his orientation to Billy. He noted that because of his training, he tended to see people's lives as evolving stories, and the goal of treatment was to help people figure out, and often change, their life scripts. The social worker said that while he was trained in this particular method, he was eclectic in the techniques that he relied upon. He stressed to Billy that the client ultimately drives the therapeutic process and that the social worker would be a guide in helping Billy figure out the next chapters in his life.

During their first session the social worker asked Billy to tell him the story of his marriage and the story of his life. He quickly realized that to Billy, the central theme of both stories was that Billy was a failure and that he was to blame for all the negative events that occurred in his life. He had little to give, little to offer, and felt lost and hopeless. The therapist asked Billy if he could tell the story by using a different central theme and have it still be "true." Billy said, "All I can say is that I really worked hard at the marriage, and I really work hard all the time." The therapist asked Billy to tell the story of a marriage and life of a guy named Billy who really tried hard, who really worked at things, and took such care and responsibility for himself that he sometimes blamed himself for things that were not his fault. At this point Billy began to cry. His therapist was careful not look to directly at Billy, as he was not certain how Billy would feel about crying in front of another man. At the same time the therapist deliberately leaned toward Billy, to signal attentiveness and openness. Billy sobbed silently for several minutes. After some time the therapist told Billy that they could remain in silence for as long as Billy wanted but that if Billy needed anything from him to please say so. Billy responded that it felt good to cry, that he had been "emotionally constipated" for a long time, and this is what he seemed to need. The therapist said that it seemed that part of Billy's story would also be knowing what his needs are, and that two of his strengths were emotional openness and sensitivity. Billy said it was too bad his ex-wife did not appreciate him for these qualities and that she saw him as weak when he did not "control" his feelings. Billy explained that his wife was Vietnamese and that her idea of what men should be was far different from where Billy was "moving on this journey."

The therapist remarked that he had once read that the two most important things a man needed to know were where he was going and who was going with him. He told Billy that the order of these truths, as presented, was part of the key to happiness and fulfillment. As Billy spoke more about the marriage, the therapist began to see that Wynn had been quite judgmental and that, given her cultural perspective, perhaps she was not able to recognize Billy's qualities. Billy said he thought this was true and that perhaps she was not the person who was supposed to be his life partner.

The therapist was using two techniques from narrative therapy (see chapter 5). First, he was asking for details, helping Billy to explore his story and make it more his own. This is called "thickening the plot." Also, the therapist was asking Billy to explore "unique outcomes," examples of when the dominant metaphor of the story, Billy as failure, would be found to be untrue. Through his work with his therapist Billy began to slowly reconstruct his story as one of a man who has succeeded at much of what he has tried to do and is responsible for and accountable to his own feelings and truths. Billy experienced relief from his depression as he began to view his life from this strength-based, reality-driven story.

FOR WRITING AND REFLECTION

1. As you read the story, what judgments came to your mind?
2. How might these judgments influence your work with a man such as Billy?
3. What might be some additional ways of working with Billy?
4. What values would guide your work with Billy, and how would you put these values into action?

Understanding the Worlds of Men

PART 1

Men's Psychosocial Health in a Global Era | TWO

A central premise of the gender and development discourse since the 1970s has been the ways in which men exercise power over and dominate women. Virtually all the main actors in international development subscribe to this basic premise. This is only half the story. Gender is also about the way social structures and authority give men power over other men, resulting in their marginalization, discrimination, and subordination. To ignore this other notion of gender is to ignore a critical variable in some of the most pressing issues that men face (Correia and Bannon 2006:245).

Globally, various groups working for the betterment of humanity are exploring the roles of masculinity and men in the creation of a better world. Greig, Kimmel, and Lang (2000:2) contend that "Examining masculinity and the role it plays in the development process is not simply an analytical exercise, but has widespread implications for the effectiveness of programmes that seek to improve the economic and social outcomes in virtually every country." These and other authors have noted the importance of including men in social welfare programs internationally. Increasingly, scholars and practitioners have recognized that social and economic development must account for the needs of women and men alike. While men have certainly benefited disproportionately from the fruits of most societies, the fates of men and women are profoundly interconnected. The importance of exploring the global implications of masculinity and its various conceptions are more important than ever.

It has been observed that the rate of social change has accelerated greatly over the last several centuries (Postman 1992). In fact, the pace of technological and social change has accelerated to the point that each generation has a hard time understanding the technological innovations that shape the social lives of the next generation. For instance, many teenagers organize their social life around social networking sites like MySpace and Facebook, forming social connections, exchanging messages, posting pictures, referring friends to one another, and engaging in Internet chats. My daughter spends a great deal of time online and seems to feel a sense of connection to those with whom she communicates. My wife, on the other hand, has a difficult time figuring out the basics of e-mails. While I communicate frequently via e-mail and use it to stay connected to friends and colleagues on a daily basis, I have little desire to engage in text messaging. My daughter cannot imagine living without it. Humans invent technology, and technology shapes human beings.

One of the most important lessons from sociology, science, and other disciplines is that grand-scale social changes affect the very nature of what is possible for humans, and in fact the very nature of human consciousness (Capra 1983; Postman 1992; Henderson 1995). This chapter explores several key areas in which global social transformations have altered the personal and social lives of men. The first section touches briefly on the history of men and masculinity in the twentieth-century United States and provides a context for the next section, which looks at the effects of postindustrialization on men. The third section deals with the relationship between globalization and changing masculinities, introducing conceptualizations of masculinity that will be expanded more fully in chapter 3. The fourth section briefly explores how technological changes themselves have shaped and continue to shape the lives of men.

The case studies in this chapter focus on the lives of two men residing outside the United States: an American living abroad and a Peruvian taxi driver whom I met while I was conducting research in Lima. As social work becomes increasingly transnational (Furman and Negi 2007), it is more and more important for social workers to understand the lives of men in other countries. The Peruvian case is also a good illustration of how complex global forces invisibly affect men's experiences. It is difficult for individuals to contextualize the confusion and pain of highly personal problems that may be indirectly caused by global forces, so it becomes the role of the social worker to help people understand the social context of their problems. Doing so helps them externalize their issues, thereby making them easier to face. Take, for example, the case of an unemployed, semiskilled industrial laborer in rural, upstate New York. The company for which he had worked for two decades had recently closed because of competition from China, where the parts the company made could be produced far more cheaply due to inexpensive labor and lax environmental standards. This man may not have been fully aware of the dynamics that resulted in the loss of his job, had a profound effect on his family, and affected his feelings about himself and his sense of efficacy as a man. Without properly positioning his personal struggles within the context of globalization and changing world markets, he experienced profound shame, demoralization, and a diminution of his masculine identity. While contextualizing these personal problems as global social issues does not eliminate them, it can help men begin the process of moving from self-blame and incrimination to empowerment. In this case a social worker helped organize a group of other displaced workers who may be able to gain personal and political power from collective action. In the twenty-first century social workers will need to be able to move deftly between direct/micro and indirect/macro services to help resolve the personal and social problems created by unprecedented globalization. As the United States adjusts to these rapid changes, new services will need to be conceptualized that help diverse groups of men find their places within the new global order.

Historical Considerations of Services to Men

It can be argued that the written history of the world, up until the middle of the last century, has been the history of men. It is most certainly true that men's domination of most social institutions and millennia of sexism and patriarchy have placed men at the center of recorded history. The achievements of countless heroic women and women of genius have been lost forever. Yet too few people understand the history of the average man and what it has meant to be a typical man throughout time. Most historical explorations discuss leaders; most men recede into the background of history. As such, some historical conceptions of masculinity will provide a context for the study that follows.

In many ways, the history of men's lives in the United States can be viewed as two separate histories. White landowners had extremely different experiences from those of other men. For 250 years the majority of men of African descent in the country lived as slaves. The lives of male slaves were harsh at best, and their treatment was typically unbearably inhumane. Male slaves lived under constant threat of cruelty and were subjected to extreme violence and repression (Genovese and Fox-Genovese 1983). African American men were property and were frequently were bought and sold, separated from their families, and treated as objects. The art, literature, music, and other cultural practices that African American slaves developed are a testimony to their indomitable spirit, resiliency, and strength.

Newly immigrated men also found the American landscape challenging. Chinese laborers, seeking to flee an economic downturn in Canton, began to immigrate to the United States in large numbers the 1860s. Subjected to prejudice at the hands of white Americans, Chinese men were viewed as weak and effeminate. Even so, they took some of the most difficult jobs, including laying track for the expanding American railroad. Many workers died from heat exhaustion, explosions, and other hazardous conditions.

In the last twenty years of the nineteenth century, the industrial revolution forced many men to abandon their lives as farmers or artisans and move to the cities where they took factory jobs. The nature of the family also changed, as the extended family began to be replaced by the nuclear family, a smaller, more nimble unit more capable of relocation. Traditional extended families and more tightly knit communities were in fact informal systems of social welfare that allowed the family to survive vicissitudes in the labor market, illness, and other personal and familial crises. Without the supportive mechanisms of the extended family and organic community, the consciousness of American men shifted from a communitarian belief system to more individualistic ways of thinking. As the head of the nuclear family, a man was under a great deal of pressure to ensure the survival and well-being of his loved ones. This movement toward individualism continued a trend in American psychosocial life; roots of anticollectivist thought and rugged individualistic tendencies are found throughout American history (Gilbert and Terrell 1998) and have had a profound influence on the role that men adopt in society, and on their conceptions of their own masculinity.

The start of modern social work can be traced to charitable responses to the social transformations caused by the industrial revolution. Historically the community and the church had responded to the needs of members who experienced problems that challenged the functioning of the group. However, in the impersonal city, distanced from their organic communities, more organized and formal means of helping were needed to respond to mental illness, poverty, unemployment, violence, and other social concerns. Social welfare slowly began to shift from informal, community-based responses to being more structurally woven into modern capitalist societies (Titmuss 1959).

The industrial revolution and the factory jobs that many men held were not easy on American men. The working conditions within unregulated factory environments were brutal. Long hours and unsafe conditions characterized the daily life of men. The work was often backbreaking and provided little opportunity for personal growth and advancement. Ollman (1971) describes the consequences of such alienation conditions. As I noted in a previous work (Furman 2008:10):

> Alienated labor is labor that fissures various aspects of the self. The factory worker thrust into the traditional model of capitalist labor is meant to act in the same rote manner for countless, expendable hours. Thinking by the worker is discouraged; the ruling class do the thinking and the working man his bidding. The worker is viewed as a machine, and indeed, is replaced by machines if technological innovation allows for it. Perhaps the best symbol of alienated labor is the tie: a piece of cloth tied tightly around the neck, separating the head from the torso, the body from the mind.

Alienated labor leads to a spiritual malaise and can be the cause of many additional psychosocial problems that are explored throughout this book.

World War I was the first significant war on foreign soil for American men in generations. Americans were called on to help defeat German expansionism in Europe. The nation emerged healthy and victorious from the war. Since Europe was largely devastated by the war, the United States had a significant strategic advantage over European countries in terms of economic health and infrastructure. As such, the country entered a period of heretofore unknown economic prosperity. However, many investors, speculators, and ordinary citizens took this prosperity for granted, and stock speculation drove up the value of companies far beyond their actual worth. A great deal of the wealth that was supposedly created in fact existed solely on paper.

The stock market crash in October 1929 marked the official end to this relativity prosperous period in the lives of American men. The date dubbed "Black Thursday," October 24, marked the end of a period of optimism and hope. Over the next several years, unemployment rose to 15 percent for non-farm workers, and the gross domestic product was cut nearly in half (McElvaine 1993). The Great Depression was a time of extreme social and personal upheaval for men. For the first time in American history, mass unemployment swiftly struck men who had the skills, inclination, and other resources to find employment under normal circumstances (Karger and Stoesz 1998). Not being able to find work was no longer seen merely as a sign of individual weakness but began to be viewed as a problem within the American economic and political system (Piven and Cloward 1993). Regardless, the Depression was a time of pain and suffering for many men who could not support their families. The

New Deal marked an important era in the life of the nation and in the expansion of social welfare supports and services. New Deal programs created employment through public works and established a system of securities designed to cushion American workers from vicissitudes of the market. The modern social welfare system had been created (Popple and Leighninger 2004).

The beginning of World War II marked the actual end of the Depression. Many men felt ineffectual and lost during the Depression because they no longer had access to the traditional ways of performing their masculine roles. But with the war, American men were not merely called to the armed services, they were called upon to fight evil. The advances of the Axis powers meant the encroachment of fascism and Nazism on democracies, so American men were called upon to protect their very way of life. The impact of the war on men was complex and depended greatly on war experiences, class, and race. While war may have had profoundly negative impacts on individual men, for American men in general it provided a sense of purpose and mission that had been missing in their lives. The end of the war saw the rise of the American suburb and perhaps the heyday of the American dream of prosperity and a better way of life. The United States emerged as the clear world leader and superpower. When men returned from the war, they resumed their privileged positions within families and in the marketplace. It was viewed as patriotic for women to leave their jobs and return to the home, although the war had opened up the world of work to millions of women who maintained their positions. The generation of men returning from the war has frequently been viewed as being one of the most successful, innovative, and skilled cohorts in American history, with the term "the greatest generation" being coined to describe them (Brokaw 1998). Indeed, the careers of many men were launched by their war experiences. Those men who were perceived to be war heroes were often afforded respected positions in industry and politics.

However, this dream was not available to all men. For example, African American men returned to an environment characterized by Jim Crow laws and segregation. African American men who were respected in the military returned to a social context that often left them feeling mistreated and oppressed. Having fought bravely in the defense of their country, many African American men returned to the racism and discrimination that characterized the American South. Out of this pain and frustration was born the seeds of the civil rights movement.

The 1960s marked a period of great social upheaval in American life, and American men found themselves in the beginning of a firestorm of social change. Men of color, often excluded from the economic and social rewards of postwar life, began to challenge mainstream American society. African American and Chicano (Mexican American) men were finding new voices and new power. Cesar Chavez, a Chicano advocate for migrant farmworkers, challenged men and women alike with his call: "Si se puede"—"Yes we can." Chavez meant that Chicanos and other minorities could indeed change their conditions, and would indeed become fully recognized and valued participants in society.

The women's liberation movement of the 1960s and 1970s also had a profound impact on men's lives. Previously, many men ascribing to the hegemonic idea had believed that they were being good husbands and good men by "taking care of their wives." Most probably did not view themselves as oppressors, as violators of the rights of the women they loved. With the arrival of feminism in the American mainstream, men were informed that their behavior contributed to the oppression of women, that they indeed were the problem. Consider for a moment what this must have felt like to the average man in his forties, who had been working hard for fifteen years to provide for his family. In all likelihood he felt a sense of shock and disbelief. In effect, he was being told that everything he had worked for was untrue, that he was the enemy. Even for the most enlightened and open person, this is a hard message to take in. Since he was most likely not the best at expressing his "softer" feelings of sadness and invalidation, he might have responded with defensive anger. He might have been dismissive of these new ideas.

Throughout the 1960s and 1970s, men continued to struggle with changes in the cultural landscape. The Vietnam War was the most powerful and defining event in this period for men. Unlike the previous two wars, the Vietnam War was unpopular. Men who fought in Vietnam did so without the social sanction that other American wars have had, and without ultimate victory. Thousands died during the war, and many more returned hurt, ill, and broken. A society not wanting to look too carefully at its own mistakes largely abandoned the American soldier returning from Vietnam.

The start of the global era may best be symbolized by the destruction of the Berlin Wall in 1989. The Cold War officially came to an end, and barriers to open trade were rapidly dismantled. This coincided with the proliferation of the Internet as a means of communication, giving people greater access to information and knowledge of all sorts.

This brief history is not meant to explain the behavior of men during these periods or fully depict the social forces that shaped and were shaped by men. Social workers use knowledge of history, economy, and other social and behavioral sciences to help contextualize the individual lives of people with whom they work. The next section explores globalization, an important trend in social organization that social workers must also begin to understand.

Globalization and Men

The concept of globalization has become almost passé. It is now taken as a given that changes in world political and economic structures, the Internet and other hypertechnologies, along with unprecedented migration have made citizens of the world increasingly connected (Jackson, Crang, and Dwyer 2004). Events that occur in another country have a far greater impact on our daily lives than ever before (Munch 2004; Kastoryano 2000). Changes in labor laws in Asia may have a profound impact on employment opportunities for poor people in the United States. War, hopelessness, oppression, and fanaticism in one region of the world now affect the safety and security of us all (Stoesz, Guzzetta, and Lusk 1999). Whether we like it or not, the world truly is becoming smaller.

It is important to note that the processes of globalization are not entirely new, nor are its consequences. In writing about the health of Native American men, Joe (2001:237) observes that "Poverty, poor education, high unemployment, unhealthy lifestyles, and voluntary and forced culture change are among the reasons for the premature mortality of Native American men. Although decades have passed since initial European contact, the consequences of colonization that followed this contact have forever altered tribal lifestyles, and, in particular, the traditional role once held by young men."

The lives of men in the United States have been greatly affected by globalization, and vice versa. Globalization has also challenged and changed the conception of what it means to be a man (Connell 2005; Hooper 2001). Transnational encounters between people around the world have brought men into contact with those who have differing notions of masculinity; identity is now globally constructed (Kearney and Beserra 2004). Global capitalism and consumerism are packaging images of men and exporting them to all parts of the globe. This section seeks to situate the lives and social welfare of American men in a global context and to explore how Western—particularly American—conceptions of masculinity are affecting men in other parts of the world.

Central to understanding masculinities in a global environment is an understanding of the concept of hegemonic masculinity (Connell 2003). This highly contested concept has played an important role in gender studies for over twenty years (Connell and Messerschmidt 2005). It refers to a dominant form of masculinity that cuts across cultures and groups and is a product of the power structures of societies; it has been created by and perpetuates class and power arrangements. Hegemonic masculinity becomes a model to which men can and should aspire. When we speak of a traditional masculinity or of being a traditional man, we are usually referring to an accepted ideal of hegemonic masculinity. There is no official standard, yet the model is transmitted through social structures, the media, education, parenting messages, and other means of socialization. There is a sense of social agreement on what constitutes such patterns and norms. Both men and women internalize hegemonic masculine ideals and engage in behaviors that push men to aspire to this model. Through early socialization roles parents reinforce what is viewed as acceptable behavior for young boys. However, it is not easy for men and boys to achieve these ideals. Connell (2003:2) contends: "Not all men actually embody the hegemonic model, in fact, probably only a minority do. Yet the hierarchy around this version of masculinity is an important source of conflict and violence among men."

Correia and Bannon (2006) observe that hegemonic masculinity becomes the yardstick by which men are judged, and by which they can achieve meaning in their lives. They note that the majority of low-income, poor, and nonwhite men do not measure up to this dominant model. They note that chronic poverty, oppression, discrimination, and social exclusion all conspire to prevent men from achieving this model. In fact, since material success is a powerful component of the hegemonic ideal, poor and many working-class men by definition are not able to reach this standard, particularly in times of economic downturn or economic transformation. Men who are thwarted in this quest often engage in self-destructive behaviors or violence against those who are less powerful than themselves, usually women and children (Dutton and Browning 1988).

Gil (1990) refers to the origin of violence of this nature as "structural violence." That is, violence becomes embedded into a system that thwarts the fulfillment of needs. When social institutions block people from meeting social, physical, and existential needs, people tend to act in regressive and repressive ways. The more disengaged and disconnected men become from their traditional sources of meaning, from social institutions, and from their capacity to conform to social expectations about what it means to be a man, the more likely they are to act out their emptiness, pain, and angst. Self- and other destruction can take the form of alcoholism, criminality, and other problem behaviors, which are explored throughout this book.

Correia and Bannon (2006) explore several key aspects of hegemonic masculinity. First, a prerequisite for being a man is financial independence and being successful in the economic realm. Second, a man is supposed to be a good husband and father and have control over his family. Third, men are taught that they must conform to the specific mandates of their social group. Fourth, power is a key aspect of hegemonic masculinity in most cultures, specifically power over women. Other roles and scripts that characterize the hegemonic ideal will be discussed in the next chapter.

However, not all scholars agree with the notion of a hegemonic masculinity. For instance, Gutmann (1996) found a great deal of diversity in the manner in which Mexican men express and experience their masculinity. He contends that many interpretations of Latino masculinity are based on inaccurate stereotypes that focus on more aggressive expressions of such masculinity. He also notes that Mexican men ascribe to diverse conceptions of masculinity in terms of work roles, fathering, and intimate relationships.

The notion of what it means to be a man has been greatly influenced by globalization. Images of modern, postindustrial Western men have found their way to the far reaches of the globe. American films are frequently shown in countries throughout the world. American television shows present caricatures of American men who are effortlessly successful, affluent, and desirable. The media usually portray men as having easily figured out their livelihoods and that material success is the most important kind of success for a man.

Not only does the United States, through its business and media interests, export masculinity, but it also exports important different conceptions of masculine identity. In 2007 the United States had 37.9 million first-generation immigrants, and the number is growing (Camarota 2007). These new Americans bring with them their own means of expressing masculine identity. As they increase their role in the American cultural milieu, their images become part of what it means to be an American male. For instance, Ricky Martin and Marc Antony have become cultural icons that have influenced notions of male sexuality and appeal. Increasingly, men of diverse backgrounds are portrayed in the media—often in roles that are similar to the dominant cultural norms, but sometimes in other roles as well. For instance, in the television show *Ugly Betty*, the father of the protagonist, Betty, is unemployed yet is strong, responsible paternal figure to his adult Latina daughters. He is shown to be successful and of value in spite of his lack of economic production. Such portrayals represent an expansion of the media's portrayal of what it means to be a man.

Globalization has become one of the key vehicles by which companies increase their sales; the booming markets of China and India are seen as two of the most important markets for a variety of products and services. Perhaps the commodity that is exported most fully is identity: the conception of what it means to be human, of what it means to be male (United Nations Conference on Trade and Development 2002). A key component of global marketing is to package American consumer goods with images of American style success. Many exported products sell images of masculinity—the classic example is the packaging of the Marlboro man, the cowboy characterization used to advertise Marlboro cigarettes. The Marlboro man was the embodiment of hegemonic masculinity: strong, silent, detached, individualistic, virile. The cigarettes were marketed globally by creating an association between the product and the hegemonic masculine ideal of the American male.

In media representations, portrayals of men's lives and relationships are often inaccurate and harmful. An example is a television commercial for one of the major automobile companies. The commercial shows men working hard on a construction site, throwing large pieces of concrete into the back of a pickup truck. The men heave the broken slabs, dust and rocks flying everywhere; the outside of the truck is covered in dirt. When the men have finished, two get into the truck, presumably to haul away the concrete. The man in the passenger seat, clearly tired, puts his foot up on the dashboard, leaving a large grease smudge. The driver chastises his coworker for making a mess of his truck and hits him in the back of the head. The blow is not damaging, but it is dominating and humiliating and clearly would sting. The message is clear; real men express their feelings of anger or annoyance with violence and domination. When a man feels harmed he must harm or shame the offending party. There is no discussion of why there could have been a misunderstanding; it is clear that the recipient of the blow has to either accept the abuse or retaliate with greater force.

Globalization has influenced psychosocial health and masculinity in other ways as well. Altman (2004:66) presents a powerful example.

The most dramatic examples of the effect of globalization on sexuality come through the rapid growth of the HIV/AIDS pandemic. In many senses AIDS is an epidemic of globalization, both in terms of its spread and its response. It is symbolic that the epidemic, first identified in the hospitals of the United States, is most prevalent in the poorest countries of the world, and there are effectively now two epidemics, a small one in rich countries, which is growing slowly, and a rapidly expanding one in much of the poor world where the huge advances in medical therapies are largely unavailable. The epidemic is spread by the relentless movement of people, the breakdown of old sexual restraints, increasing needle use, and the unwillingness of authorities, both governmental and religious, to confront the real needs of prevention.

Over the centuries, technological innovation has had powerful impacts on masculinity, and vice versa (Mansfield 2006). As the world becomes more integrated through Internet technologies, at least for those with access to technological resources, men are increasingly influenced not only by the messages transmitted through technology, but by technology itself. The Internet and other hypertechnologies may expand the means by which men receive social work services. Perhaps one of the most profound changes is how such technologies have changed the nature of communication. As geographical or organic communities deteriorate, social work could lose its context for service provision, spelling the "end of social work" (Kreuger 1997).

E-mail, instant messaging, and text messaging have changed the ways people communicate. E-mail has several advantages and disadvantages as a means of communication. It allows people to communicate with others across the world at any time, but it also has some potentially negative effects. It may reduce the actual time that people spend in other types of communication and lead to reduced intimacy in personal relationships. E-mail may help men maintain or increase the number of contacts, as men typically are not good at calling their family and friends. Not surprisingly, however, recent data show that men may not value the use of the Internet as a tool for maintaining social relationships as much as women do. Some 42 percent of men in a recent survey stated they valued the social aspects of the Internet (keeping in touch with family and friends), compared to 57 percent of women (Fallows 2005). This is in spite of the fact that the same data set showed that men are likely to spend more time on the Internet.

Men are often socialized to have impersonal and nonaffective communication, so in some ways the new technologies are well suited to the communication needs of men. On the other hand, they may also further the social isolation of some groups of men. The results of research are preliminary and inconclusive. Kraut et al. (1998) observed what is termed the Internet paradox, the notion that one may have increased interaction with people through the Internet yet feel a decrease in social connectedness. However, several years after their first study, the authors found opposite results. It is posited that the evolution in how people use the Internet may account for some of this change.

More research is needed to understand the nature of how men use the Internet, and the effect of this use on their communication.

The potential exists for both benefit and harm. For instance, John, a 45-year-old construction worker, moved from the Northeast to the mid-South, where more construction jobs were available. John was from a working-class background and was unfamiliar with computers. However, shortly after his family moved, his daughter showed him how to use e-mail. He found that many of his old friends had e-mail accounts, and he was able to maintain contact with them. Maintaining these relationships has provided John with a sense of connectedness and support. While he does not normally express deeper emotions to these friends, it is the communication itself, not the type of communication, that provides him this sense of social support. On the other hand, an example of the negative impact of the Internet is the case of Chuck, who finds himself increasingly isolated from his family as he spends countless hours on gambling and pornography websites. Chuck has lost thousands of dollars playing online poker and is at risk of losing his home. Chuck's wife recently threatened him with divorce if he does not seek help. One of the potential detrimental effects of the Internet has been the proliferation of addiction to such gambling and pornography sites, which will be discussed in chapter 13.

In his exploration of pathological intent use, Davis (2001:193) cautions against the notion that all Internet use is negative. He describes healthy Internet use as "using the internet for an expressed purpose in a reasonable amount of time without cognitive or behavioral discomfort. Healthy internet users can separate internet communication with real life communication. They employ the internet as a helpful tool rather than a source of identity."

The Men's Movement

The men's movement is often discussed as if it were a singular phenomenon. However, the men's movement can really be viewed as several movements, each with its own historical roots, views about the nature of men, and understandings of the problems of men in the modern era. This section will briefly explore these movements and highlight some of their potential implications for social work practice.

The men's movement overall was a response to the feminism of the 1960s. Early men's movement proponents, responding to the new feminist critiques of dominant society, explored the impact of a patriarchal society on women and took on the task of changing men according to an antiviolence, antisexism platform (Kimmel 1996). These groups largely adopted a feminist, gender equity position. Their focus was on exploring the ways in which men perpetuated sexist behavior that led to the oppression of women. Some gender equity authors were able to effectively describe the negative impact that sexism and patriarchy had on men as well (Goldberg 1977). While early men's movement proponents made important gains in helping many men and groups of men change, they were often discounted by mainstream men. It has been noted that while they provided the valuable service of advocating against the most harmful effects of patriarchy and traditional male culture, they shunned any focus on the lives and identity of individual men and the demands that society was placing upon them in terms of their identity (Seidler 1989). Because men and masculinity were viewed as the problem, men were discouraged from joining with other men and exploring the impact of the seismic social changes upon themselves. Seidler (1997:5) notes that "The idea was that men were also limited and in some ways oppressed by dominant masculinities. The lives of men were impoverished through the disconnection they have to make with their bodies and emotions. Within an Enlightenment vision of modernity, men were expected to be independent and self-sufficient. Emotional needs were a sign of weakness and therefore were often suppressed as a threat to male identities."

The early proponents of the men's movement were often not able to incorporate a strengths orientation toward men. Instead of carefully dissecting the negative and positive aspects of masculinity, they adopted a position that was often too dogmatic and rigid and failed to engage everyday, working-class men or men of color. These groups failed to resonate with poor and disenfranchised men, who were in touch with their own historical experiences of oppression and were often alienated by the assertion that their realities were characterized by power and privilege.

In the 1970s and 1980s men's groups that were not associated with feminist movements began to explore the needs of men. Some of these groups identified themselves as being in favor of males and men's rights. Men's rights groups varied greatly. Some appeared to have a strongly political, antifeminist orientation. Others advocated for men to have equal rights as noncustodial parents. These groups were characterized by a desire to help men reposition themselves in terms of their power and position. In some ways they were seen as being reactive to changes in American society, and they have often been referred to as being part of an antifeminist backlash (Heath 2003).

A different type of men's movement was the mythopoetic movement, which was jump-started by an interview of the poet Robert Bly (Thompson 1982). In this article and in his subsequent book, *Iron John* (1990), Bly posits that men suffer from deep confusion about what it means to be male. He asserts that prior to the industrial revolution, men were initiated into manhood by working side by side with their fathers and other men. Farmers worked with their fathers in the fields, and artisans apprenticed at the feet of their fathers. The industrial revolution shifted the means of production toward the factories, where labor was characterized by routine movements that needed little mentorship. While the field or the workshop may be an ideal context for conversation, dialogue, and behavioral modeling, factories are made for efficiency. Factories were designed to keep people focused on their work. Subsequently, men lost many of their opportunities for mentorship. Fast forward to the 1950s and the return of many American males from war. Consumerism was rampant, and the machine of American capitalism rewarded the working male with material goods. As good as the 1950s male was at making a living, he was not wonderful at relationships. He was not able to talk about his feelings, and he often felt meaningless and expendable. The next generation rebelled, becoming more sensitive, more in touch with their own feelings. Yet, according to Bly, this male was as confused and disconnected as was the 1950s male. The male of the 1960s was in touch with his feminine, feeling side yet unable to claim and own the more masculine parts of his personality. Herein lies the problem: men had lost the capacity of being whole, integrated men. They lost their sense of wholeness. Through stories and metaphors, Bly challenges men to find ways of integrating their deep, masculine selves. Mythopoetic men's groups engaged in various methods to help men explore their identity. Discussion groups were formed, and men were encouraged to talk together about their experiences of being men in society. Men's movement groups also created rituals of initiation, where men would attend weekend retreats, and followup groups that helped them understand their experiences of loss, reconnect to the world of men, and work toward continued growth and healing in the company of other men. While psychodynamic in orientation, mythopoetic men's groups seek to encourage men to explore their own sense of masculinity, and they approach men from a strengths perspective.

Harry Brod has several critiques of the mythopoetic movement. He notes that the weekend retreats that men in the movement attend are just that—retreats from women, from communities, and from children (Nangeroni and Mackenzie 2002). He believes that the changes that men need to make must be made in partnership with women. As an example, he notes that men who attend such meetings in response to feeling disempowered are disempowered not because of their relationships with women, but because they are entrenched within competitive capitalist systems.

Over the last twenty years, another men's group, the Promise Keepers, has become prominent. This Christian group seeks to return men to their "traditional" role within families and reposition their relationships with women (Heath 2003). Explicitly antifeminist, the Promise Keepers have been criticized as espousing a "fundamentalist gender politics" (Connell 2003:11). Connell positions these groups within a broader global movement to preserve the power of men. These groups are often homophobic in orientation and are explicitly antiequity.

New gender equity and profeminist men's groups have been gaining in strength during the last decade. These movements have focused on the nature of men's privilege and the impact of this privilege on both men and women. One of the primary aims of these groups has been to end violence against women, and to challenge patriarchy as it plays out on the local and national levels. One of the key groups is the National Organization of Men Against Sexism (NOMAS). According to its website, NOMAS

> advocates a perspective that is pro-feminist, gay affirmative, anti-racist, dedicated to enhancing men's lives, and committed to justice on a broad range of social issues including class, age, religion, and physical abilities. We affirm that working to make this nation's ideals of equality substantive is the finest expression of what it means to be men. We believe that the new opportunities becoming available to women and men will be beneficial to both. Men can live as happier and more fulfilled human beings by challenging the old-fashioned rules of masculinity that embody the assumption of male superiority. Traditional masculinity includes many positive characteristics in which we take pride and find strength, but it also contains qualities that have limited and harmed us. We are deeply supportive of men who are struggling with the issues of traditional masculinity. As an organization for changing men, we care about men and are especially concerned with men's problems, as well as the difficult issues in most men's lives.

Brod explores the tasks of a profeminist men's movement in a powerful radio interview (Nangeroni and Mackenzie 2002). He notes that men must become more fully aware of the feminist slogan "the personal is political" and develop an understanding of the negative consequences of their power and privilege. He notes that men are alienated from their feelings, their families, and each other. He notes that "society confers very real rewards to men that will conform to self-destructive and self-alienated behaviors." Men who appear less emotionally available seem to be more rational and are more likely to be placed in positions of power.

The men's movement is at something of a crossroads. To date, few groups seem to have successfully found a way to adopt strengths-oriented attitudes toward men—including men from diverse economic and religious traditions—oriented toward gender equality, while at the same time being supportive and nurturing of the individual, psychological needs of men. While the creation of such groups may be a tall order and largely has come from the self-help movement, social workers should encourage the exploration of models for meeting these aims. Helping men to create and develop self-help groups that enable them to validate their strengths and explore new conceptions of masculinity will be an important task of masculinity researchers and practitioners in the coming years.

Case Example

Jorge Leon is a 28-year-old taxi diver in Lima, Peru. He has a college degree in accounting, but for the past several years he has been unable to find other work. After college he worked for a federal agency, but he lost his job when his position was cut. As Peru has struggled to respond to the demands of international lending agencies and changes in the global economy, it has eliminated various public-sector services. Also, while the Peruvian economy has been doing well, life for many middle-class Peruvians has become more complex. Increases in unemployment and crime have made life increasingly difficult.

For the first two years after Jorge lost his position, he did not work. He said he mostly stayed by himself in his room in his family of origin's home, where he would drink a great deal of Pisco, Peruvian brandy. Jorge's situation changed when he met Elisabeth, an artist with a bubbly personality and a zest for life. Still unable to find an accounting job, he decided to drive a taxi to show his new girlfriend that he was worthy of her affection—being industrious and hard working are important values that Peruvian women hold for their men. Being a taxi driver in Lima has been stressful. Lima is a hectic city of nine million people, and drivers are far less attentive to traffic rules and lanes than most Americans are accustomed to. Traffic in Lima can be intense, and competition for passengers can be fierce. Accidents are frequent, and one must work extremely hard in order to earn a living. Typically, Jorge works twenty-four hours, takes a day off, and then works another twenty-four hours.

For the first year of their relationship, things went well for Jorge and Elisabeth. Influenced by Western and modern values, which have been rapidly changing Peruvian society, the two moved in together without being married.

This was difficult for both of their families, yet both sets of parents ultimately gave their blessing to their seemingly happy adult children.

Elisabeth was not able to earn enough money selling her paintings, so she worked in an art gallery for a woman who sold the work of indigenous women painters. A descendant of the Incas, Elisabeth reflected both indigenous and modern themes in her own work. After a while, Elisabeth's boss decided to make her a full partner in the business. She quickly went from having a salary about half of what Jorge was able to make to more than double his income. While he would not admit it, Jorge began to feel jealous and angry. As with many men, Jorge's anger served as a cover and replacement for more difficult and less traditionally masculine feelings of inadequacy and humiliation. Jorge was struggling with the success of his increasingly modern and successful girlfriend, who gained power and status. He no longer felt like "the head of the household" and silently contrasted his own unused professional training with his girlfriend's success. Jorge began to drink excessively again. He refused to let Elisabeth go out with her friends and demanded that she be home from work in time to cook dinner. Elisabeth was dismayed. She had believed that her boyfriend had more equalitarian views, but she began to worry that he was becoming increasingly "machista" (macho or chauvinistic). One evening during an argument, Jorge was feeling out of control and forced his unwilling girlfriend to have sex with him. He then called her a whore and told her to have sex with her other feminist, artist friends. Jorge passed out from the alcohol, and Elisabeth packed her bags. She moved back to her parents' house the following day. Elisabeth called the following week and asked Jorge to go with her to see a therapist. He refused, saying that only those who are weak seek help outside of themselves, and said he never wanted to see her again. Elisabeth was deeply saddened that her formerly loving boyfriend could be so cold, hard, and detached. He continued to ignore her calls but would periodically call her when drunk and would blame her for their breakup and problems.

Jorge was not able to face his own inadequacy and pain. Instead, he defended against his failure through anger and blame. He constructed an intricate narrative in which he accepted no responsibility for his feelings but made Elizabeth the antagonist of his story. It is tragic that Jorge was not willing to seek help. Had he done so, he may have been able to understand that while Elisabeth was not to blame for his fate, he too was not entirely at fault. Jorge found himself caught between many of the forces that affect men in the globalized world: economic changes that impact the lives of individual men, changes in sex roles based upon women's developing sense of their own potential, and the influence of some of the darker characteristics of male identity and help-seeking behavior of the hegemonic male (in this case, of the Latino hegemonic ideal). He was, of course, to blame for his sexual assault of his former girlfriend, yet by not being able see the social influences behind some of his behaviors, it was too overwhelming for him to accept any responsibility. Caught in a world that is rapidly leaving him behind, Jorge may continue to drink and live alone.

FOR WRITING AND REFLECTION

1. Suppose that Jorge came to you while you were the social worker in an employment training program and, in a moment of honesty and openness, told you his whole story. What services might be beneficial for him to explore?

2. How might the four theories outlined in the last chapter inform your work with Jorge?

3. Which of the four theories would you be most likely to use, and why?

4. How does Jorge's culture impact the choices and recommendations you explore in the previous questions?

Case Example

Cal Jones is a 55-year-old American man who has been living in Colombia for the last four years. In a very real sense, Cal moved to Colombia in an effort to save his life. For many years, Cal had been struggling with extreme depression. He had tried therapy but never found it successful. Cal was frustrated that the three therapists he saw wanted to focus on his childhood and family of origin. He felt invalidated when they attempted to steer conversations toward those issues, in spite of his clear description of good relationships with his siblings and parents. Cal had hoped to discuss specific strategies for handling his depression, and he wanted to talk about his frustrations with meeting women. Each time he attempted to discuss these concerns, Cal's therapists would try to draw connections to hypothetical childhood events and issues, which for him did not exist. Cal wanted to talk about what he saw as the real issue: most women found him physically unattractive. He understood this, and while he had largely come to terms with what it meant in his life, he felt the need to discuss ways of overcoming this limitation. He understood that his lack of classic physical attractiveness was complicated by his personal tastes. Like many men, Cal has internalized standards and mandates for physical attractiveness for his potential partners; Cal is very picky. Cal was married briefly, during his late thirties. Cal was thrilled that Vanessa, a Latina woman in her mid-twenties, was interested in him, and they married after they had dated for just a few weeks. Vanessa was born in Colombia and had moved to the United States several years before. She had a 6-year-old son by the American man who brought her to the United States. Cal ignored early signs that Vanessa might not be the best partner for him. She had a nearly violent temper and was prone to bouts of severe depression and periods of mania. She did not inform him that she was indeed bipolar until after they were married. During their stormy six-month relationship, Vanessa and Cal visited Colombia several times. He immediately felt comfortable there and liked the slower pace of life and the warmth of Vanessa's family. He enjoyed the closeness and intimacy that people seemed to share. However, Vanessa's untreated mental illness prevented her from expressing a great deal of affection. She was also extremely hostile and would break objects when angry. During her depressive moods, she would hide in her room for days. Cal asked her to move out when she took his credit cards to Las Vegas and spent eight thousand dollars in three days.

Even though he had a college degree, Cal had worked as a limousine driver for many years. The company Cal worked for catered to the very wealthy, and between his salary and tips he made a very good living. However, he was not happy. He found himself torn between doing what he did for work and doing what he loved to do, which was writing and journalism. After his marriage dissolved, Cal found himself thinking about Colombia more and more. Over the next several years, he traveled to Colombia on his vacations, making friends and connections there. He found that Colombian women seemed far less interested in his physical attributes, and more interested in him as a person. For a decade he saved his money and invested well. His house had skyrocketed in value. At age 50 he had saved enough money to move to Colombia, if he could find a part time job. Cal found a job working in an American-owned travel agency and made his move.

Cal has very mixed feelings about living in Colombia. On one hand, he enjoys the quality of life that is afforded by being able to life comfortably though working only twenty-five hours a week as the manager of the travel business. He also enjoys the fact that he has been able to frequently date and have intimate relationships with local women. However, he also believes that the main reason these women are interested in him is that they see him as a potential way out of poverty. Cal understands the power and control that this gives him over these women, many of whom are twenty years his junior. He also worries that they are not being honest with him, and that his relationships are often not authentic. When Cal is honest with himself, he has great ambivalence about these encounters. He finds them pleasurable, but he also feels a bit exploitative. He also admits to liking the power and control that this gives him. Cal has felt relatively happy for the first time in many years, and he enjoys his job and the Latin American lifestyle.

FOR WRITING AND REFLECTION

1. On a month-long vacation back to the United States, Cal asks to see you in treatment. Knowing his story, what would you see as his treatment goals?

2. Cal expresses to you that he wants to talk about his physical appearance, and that social workers in the past have avoided the topic. Would you be comfortable talking to him about this topic? How would you approach it?

3. In what ways do you feel you might be effective with Cal? In what ways might your own history, background, and skills not be well matched for working with him? How might you overcome these deficits?

4. As Cal moves into older adulthood, what issues must he begin to consider?

Conceptions of Masculinity and the Development of Men

Connell (1998) observed that masculinities are not homogeneous. Even within supposedly homogenous groups, masculinity often differs in how it is expressed and lived by individual men. Holding rigid notions of what it means to be a man is a significant problem for many individual men. The adoption of dogmatic, rigid, and overly restrictive notions of masculinity has been found to be a central cause of gender role strain, the pressure that men feel when they attempt to conform to gender norms that are often extremely difficult to achieve (Pleck 1981).

These rigid conceptualizations of masculinity are deeply ingrained within social institutions, such as family and the workplace (Walby 1997). In fact, social workers and other helpers may hold unrealistic and harmful expectations for men. These sometimes subtle expectations can greatly affect the helping relationship, as social workers compare and contrast individual men to their own internalized schema of what men should be. These expectations can lead social workers to underestimate the capacity of some men, and they may lead men to feel undervalued and unappreciated for who they are. For instance, a man who has struggled with developing and maintaining a stable career is often judged more harshly than a woman in a similar situation (Sommers 2000). This chapter examines various conceptions of masculinity and adult male development. The exercises and case studies at the end of the chapter will help you examine your own beliefs about notions of masculinity and assess how this may affect your work with men.

Men Becoming Men

One desired outcome for working with men is to help them develop their own conception of what it means to be a man. This is a difficult task, as men may feel threatened if the social worker does not accept their traditional male values and behavior. This theme—the balance between accepting men's views of masculinity and helping them explore the positive and negative consequences of these conceptions in their lives, their health, and their relationships—will be revisited many times throughout this book. Men may be negatively affected by some of their more rigid beliefs and notions about what it means to be a man. Social workers must develop skills for helping men evaluate the costs of these beliefs and values, while at the same time assuring that their clients experience "unconditional positive regard" (Rogers 1961). Yet this is often easier said than done. Shay and Maltas (1998:98) explore this theme realistically when, referring to men in couples counseling, that "It is a paradox that the very expectation for deep understanding and intimate communication is directed towards someone whose gender socialization is so different as to require skills in a kind of cross-cultural communication." They note that a goal for many men in counseling is to help them "become more aware of the cultural forces, mediated through their families, which shape their gender ideologies and their relationship behaviors. Such heightened awareness makes possible a more conscious evaluation of the implicit choices they have made about their behavior in intimate relationships and an exploration of the costs and benefits of continuing on in the same fashion."

At no time do Shay and Maltas discuss making men change. They recognize that when one is dealing with internalized values that are culturally ascribed, one must give men the opportunity to explore how their beliefs and behaviors affect their dreams and goals. The temptation of many social workers, particularly women who have witnessed the effect that many of these beliefs and behaviors have had upon themselves and other women, is to directly and forcefully confront men about sexist attitudes. Some social workers may view their primary ethical responsibility in such situations as being toward social change. I fully agree that an important goal of our work with men is to help them behave lovingly, responsibly, nonviolently, and ethically toward women. Yet taking a confrontational approach with men may alienate them from working collaboratively with you and with professional helpers in the future. The costs of this alienation could have grave consequences for men and their loved ones. Change is a slow and often painful process. For now, it is important to understand that masculinity is a complex, multicultural phenomenon, and that men often are stuck between multiple domains and expectations about how they are supposed to behave.

Conceptions of Masculinity

This section looks at different conceptions of masculinity and how masculine identity is developed. Some of the discussion hinges on research in the behavioral and social sciences, and some comes from gender studies and other disciplines in the humanities. It is difficult to explore identity and development separately, as they are highly intertwined. I start with the notion of identity, allowing for a more complete discussion of other developmental issues later in this chapter. Clearly, the development of masculine identity affects and is affected by the biological, psychological, and social forces that influence other aspects of development. While I discuss these issues separately to deconstruct and illuminate several key perspectives, the confluence of these factors is evident in many of the case examples that I present in this book.

As mentioned, men and their social workers must grapple with acceptance (both men's self-acceptance and acceptance by the social worker) versus the known effects of traditional masculine norms. On one hand, it is essential to treat men who ascribe to traditional values as a culturally different group whose values must be accepted and cherished. Social workers must "start where their clients are" and be accepting of values that are different from their own. On the other hand, some traditional male beliefs, values, and behaviors are associated with numerous poor outcomes for men, including disease, illness, and even shorter life expectancy (Brooks and Silverstein 1995). Some traditional male values have been associated with discrimination and violence against women. I will argue that what is necessary is to help men reflect upon their values and make choices for themselves based on a reasoned review of the consequences and costs. Additionally, what Freud believed about mechanisms of defense may hold true for traditional masculine values and behaviors; they may have functionality to the degree to which they are flexibly and selectively "used." For instance, stoicism is extremely helpful when dealing with a crisis, yet less so when a man is called upon to express empathy in intimate relationships. Several concepts that I consider below will lend insight into how to approach men around these issues.

Connell (1998) posits that masculinity studies in the 1970s and 1980s often consisted of oversimplifications about notions of the male sex role. In this work, the author contends, specific variables were measured in female and male populations to ascertain what behaviors were correlated with men. The work was often limited in that it did not account for the role that power plays in the construction of masculine identity. Newer research and scholarship focuses on the social construction of masculine identity. In these approaches, masculine identity is not viewed as one fixed, context-free phenomenon, but as a complex and shifting set of cognitive, emotive, and behavioral possibilities. Consistent with nondeterministic views of human behavior, social constructionist perspectives lead to the potential for men to critically examine, and therefore alter, behaviors that were heretofore viewed as inherently male.

Hegemonic masculinity is a concept that helps us understand masculine identity as it is socially constructed. The previous chapter explored the notion of hegemonic masculinity and its relationship to men and globalization. While not without its problems, understanding the concept of hegemonic masculinity, or perhaps competing notions of masculinities, provides social workers with a tool by which to understand how men view and judge themselves, and how they are viewed and judged by society. As Oliffe (2005:2250) contends, "Hegemonic masculinity also signifies as positions of cultural authority and leadership, not just in relation to other masculinities, but in relation to gender order as a whole."

The concept of hegemonic masculinity helps us focus on the aspects of masculine behavior that are expected of men in society. This may at times be overstated, as masculinity does tend to be contextual. Behaviors that the dominant culture does not accept may be valued and cherished within ethnically diverse communities. For example, harmony with others and cooperation are traits valued in most Native American cultures, yet they may not be valued in mainstream social institutions (Krech 2002). The notion of hegemonic masculinity assumes that men will experience conflict when their behaviors conflict with norms of dominant male behavior. However, within their own communities these behaviors are accepted. Where problems occur is when men who ascribe to different models of masculinity inevitably engage the institutions of the dominant culture, which often do not accept alternative ways of being a man. For example, the collectivist traditions of indigenous men may not lend themselves to success in the competitive, individualistic world of most American universities. The inability of these institutions to incorporate other models of masculinity may in part account for the low university attendance and graduation rates of some diverse populations. This is not surprising, as the process of promoting the hegemonic masculine idea in the educational system starts in elementary and secondary schools. Nunn (2005) identifies seven structural mechanisms that reinforce hegemonic masculinity in school settings: textbooks; the legitimation of sports; orientation toward writing; teachers as leaders; school as a space of mandatory congregation and interaction among students; and normative heterosexism. While Nunn notes that some diversity of masculinities is accepted in some schools the hegemonic idea is usually reinforced and privileged.

Connell (1998) observed that the study of masculinity has reached what he refers to as an "ethnographic moment" in which the study of the lived experiences of individual men, culturally diverse men, and men whose masculinities do not conform to the hegemonic idea must be championed. This appeal has relevance for social work and social work practitioners, as we need to guard against preconceived assumptions, stereotypes, and prejudices in our work with men. As I shall stress several times in this book, social workers should use research and ideas about masculinity as hypotheses yet must be guided in their practice by the truths of their individual male clients.

This socially constructed notion of masculinity is one of the domains of research that Connell (1998) suggests are key to understanding masculinity. They include plural masculinities, hierarchy and hegemony, collective masculinities, bodies as arenas, active construction, and contradictions. As discussed earlier, various social influences affect the development of masculine identity. There is not one masculinity, but multiple or plural masculinities. Within each society, within each culture, and even within each man, multiple masculinities exist. A man's perceptions about his own masculinity and behavior shift and change over time. Masculinities are also created collectively in the context of social groups. Men's bodies are often the places where conceptions of masculinity are played out. Notions of what a masculine body is often change over time. Further, what a man will do with his body and what his body will tolerate also vary by culture. In accordance with their collective and socially constructed natures, masculinities often conflict, particularly when men's different cultural realities come into contact. A college professor, for example, is expected to express his masculinity in one way with female colleagues yet differently with male friends while engaging in workouts in the gym. That men are able to move between these worlds and still function well is indicative of the strength that comes from this form of biculturality.

In their important synthesis of research on gender differences and the clinical implications that can be derived from this research, Mahalik, Good, and Englar-Carlson (2003) present a number of masculine scripts by which men live their lives. These scripts each represent aspects of the hegemonic idea that research has suggested guides male development and behavior. The scripts are metaphors that help explain key aspects of male identity.

- The strong-silent-type script leads men toward emotional restriction and stoicism. The authors note numerous consequences of adherence to this script, including depression, anxiety, and social isolation.
- The tough-guy script is learned by boys, as they must show bravery and suppress their vulnerability. Boys learn to not back down from fights, thereby placing themselves at a higher risk of violence as they mature. Not developing the ability to directly express emotions predisposes men to relationship problems and substance abuse.
- The give-'em-hell script, related to the tough-guy script, suggests the ideal that men do not back down from conflicts but demonstrate their power and willingness to use violence as a means of exerting control and their will. Men who conform to this script are at high risk of engaging in violence in intimate relationships and may have legal problems as well.
- When men attempt to conform to the playboy script, they seek sexual relationships outside the context of emotional intimacy. Having suppressed the capacity to feel and express their own emotions, they use sex as a primary means of achieving connections. Such men equate their ability to make sexual conquests with their own personal worth. Sexual conquests become a means of achieving personal acceptance. Adhering to this norm predisposes men to problems maintaining long-term, loving partnerships and places them at risk for sexually transmitted diseases.
- The homophobic script has powerful consequences for men and their capacity to form intimate relationships with each other. Men adhering to this script seek to prove their own manhood by shunning connections with other men, in fear of being viewed as homosexual. Since according to the hegemonic ideal homosexuality is antimasculine, many men will go to great lengths to prove they are not gay, often eschewing any type of relationship that could be construed as homosexual. The homophobic script leads to isolation and often to denial of aspects of oneself.
- The winner script is important to American culture, in which men are expected to be competitive and successful. While competition has its place, and material and career success are of value, rigidly holding this script as the only way to achieve valuing and meaning can be associated with heart disease and other health concerns. It may also make it difficult for men to connect to others in noncompetitive contexts.
- The independence script refers to men's adherence to a hyperindependent relationship style that leads to isolation and disconnection. This script also has strong consequences for men's health, as men who follow this script

believe that they can solve their problems on their own. Seeking and receiving help are viewed as weaknesses.

One of the most important theorists in masculinity, Pleck (1981) developed the concept of gender role strain. According to Pleck's theory, men internalize socially constructed norms about what it means to be a man. The previous generation of parents, teachers, and other adults transmit these stereotypes through their expectations to developing boys. Boys begin to develop an understanding of the proper way to be masculine and what behaviors are seen as feminine. They learn the rules of the game and attempt to match their own behavior and personality to these rules. However, these guidelines often conflict with one's own sense of self. They are often contradictory as well, so no matter how hard a boy or man may attempt to fit the model, achieving "perfect" masculinity is impossible. The discrepancy between these internalized ideas and a man's inability to achieve them causes a great deal of strain, emotional conflict, behavioral problems, and pain. Pleck asserts that these conflicts actually create trauma in men that is partially responsible for men detaching from their emotions.

A colleague recently told a story that serves as a perfect example. Her nephew, a child care worker in a recreation center, was experiencing conflict with one of his female colleagues. Apparently she felt that he was too easily influenced by the children's emotions and was not firm and stoic enough. Feeling particularly frustrated with him, she said that he was acting "way too girly." Messages such as this send men mixed signals. Our socialization teaches us to be firm, stoic, detached, and emotionally uninvolved. However, certain social roles mandate that we develop other aspects of our personalities. Yet when we exhibit these behaviors, we are often censored, shamed, or punished for them.

Lazur and Majors (1995) focus on the impact that this gender role strain has on men of color. They argue that the normative masculine model is that of white, middle-class, heterosexual, employed, able-bodied men. Men of color and other men do not fit this model and thus find themselves stuck in a difficult double-bind (Phillips 2006). On one hand, a racist model leads men of color to judge themselves against an ideal they will never achieve. However, social acceptance pushes men to attempt to adapt to the hegemonic ideal. On the other hand, the degree to which they do achieve these norms may distance them from parts of their own culture.

When a man of color acts according to the prescriptions of dominant masculinity norms, he often finds that other people in his particular ethnic group may consider that he has "sold out." He has bought into a cultural concept that, in effect, negates him (Philips 2006:412).

Within Latino society, machismo is considered the constellation of ideal male characteristics, which include physical power, social domination, and a discounting of feminine characteristics. The roots of machismo have been traced to the influence of Catholicism on indigenous peoples and the reaction of indigenous men to their own subjugation at the hands of Spanish conquistadors (Hardin 2002). Taylor and Behnke (2005) contend that central components of machismo are the role of the Latino father, his capacity to provide for his family, and the lengths he will go to do so. Latino men who for socioeconomic reasons are unable to engage in this prosocial aspect of machismo may engage in other, less positive ways of proving their worth and masculinity.

Developmental Theories

> When a man of forty falls in love with a girl of twenty, it isn't her youth he is seeking but his own.
>
> —Lenore Coffee

Traditional developmental theories conceptualized adulthood as the final stage of human development (Zastrow and Ashman-Kirst 1997). Regardless of differences in focus and in the actual delineation of stages, human beings are viewed as progressing through clearly defined stages of development during childhood and adolescence. Traditional developmental theories view adult personalities as being relatively fixed (Miller 1993). From this view, actual changes in adults' lives are due to changes in social context, and the degree to which the relatively fixed personality structure of the adult is able to fit into the world. In terms of physical development, classical developmental theories present clearly defined patterns of growth and development during childhood and adolescence but mainly view adulthood as a state of ever-accelerating physical decline, which culminates in death. In other words, adulthood traditionally has been viewed not as a time of growth and development, but as the culmination of prior developmental states (Park and Schwarz 2000). The already developed adult must use what he has in order to meet the responsibilities and tasks of adulthood.

However, the modern field of developmental studies has revealed that adulthood is indeed dynamic. Individuals grow, change, and develop throughout their lifespan (Colarusso and Nemiroff 1987). Personality traits and structure developed in early life may certainly predispose men to certain behavioral and affective tendencies, but adults have a profound capacity to develop, grow, and change. Men are capable of adding new relational responses and behaviors to their repertoire. They can develop new capacities for self-expression and learn to deeply feel emotions of which they previously were unaware. Personality structures should be viewed as tendencies, but adults are capable of maximizing their strengths and working on their limitations. For example, the adolescent boy that was once diagnosed as being antisocial may develop (or perhaps reacquaint himself with) new capacities for empathy, deep caring, and a prosocial lifestyle. What was thought to be a clear psychiatric diagnosis may have been an environmental response to a social world that taught him that it was emotionally (and perhaps physically) unsafe to care about others. The boy who was lazy and underachieving may find the strength within himself to work hard toward his goals and dreams. During his adolescent years, he may have lived according to a life script in which he played the role of an underachieving, uninterested, and disengaged loner. Over time he may have learned on his own (or perhaps in collaboration with a good social worker) to write a new script for himself in which he is motivated, hardworking, and engaged in life. Those who know him in adulthood may be shocked to learn about his former self.

The next section explores some of the theories and research on adult development as they pertain to men, focusing on stage theories. Stage theories help us view men's lives as evolving stories and narratives within a developmental period. Each stage can be viewed as a chapter of an evolving journey in which biological, psychological, and social seasons shape the context and potentialities of being. Being able to view men's lives as stories is important, as it is through the construction of individual men's stories in practice that social workers can help those men achieve their goals and dreams. While each man will ultimately teach you what is important in his individual life course, by understanding some of the developmental stages and needs you can help him place his personal story within a universal, human context. Knowing this developmental context helps men make sense of their lives and experiences and helps them see themselves as connected to humanity as a whole. Other perspectives and theories that help us understand male development are also addressed in this section. The case examples at the end of the chapter will help you view the relationship between the developmental norms that are presented and the manner in which individual men live and express them.

I would like to preface the discussion with a warning. As with many theories, it is good to view stage theories as hypotheses. Theories of development should be used to help improve your understanding of masculinity and what it means to be a man, yet only provide guidance. When attempting to understand a particular man, these theories must be used in conjunction with other approaches, such as "other" developmental theories and general clinical theories. It is also important to remember that the best guidance for understanding a man is the man himself; theories are only approximations that help guide our practice.

Elder, Shanahan, and Clipp (1994:5) highlight this notion when they observe that "the life-course implications of drastic change for adult development and health vary according to the personal experiences that people bring to new situations. These are determined in part by a person's life stage or social age, whether childhood, young adulthood, or late life. Any stage of life indicates potential life experiences, developmental assets, social roles, and options and reveals by comparison the variable meaning of events across the life course."

When a man's experience does not fit your theories, it is important not to push him into a box in which he does not fit, but to look for alternative explanations. Often the most appropriate place to look for this explanation is within the words and story of the client himself. Stage theories are tentative explanations that help us provide structure to the story of lives.

Stage Theories

Stage theories are valuable means of understanding adult development (Austrian 2002). According to stage theories, all human beings undertake key developmental tasks at specific stages of their lives (Ashford, Lecroy, and Lortie 2005). These theories posit biological and psychosocial patterns and tasks that characterize each period. For instance, one of the key developmental tasks of late adolescence and early adulthood is the development of autonomy and individuation (Crokett and Silbereisen 2000). This psychosocial development occurs along with, and is facilitated by, physical developments that enable young men to gain the capacity for self-care and independence (Lyons, Wodarski, and Feit 1998). Brain structures and the capacity for complex reasoning allow for the development of more advanced cognitive processing and more mutual and adult relationships. The biological, psychological, and social developmental realities are intertwined and support and/or inhibit each other (Hutchison and Charlesworth 1998).

Stage theories are based on attempts to describe what all human beings have and do in common at different times of their lives. Yet stage theories are not without their limitations. Schriver (2001:185–186) notes that these theories "are incomplete, they exclude many people, and they reflect biases due to the value assumptions and historical periods out of which they emerged. . . . The developmental modes we have historically used are not representative of even most people when we compare the race, gender, and class diversity of the people with whom social workers work and the race, class, and gender reflected in traditional models. This is to say nothing of differences in sexual orientation, age, and disabling conditions completely ignored or specified as abnormal in many traditional models."

For example, autonomy and individuation as they are classically constructed are very much white, middle-class phenomena. It is not uncommon for first-generation male Latino immigrants to live at home until they are married; often they will live with their wife and children in their parents' home. This is not a sign of a young man's lack of development; cultural realities shape human development in powerful ways. Therefore, while stage theories may often be overgeneralized and based on assumptions that are not applicable across ethnic groups, they are valuable in pointing out the universal developmental realities that tend to influence men across their lifespan. For instance, all groups of men will experience a slow and gradual decline of their physical abilities after the age of forty, yet the meaning, significance, and expression of this decline will differ based on race, ethnicity, and class. A middle-aged housepainter with only a sixth-grade education will experience physical decline and the development of arthritis far differently than an executive with an MBA and a host of resources. From a practice perspective, it is perhaps best to see stage theories not as providing clear-cut rules, but as guides to sensitize practitioners to the potential issues that their clients may face. To place stage theories in their proper practice context, social workers should attempt to understand the culturally specific realities of their clients. This will include class, race, ethnicity, level of assimilation and acculturation, sexual orientation, ability/disability, and masculine identity scripts. Each of these will provide guidance on how to "read" the developmental stages as they apply to a man's life.

Erik Erikson (1959) created one of the most influential models of lifespan development with profound implications for the lives of men and for social work practice. Core to Erikson's theory of psychosocial development is the concept of the developmental task. Erikson observed that during each developmental stage, a person would need to master key developmental challenges in order to move successfully to subsequent stages. The key tasks were juxtaposed to a countervailing concept that would serve, in some ways, as a foil to the task to be mastered. When a task is not successfully mastered, individuals will revisit and struggle with them throughout their lifespan. While the notion of men being stuck in a subsequent stage may not be fully supported by the literature, it may be valuable to look at Erikson's psychosocial tasks as existential themes that many individuals must contend with throughout their lifespan. Regardless of whether men are classically "fixated" in a developmental stage, being able to identify these core developmental deficits of men can be helpful during the process of assessment. Below I briefly explore the developmental tasks, as a lack of resolution of these can shape the life context of men. These crises, as Erikson referred to them, include trust versus mistrust, autonomy versus shame and doubt, initiative versus guilt, industry versus inferiority, and identity versus role confusion.

The early infant must learn to develop trust. Those who do not may develop problems with attachment that can have profound influences throughout their lifespan (Schore and Schore 2008). Not being able to trust can lead men to struggle with forming intimate bonds, relying on workplace colleagues, or developing supportive friendships.

The developmental task of the toddler, autonomy versus shame, is crucial for later development of security and independence. Children who successfully learn that their feelings, thoughts, and behaviors are different from those of others, and that they are supported in their development of autonomy, come to understand that they can be separate yet still have their emotional needs met. Children who are shamed for their developmentally appropriate need for increased autonomy can develop feelings of shame or a global feeling of guilt for their independence. Men who feel shame for autonomous action may overcompensate with hyperindependence and rigidly adopt a go-it-alone masculine script.

Children who are supported in their ability to initiate may develop feelings of mastery and confidence in their ability to successfully handle life's challenges. Children who are thwarted during this stage may come to feel insecure and spend a lifetime attempting to prove that they are successful. A focus on proving themselves can lead men to neglect other facets of their lives and may be accompanied by consistent feelings of insecurity.

Adolescents should be given the space to explore their own identity and sense of self. Adolescent boys experiment with various roles, searching for a sense of who they are. If their social environment provides enough stability, boundaries, and "containers" to keep them safe, yet enough freedom and validation for their own developing ideas about themselves and the world, they can successfully enter early adulthood with the beginning of a conception of themselves as men.

The first adult stage is early adulthood, lasting from age 18 to 34, with its associated crisis of intimacy versus isolation. Erikson conceptualized the main task of this phase as the establishment of intimate, lasting relationships. Young men who emerge from adolescence with a clear sense of their own identity more easily allow others to become close; they do not perceive as a threat the giving away of the self that is needed for successful relationships. Having learned to trust and feel a sense of autonomy in childhood, young men are able to let down their boundaries and walls and allow others in. Poa (2006:29) observed that "for many persons, the period of young adulthood is an exciting time as they negotiate the transition from adolescence to adulthood and begin to grow and develop into their new roles as more independent individuals. However, this can also be a troublesome time, as the process of transition leaves them vulnerable as they attempt to consolidate their identity and exercise their recently acquired rights and responsibilities."

Young men in early adulthood have many choices to make. They must figure out their career in an ever-changing world and experiment with establishing new emotional bonds. Working toward establishing intimacy is not a linear process for most men. Most men, regardless of their sexual/affectional orientations, develop early relationships that do not stand the test of time. These "practice" relationships can be the context through which men learn how to express their needs and meet the needs of others. Men who do not have these early relationships may struggle to build intimate connections and can begin to feel a sense of despair. This despair may become more pronounced as they move toward the next stage. Men must also learn to negotiate their relationships to their families of origin in culturally appropriate ways. Men from more communally based cultures who find work and careers within mainstream American society need to reconcile the expectation for individuation associated with the hegemonic masculine ideal and the values of their culture.

The second stage in Erikson's model is middle adulthood, from 35 to 60 years old. The main psychosocial crisis is generativity versus stagnation. In this stage, the adult seeks life satisfaction through productivity. This productivity can occur within several domains, such as work, community involvement, and family. For men in the United States, work is the central means of achieving productivity. As with the other stages, this stage is very similar to one of the stages of child development: industry versus inferiority. The common thread that runs between both is the importance of feeling competent in relationship to oneself and to one's family, friends, and peers. Men who previously suffered from feelings of incompetence in one domain of life may be attempting to overcompensate and compulsively strive for success in the workplace. For instance, a man who struggled with achieving at school may also have a difficult time achieving success in work or may work compulsively to demonstrate to an internalized "other" that he is worthy. Men who are doing well in this phase of development will hopefully learn to balance family, work, and other social obligations. A man who is able to develop meaningful family and creative (career) achievements is able to heal many of the wounds of the past through coming to view himself as a competent and productive member of society. Men who fail to achieve success in these domains often slip into self-absorption and stagnation. To Erikson, a great deal of life's purpose is to prepare for the middle stage of life. He believed that the end of life is a time in when the aging adult looks back upon his life and assesses the meaning and value of what he created.

The meaning of production and generativity will vary by culture, and for each individual man. Men may also develop a conception of their own worth that is more reliant on family, religion, political activism, or alternative sources for generativity. The traditional conceptualization of generativity must be expanded. For instance, new research on fathering suggests that men may receive numerous benefits from fathering, including increased self-worth, improved quality of health, overall well-being, and an enhanced relationship with their spouse (Palkovitz 2002). Social workers working with men in midlife can help them negotiate the complex web of developmental life-stage needs for generativity and production within a complex, changing, postmodern world. Social workers will frequently encounter men who have not, in their perceptions or in the perceptions of those around them, successfully met this developmental stage. Men may experience stagnation as depression, sadness, a fear of the future, or preoccupation with the past. The existential perspective, as it is applied in various chapters throughout part 2 of this book, provides especially relevant guidance in helping men work through stagnation. With its focus on helping men develop a sense of responsibly, its here-and-now orientation, and its mandate that each man find his own personal meaning, the existential perspective may provide the means by which social workers can contextualize these developmental stages within the context of personally constructed development.

The last phase is late adulthood, beginning at age 60 and lasting until death. The psychosocial crisis of this stage is referred to as ego integrity versus despair. If a man is able to look back on his life and derive a sense of satisfaction, if he believes that he was able to positively contribute to existence, then he will feel a sense of wholeness, or integrity. If a man looks back on his life and fears that he has not contributed well, that he experienced more failures than successes, he may slip into despair. The pain of not having lived a life that he perceives as being of value is one of the most tragic experiences that a man can endure.

Erikson was in his forties when he conceptualized this stage, and he wrote at a time when biomedical advances were not as sophisticated as they are today. For many men today, the ability to be productive and achieve extends well beyond the age of 60. Men tend to work far longer and are physically more healthy and vital than they were just a generation ago. This improvement in physical health is not without its complications. Men may often have to work far longer in order to prepare for retirement. Men who retired early from unsuccessful careers, who may struggle with despair, may find themselves living with financial deprivation and insecurity far longer. Concerns and fears about the financial health of the social security system have increased social concerns about our capacity to care for older adults. The anticipated social security shortfalls may occur at a time when the relative wealth and prosperity of the United States is declining relative to many other countries, and after decades of soaring health-care costs.

However, when a man is able to feel good about his life in this stage, he is able to find new ways of engaging the world. Less concerned with the views of other, with social norms and rules, many men are able to shift gears and create a new sense of self and meaning. During this time, an important task is to contribute to subsequent generations. One of the ways that this can be accomplished is for men to be provided with opportunities to mentor other men or boys. Mentoring programs have been shown to have many positive benefits for both mentors and mentees (Flaxman, Ascher, and Mahaley, 1992; Greim 1992).

One of the most important early studies of adult male development was undertaken by Levinson (1978) and his colleagues and culminated in the classic *The Seasons of a Man's Life*. Based on a sample of in-depth qualitative interviews of forty men, the researchers developed a theory of male development using the metaphor of seasons:

> To speak of seasons is to say that the life course has a certain shape, that it evolves through a series of definably forms. A season is a stable segment of the total cycle. Summer has a character different from that of winter; twilight is different from sunrise. To say that a season is relatively stable, however, does not mean that it is stationary or static. Change goes on within each, and a transition is required for the shift from one season to the next. Every season has its own time; it is important in its own right and needs to be understood in its own terms. No season is better or more important than any other. Each has its necessary place and con-

tributes its special character to the whole. It is an organized part of the total cycle, linking past and future and containing both within itself. (Levinson 1998:7)

While the precise time periods that Levinson and his colleagues developed has been challenged over time, and certainly was based on a sample that was too small and perhaps too heterogeneous to include the realities of all cultural groups from varied historic periods, the notion of seasons is indeed important. Levinson viewed early adulthood as lasting from the end of adolescence, between 18 and 22 years of age, until around 40. From 40 to 45 years of age, men make the transition from early adulthood to midlife. At approximately 60, men transition to older adulthood. One of the key findings of Levinson's work rests on the notion of a transition period. During this period between seasons, men are living between two worlds, life structures, and ways of achieving meaning. These transition points are often when men find themselves seeking or are referred to social work services as their old ways of living may not work, and they experience psychosocial or physical problems that are the result of living between these two spaces.

For instance, I am currently in the transition between young and midadulthood. I have put on some weight, normal for men during this transition. This extra weight and physical decline, combined with not recognizing my new limitations (i.e., I can no longer push my body as I did ten years ago without consequences), has led to the development of tendonitis in my feet. This intermittent, painful condition has affected not only my health but also my mobility, my capacities at work and for housework, and my sense of identity. No longer am I the young man who could push through exercise pain and eat what he wanted without weight gain. This process has forced me to explore my own mortality (and lose forty pounds!).

Other Theories

While not normally viewed as a developmental perspective, existential theory is a valuable means of understanding male development, with important implications for practice. In particular, existential theory's focus on the importance of meaning, and the construction of meaning as a core organizing principle in adult life, holds special value for adult male development. Sartre (1965) contended that the fundamental nature of human existence is that it is inherently meaningless. That is, there is no one set meaning and purpose of life that each person can choose to build a life around. To Sartre and many other existentialists, the very mission of our lives is to work toward the development of our own purpose and meaning. Too often men hide from taking responsibility for developing their own meaning by engaging in what is referred to as "bad faith" behaviors, such as addiction, blaming others, or spending countless hours watching television, that help us hide from the difficult work of creating our own lives (Krill 1969). Existentialists believe that the emotional consequences of choosing to be free and responsible often compel people to act in ways that may lead to life being easier, yet far less authentic and rewarding (Jourard 1968; Kierkegaard 1954). Examples include not being able to blame others for one's fate, and understanding that the centrality of one's own role in creating one's existence leads to a sense of anxiety. Existentialists view this anxiety as part of the cost of being fully alive, fully human, and fully autonomous (Buber 1955). This is not to be confused with clinical anxiety, which is a debilitating condition and will be addressed later. Additionally, a man being responsible for creating his own sense of meaning does not mean that he is responsible for having "caused" his social context. Historically disadvantaged men are not responsible for being subjected to discrimination, oppression, and other social factors. However, existentialists argue that a key part of development, of personal and emotional growth, is taking responsibility for choosing to create meaning within the context of such obstacles. Frankl (1963; 1967) posited that his ability to survive the Nazi concentration camps was in part facilitated by his capacity to find meaning even within the horrors of a death camp.

The ability to transcend difficulties and create meaning from them is an essential aspect of healthy male development. In a real sense, this capacity lies at the heart of what it means to be resilient (Furman, Jackson, Downey, and Bender 2002).

One of the advantages of the existential approach, as well as other non–stage theories, is that stage theories break down when issues of disease and illness shorten the life span. When a younger man has a life-threatening disease, he faces developmental issues differently than other men. Recently I watched a video of the last lecture of a computer science professor who, at age 46, was dying of pancreatic cancer (Pausch 2007). The video illustrated a man who was forced to struggle with end-of-life issues in a way that most men his age do not. His powerful lecture highlights how important it is for people to make sense of their lives when faced with death, and how important existential themes are for men.

Ashford, Lecroy, and Lortie (2006) present a powerful perspective that they refer to as the multidimensional approach. This approach adopts an eco-systems perspective in which the major domains of a person's life are viewed as interacting with and affecting each other. As with other systems-oriented approaches, the metaphor of a mobile can be useful. When one part of a mobile is touched, other parts are impacted. So it is with a man's life, when one domain of experience is affected, so too are the other domains. According to this approach, the main domains of human life consist of the biological, psychological, and social spheres. The authors note that human behavior can be viewed from this perspective in terms of a hypothesis regarding the etiology of the problem: "It is helpful to take a hypothesis approach to each primary dimension and its underlying functions. Hypotheses from biophysical, psychological, and social dimensions are posed in order to examine possible etiology and explanations of the client's functioning" (17–18).

In my social work practice courses, I have used this approach as a means of teaching assessment. A concept that students have found valuable is the importance of the intersection between the different domains. That is, human behavior can be viewed as not being "caused" by any one event that occurs within one particular domain, but by the interaction between different domains. These intersections are graphically illustrated in figure 3.1.

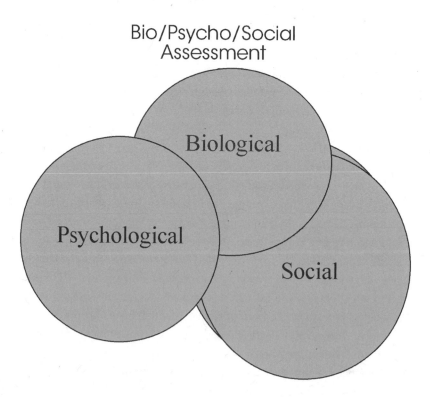

Figure 3.1 Bio/psycho/social assessment.

As an illustration, consider a biophysical illness, such as diabetes. Many social and psychological factors overlap and intersect with biological processes that affect how diabetes will be experienced, the course of the disease, and potential treatment options. Let us take the case of an African American man who finds out he has diabetes at age 45 (a similar case will be discussed in another chapter). Hearing his diagnosis may trigger feelings of inadequacy and sadness. He may for the first time "come out of denial" and come to see himself as obese. This may contribute to a biological tendency to feel depressed. This depression may make it harder for him to want to take care of himself, thus inhibiting his ability to comply with his doctor's orders. Over time his depression and his untreated diabetes have an impact on his capacity for work. He therefore begins to experience work problems, which exacerbate his level of stress. His increased stress leads to compulsive overeating and poor self-care, and he winds up gaining a significant amount of weight. Gaining weight not only affects his diabetes but his relationship with his wife, who no longer wishes to be intimate with him and is increasingly afraid and angry over his seeming inability to take care of himself. He also becomes isolated from his friends, his church, and the rest of his social network, thereby increasing his sense of isolation and shame. As is clear from this example, the three domains of human functioning overlap and intersect, and they act upon one another in a reinforcing manner. There is a sense that this man's life is spinning out of control.

Understanding this relationship is not merely an academic exercise but has important implications for social work practice. Social workers working with men will find that since all three domains of human behavior are implicated in nearly all human problems, social workers have multiple entry points through which to help men resolve their problems. That is, regardless of which domain a particular problem "started" in, many potential actions can have a profound impact on specific problems. Not only do these domains intersect in the perpetuation of problems, but they are a powerful force in the maximization of client strength and resiliencies, as subsequent chapters will make clear.

Case Example

This case example presents the life story of a man who recently has "come out of the closet" and affirmed his homosexuality. A long and painful process, Chip's story encapsulates several important aspects of this chapter's discussion of masculinity.

Chip Botch is a 49-year-old man living in Kansas City, Missouri. Chip was brought up in a small town in Wyoming. His father was a day laborer and a cowboy. Both his father and his mother were quiet; Chip said that, growing up, his house "like a morgue." Chip's mother and father watched television for several hours most evenings. Chip believes that his father was an alcoholic—he often sat in his chair and drank until he fell asleep.

Chip did fairly well in school until the age of 9, when his father announced to the family that he was moving in with another woman. Chip's father moved a hundred miles away and rarely saw his family. When he died several years later of cancer, it had been two years since Chip had seen him. Chip heard about the death from a family friend.

Chip reports that as sad as his childhood might have been with his father in his life, it was far worse without him. His mother became increasingly angry and paranoid. She developed extremely dogmatic religious beliefs. Over time, she became something of a fanatic; even her minister seemed to feel uncomfortable around her. She compelled Chip to read the Bible for two hours a day. Combined with his increasing responsibilities around the house, this cut into his schoolwork considerably. Chip lost interest in school during his early adolescence and barely passed most courses.

Chip said that he always felt different, and he realized fairly early on that he preferred doing "girl stuff" to boy things. In junior high, he began to realize that he was more attracted to boys than to girls. This realization was simultaneously painful and liberating. He believed that his feelings explained why he was different. He felt liberated, in that one of his greatest fears was that he would eventually have a relationship that mirrored that of his parents. Since he was not interested in women, he felt great comfort that he would not be destined to repeat his father's path. However, Chip also was troubled by the contradictions between what he was learning in Sunday school about homosexuality and his developing identity.

One summer night, when he was 16, Chip was out drinking with his friends. They began to tease him for never showing interest in girls, and one of his friends wondered out loud if Chip was gay. Realizing that he had to make a bold statement against what seemed like, on many levels, a very threatening accusation, Chip hit the boy over the head with a small tree branch. The boy slumped over and died from the blow. Chip and two of his other friends began to panic and wanted to go to the police. However, one of the other boys convinced them not to, but instead to say that the boy fell and hit his head while they were playing tackle football. Everyone agreed, so the boys took their dead friend to the hospital.

After this time, Chip became more isolated and spent most of his time by himself in his room. He rarely spent time with his family, and he stopped going to church. Chip became increasingly withdrawn in school. He developed the habit of going to sleep shortly after dinner and waking up at one or two in the morning. In this way, he was able to get the sleep he needed and avoid human contact as much as possible. Chip was tormented by feelings of guilt and shame. He was also extremely anxious that the police would find out about his having killed his friend. He also had other complex and painful feelings. At times, he was able to identify the sources of his feelings: his father's abandonment, his own sexual attraction toward men, and his having killed his friend. However, most of the time he just felt lost within himself, sad and disconnected. He wrote daily in his diary about his feelings, usually about his depression. He also wrote poems and stories about what it would be like to be someone else.

The day after Chip graduated from high school, he took a bus to Denver and began to look for a job. For years, he had stolen several dollars a week from his mother's purse and hidden it in the wall. With nearly two thousand dollars saved, Chip took a room in a skid row flophouse. After about three weeks, he found a job repairing equipment for a large copy machine company. He had developed mechanical skills as a young child, helping his father fix the car and household appliances, so he did very well in the company's training program, quickly learning about the various machines. The job seemed perfect to Chip. He was able to make a reasonable living and did not have to spend much time with other people. Each night he came home and wrote his poems. He soon saw himself as a poet and thought that perhaps one day he would become a writer. However, these positive aspirations would always be overwhelmed by his feelings of shame and worthlessness.

Chip lived this way for five years. One day, while he was walking home from the store, a young woman named Brenda began flirting with him. Soon they were talking, and within a half hour they were embracing and kissing. Chip felt a strong and powerful connection to Brenda, something he had never felt before. The two started spending all their free time together. Chip felt ecstatic. Not only did he feel a real and deep connection to another human being, but it was to a woman. He believed that this helped him reconcile his feelings toward men, which he had denied for many years. Perhaps he was not a pervert, he would tell himself. Within two months, Chip and Brenda drove to Las Vegas and got married.

For several years, the couple was happy. They partied a great deal and had a simple life of loving each other. However, years of heavy drug use eventually caught up to them. They began to feel estranged from each other. As Chip and Brenda grew apart, Chip recognized that he still wanted to be with men. He started meeting men for sex in various public places. One night, after drinking heavily, he told Brenda about his behavior. Intuitive and nonjudgmental, Brenda said that she strongly suspected that something was going on, and that Chip was indeed gay. The couple's relationship moved more toward a friendship, although they continued to live together.

While Brenda professed to accept Chip, she began to drink more and more. Her drinking soon became out of control, and Chip asked her to go into a rehab program. For a couple of years Brenda went in and out of rehab. Her sister, to whom she was very close, had been diagnosed with cancer, and this sent Brenda into an emotional tailspin. Her drinking became worse and worse, and she entered rehab once again. When her sister informed her that her cancer was getting worse and the doctors were recommending palliative chemotherapy, Brenda said she wanted to leave rehab, but her sister asked her to stay and to become clean, for her.

At this point, Chip became extremely confused about his own life. He wanted to be supportive of the woman he loved deeply and had shared many years with, but he also realized that he was not happy with her. He wanted to pursue relationships with men. He was conflicted about how to reconcile these two very different impulses. Chip also began to realize that after nearly twenty years at his job, he might be interested in trying something else. He had become confident in his skills and abilities and felt that he could grow in new ways. Chip also knew that while his drinking was not as out-of-control as Brenda's, he still drank too much. When he did not drink, he was plagued with his old feelings of guilt, sadness, and rage. He decided to seek counseling at an outpatient substance abuse treatment center.

FOR WRITING AND REFLECTION

1. You have been assigned as Chip's clinical social worker. Having heard Chip's story, what is your initial impression of his needs?
2. How would you help Chip deal with his feelings of guilt over having killed his friend?
3. How would you help Chip deal with his sadness about his father?
4. What techniques and methods would you use to help Chip sort out his relationship with Brenda?
5. What other services might be of help to Chip?

Case Example

Sam Wong is a 35-year-old Chinese/Vietnamese American man who lives in the South. He is a computer programmer and is married with no children. Sam was born in Vietnam, but his family left during the 1970s, moving to Guatemala City. After Sam's father paid for the family to leave Vietnam, they had only two thousand dollars to begin a new life in a place where they did not speak the language, did not know the customs, and had no work prospects. After spending several weeks in a hotel, the family was able to rent an apartment. Without any employment prospects, Sam's mother and father began to bake pastries and sell them in the street, a practice common in both Vietnam and Guatemala. They worked day and night and did not have much time to spend with their children.

After three years, a friend of the family sold Sam's parents a Chinese restaurant. Although they had saved very little money, the man said they could pay him when they were able. They ran the restaurant for six years and were able to build a good life for the family. Still, they never quiet felt at home in Guatemala City. While they were ethnically Chinese and had friends in the Chinese community, their years in Vietnam had left them culturally different from other Chinese Guatemalans. Sam's father dealt with this isolation through hard work.

Eventually the family saved enough money to buy into a Chinese/Vietnamese restaurant in a large city in the American South where several family friends and relatives were living. The family emigrated to the United States when Sam was 12 years old.

While worried about how he would fit in in his new country, Sam actually made friends quickly and adapted well. He found friends in the Latino and Asian communities and, having studied English in school, picked up the language fairly quickly. His older brother and sister soon went off to prestigious universities; the family had achieved happiness and stability. Sam was mostly happy and well adjusted, though he felt a sense of sadness about not knowing his father well. Sam's father continued to work hard in the United States. He was not a demonstrative man—he lived in cultures in which men controlled their feelings. He was shy, reserved, and highly logical by nature. Besides this pain, Sam's life was going well. Over time, he attended an excellent university, studied computer programming, and accepted a good job when he graduated.

Sam met and married his wife, Sally, six years ago. Sally is white, has never been outside of the south, and is religiously conservative. They are now at a crossroads in their marriage. Sally has wanted to do something with her artistic talents for work—she dreams of writing children's books and other artistic pursuits. However, she has not been able to fully dedicate herself to starting her career. Over the last few years, Sam has grown increasingly frustrated with Sally and her unfulfilled professional pursuits. He believes that she has done little to make her career happen, and he is angered and pained by this. A strong work ethic is one of the most important values to Sam. Not only is this an essential part of Chinese culture, but Sam grew up watching his parents work extremely hard at creating a life for their family. He watched their dogged efforts and appreciated their willingness to do whatever it takes to get ahead. Sam perceives Sally as uncommitted and lazy. Her lack of effort has made him respect her less and less.

While Sam cares deeply for his wife, he admits to wondering if she is the right person for him to have a life with. Sam has grown increasingly disinterested in their sex life and is now asking his wife to get "a regular job." Recently Sam spoke to Sally's parents about his concerns with her. While they like and respect Sam very much and in fact agree with him about many of his concerns, they were uncomfortable speaking to him. They saw this as a personal and private matter between Sam and his wife. Sam was perplexed by their behavior. Even though he has lived in the United States for many years, he is very much culturally Chinese. In Chinese culture, bringing elder family members into such discussions is a sign of respect. Sam sees it as the role of Sally's parents to help him influence her so she can be a "better woman and wife."

When Sally heard that Sam had spoken to her parents, she was extremely upset. She was able to recognize that this was another example of cultural differences that had made resolving their problems difficult. For many years, Sally had wanted Sam to go to couples counseling with her. However, Sam did not see the point of counseling. To Sam, one merely identifies problems, comes up with alternative solutions, and then makes thing happen. Sam said that he had no desire to talk to a stranger about how he felt—he just wanted Sally to follow through on her commitments to him. Sally told Sam that if he went to counseling with her, she would get a full-time job. He saw this is a positive step on her part and thought it a reasonable trade-off. However, Sam was reluctant to talk to a counselor. He worried that he would have to talk about things that were uncomfortable. His father, as his role model, had taught him to keep family problems in the family. Sam also has a hard time talking about his feelings, and he worried that the counselor would see this as the problem in their relationship. Recognizing that Sam might be more comfortable with a male counselor, and one from a culture similar to his own, Sally was able to locate a Japanese American male counselor. She reasoned that while he was not Chinese, he would be able to understand some of Sam's cultural issues better than a non-Asian helper.

FOR WRITING AND REFLECTION

Develop three questions that Sam might want to ask a social worker, and three questions his wife might ask. Write out the answer to each question.

The Relationships of Men | FOUR

Who is the happiest of men? He who values
the merits of others, and in their pleasures take joy,
even as though they were his own.
—Johan Wolfgang von Goethe

At the outset, it is important to note that despite the ubiquitous notion of the "dysfunctional relationship," significant research has demonstrated that the majority of human relationships are positive (Reis and Gable 2003), and people experience three times as many positive interactions as negative interactions in their close personal relationships and more casual social encounters (Gable, Reis, and Elliot 2000). From an evolutionary perspective, it may be advantageous to focus on negative stimuli in one's environment, for example, to protect against physical or emotional harm (Gable and Haidt 2005), yet our collective biases seem to have skewed our understanding of human relationships. This is certainly true of the relationships of men. Most men have positive and functional relationships with many people.

This chapter focuses on the significant relationships that men possess, and their roles in these relationships. Men are fathers, friends, husbands, sons, and lovers. While I discuss both heterosexual and homosexual relationships I pay special attention to the former because other authors have produced excellent studies of the relationship issues of gay men (De Cecco 1987; Isay 2006; Peplau and Fingerhunt 2007; Seidman 1996). The same is not the case for heterosexual men and their relationships, as Rowland (1996) and Warren (1992) note. When the relationships of heterosexual men are explored in the social work literature, it is usually as it relates to some severe psychosocial problem, such as domestic violence, divorce, or "deadbeat dads."

Yet every social worker who has worked with male clients knows that many men are lonely. Many men have too few social relationships, and the ones they have may not provide nurturance, support, and fuel for personal growth and support. There are powerful costs to this loneliness and disconnection, as I explore in this chapter and throughout this book. The interconnectedness of masculinity, health, relationships, and general well-being are palpably described by Mahalik, Lagan, and Morrison (2006:67) in their comparison of the health behaviors of American and Kenyan men: "Our results suggest that what may be distinctive about American masculinity in relation to health behaviors is interpersonal isolation and how men manage stress. American men's masculinity is related to being less likely to have a close friend or family member whom they could talk to about things that are bothering them, being more likely to report that they had been told that they use alcohol or drugs too much, and being more likely to get angry and annoyed when caught in traffic."

Some research has demonstrated that men's relationships are less satisfying than are those of women (Osherson 1992). However, even this research is controversial, as other studies demonstrate that many men have different relational needs than women do. Yet before I turn to the problems men have in relationships, I should note again that many men do have extremely nurturing and positive relationships in their lives. Many men and women have much in common in terms of their capacities, desires, and needs for intimate relationships, as well as their skills in developing and maintaining such relationships.

One way of viewing the different relational needs of men and women is to see men and women as two culturally different groups. In fact, the metaphor has been extended, with men and women being portrayed as two different species from two different planets (Gray 1992). While this metaphor may be somewhat exaggerated, it does help us understand men and women as being culturally different enough that our worldviews, and therefore our relationships, will be different.

Shye et al. (1995:936) provide an important overview of essential differences in men's and women's relationships: "Considerable data indicate that women's social network interactions fulfill feminine social role prescriptions for expressive, affiliative, supportive behaviors, while men's conform to masculine role norms of independence and instrumentality." In other words, traditional interpretations of data on sex role differences find that men are inclined toward separateness (independence) and view relationships in terms of what they can practically provide (instrumentality).

Baumeister and Sommer (1997) give an alternative interpretation of some of these key relationship needs and tendencies:

> Our view is that men, like women, are powerfully and deeply driven by the need to belong—only that men tend to understand and realize this need within the context of a broad sphere of social relations (unlike women). Whereas the female view focuses narrowly on a small number of intimate didactic bonds, the male view embraces a broader social structure with a larger number of people. This larger number of people entails that the male orientation cannot pursue intimacy as effectively as the female approach. As a partial replacement for intimacy, the male quest for belongingness may emphasize hierarchies of status and power. Indeed, status and power structures may be almost inevitable issues in larger groups (unlike communal dyads), which cannot avoid certain problems of social organization such hierarchies may solve.

The authors view certain aspects of men's relational style not as attempts to distance, as posited by some researchers (e.g., Cross and Madison 1997), but as attempts to connect. For example, they note that when men engage others in hierarchical relationships, characterized by expressions of power, the very act of attempting to exert power closely bonds them to others. This analysis of the relationship style of men whose behavioral patterns conform to the American hegemonic idea is a significant departure that challenges many interpretations of men's relational styles. While this controversial view is open to debate and has been critiqued as not being fully developed or not having enough operational definition to help us fully understand masculine identity (Wetherell and Edley 1999), it may have relevance in explaining the importance of relationships to men. An expanded definition may help us truly understand the motivations of men in their perception of relationships with others and provide us with additional information by which to make assessments. However, this does not imply that this relational motivation and style will be effective in all social settings. As with other behaviors, it may be a historical anachronism that is useful in some social contexts but not in others. Using such an analysis, social workers may wish to help some men develop new relational styles and to improve their ability to adopt different roles in different social contexts.

One might be concerned about condoning relationships based on unequal power dynamics. I strongly sympathize with this concern and believe that in macro social work, practitioners should promote more egalitarian, non-power-based relationships. However, in working with individual men on their relationships, such an approach may not prove effective. Change is often a slow process, and helping men to develop different skills and tools without shaming them for who they currently are must be a central guide to practice. Clearly, these are complex issues for which easy answers cannot be found; they call for creativity and further exploration and research.

It does seem clear, however, that some of the traits of hegemonic masculinity do impede the formation of intimate relationships. Competition, unequal power differentials, stoicism, intolerance for "softer" emotions, and the valuation of isolation and independence all make some types of relationships difficult. In intimate personal relationships with children, the ability and willingness to express oneself emotionally is crucial. Intimacy demands a level of sharing of our real selves—selves that make mistakes and have fears, concerns, and regrets. This type of sharing is key to the formation of trust in relationships. With children, it helps establish connections and fosters a sense of warmth.

In relationships with significant others, both heterosexual and homosexual, if a man can share difficult emotions and personal flaws and trust that he will not be rejected, he can develop a sense of increased security and confidence in his relationship. Being able to trust a significant other on this level also provides a man with a feeling of psychological safety. When men feel that they are accepted as they are, they are less worried about being abandoned (feelings that men may frequently experience but not typically admit). The give-and-take of sharing of emotional truths, feelings, and vulnerabilities is important to the formation of many relationships, in particular relationships with significant others.

However, many men have a hard time with this type of expression. Sharing vulnerabilities goes against the cultural norms of the hegemonic masculine ideal. To admit to having these less "masculine" and assertive feelings is to admit weakness. As discussed in earlier chapters, the masculine ideal is predicated on power, domination, and control. The hegemonic masculine ideal views the expression of sadness, doubt, guilt, remorse, shame, concern, worry, and other feelings as signs of weakness. A man who is asked to share his vulnerabilities is being asked, in a very real sense, to be less of a man.

The scripts explored previously often make it hard for men to overcome these difficulties. The strong-silent-type script encourages stoicism and makes it difficult for men to want to develop new relationship capacities. Men learn that it is cool to be distant and aloof. Among African American men, the "cool pose" becomes a similar script (Pierre, Mahalik, and Woodland 2002). Among Latinos, a component of machismo is to not express weakness and vulnerability.

The costs of disconnection may be significant. While it seems obvious that relationships are important, benefits of relationships are tangible, and their absence is costly. In their cross-cultural exploration of the connection between health and relationships, Shye et al. (1995) found that the mortality rates of unmarried men are significantly higher than those of unmarried men. They noted that the web of personal relationships, or social networks, provides individuals with assurance, guidance, satisfaction of emotional needs, and physical survival.

Men in Families

The research on men's involvement in family life suggests that historically men have been less involved in family life than women. Juster and Stafford (1985) found men's involvement in child care and housework to be approximately 20–30 percent of the total workload of these activities between the mid-1960s and 1980. While the percentage continues to rise slowly, certainly such low involvement is a concern. Pleck, Lamb, and Levine (1986) present a model of four factors that contribute to men's lower levels of family involvement. These factors—personal motivation, skills, social supports, and institutional barriers—are all important to consider when creating programs for increasing men's involvement in parenting and also for work with individual men. The authors posit that while an analysis of social variables is key to understanding the problem, the motivation of individual men should not be discounted. For instance, they note that some men increase their level of motivation in response to a midlife reassessment of what they have missed vis-à-vis family life, and a desire to improve family relationships. It may also be, as I discuss later, that men's personal motivation is influenced by the degree to which they hold hegemonic masculine views about the nature of "women's work."

The second factor mentioned by Pleck et al.—skills—also has important clinical implications. Men who do not feel capable or competent in caring for children or doing specific household tasks may avoid these tasks because engaging in them may be an affront to perceptions of their self-efficacy. Devising interventions that help men assess and improve their skills may be valuable.

Social supports also clearly influence a man's involvement in his family and with family work. Social supports that reinforce a detached, disengaged relationship with family or family work can increase this tendency. Reinforcing involvement will help support a man in being involved.

Of particular note to social workers engaged in macro practice are the institutional barriers that may influence men's involvement in families. Work is the primary institutional context that provides incentives, though often disincentives, for men to become more involved in family life. Most work contexts do not support men having time off to spend with their families. Universities and government jobs are increasingly making parental leave open to men. However, many jobs, particularly those in traditionally male careers, are less likely to do so. However, providing institutional support for men's involvement with families can have powerful effects. Winett and Neale (1980), as cited in Pleck, Lamb, and Levine (1986), found that when flex time was introduced into the workplace, half the men to whom it was available would modify their work schedule to spend more time with their families.

The hegemonic model of masculinity tends to promulgate an individualistic view of men. Men, particularly white men, who most approximate this ideal, tend to view themselves as individuals first. Movies are full of images that portray an individual hero against a collective, shadowy enemy. The valiant, courageous man stands alone and fights for what is right. Yet systems theory teaches us the limits and risk of perceiving the world in too individualistic a manner. While perhaps congruent with and indicative of the way many men see the world, men are profoundly influenced by the important systems in their lives. The family is the primary system for most men: so ingrained is the notion of individuality that the temptation for men is to talk about families being the context of relationships, not the relationships themselves. Women tend to be far more comfortable with collective and group relationships than men are. Family group experiences are predicated on give and take, the sharing of control, and collaboration rather than competition. The classic image is the man who sits silently in his "big papa chair" while life goes on around him. The other members of the family are talking, laughing, and playing. The man becomes annoyed at all the noise and attempts to exert some control over his domain.

The scenario above was presented in such a way that it clearly pathologizes the needs, roles, and abilities of men. The man is seen as distant, incapable, unemotional, and disengaged. His behavior is clearly unhealthy. Situations such as this represent the complexity of working with men. On one hand, it is true that these behaviors and traits, in the extreme, are problematic. Yet it could also be argued that the problem exists in a system that will not accept the man for who he is and respond to his needs. Two key concepts help us negotiate these relationship issues: flexibility and balance. A man who can flexibly choose other potential behaviors will be able to meet the needs of his family and better engage with them. Masculinity in this sense becomes less hegemonic and more a cultural difference. A man can at times compromise and spend time with his family but at other times find a quiet place in which he can be the stoic bear.

Men as Fathers

The role of fathers in the lives of their children may often be underestimated (Snarey 1993). Research has shown that fathers significantly influence, and are influenced by, the development of their children. For instance, one study showed that men actually undergo hormonal changes before and after their children are born (Storey et al. 2000). Fathers provide their children with a sense of stability and with alternative male perspectives. Affirming the importance of men and fathers in the lives of children has become controversial, in that it may be perceived as being a slight against mothers, in particular single mothers. However, it is not my intention to slight the importance and value of motherhood. Additionally, many children raised by single mothers do indeed thrive. That being said, male ways of being and behaving are different than those of women; each gender brings important skills to the table.

Fathers and children affect each other in many mutually reinforcing ways. A qualitative study by Shears, Furman, and Negi (2008) explores this reciprocal relationship with Mexican men. Through one of the questions asked in the study, these authors seek to understand how fatherhood has changed the men. Some 72 percent of the men reported that fatherhood made them become more responsible. One respondent observed: "Knowing you have a child makes you more responsible. It makes you think before you act. I never had much of a problem getting into trouble before he was around, but certain things were a lot less important before him—job security. Nowadays it's . . . actually a lot of weight being responsible for a child and everything from, 'Does he have enough diapers and do we have enough milk in the fridge?'"

The study also asked what being a good father meant. The research identified several themes, including being there for their children, teaching them, being a good role model, and offering emotional support.

Media stereotypes of fathers often portray them as bumbling and incompetent. Fathers are obstacles that must be circumvented; they are shown as distant and uninterested, or overcontrolling and demanding. However, research has demonstrated that fathers are attentive, skillful, and intentional in their parenting (Shears et al. 2006). Instead of being distant and uninvolved, fathers are highly involved in their young child's life as stimulators of gross and fine motor development, socializers, and sex role models and behavioral models (Shears and Robinsons 2005). Recent research has highlighted that fathers are not inferior to mothers but may meet different psychosocial and developmental needs. Some studies have found that fathers are more likely to participate in physical play with their toddler, whereas mothers are much more likely to participate in cognitive activities (Redina and Dickerschied 1976; Shears 2007).

In spite of these strengths, men are often at risk as fathers. Dudley and Stone (2001) contend that increasing numbers of men are at risk of being absent from the lives of their children, or of not being able to adequately perform the role of father. They contend that this problem has been growing over the last several decades, as men are often asked to take on new and conflicting roles. Goldberg (1976) contended that society often demands that men simultaneously be aggressive and nurturing, dominant yet egalitarian, sensitive yet stoic.

Mahalik and Morrison (2006) describe masculine schemas that at times may interfere with men's ability to be effective fathers. Their schemas are similar to the scripts that influence men, discussed previously. Mahalik and Morrison note that not all men are affected by each schema, and that cultural differences influence the prevalence and acceptability of different constellations of schemas. They stress that their framework does not represent all masculine schemas—only those that interfere with men's capacity to be good fathers. Their schemas are emotional control, primacy of work, pursuit of status, self-reliance, power over women, the need to win, dominance, and homophobia. The major themes contained within each have already been explored, but it may be instructive to highlight several as they relate specifically to men's involvement as fathers. For instance, the authors explore the effects of men's tendency for overemotional control: "Fathers who overregulated their behavior according to this schema may have difficulty telling their children that they care about them, modeling emotional development, and supporting and nurturing their children" (65). Overadherence to this schema may make it difficult for men to accept the feelings of their children, thereby inhibiting their children's' capacity for self-expression.

Several of the schemas inhibit the father's presence and involvement in the life of his children. The pressure to be a winner, the primacy of work, and the pursuit of status all lead to men's' privileging of their work life over their family encounters. These schemas are difficult for men to overcome, as each reinforces the others in creating a tendency toward workaholism. Later in this chapter I discuss how Mahalik and Morrison have used cognitive therapy to challenge these schema.

Men as Sons

One of the most powerful poems I have read is "The Lost Pilot," by James Tate (1967). Tate wrote the poem about his father, who died during World War II, while Tate was still in utero. The poem expresses the complex emotions that Tate feels about a father that he has never met. He candidly depicts his relationship to a specific father and to the mythological, archetypical father. The poem poignantly portrays the sense of loss and grief felt by many men whose fathers were not part of their lives or were only part of their lives only intermittently.

> If I could cajole
> you to come back for an evening,
> down from your compulsive
> orbiting, I would touch you.

This distance, and a desire to bridge this distance, holds currency even for men who grew up with their fathers. Tate continues and presents an evocative description of how his loss affects his own sense of self and identity.

> I feel dead. I feel as if I were
> the residue of a stranger's life,
> that I should pursue you.

Being a son in America is a complex experience that depends on a person's age and generational cohort. Understanding what it means to be a son is influenced by culture, level of acculturation, class, masculine norms and ideals, and personality traits of the father–son pair.

Bly (1990) contends that many men's most significant pains and emotional blocks stem from a disconnection from their fathers. He and others have observed that men became increasingly separate from their fathers during the Industrial Revolution. Prior to that time, the work of most men was near the home; sons were able to spend time with their fathers, develop close bonds, and learn what it means to be a man. As the twentieth century progressed, young boys no longer spent time during the day with their fathers. Industrial jobs in the late nineteenth and the twentieth centuries demanded long hours at work; men returning home had little energy for parenting.

Generational differences also make it difficult for men to relate to their fathers. Men who were brought up aspiring to the hegemonic masculine ideal may not understand sons whose behavior seems to them more feminine. For example, when one 15-year-old came home with an earring, his father, without thinking, immediately blurted out the word "faggot." He was shocked that his son was engaging in behavior that to him indicated an alternative form of masculinity. The father felt threatened by the son's behavior and wondered if he somehow had failed. The son, on the other hand, felt rejected by his father and felt his masculinity being challenged. A strong and powerful teen, he stepped up to his father and said, "Say that to my face, pussy." This act of rebellion made the father angry yet also provided him with a sense of comfort that his son, in spite of the feminine symbol of the earring, would still behave in accordance with masculine norms, that is, respond with anger to challenges to his masculinity.

Research has demonstrated the complex feelings that men have about their fathers. A qualitative study of men's perceptions of their fathers, presented in the form of research poems, illustrates these complexities (Furman, Shears, and Badinelli 2007:148). Here are two examples:

Just because my father was an alcoholic,
it does not mean he wasn't there.
I'm going to take care of my child,
I'm going in a different direction.
It does not mean he wasn't there,
he didn't have nobody to love him.
I'm going in a different direction.
He started drinking cuase' [sic] he was hurt.
He didn't have nobody to love him.
I'm more grown up than him.
He started drinking cuase' [sic] he was hurt
I stopped drinking, got my medicine, respect life more.
I'm more grown up than him.
I'm going to take care of my child.
I stopped drinking, got my medicine, respect life more,
just because my father was an alcoholic.

I would have liked, getting a hug or something.
Dad kept to himself a lot,
didn't show much emotion, day to day
he gave us what we needed.

Dad kept to himself a lot.
He worked long hours,
he gave us what we needed.
Wished he'd play with me more.
He worked long hours,
I did not know what he was like,
wished he'd play with me more.
I try to be more loving.
He worked long hours,
didn't show much emotion, day to day
I try to be more loving.
I would have liked, getting a hug or something.

Men as Partners

In general, social stereotypes of men as partners have not been kind. Television programs parody the less acceptable aspects of masculine identity, turning men into caricatures. In their relationships, men are portrayed as disinterested or hostile. Television shows have portrayed them as incapable of being caring and supportive.

Social science literature has observed men as being less capable of commitment (Ehrenreich 1983), less able to support their significant others emotionally (Balswick 1988), and less capability of intimacy than women (Abbott 1990; Berlant 2000). It certainly is true that many men struggle with intimacy and find it difficult to attend to the affective needs of others. As previously discussed, social workers should help men expand their emotional and behavioral repertoire when it comes to the more affective types of supports. However, several studies have demonstrated that many men are able provide emotional support for their partners.

Additionally, men offer types of support to their partners that may often be underappreciated. For instance, the stoicism, emotional control, steadiness that many men possess may be extremely valuable in times of crisis. When a man's partner feels as if life is out of control due to painful events or illness, having steady, nonemotional support can be very grounding. For example, one man's wife recently lost her mother to a prescription drug overdose, at the same time as she was going through a career change. Her husband's steady, nonemotional response helped her feel a sense of safety and stability when everything around her felt out of control.

The rights of gay men to marry vary from state to state. Gay marriage is currently legal in a small number of states. Additional states allow same-sex couples to enter civil unions, in which the partners hold many of the same legal rights as married couples. Vermont was the first state to allow gay couples to enter legal civil unions, with the passing of the Act Relating to Civil Unions in 2000. While this landmark decision provided gay partners with some legal rights, rights are granted on the state level (Solomon, Rothblum, and Balsam 2004). Not having federal-level rights means that gay men cannot receive social security, inheritance, and many other privileges that are afforded to married heterosexual couples. This may place many gay men at risk, as they are less able to share resources during difficult times, or provide as completely for their significant others in the case of death.

Social work values and ethics clearly support the equal rights of all people (NASW 1999), and gay marriage should fall within this domain. Additionally, arguments against gay marriage are largely based on moral reasoning within an increasingly reactionary social context, as studies shave shown that homosexual relationships are certainly as functional as heterosexual relationships, and in some cases more so (Kurdek 2004). Kurdek found that the mechanisms by which heterosexual and gay relationships operated were very similar. The one measure in which gay men did fare poorly was their perceptions of social support, which may be accounted for by social stigma against gay unions. This is supported by Green (2004), who posits that the supportive, loving relationships of gay men are actually a sign of resiliency; many have been able to maintain functional, healthy relationships in spite of stigma and less social support. As Green notes: "To reach that point of 'outness,' lesbian and gay partners must have successfully challenged in their own minds the negative views they were taught about homosexuality and their fears of being seriously harmed by discrimination. Successfully countering homophobic messages requires attributing them to social ignorance, prejudice, fear, and the human tendency to conform to dominant norms" (291).

Marriages and other long-term relationships do not always succeed. And given that heterosexual men tend to receive a great deal of their emotional support within the context of families, they often have a difficult time adapting to divorce. Baum (2004:179) observed that "most divorced men respond to their loss by increased activity, especially by throwing themselves into their work, hobbies or social life, and by somatization, and/or self-medication with alcohol and drugs; and they are much more likely than women to quickly replace the marital partner with other sexual partners."

For men with children, working through custody issues involves the legal system. Men who are going through a divorce should be encouraged to investigate their rights and responsibilities, which vary from state to state. Social workers should encourage men to seek appropriate legal counsel. While the impulse to not get an attorney and to settle things in an amicable manner is commendable, and both parties should be encouraged to be as nonconflictual as possible, legal counsel can help those undergoing divorce to understand the parameters and boundaries of their rights and responsibilities.

If social workers are involved, they should help explore how their clients are feeling about being separated from their children. Social workers may also help a man assess his current psychosocial needs, and they may make referrals to additional services as needed. Some men are embarrassed and ashamed at some of the life-skill deficits they may encounter in themselves. For instance, some men may not know how to cook or do laundry. Talking to men about how they can learn these skills can be difficult, but it is important and potentially empowering for them. Many good resources are easily available on the Internet. During a divorce, men's other social relationships become especially important. This may be particularly true of friendship.

Men as Friends

"In America a man's success is almost always seen in terms of his role as a professional, as a lover, as a husband, and as a father. A man's success in love seems to be viewed only inasmuch as it is about his wife or lover. Rarely do we gauge a man in terms of his success as a friend. American men are celebrated not for the achievement of a loyal, lasting, and significant friendship with another man but for the achievement of a significant career, and possibly for the achievement of a loyal, lasting, and fruitful marriage" (Michaelis 1983:9). This quote highlights one of several barriers that block men's desire, willingness, and ability to establish, deepen, and maintain friendships. This is lamentable, as a great deal of research has shown that friendships are key to healthy development and resiliency throughout the lifespan (Clark and Ayers 1991; Hartup 1979, 1983, 1989; Hutter 2001; Linden 2003; Roff 1963). Men's devaluation of friendships can be clearly found in adolescence. Blyth and Foster-Clark (1987) discovered that teenage girls reported a same-sex friend as their most intimate relationship. Boys ranked friends third for intimacy after each of their parents. However, the researchers found that boys' relationships with their siblings and other family members were actually less intimate than with their friends. Boys' perceptions of their friendships, or at least their willingness to acknowledge the intimacy in their friendships, did not match the actual nature of these relationships. By the time boys are teenagers, they have learned that expressing love and affection toward men who are not their relatives is taboo. Along with competition, homophobia may be one of the most significant impairments to men's being friends with other men.

In the hegemonic idea, men are in competition with one another. If power is the goal, then a man achieves power through domination of women, and domination of weaker men. This makes it far less likely that a man will share the softer feelings with a peer, in fear of being seen as weak. With other men, anger is the primary feeling that is permissible to share.

Friendships are not built on anger. They are built on a sense of trust and intimacy. The power of friendships is that they are perhaps the most voluntary of all social relationships; we choose to be in friendships, and we may also choose to leave them. Keen (1991) notes that in ancient Greek society, platonic relationships between friends were viewed as the most important relationships that one could have in life. Michaelis (1983) also explored the importance of friendship to successful men. He interviewed pairs of men about the role that their friendship played in their success. In each example, the friends were able to describe how their friendship contributed to their growth and development. At times friends helped console them in their losses. At other times friends challenged them to live more authentically, often through direct confrontation. Men's friendships are often different from those of women. Men are more likely to be confrontational and challenging. Yet between close male friends there can also exist a great deal of gentleness and compassion.

As stated, homophobia is a significant barrier to men having close friendships. According to the hegemonic ideal, only heterosexual men are real men. Real men do not express feelings of love to other men; these are our competition for valuable resources (including women) and power. To be seen as being close to another man is to risk the perception of being gay, of not being a man. Even men who see themselves as enlightened and as attempting to free themselves from the shackles of overly ridged gender roles are highly influenced by the specter of homophobia.

Practice Considerations

Helping men improve their relationships is an important task for nearly all social workers who work with men. While men are socialized to value relationships less than women do, men still feel the existential and human need to be deeply connected to other human beings in a positive manner. While men may possess blocks that inhibit their relationships and may at times deny the desire for relatedness, these thoughts may often serve the purpose of keeping them safe from rejection, frustration, and other types of hurts. In this section I consider how each of the four theories explored in this book are helpful in social work with men.

Mahalik and Morrison's work on cognitive schemas leads them to assert that a goal for helping men can be to "improve men's lives by challenging some of the traditional norms of masculinity that contribute to interpersonal disconnection and psychological distress (2006:63).

The behavioral side of cognitive behavioral therapy (CBT) stresses the importance of modeling in the shaping of human behavior. At a very basic level, the helping relationship provides an opportunity to model healthy relationship patterns and connectedness. In working with men, practitioners should demonstrate respect, trust, empathy, and acceptance. Through a quality helping relationship, men may learn that they will not be judged for their faults. For some men, being engaged in a quality helping relationship may represent the first time they have had a relationship where they could be themselves. The social pressures that men feel are enormous. Sometimes men hide their true natures behind socially constructed and accepted façades, many of which even hide parts of their beings from themselves.

Also from a CBT perspective, men may hold several irrational beliefs that can interfere with their relationships. Ellis (1985) has observed a desperate need for approval as a typical irrational belief that harms relationships. Many men certainly have this profound need for acceptance. They often learn that they must be perfectly strong, capable, and competent in all aspects of their lives. When they invariably fail to meet the high bar that they have set for themselves, they are susceptible to self-doubt and feelings of worthlessness. Sometimes they experience their feelings as depression; other times they cover up their feelings in reactive anger. Certainly it is healthy to want to be respected and loved by our loved ones most of the time, but when men cognitively turn this desire into absolutistic internal demands, they experience extreme anger and disappointment. Because men believe that they need to be perfect, they may worry that not meeting these aims will lead to rejection or even abandonment. Preferring to be in control, they may also disengage from relationships, not waiting until their feared abandonment occurs. This is congruent with the hegemonic male norm of attacking before you are attacked. According to this norm, it is better to hurt others than to be hurt yourself. One who waits to be hurt is a "sucker" or "chump."

The belief that one must be in charge and control at all times is antithetical to mutual and reciprocal relationships. Good relationships demand compromise, give and take, and at times letting go of control. By its very nature, love means giving up control. Intimacy involves taking chances, risking being hurt, and allowing another person to deeply affect how you feel. To establish relationships, one must risk abandonment, rejection, and hurt feelings. To open oneself up to these experiences is to give control over one's internal life to another.

Case Example

The case example below originally appeared in Furman, Collins, and Swanson (2003).

Dan is a 37-year-old single male. He has worked as a computer repair person for the last several years. Dan sought treatment for feeling isolated and depressed. He has been lonely much of the time and does not feel a sense of connectedness to others. During a previous course of treatment, Dan was placed on medication that decreased, but did not eliminate, his depression. He also was able to improve his relationships with his family of origin, joined a book club, and started to date a woman whom he saw about once a week. In spite of these changes, Dan still felt somewhat depressed. While his new social contacts were important, Dan longed for more meaningful and intimate friendships.

As a child Dan was often lonely and sad. He had few friendships and was the youngest child in a distant and detached family. The friendships that he developed as a young man in college and in the navy provided his first reprieve from the loneliness that he felt in his life until that time. During therapy he began to realize that the close friendship bonds he experienced during those earlier years were the missing piece that he needed in order to feel a sense of wholeness. In spite of this realization, Dan was not certain about how to make friends at this stage in his life, or if he wanted to do the work necessary to start a relationship. He was also deeply afraid of being hurt and rejected by others. Several years earlier, Dan attempted to start a friendship with a coworker at a previous place of employment. He and this other man began watching football together on Sundays, and then began to talk about their lives, pains, and dreams. Just as they were beginning to become close, his friend informed Dan that he was "strange" and that he did not want to be his friend anymore.

Developing meaningful and supportive friendships became a primary goal in therapy. One of the early steps in helping him work toward this goal was to point out his strengths regarding forming relationships. Collaboratively Dan and his therapist developed an inventory of Dan's strengths that included being able to talk to people easily, having interesting things to say, being able to talk about his feelings, having a history of making friends, being a loyal person, being a kind person, and having a good sense of humor. Helping Dan recognize his strengths was instrumental in helping him become more invested in the process. By focusing on his strengths and not only his deficits, Dan began to perceive himself as being more socially competent and less fearful of increasing his social contacts. Soon he was able to ask a fellow member of his book club out for coffee. After meeting several times for coffee, Dan stated that he believed this man would become a friend of his. He reported feeling less isolated and more hopeful.

During his final three months of therapy, Dan was able to explore difficulties he experienced with reconnecting to friends. For example, one day he and his new friend had an argument over where they would have dinner. Dan gave in to his friend's demands but felt mistreated and resentful. He believed that the friendship would soon be over, and that he would go back to being alone. Collaboratively, he and his social worker explored alternative meanings for the conflict. Dan decided that the struggle with his friend really was more about both of them being afraid of intimacy, even though it was manifested as being about control. Addressing the issue with his friend allowed them to develop a greater sense of trust in their relationship. They both learned that their friendship could survive conflict, and that they could be closer for it.

FOR WRITING AND REFLECTION

1. What hegemonic masculine traits are affecting Dan's relationships?
2. In what ways might you approach this case differently if Dan were ten years older, or ten years younger?
3. What relationship issues explored in this chapter are important to understanding Dan's relationships?
4. What might be some alternative ways of helping Dan? In other words, what might you have done differently?

Case Example

Carlos P is a 48-year-old, second-generation Mexican American/Native American man. He identifies primarily as being Mexican (his maternal grandfather was Native American and was not influential in his life). He has four children—two by one woman and two by another. The woman he has recently been dating asked him to go to counseling because she says that he has too many "issues." Specifically, Carlos's girlfriend is concerned about his temper and his lack of relationships with his two sets of children. She is ten years younger than he is and would like to have children of her own; she is worried about Carlos's history of abandoning his children.

While Carlos has never been to therapy before, he has been involved in "new age" spiritual experiences and a men's movement group. These experiences have helped him understand himself, grow, and develop, but he has found himself in a personal crisis. He deeply cares for his new girlfriend but finds that he is repeating the same mistakes that he has always made in relationships. While Carlos at times is able to recognize these patterns, he frequently behaves in a reactive manner and utilizes a great deal of aggressive defensiveness. When his girlfriend attempts to talk to him about her concerns, he becomes angry and blaming or retreats into silence. He finds it extremely difficult to listen to her feelings and concerns and only is able to admit to and address her concerns through e-mails.

Each of Carlos's marriages ended in divorce due to Carlos's difficulty with intimacy, problems with commitment, and substance abuse. For instance, during Carlos's second marriage, he sold one of his wife's family heirlooms, her grandmother's wedding ring, for drugs.

Carlos has not spoken to his second set of children in four years. His second wife has remarried; she and Carlos separated when their children were 1 and 5 years old. For the first year he maintained a relationship with his two girls. However, when his ex-wife started dating and subsequently remarried, he began to distance himself from his children. When his ex-wife's new husband attempted to reach out to him, he sent e-mails calling his ex-wife degrading names and belittling her. He began to make up stories about her marriage and her treatment of the children. He went as far as intimating that her husband was physically inappropriate with his children, which he did not believe and had no evidence of. By pathologizing her marriage and family life, Carlos was able to defend against his own personal feelings of failure and inadequacy. Over time Carlos's behavior pushed his ex-wife and her husband away; they eventually moved out of state, in large part to avoid his abusive and disruptive behavior. During this time Carlos began to drink heavily again and would periodically do cocaine. On these nearly monthly binges, he would drive to a Native American casino and gamble, often losing as much as five hundred dollars.

Feeling out of control and wishing to preserve his current relationships, Carlos has decided to seek counseling.

FOR WRITING AND REFLECTION

1. Based on what you have read, what additional information would you want to know about Carlos?
2. How would you approach Carlos about his children?
3. What are Carlos's current developmental challenges, and how would these influence your work with him?
4. Write about some potential interventions that you might explore with Carlos.

Theoretical and Practice Guidelines | FIVE

This chapter presents some general guidelines for working with men, focusing on direct practice issues for social workers. Macro practice will be briefly explored here, examples of which can be found throughout this book. All social workers, even those whose positions are more clinical in nature, must be willing to engage in the macro issue of social change. When they find patterns in their clinical practice, they can prevent future micro problems by engaging in macro interventions oriented toward social change. Also, helping empower men to engage in social change is personally empowering and can help ameliorate many symptoms typically associated with other causes.

The focus of this book, however, is primarily on the domain of direct practice. Thus in this chapter I first briefly discuss basic conceptions of micro (including mezzo) and macro practice. Next I turn to some of the help-seeking barriers and behaviors that can make it difficult for men to engage in the helping process. Then I take a look at key cross-theoretical principles that inform the basic practices and concepts that are applicable for work with most men in most contexts. Finally, I present a general discussion of how cognitive therapy, narrative therapy, existential theory, and the strengths perspective can be implemented in practice with men. Of course, it is impossible to make generalizations about working with a population as diverse as men without there being exceptions. The needs of men often vary by race, class, and ethnicity, and different problems call for different approaches, discussion of which will form the basis of part 2 of this book.

General Services Provided to Men

Social work services are typically conceptualized as occurring on the micro, macro, or mezzo (family) levels. This section considers the general domains of service domains as they apply to men. More details about the specific intervention approaches for different problems will be found in subsequent chapters.

Micro Social Work Practice

Direct social work services are provided to men in a variety of situations. Men encounter social workers both as voluntary and involuntary clients. While men are less likely than women to voluntarily seek services, they still frequently do so. Men come for help for problems including substance abuse, mental health concerns, family stresses, work issues, as well as many others. Men voluntarily seek social work services through community mental health centers, their employee assistance programs, work training centers, and other community-based groups. However, whether or not a man is voluntarily or involuntarily seeking services is not merely an either/or distinction. For instance, a man who is told by his wife that she will leave him if he does attend therapy may technically be a voluntary client (i.e., not mandated by some legal authority) yet may feel compelled to seek services and may be less than thrilled at the prospect of professional assistance. He may feel extremely resistant and resentful about engaging in services; traits typically associated with involuntary clients. Therefore, the degree to which a man feels he is seeking help by choice is an important factor to consider during intake and initial sessions.

Often men are mandated by outside authorities to seek treatment. For instance, a man who was convicted of driving while under the influence of alcohol or drugs may be ordered to attend substance abuse treatment, a psychoeducational group, group or individual therapy, or a combination of these. A men who is on probation for domestic violence may be mandated to attend an anger control group or a group for batterers. Men who are incarcerated are often also mandated to engage in treatment (although many men who are incarcerated do not receive sufficient help for the variety of mental health or psychosocial concerns that contributed to their incarceration).

Group work is an important intervention with men. The group experience, in which clients are treated together, can provide a context that can be used to help men resolve many of the problems which they face. For instance, interpersonally oriented groups give men the opportunity to establish relationships, decrease social isolation, understand how they are perceived by others, and practice new skills in a safe and accepting environment. Groups may provide an ideal setting for helping men confront and change some the most problematic effects of hegemonic masculinity. Men who have a difficult time expressing their feelings can observe other men explore their emotional reactions, thereby helping them to work toward change. Men who have a hard time with intimacy can take chances on receiving and giving support to others in a controlled environment.

However, it is important that groups are not overly focused on affectual content but include behavioral and solution-focused cognitive behavioral interventions as well. A more action-oriented, results-focused group can prevent men from being too uncomfortable with the affective nature of group work and can demonstrate to them the benefit of groups. Many men want to see results quickly, and they may deride a total focus on affect or on the exploration of insight as "touchy feeling" or "navel gazing." As with other interventions, practitioners want to balance interventions that play to men's strengths with some gentle pushes toward expanding their affective and social repertoires.

Yalom (1995) is one of the most important writers on group work; his therapeutic factors have been particularly influential in the development of group therapy practice. While Yalom is known for his work in existential therapy, his group approach is far more generic and incorporates many research-based ideas that are congruent with each of four perspectives highlighted in this book. His therapeutic factors are instillation of hope, universality, imparting information, altruism, the corrective recapitulation of the family experience, development of socializing techniques, imitative behavior, interpersonal learning, group cohesiveness, catharsis, and existential factors. Several of these are discussed below in some detail as they pertain to men.

Instillation of Hope

Hope is one of the most powerful therapeutic factors and is strongly correlated to positive treatment outcomes. An element of the famed placebo effect may have to do with one's capacity to experience hope in relation to a potential solution. Helping men feel hopeful is one of the most important things that a practitioner can do in groups or in other practice settings. Men who come to treatment rarely do so until problems are acute; they often experience a profound sense of hopelessness and shame for needing assistance. Helping men feel hope activates their internal strengths, capacities, and resiliencies. It helps them become willing to take actions that may often go against what they have learned to do.

Universality

Not sharing your feelings with others has many costs. Perhaps one of the greatest is that men often believe that they are the only ones who are experiencing the problems they face. When a man believes that he is the only one who has made the kind of mistakes that he may have made, that he is perhaps flawed for not having been able to solve his own problems, he may become depressed and ashamed. Groups can help men face and work through shame by helping them universalize their problems; that is, groups can be used to assist men in understanding that many of the problems they experience are also experienced by others. Their problems are often universal, part of the drama of human existence. Men usually respond to feeling shame with defensiveness; helping them decrease their shame will allow men to face their other concerns without becoming overwhelmed.

Imparting Information

Groups can be excellent places to encourage men to share information that may be valuable to others. Instead of receiving only the perspective and opinion of the group worker, being a member of a group allows men to receive multiple ideas from many different perspectives. Some men may listen to information that is shared not as direct advice but is provided in the context of group dialogue. For instance, in a hospital group for men who recently have had significant health concerns, one member shared his fear of dying, and how his obesity led to his heart attack. He began to share information that his doctors had given him about diet and exercise but expressed ambivalence about whether or not his doctors' suggestions would work for him, or if he would be able to follow their guidelines. Other men empathized with his concerns, and the group soon began to discuss alternative ways of losing weight. One of the suggestions that resonated with the original speaker was the thought of riding an indoor exercise bike instead of walking. During the discussion, he realized that he was too ashamed of his appearance to walk in public. He decided to ask his doctor about the advantages and disadvantages of riding an stationary bicycle.

Corrective Emotional Experience

Facilitating a corrective emotional experience is an important aspect of group work. Corrective emotional experiences can often be facilitated by helping members increase their social contacts and improve their connectedness to others. At times this runs counter to traditional notions of social work boundaries and the preferred relationships between group members. In his work with gay men in groups, Behan (1999) observed that in helping men find these corrective emotional experiences, close relationships should be strongly encouraged. Given the isolation of many of these men, Behan found it inappropriate to ask participants to abide by the common group therapy norm of not allowing outside contact between members. Indeed, he saw the group as a potential vehicle for helping gay men meet their social needs within and outside the group. Given that relationships were formed during the group process, he was able to help participants explore their new connections during group sessions, allowing for in-vivo learning and exploration.

Family Therapy and Family Work

Men are often part of social work services geared toward families. Men frequently become involved in the child welfare system when they or their partners abuse, neglect, or abandon their children. Becoming involved in the children welfare system is particularly problematic for many men. Believing that they should be able to resolve their own problems and those of their family, men frequently feel shame, humiliation, and anger at being referred to a child protective services agency. Workers often misinterpret this anger as merely a component of a man's pattern of violence and abusive behavior. While a man's anger many certainly be an important ingredient in the family's problems, it is often true that men have an easier time expressing anger to social workers than the "softer" and "more vulnerable" feelings of guilt, shame, humiliation, or inadequacy. It is important that social workers not make quick judgments based on first encounters; the social control aspects of social work practice are known to contribute to defensiveness (Rank 1945).

When selecting a model of family therapy, social workers should take into account the degree to which a man ascribes to the hegemonic ideal, and other cultural factors. Models that are more behavioral or structural in orientation may be especially appropriate for more traditional men. For instance, in structural family therapy the therapist helps the family work on appropriate boundaries and family hierarchies (Minuchin and Fishman 2004). In this approach, parents are placed on top of the hierarchy, and work together to develop methods for raising their children and resolving family problems. Men who ascribe to the hegemonic ideal may view these approaches as being congruent with their values. It is important to note, however, that such approaches have been criticized as overly restricting gender roles in their conceptualization and practice (Hare-Martin 1987).

Macro Social Work Practice

Macro social work practice focuses on larger groups and social systems. Typically macro practice entails community organization, advocacy, policy development, administration, social development, and other social change practices (Kirst-Ashman and Hull 2006; Long, Tice, and Morrison 2006). Estes (1992) notes the trend toward world building: the need for social workers to help develop transnational organizations and structures to promote peace, justice, and human rights. Macro practice identifies the structural social causes to problems that are experienced on the individual level and seeks structural solutions for them.

Macro social work practice with men is not as developed as it is with women. Perhaps because men already have considerable rights, privileges, and power, macro practitioners have focused more on the rights of women and minorities. Yet men constitute half of minority populations, so much macro practice has been geared toward men, however indirectly. In my discussion of globalization, I explored the importance of including men in social development programs as a means of working toward progressive social change for all people.

The HIV/AIDS and gay rights movements have been two important areas of advocacy and social change for men. Several groups have played an important role in advocating for the rights of gay men. One of the most influential groups has been Act Up, which started in 1987 as a challenge to the federal government's early response to the HIV/AIDS crisis. The group began to organize demonstrations in highly visible places to protest the lack of care and fiscal resources available for people living with HIV/AIDS. By engaging in acts of civil disobedience, the group brought to the attention of the media and mainstream Americans the grave problems experienced by people suffering with the disease. The ACT UP Oral History Project (Act Up 2007) tells the courageous stories of many of the men (and women) who were involved in this advocacy/social change movement.

Help and Help Seeking

Men present social workers and other helping professionals with several interrelated dilemmas in regard to their help-seeking behaviors. First, as I discuss in greater detail later, men disproportionately experience several debilitating psychosocial problems that are typically treated through clinical services. Second, traditional masculinity has been associated with less frequent help-seeking behavior and with negative attitudes toward seeking help (Mahalik, Good, and Englar-Carlson 2003). Rochlen, McKelley, and Pituch (2006:1) refer to this problem as a "lack of fit between the culture of masculinity and the therapeutic process."

Numerous authors proposed different conceptualizations of what factors influence help seeking by men. Pollack and Levant (1998) deduce six main factors that stand in the way of men in need of help:

1. Difficulty admitting that they have a problem, which stems from men's difficulty with accepting weakness
2. Difficulty asking for help and an intolerance of depending upon others, which stems from men's strong valuation of autonomy and independence
3. Difficulty in accepting, identifying, and processing the more tender or "softer" emotions
4. Fear of intimacy and vulnerability
5. Sexualization of female helpers and homophobic feelings that block opening up to male helpers
6. A paucity of treatment approaches that are sensitive to men's need and dilemmas

Kosberg (2005) notes the values and personality characteristics of independence, stoicism, control, and self-reliance as being key factors to consider, especially for lower-income and culturally diverse men. However, help seeking by men is complex; some evidence calls into question some of the notions presented above. Cusack et al. (2006) found a relationship between therapeutic bonds and perceptions of treatment helpfulness in a sample of men currently in psychologically oriented counseling. Contrary to some stereotypes of more traditional, stoic men, the authors found that men characterized by "restrictive emotionality," or the lack of comfort and willingness to express affect, were different from other men in terms of help seeking. Alexithymic men, or those who do not have the ability to identify and express emotions, did perceive therapy as less helpful than other men. The authors note that further research is required on how to improve therapeutic bonds with this group of men.

Several studies have indicated that when men perceive a problem as "normal," they are more likely to seek help for it (Addis and Mahalik 2003; Brooks 1998). Many men are extremely self-conscious about having their behavior seen as deviant or "crazy." A recognition of this dynamic can be found in television ads in which celebrities promote medication for depression, sexual dysfunction, and other psychological and physical problems. Preventative programs in physical and mental health often attempt to normalize the problem in their campaigns. Normalizing problems is also an important clinical tool for social workers practicing with men. Early in the process, social workers can discuss with their clients the prevalence of a problem or the likelihood of a problem occurring given a high concentration of life stressors.

Research has thus demonstrated that men have significant barriers to help seeking help. However, what might be most significant is that clinicians, researchers, and the helping professions in general tend to subtly or not so subtly blame men. Professionals tend to pathologize the attributes that make men less likely to seek help, thereby increasing the isolation they may experience, which in turn may increase their presenting problems and make them reticent to seek and receive help. By focusing on men's deficits and their relationship to help seeking, bonding, and ultimately therapeutic success, professionals abdicate responsibility for creating services designed to meet needs of men. That many traditional men do not fit the standard models of therapeutic services indicates not only that there is room for growth for some men, but that the profession needs to develop new, more culturally competent models.

It is essential that social workers become able to accept their male clients and their clients' reluctance toward specific types of services. To accomplish this aim, it is valuable to view men as a culturally different group with their own unique norms, values, and socialization. Social work wisdom tells us to "start where the client is." Too often when providing services to men, social workers forget this time-honored maxim. They must be able to view male behavior, including help-seeking behavior, in all its complexity. Many behavioral patterns contain both positive and negative aspects. For example, take the traditional male trait of stoicism. While there are clear emotional problems with not expressing one's feelings, there are clear benefits as well. For instance, a man who is able to control his feelings under high-pressure situations may be an excellent negotiator or may be able to survive a crisis. During the tragedy of September 11, 2001, the calm and collected behavior of many firefighters and other emergency personnel led to the rescue of many people.

Mahalik, Good, and Englar (2003) explore this dynamic in their description of the scripts that men adopt that affect their ability to receive traditional clinical services. These roles include the "strong silent script," the "tough guy script," and the "independent script," among others. The authors note that practitioners must be able to validate and explore the strengths inherent within each of these roles. They also note that the goal of therapy is not to compel men to abandon their scripts, but to help them employ their scripts in flexible ways that meet their psychosocial needs. Men are aware of the attributes that lead to their success. To deny the positives of masculine scripts and behaviors and critique a trait as being maladaptive will lead to a decrease in social workers' credibility and an increase in client defensiveness. After social workers validate men for this strength, they may then inquire about the potential consequences of using these attributes in all social contexts. The goal should be to help men develop new skills and tools and learn to view their strengths as being situationally positive but inappropriate for other situations.

Closely related to the notion of roles and scripts are several key concepts that transcend theoretical perspectives and that social workers must understand in working positively with men. I describe some of these cross-theoretical concepts below, prior to a more detailed exploration of the four key approaches that form the core of this book.

Responsibility versus Blame

Mooney (1998:58) says that "One of the basic assumptions of cognitive behavior therapy centers around the notion of a non-blaming sense of responsibility for self which includes one's thoughts, feelings, and behaviors." Although Mooney's statement is meant to apply to cognitive therapy, it is an essential general principle for working with men. Social workers should nonjudgmentally help men accept responsibility for their feelings, thoughts, and behaviors. In practice with men, I have used metaphors that are consistent with a narrative and cognitive perspective to help them take responsibility for difficult behaviors and feelings. For instance, as a means of helping men begin to take responsibility for their beliefs, I liken social learning to the process of brainwashing, or even alien abduction. Let's take the case of depression, I tell them. I ask them to imagine that nefarious spies had brainwashed them into believing that they were worthless. I assert that they are not at fault for being brainwashed, but that it is now their responsibly to work collaboratively with me on their reprogramming. I have found that men like this metaphor, as it helps them explore and ultimately accept their feelings through nonjudgmental dialogue, while acknowledging that they will have to take ownership for the process of change. In other words, they learn to accept responsibility without shame or self-reproach. Helping men find ways to take responsibility without blaming them helps them be less defensive and more focused on behavioral change.

Redefining Basic Helping Skills

Successfully working with men demands that social workers make adjustments to their repertoire of basic helping skills. The typical core of the helping interview is reflective listening, specifically reflection of affect and emotions. While it is important to use self-reflection with men, it can easily be overused. Men tend to respond to an overreliance on reflective listening with annoyance and discomfort. Social workers must learn to express unconditional positive regard without a formulaic reliance on reflection of affect. In fact, comprehensive empathic responses do not merely focus on affect but include attention to the cognitive and behavioral realms as well (Egan 2004).

Focusing solely on feelings may also turn men off to the helping process. Practitioners should not repetitively ask men "how do you feel?" A better question usually is "what is that like for you?" Men tend to relate to this question better, as their experience may typically focus on behaviors and thoughts more than feelings. Asking a man what something is like invites them to explore any aspect of their experience. When social workers want to help men learn to identify their feelings and thoughts, they may do so through reflections that are more naturalistic, and that attend to the entire message that the man is presenting. Working with feelings should be only a part of the overall therapeutic process when working with men, regardless of the theoretical orientation that is being used.

Men typically prefer a more direct approach to helping and may often appreciate direct feedback. Advice is typically considered a lower-order helping skill; indeed, there are several reasons to be very careful when giving advice, and why advice giving has often been counterindicated. If a client follows advice and things go badly for him, he may blame the practitioner and lose trust in him or her. Additionally, giving advice too often can be disempowering; one of the key goals of most practice is to help clients become better problem solvers and decision makers. Workers want to help encourage maximum autonomy and independence for all their clients. Yet men value a more direct, forthright approach. When a man asks your opinion about something, there are times when it is not appropriate to turn the question back to him with "well, what do you think?" I have found that a good preface is "I will tell you what I think, but remember, it is just my opinion, and it might not work for you," or "I would be glad to tell you my opinion, but I would like to hear your thoughts on the matter first."

Men will often ask for direct feedback, especially once they become comfortable with their social worker. A former client of mine would repeatedly ask me to tell him when he is "screwing up." One session I told him that some of his behavior might not be serving him well. He replied, "Does that mean you think I am messing up? Come on, Richie [what he called me], you can be more straight up with me, I can take it." At that point I spoke in a bit more pointed tone, using language that was somewhat more colorful. He listened carefully, knowing that I was seriously concerned about his behavior. My willingness to be direct and communicate in a manner to which he could relate let him know that I cared about him, and that his needs and desires were important. By speaking to him in the direct manner he desired, I communicated to him that he was responsible for his own change. I was starting, and ending, where the client was.

Social workers should always adapt their approach to the needs of their clients. In a sense, everything we know about human behavior can be seen as hypotheses. Sometimes our hypotheses are correct; other times they are not. It is important that our clients provide us with clear feedback on the relevance of our hypotheses, methods, and helping skills.

Metaphors

Metaphors are extremely useful in the helping process (Carter and McGoldrick 1989; Furman, Langer, and Anderson 2006; Goldstein 1984; Nichols and Schwartz 1995). A metaphor is a linguistic device that compares and relates two seemingly unrelated things or events. A metaphor allows aspects of one phenomenon to come into focus by comparing it to the other phenomenon. For instance, the title of a book by Carson McCullers, *The Heart Is a Lonely Hunter*, is a powerful metaphor that speaks of loneliness, longing and emotion. The heart is not literally a lonely hunter, yet the metaphor evokes images and ideas about love and desire more powerfully than would a narrative description. Metaphors help focus clients on salient aspects of their situation and can help them view their possibilities in a new light. Metaphors allow workers to help clients view their situations in a nonthreatening manner. By removing their behavior or situation from its particular context and placing it in the abstract, men may be helped to objectively and dispassionately approach their concerns.

For instance, Geer (1983) describes his work with a Vietnam veteran who struggled with a violent history. He helped the veteran to see that his way of dealing with the world could be represented by the metaphor "marine/machine." This metaphor captured the man's two primary ways of relating to others: with intensity and aggressiveness or with a cold, mechanistic detachment.

During therapy he was encouraged to develop a new metaphor to help guide his growth and healing. He began to refer to himself as "the poet of the rocks," a metaphor that honored his love of creativity and nature. Over time he began to use this metaphor as a means of assessing his current behavior, and he began to accept a potential new identity that was free of violence, and one that allowed for greater emotional expression. His new metaphor symbolized and made concrete a complex set of feelings, thoughts, and behaviors to which he could aspire.

Men tend to be more instrumental than emotional in their preferred manner of problem solving and change. That is, men seek to "act" their way out of problems, and to see the process of change connected more to doing than to feeling. As such, metaphors that focus on action and behavior can be effective. For instance, when men are feeling afraid to change, or believe that actually changing means that they are somehow weak and inadequate, it is important to help them see that the goal of helping is not to "fix them." In such situations, I have found it valuable to inform a male client that the goal is for him to merely add another "tool to his tool box." A man who is handy with tools will understand that attempting to refinish a floor without the proper equipment is next to impossible. A man who bowls will understand that using an aggressive bowling ball on a dry lane is not a wise choice; the right tool is needed to do a job well. By becoming willing to use new emotional, cognitive, and behavioral tools, men can focus on the process of learning a new skill or new ways of using existing resources.

The next sections chapter explore our four theories in more depth. I begin with cognitive behavioral approaches, which serve as an umbrella or organizing approach that connects the other theories and perspectives. Again, please do not view this centering of cognitive therapy to imply that it is more valuable than the other approaches. It can, however, be an extremely valuable theory in its capacity to connect other approaches.

Cognitive Behavioral Approaches

There are several reasons why cognitive behavioral therapies are a valuable method for working with men. One of the key reasons stems from the manner in which gender role socialization occurs and affects men. As Mahalik and Cournoyer (2000:109) explain, "An often overlooked source of these cognitive structures is the process of gender role socialization that teaches males and females about expected societal roles for men and women and how they are expected to act, think, and feel in those roles. In a similar way to Beck's description of the development of cognitive structures, gender role theorists have observed that males and females are socialized to be masculine or feminine by learning 'shoulds' and 'musts' from important individuals and to adopt traditional gender role attitudes."

The approaches associated with CBT may be particularly well suited for working with many men. These approaches emphasize logic, rationality, and the desire to "do" things in therapy, areas that have been shown to be congruent with how men want to receive help (Silverberg 1986). While it certainly is an appropriate therapeutic goal to help men learn to be increasingly in touch with their feelings, it is important that treatment maximizes what men do well. This section explores the core elements of CBT and how they can be helpful to men. I focus on the approaches of some of the most important theorists and provide a general understanding of the central ideas of the theory. Different authors tend to focus more on either the cognitive or the behavioral domains; I spend more time on theories that are slightly more cognitive in nature. These approaches are more constructivist and more congruent with the humanistic thrust of social work practice.

Cognitive behavioral therapies in general focus on the connection among thinking, feeling, and behavior (Walen, DiGiuseppe, and Dryden 1992). CBT focuses on the centrality of the role of cognition in shaping human behavior and emotion (Dryden and Neenan 2004; Mahoney 1991). At CBT's core is the notion of cognitive restructuring: that human thinking can be changed, and that these alterations will subsequently lead to changes in feeling and behavior. Corcoran (2006) notes four important steps for facilitating the cognitive restructuring process: educating clients about the connection between thoughts and feelings; helping them identify their thoughts; examining the validity or rationality of their thoughts; and, replacing irrational thoughts with those that are more functional. Increasingly, the relationship among feeling, thoughts, and behavior has been understood as extremely complex; yet most CBT approaches still stress the importance of changing cognition as a key task in the therapeutic process (Safran and Greenberg 1991).

The three dimensions of cognition that are addressed in CBT approaches are content, structure, and process (Blackburn and Twaddle 1996). Content refers to the actual messages and meanings that clients present; structure, to the nature of cognition, the different layers or levels of thought; and process, to how clients think. Most cognitive therapists focus on the content and process of cognition. By helping clients change the content of their thinking, social workers help them adopt beliefs that are more reality based and congruent with their values. Focusing on process helps clients explore different ways of thinking and develop new skills and tools for managing their behaviors and feelings by expanding their cognitive repertoire.

David Burns (1989) explores ten cognitive distortions that represent faults in the manner in which people think and the content of their thinking:

- All-or-nothing thinking: in this cognitive distortion, people see things in black-and-white terms that do not reflect the gray nature of reality.
- Overgeneralization: when one specific detail becomes evidence of a pattern. For instance, one mistake becomes evidence of a total pattern of failure.
- Mental filter: when someone picks out one negative aspect of a situation and focuses solely on it, neglecting other relevant data. For instance, someone may receive positive strokes from a significant other but will dwell on one comment that was not particularly positive.
- Disqualifying the positive: when someone rejects positive experiences, attending only to negative stimuli as reflecting the reality of a situation.
- Jumping to conclusions: a type of distortion in which one makes assertions that are not based on facts.
- Magnification: exaggerating the importance of a problem, or minimizing of good things that are occurring.
- Emotional reasoning: when one thinks something is true based upon how he or she feels about things or events. For instance, someone who feels nervous or anxious about a situation reasons that it is dangerous due to how he feels.
- Should statements: when one makes rigid demands and expectations on the world. One thinks that something "should" and "must" occur—evaluations based on a dogmatic assessment of the world that usually lead to anger.
- Labeling and mislabeling: often thought of as a form of all-or-nothing thinking. One places an all-encompassing label on a situation or event based on a limited number of occurrences or information. For instance, if someone rejects someone else, that person labels himself or herself as "unlovable."
- Personalization: when someone sees himself or herself as being responsible for events that lie outside of his or her control or purview. For instance, a husband blames himself for not being home when the family pet has a stroke. While it would be normal to feel some sadness and regret about this event, holding that belief so strongly that one beats oneself up for it is not helpful or productive.

Rational emotive behavior therapy (REBT) is one of the cognitive behavioral approaches that holds particular promise for men. REBT is a structured approach to change that focuses on how "irrational" thinking leads to behavioral and emotional problems. Research has demonstrated the effectiveness of this approach with men (Haaga and Davison 1989). Developed by Albert Ellis (1958), REBT's main premise is that people are not directly influenced by events, but by the views they hold of these events. Practitioners using REBT encourage growth and change by teaching clients to replace their negative, self-defeating thoughts with more rational, reality-based patterns of thinking (Gullo 1977). REBT focuses on self-help and empowerment; the goal is to teach men the skills they need to help them resolve their own problems.

One of the most powerful techniques of REBT for working with men is the ABCDE method. The "A" in the approach represents a client's activating event, or the situation or context in which the client is experiencing distress. "B" represents clients' beliefs, including images, values, and perceptions. Clients are taught a systematic method for evaluating the problems in their lives, which are represented as "C" (or consequences, either emotional or behavioral) in the paradigm. According to Ellis (1994), clinicians must disrupt (D), the irrational beliefs of the client, in order for the client to enjoy (E), his or her newly discovered rational beliefs. Clients are helped to assess the connection between their beliefs and the difficult feelings and behavioral consequences that are transpiring in their lives (Ellis 1958, 1973, 1994).

Traditional approaches to psychotherapy tend to focus mostly on events and their emotional and behavioral consequences. In the assessment phase of REBT, practitioners spend most of their time assessing and understanding the nature of clients' beliefs. Treatment focuses on helping clients change their beliefs so they can have more positive emotional and behavioral outcomes.

At the core of REBT is the notion of irrational beliefs—those that do not reflect reality (Higbee 1997). They represent core philosophies that are untrue and lead to problematic feelings and behaviors. Irrational beliefs are often rigid, overgeneralized, and dogmatic. According to Ellis, there are four core irrational beliefs: demandingness, awfulizing, low frustration tolerance, and global evaluation of self. Each of these classifications leads to different "dysfunctional emotions."

Demandingness reflects unrealistic expectations regarding events and other people. It can be identified by cue words such as "must," "should," "ought to," and "have to." Demandingness is the irrational belief that is most associated with anger and can be contrasted with desire or want. If I merely wish for things to be a certain way, when they do not occur I may feel more appropriate and more functional emotions such as disappointment or annoyance. Yet if I demand that the world and others behave other than they do and I dogmatically and rigidly insist that these behaviors and events are "wrong" and "must" change, my response will be moderate to extreme anger.

Awfulizing is the process of exaggerating the consequences of an event in an extreme manner. Difficult and unfortunate events become "the worst thing that ever happened to me" or "the most terrible thing I can imagine." The man who awfulizes turns the metaphorical broken fingernail into a catastrophe. Awfulizing is associated with feelings of frustration, depression, low self-esteem, and overall lack of well-being. When awfulizing, men tend to ignore other important information, such as the good things that are occurring in their life, or the relative importance of specific situations.

Low frustration tolerance stems from demands for comfort or ease and represents sets of beliefs about one's capacity to tolerate situations. When a man engages in low frustration tolerance, he inappropriately assesses his internal resources and his capacity to tolerate difficult feelings and external events. In other words, he believes that he cannot tolerate a specific situation or event. He tells himself that he "can't stand" a situation and thereby experiences feelings of dread or anxiety. Over time, evaluations based on low frustration tolerance tend to lead to generalized feelings of anxiety. Additionally, by holding negative beliefs about one's capacity to tolerate and cope with situations, men begin to develop negative appraisals about their self-efficacy, which can exacerbate feelings of low self-worth and depression.

Global evaluation of human worth occurs when a man bases his overall evaluation of himself or others on too little information. For instance, if a man fails to get a raise at work, he may tell himself that he is stupid and unworthy of the job. These types of self-evaluations usually lead to the internalization of these messages, where over time a man comes to believe that he is worthless, stupid, and undeserving. Alternatively, these global evaluations can be combined with low frustration tolerance. For instance, a man not able to tolerate the emotional pain of holding these self-doubting beliefs reacts with defensive anger, blaming others for his own shortcomings. This type of defensive reaction makes it difficult for men to gently accept themselves as being fallible, thereby decreasing their willingness to work toward change. Global evaluations can also be directed at others. When a men globally evaluates others, he extends faults and mistakes made in one situation to general character defects. Men who globally evaluate others become very judgmental of others and struggle in establishing and maintaining relationships.

Cognitive methods not only are useful in traditional talking therapy but can be used creatively as well. Jacobs's (1992) use of creative props in CBT-oriented treatment can be extremely useful. Through his impact therapy approach (Jacobs 1994), he has taught many clinicians the use of creative props and kinesthetic exercises to help enliven the therapeutic process. I was trained by Ed Jacobs at a three-day conference fifteen years ago, and the techniques that he demonstrated continue to influence how I view practice. I have used and adapted several of his techniques in my own practice. Using props allows practitioners to make metaphors and lessons concrete and real. Through the use of methods that extend verbal communication to include other senses, counseling can help create a greater impact on clients (Jacobs 1994). For instance, automatic thoughts can be likened to a tape loop that repeats in one's head. It is one thing to ask a client what he is "telling himself," but to hand a man a tape and ask, "What message keeps playing in your mind when you are feeling X?" can be far more powerful. In addition, the metaphor can be extended to the cognitive disputational process. Since a tape can be recorded over, thoughts can be changed. A client once shared with me that his parents would always tell him how stupid and worthless he was. He said he could actually hear them saying "you are too stupid to learn." He said he still could hear that "tape" every day, and that it still "played very loud." I asked him what that tape really should say, and he responded, "That you are smart, you just had a learning disability that was not diagnosed." We spent a significant amount of time practicing and rehearsing this more realistic, life-affirming "tape."

Creative props can be combined with REBT in other ways. I have had clients move between two different chairs, each chair representing a different constellation of beliefs. When they sat in one chair, they would speak form the voice of their problematic beliefs; when they sat in the other chair, they would work to dispute and alter the irrational thoughts and beliefs. These are empowering techniques for men, as they learn that they can very much be responsible for their own change process. As stated previously, men often fear that therapy is something that is done to them; many men fear and resent being in a position that feels submissive. By helping them do their own work through creative methods, a social worker can enable men to feel empowered in the process of change.

Krech (2002) explores approaches that can be used with Native American men. He outlines the psychosocial problems that that have reached near epidemic levels among Native American men, both on and off reservation, including unemployment, hopelessness, depression, and substance abuse. Krech contends that a history of systematic and accidental destruction of the cultural norms and rituals of many Native American men, in conjunction with their being frequently denied access to meaning, value, and resources within mainstream institutions due to racism, has created unhealthy belief systems in some of them. In his exploration of approaches to treat these problems, he notes the need to help such men restructure their belief systems, using methods that seek to help them integrate traditional Native American values and connections to their own culture. Each method he advocates has a strong cognitive change component. Krech cites Williamson (2000), who posits that intergenerational mentoring programs can help restructure the core beliefs of youth. Krech explores how traditional storytelling and narratives can "actively restructure the listener's views and provide problem solving methodology" (89).

Education and psychoeducation are an important part of most CBT approaches and are often important in working with men. Kim et al. (2000), in their qualitative analysis of therapy transcripts, note that Kenyan men who were seen in family counseling found the information that was provided in therapy to be the most important aspect of their treatment. They especially valued information that allowed them to make better decisions. Part of most cognitive behavioral approaches involves teaching. For instance, practitioners often teach men early in the helping process the relationship between thinking and feeling (Harvey et al. 2004), and the nature of the cognitive behavioral change process (Wills and Saunders 2003). The teaching of new skills does not need to imply a hierarchical relationship, as is often the case with traditional models of teaching and education. Instead, practitioners may view the development of information acquisition as a collaborative process, where men may be actively involved in investigating the things they wish or need to learn. In my work with Latino men with histories of substance abuse, we developed homework assignments in which they conducted research on topics important to them. For instance, a man who struggled with anxiety and stress explored the causes and potential solutions of stress. By taking charge of his own psychoeducation, he was able to acquire new information that was subsequently explored in therapy. Therapy helped him evaluate his new knowledge and learn to apply it to his own concerns and life context. Other skills that are taught in the context of CBT are relationship building, problem solving, and relaxation methods.

Narrative Therapy with Men

Narrative therapy is a relatively new approach that has become influential in social work practice and education, particularly in Australia, New Zealand, and Great Britain. It is largely constructivist in nature; human beings are seen as actively creating their lives and their perceptions about themselves and others through the language that they use (Freedman and Combs 1996). More important than what "really happened" is how clients construct their world and construct meaning from it (Speedy 2005). The narrative approach is congruent with cognitive therapy in that it focuses on how men create mental representations of their world, with the strength perspective in that men are viewed as far more than their problems, and with the existential approach, which highlights the importance of individuals choosing their own realities.

The narrative approach was developed by David Epston and Michael White. These therapists believed that the stories that people internalized about themselves and the nature of their problems led to personal dilemmas and social oppression (White 1997, 2002). The goal of therapy is to help clients deconstruct the "pathologizing" stories they hold about themselves and change them into more liberating and freeing narratives. Changing the narratives and stories that people hold about themselves is not a small task but is a powerful part of the process of change. Carr (1998:486) notes: "The process of therapeutic reauthoring of personal narratives changes lives, problems and identities because personal narratives are constructive of identity."

In his exploration of the work of Michael White, Carr (1998) notes nine practices of narrative therapy that I discuss in detail below: position collaboratively, externalize the problem, excavate unique outcomes, thicken the new plot, link to the past and extend to the future, invite outsider witness groups, use re-remembering practices and incorporation, use literary means, and facilitate bringing-it-back practices.

Position Collaboratively

Narrative therapists stress the positioning of the therapist in relationship to the client (Payne 2000). They insist on a collaborative and egalitarian relationship that may differ in nature from the type traditionally advocated by social workers. For instance, social workers' concern for clear boundaries is less important to narrative therapists. Powerful and evocative self-disclosure by the therapist is not viewed as a negative within the context of narrative work. In one account of a narrative session, a therapist made a deal with a resistant adolescent girl that for every question she answered, she could ask him a question. The therapist never set limits on the types of questions the girl could ask, any more than she would impose limits on the questions he could ask. In narrative therapy, the interview is conceptualized as a conversation between two people who are equals. Narrative therapists are concerned about the oppressive nature of hierarchical relationships and the discourse of pathology, in which one person is the expert and the other is viewed as a sick person who needs to get well. Narrative therapists work hard to change the prevailing discourse or story from one of an illness to one of a person who at times struggles with problems that lie outside themselves. By positioning himself as an equal, no healthier nor sicker than the client, the narrative therapist works to counter the pathologizing structure of traditional therapeutic positioning.

Externalizing

Men often feel blamed for their problems and mistakes and feel inadequate for not being perfect or being able to solve their problems on their own. The autonomy script and rugged individualism make it difficult for men to accept their fallibility, and ultimately their humanity. Men are therefore often defensive about their difficulties and imperfections. This often appears in the language of men, where they will use the third person when referring to a difficult situation or set of feelings, such as "you know, losing your job makes you feel bummed out," or "you really get mad when someone cuts you off like that!" It is important to see this linguistic trick as a normal response to feelings of inadequacy that often will be generalized to situations in which men do not feel inadequate or less than perfect.

Social workers inexperienced with men will often make the mistake of moving too quickly toward helping a man "own" his feelings and push him to use "I" statements. Making such suggestions too early can sabotage the helping process. First, such corrections can signal a lack of acceptance of the individual man and of the manner in which men communicate. Again, it is important to see men as a culturally different group, with their own language and culture. In addition, clients have their defense mechanisms for a reason: they have protected them against perceived or real threats for many years. It is rarely the goal of treatment to immediately challenge and alter defense mechanisms; it is far more therapeutic to slowly help men understand their defenses and employ them in a flexible manner.

Further, as men are instrumental and want to be problem solvers, keeping an objective, emotionally distant stance can at times be valuable. Lessons from narrative therapy are instructive in this regard. Narrative therapy has demonstrated how professionals can actually use this externalizing technique as a therapeutic method (Freedman and Combs 1996). Narrative therapists advocate for helping people to explore problems in the third person as a means of helping them see that they are not the problem, but that "the problem is the problem" (White and Epston 1990). Since men often naturally present problems in this manner, it is wise to allow them to do so. In externalizing the problem, narrative therapists encourage men to refer to a problem in the third person, often asking them to name their problem in order to clearly situate it outside themselves. For instance, a man can refer to the angry aspect of himself as "Mr. Anger." The therapist can ask externalizing question to help the man explore feelings and concerns from an objective distance. For example, "What can you do when Mr. Anger pays you a visit?" It is often easier for a man to talk about his feelings in this manner, and to subsequently explore ways of coping with them.

Excavate Unique Outcomes

Unique outcomes are situations in which the client has been able to handle or resolve his problem differently from the way he usually does, or differently from what he believes he is capable of doing. For instance, a men who believes that he is never able to talk to women without feeling nervous may actually be able to think of times he has spoke to women without feeling anxious. People tend to minimize their capacities and forget to recognize their own triumphs. As such, one of the goals of therapy is to help clients become archeologists into their own successful behaviors.

Excavating unique outcomes builds on externalization by helping clients continue to see themselves as being less "problemed." Clients are helped to move from a narrative of an all-consuming problem that they can never resolve to one in which they are at times able to at influence and manage outcomes, and in this way to see their strengths and competencies. Breaking down the story into small movements and steps helps men learn to identify the methods by which they resolve their problems. By consciously thinking of the skills and methods they use, they can generalize their behavior and increase their self-efficacy. Slowly the plot of the story moves from the protagonist as an incompetent person with a fatal flaw to one in which he finds himself battling an enemy that he has previously defeated (or at least fought against valiantly).

Thicken the New Plot

Men in therapy will sometimes provide very little detail. Being traditionally action oriented, they may think that the experience of providing details that seem extraneous to the core of their story may be unimportant. Parsimony is considered an important male value, as illustrated by the image of a man as a "strong and silent type." In narrative work the details of how events are lived and understood are curtailed. It is often in the details that men are helped to find the source of meaning and change, opportunities for establishing connections, and the ability to create alternative outcomes. It is in the filtering through the details of their stories that men are able to find alternative outcomes. Therapists help to thicken the plot by exploring key details in regard to how men have experienced a problem in the past and, most important, how they have resolved or overcome the problem. To help men do this, social workers need to tell men why the details are important. As with most aspects of helping, deconstructing helping behaviors allows men to become increasingly invested in the process of change.

Link to the Past and Extend to the Future

In narrative work, the therapist will want to help the client link alternative views about their problem to the past and extend these alternative conceptions into the future. For instance, a man suffering from compulsive overeating can explore a time in his life when food was not the center of his world, and when his eating was healthier. This type of conversation helps strengthen the externalization of the problem. By learning to connect past coping to the future, a man is able to begin to reauthor his life and his experience of his problems in a more complex, realistic manner. This linking of the past to the future helps clients experience a sense of hope. If a man can clearly remember and understand a life in which the problem was less significant (or perhaps even nonexistent), he can begin to see an alternative future.

Questions that link the past and extend the future include: If your past were a movie and we were both watching it, what would we see that would help us understand your situation today? If we could envision you having a different relationship to your concerns a year from now, what would it look like? Picture yourself in the future: what do you see?

Invite Outsider Witness Groups

Outside witnesses are people who care about the man in therapy and can provide important information to be used in the process of change. They are those who can help him begin the process of reauthoring and restorying his life. Often outside witnesses are useful in helping a man look for new ways of understanding a problem or situation. They can also be invited to be positive supports to a man as he actively works toward change. Sometimes outside witnesses are those whom the man has mistreated in the past, and they may be skeptical about a man's developing vision of himself as someone who is more than the problem. Social worker must help the man see that these witnesses may not accept a man's new vision of himself quickly; the man will have to learn to find supports and resources that help him nurture change while he develops patience for those who many not be convinced. As was explored in the earlier discussion on men's relationships, each man brings with him a set of strengths and limitations in how he relates to others. Inviting outsiders into the treatment process can help men build and repair relationships and may help decrease their sense of isolation or shame.

Use Re-remembering Practices and Incorporation

Loss is one of the truly universal experiences. For each of us, learning to grieve and heal from loss is an important part of emotional health. Given the multiple losses that men have faced, and their difficulties contending with affectively oriented experiences, grief work may be particularly important with men. The process of working through grief and loss is different from a narrative perspective compared to other approaches. In other approaches, grief work often employs techniques that distance the griever from his or her loss. In narrative therapy, re-remember techniques are used for "maintaining ongoing relationship with the dead person and seeking comfort in keeping this person's membership current in one's 'membership club' of life" (Hedtke and Winslade 2004/2005:198).

Re-remember techniques are not merely about reminiscing or talking about the dead or a particular loss but include rituals and methods of actually positioning the dead person within the lives of those who are living. Men are frequently disconnected from their sense of community and from those they used to feel close to. Helping them remain connected to those they have lost can enable them to maintain ties and feel less isolated. For instance, a soldier can write letters to his dead comrades as a means of staying connected to them and of achieving a sense of the dead still being involved in the world of the living. This may help men with the common experience of survivors' guilt. Such methods are particularly important for working with men from cultures in which the boundaries between the living and the dead are more permeable than in the dominant culture. For instance, it is not uncommon for Puerto Rican men and women to have ongoing communicative relationships with important deceased relatives. Such cultural traits should be used as strengths and be integrated in a man's developing narrative. For those people who are not dead, such as estranged old friends, men can be encouraged to create rituals to maintain contact at a distance and maintain a sense of connection.

Use Literary Means

Traditional narrative therapy has relied heavily on the use of letters and letter writing in the therapeutic process. Letter writing has been used frequently with those in crisis, as well as in long-term therapeutic work (Tubman, Montgomery, and Wagner 2001). In narrative work, the therapist will often write letters to clients at different points in and after treatment. These letters can be used to reinforce growth and change, to summarize important lessons, or to provide hope and inspiration during difficult times. They become concrete documents of the process of growth and change.

Various literary methods can be used to help men reauthor their lives. In addition to traditional narrative methods, poetry and bibliotherapy exercises can assist men in creating therapeutic changes (Furman 2004; Harrower 1972; Lerner 1981; Mazza 1999). While it may seem counterintuitive to encourage men to write poetry, given how it does not seem congruent with traditional ideas about masculine identity, I have used poetry often in my practice with men. It is my experience that many men either write poetry or have enjoyed poetry in their past. Many men have used poetry as a means of making sense of their world, and for coming to terms with their own feelings and masculine and personal identities. While not appropriate for all men, when a social worker discovers that a man has a particular interest in writing poetry or other creative means of expression, it may be valuable to explore with the man how he has used it for their his growth and well-being. Doing so helps men seek their own solutions and allows for another powerful means of helping them reauthor their own story.

Facilitating Bringing-It-Back Practices

In bringing-it-back practices, clients are encouraged to share the construction of their new narratives and their positive changes with others. This can be done through sharing in self-help groups, therapeutic groups, conversations with other clients with whom their therapist is working, or speaking with community groups. Different from more positivist, individualistically oriented therapeutic approaches, narrative therapy encourages a community-centered approach to the change process. Bringing-it-back practices also encourage men to own their change, to develop a sense of themselves as being of worth and value to the community, and of being mentors. Bringing-it-back is an important aspect not only of the narrative approach, but also of self-help groups and the men's movement. It helps to encourage the reformulation of identity reconstruction by aiding a man to systematically share himself with others in a new and socially constructive manner.

Narrative work is consistent with approaches for indigenous people that focus on using storytelling as a means of helping men work through life struggles and traditions. Krech (2002:89) provides a cogent explanation of how this occurs, and the mechanisms that facilitate growth and change: "a successful story contains all the essential elements of a listener's concerns and then organizes these elements into a viable and replicable process. Storytelling can generate abstract outlines and relational networks for ideas that also serve as guides for action and understanding. This form of narrative may begin a process that leads to a conclusion and growth far beyond the original tale because the storyteller provides a vehicle for the listeners to comprehend in their own way and derive their own solutions."

The Strengths Perspective with Men

At its core, social work is about helping people transcend social and personal obstacles to improve their lives. The strengths perspective is an orientation to practice where practitioners seek to help men marshal their internal and external resources in service of solving their problems and living successful lives. Some of the core values of more dominant models of masculinity, such as courage, fortitude, bravery, willingness to withstand hardship, and even stoicism, may be valuable aids in helping men transcend difficult situations. The strengths perspective is grounded in the literature and research on resiliency, which demonstrates the power of individuals, families, and communities to thrive in the face of seemingly debilitating events (Kaplan and Girard 1994; Stinnett and DeFrain 1985; Wolin and Wolin 1993). While it is still relatively young and in the early stages of development, the strengths perspective can be a powerful lens through which to view social work practice with men.

Working from a strengths perspective contrasts with pathology-oriented approaches, which stress the removal of problems as the primary aim of treatment. In the strengths perspective, practitioners try to catch men "doing the right things" instead of focusing on weakness and failure. Glicken (2004:205) notes that the strengths perspective is important in framing the helper/helpee relationship: "Focusing on pathology creates a sense of pessimism in clients that is contagious to clients. The pessimism of the working and the stigma attached to many diagnostic categories have a pervasively negative impact on clients." This may be especially true for men, who often enter the therapeutic relationships skeptical of social workers' intentions. Men fearing being judged and worry about being controlled and "made to do things." Focusing on the positive aspects of men's behavior may be one of the most important things a clinician can do to build a quality working relationship. As I frequently stay to students, social workers are not paid to judge: each person has had many people in their lives who have done so, and probably very few have been helpful.

The focus on strengths, capacities, and resiliencies differs markedly from more mechanistic approaches that focus on disease (Goldstein 1990b). In those approaches, informed by the medical model, the social worker serves as an expert in diagnosing and fixing problems in the same manner in which a surgeon would remove a tumor. In the strengths perspective, social workers work collaboratively with people, focusing on their strengths, capacities, and skills. Problems are not ignored or minimized, but endless explorations of problems and deficits are not viewed as the most effective or ethical way to help people live more fulfilling lives.

Saleebey (2002) and Kisthardt (2002), two of the developers of the strengths perspective, have suggested six core principles that can guide strengths-based practice with men at risk:

1. Every person has strengths. To focus on people's strengths challenges us to assume a stance of respect and admiration. We are challenged to assume the role of a student interested in learning about the person's hopes and dreams, rather than the expert who purports to know more about what motivates a person than the person does (Kisthardt 2002:166). This fundamental stance is often difficult to adopt. A century of Freudian psychology has situated problems at the center of the helping endeavor. Current evidence-based practice asks us to focus on the identification of quantifiable problems and measure change. However, the strengths perspective asks us to reorient our way of understanding people. It asks us to view people as possessing far more strengths than limitations. Learning to approach men from this perspective is often a challenging task.

2. While traumas and injuries may cause harm, they are also the source of opportunity and potential for growth. In his exploration on how strengths-oriented approaches can be applied to people with mental illness, Jackson (2001) connects this principle with the facilitation of resiliency. Often it is within the contexts of crisis that people reach deep within themselves and find

new sources of strength, growth, and hope. Men have overcome many difficult situations, and the strengths they develop from trying times may become
fuel for resolving current challenges. Congruent with the narrative concept of
finding unique outcomes, social workers should explore the ways men have
used their skills and abilities, as well as their external resources, to meet their
goals and challenges.

3. It is important for social workers never to underestimate the capacity
of an individual for growth and change. We can never know the upper limits
of a man's potential. If we believe that all people possess the capacity to learn,
grow, and change, then we will constantly be seeking new and different strategies to create opportunities for this growth to occur. At every helping session
we should strive to learn something about the person that we did not know
before. Each new piece of information may serve as a key that unlocks the
potential that resides in all people (Kisthardt 2002:169). Social workers frequently encounter people who have multiple programs, who have had limited
success in meeting some of life's challenges. From the outside they may appear
to be failures. Encountering such difficult situations day after day can make
social workers jaded or burned out. However, it is important for social workers to develop a sense of hope about people's capacity for growth and change.
The exercises at the end of this chapter may help you develop this capacity.

4. People are best served by collaborating with them. In some traditional
helping models, the helper is conceptualized as the expert; the relationship is
essentially hierarchical. In classic psychodynamically based practice, the therapist is detached and becomes an unknowable other, ready to be the recipient
of client projections. The strengths perspective views the helping process as
a collaborative effort between two equals. Since a goal of the strengths perspective is to help people find their personal power, the helping relationship
should encourage empowerment, not disempowerment. By modeling a collaborative way of working together, the social worker helps the client view his
own knowledge and skills as being of worth. While men value expertise and
knowledge, they also want to be viewed as being the equal of their helper.

5. Every environment is full of resources. Assessing social environments
should be what social workers do best. However, the individualistic nature of
the dominant American culture contributes to most of us seeing the individual as most central organizing principle. That is, we see the individual before we
see family and community. This is especially true for social workers who adopt
more middle-class, dominant values. However, when assessing the strengths
and assets of men, we must learn to look at the richness and fullness of their
environments, or the potential richness and fullness. It is true that many men

are disconnected from their communities, from those who love them, and even from their natural environments. Ask a man who are the people who are willing to help him, and you will likely hear only a few names, if any. However, the vast majority of men are cared about by many people. They have many formal and informal social institutions that can be valuable resources to them. Part of the assessment process will be assessing not only the current support systems of men, but also their aspirational support systems, or any systems that may be of help. Many men, espousing the value of rugged individualism, may not express the desire to connect to and be helped by others. It is a key challenge for social workers to help men realize that reaching out for support is not a sign of weakness but of strength, and that regardless of what each of us believes, we are all connected together in inextricable and profound ways.

6. It is important to understand the relevance of caring, caretaking, and context. These issues are often different for men than they are for women, and they warrant exploration. Women tend to view care and caretaking differently from men and have different emotional needs when they are feeling overwhelmed, stressed, or burdened. Men in therapy may need less affective expressions of empathy and more normalization of their experiences, and guidance for action. That is, men need to be helped to understand and contextualize their problematic feelings and behavior as being "normal." This helps men reduce the shame they may feel for having discussed their experiences and can be an important step in the healing process. However, normalization is not without its counterindications. For instance, violence and behaviors that place men and those around them at risk should not be normalized. Acceptance and unconditional positive regard about the man as a human being is essential, yet this does not mean condoning violent, abusive, or inappropriate behavior. Adhering to a strengths perspective does not mean we gloss over problems, or that men should not be held accountable for their behavior. One can be guided by a strengths-oriented principles yet still be in favor of a man entering the criminal justice system; focusing on one's strengths does not preclude believing in the importance of men being held accountable for their behavior.

Glicken (2004) notes that the strengths perspective attempts to focus therapy away from mere symptom reduction. The goals of therapy should be to help men become more self-fulfilled and to develop the capacity to lead meaningful lives (Saleebey 1994; Sandage and Hill 2001). For example, it is not enough merely to help a man reduce his subjective experience of anxiety and depression if the events and circumstances, or his perspective and beliefs, are hardly changed. These troubling feelings may very well reappear.

People will experience fewer symptoms when they have full, healthy, and meaningful lives and are living according to their dreams and desires. It is this focus on meaning that is the special purview of the next approach, the existential perspective.

The Existential Perspective

While the roots of existential theory are ancient, existentialism largely grew out of the hopelessness and despair of the great wars of the twentieth century (Furman 2003a). Existential authors saw the importance of addressing humankind's capacity for both greatness and evil actions. Existentialists were concerned that modern science and technology, while capable of advancing society, also came close to leading to its ultimate destruction. In addition to responding to the catastrophic events of the early part of the twentieth century, existential authors also became concerned about the biological, psychological, and sociological determinism that began to influence Western thought during the mid-twentieth century. Whether it was Freud's notion that men were controlled by unconscious drives, behaviorists' belief in classical conditioning, or the medical professions' biological determinism, existentialists were concerned that men would abdicate responsibility, freedom, hope, and ultimately their humanity in response to these ideas. Existentialists perceived that when individual men and women give in to deterministic influences and are no longer willing to accept responsibility for their own actions, great social ills occur. While less influential in the United States, existential authors had great influence on European thought for many years. Existential thought moved into the American psychotherapeutic community in the 1960s, and into social work thought through the work of Donald Krill (1969, 1978).

While philosophical differences exist among different existential writers, existentialists focus on what they view as ultimate human truths, and the need for people to attend to these truths in the course of their lives. To not attend to the truths of existence will lead men and women to live blind, meaningless, and often destructive lives. Existentialism is very much a challenge to people to explore what it means to be human, and to put the results of this exploration into action.

Existentialism may at first seem like an esoteric and abstract theory. Even the name may leave some cold and cause others to run for the dictionary. However, existential thought holds particular relevance for social work practice. By focusing on the core truths of human existence, the application of existential theory provides practical guidance for how to live and practice social work. It helps us strip away excess and focus on the core of what it means to develop a good life, as constructed and lived by each individual. By helping people focus on the nature of existence and examine their lives through the filter of these core truths or questions, social workers enable people to live fuller, more meaningful lives. While many of its concepts may at first glance appear dark and depressing, existentialism actually is an extremely hopeful perspective that holds that each person has the capacity to develop a life of deep joy and meaning regardless of social circumstances. In this section, I hope to demystify the existential perspective and show its utility for social work practice with men. As with the other theories presented above, the theory will be further explored in subsequent chapters, as applied different psychosocial risk factors and issues.

A central notion in existentialism is the responsibility of each individual to create his or her own sense of meaning and purpose (Mullan 1992). Sartre (1965:15) asserted that "Man is nothing else but what he makes of himself." In the existentialist view, a man is born into the world very much a blank slate. Life experiences shape the views and perspectives of the child, as do personality and human biological tendencies. However, from the existentialist point of view, those internal and external forces are only influences on human behavior; it is up to each individual to engage in the process of self-definition and self-creation. Furman and Bender (2003:126) assert that "The 'authentic man' comes to grips with the reality of his/her existence; he/she chooses to define him/herself and creates him/herself in every action; develops meaning and purpose for him/herself."

At times, social workers find it difficult to reconcile personal responsibility with personal blame, and with the existence of oppressive and discriminatory social forces. Existential thought does not lead us to deny or negate these factors but pushes social workers to help clients find their authentic sources of power and control given and within the context of their social conditions. Used appropriately and nonjudgmentally, this constructivist view, congruent with the other approaches discussed in this chapter, supports the notion that people can and do change throughout the life cycle. We are not fixed; we can taken control of our lives and, with a great deal of work, create meaningful and lasting change.

Meaning

To most existentialists and existential practitioners, the creation of meaning is life's most pressing task. Existential practitioners tend to view many symptoms and problems that clients possess as ill-fated attempts at creating meaning or desperate attempts to avoid having to work toward it.

Meaning in life is not simply a global judgment made about a life as a whole, but potentially a quality of everyday existence. It may be that a meaningful life is simply a sum of meaningful days. Or the experience of daily meaning may be derivative of a global sense of meaning in life that adds a "glow" of meaning to judgments about specific life domains (King et al. 2006:181).

In social work practice with men, social workers recognize that men in modern societies are often not encouraged to develop their own sense of personal meaning. Men are encouraged to be good soldiers and good providers, to do whatever they need to get by and do what is needed. Helping men think through how their current life structures provide them meaning can help motivate them to explore behaviors that may be destructive to themselves or others. Developing the capacity to engage men in discussions around meaning or purpose demands that social workers have explored these issues for themselves. It may take practice for social workers to begin to discuss deeper issues such as meaning with clients. In truth, we are more accustomed to having discussions about meaning and life's purpose with friends. Fortunately, we can use these discussions as internal models for how we might approach such conversations with clients.

Death

To the existentialist, death is one of the most powerful forces motivating human beings. Becker (1971) observed that a great deal of human behavior can be attributed to human beings escaping from the painful specter of death. To the existentialist, the awareness of death is both a cause of anxiety and a powerful force that may push us toward authentic living. The type of anxiety that is derived from an awareness of death is not a disease process and should not be mistaken for an anxiety disorder. This anxiety is part of the cost of being aware, part of what makes us human. The man who is aware of his own death is aware of how finite life is. Life is viewed as a precious gift that cannot be wasted when one is aware of the specter of death. Somerset Maugham's protagonist in *On Human Bondage* would wake up in the morning and ask death what he had in store for him today. The implication of this question is that the more a man is able to use this awareness of death for the enrichment of his own life, the more likely he is to live fully. When he lives with an awareness of death, it is less likely that he will give in to petty annoyances and more likely that he will focus more fully on what truly matters.

Freedom and Bad Faith

In existential thought, bad faith is one's conscious and unconscious strategies for disowning personal responsibility for how one thinks, feels, acts, and lives. To the existentialist, people engage in bad faith when they wish to deny personal responsibility. In a sense it a safer and at times less emotionally risky way to live. However, the costs of bad faith are powerful. Engaging in bad faith and denying one's essential freedom also denies one access to the potential of growth and transformation. To change, one must accept a degree of responsibility for one's life in the moment and be willing to engage in uncoerced action.

Freedom plays an essential role in existential therapy. Men are seen as possessing a great deal more freedom than they often care to admit. While existentialists do not deny the constraints of social forces, they also believe that men can choose how they will respond to these forces. This notion is particularly attractive to American men, who have been raised with images of rugged individualism. While at times it is important to help men understand and increase their interdependence and reliance on others, responsibility and freedom can be powerful motivating forces that may be important therapeutic factors when providing services to men.

Struggle and Pain

One of the most important choices we can make is how to view our own struggles and pain. The maxim "pain is mandatory, but suffering is optional" successfully encapsulates the existentialist view. In this view, it is the belief that life should be pain free that creates suffering. No one escapes life without pain and loss—it is how we respond to these events that define us as people and allow us to develop integrity and wholeness. That is, we lament our own pain and add pain on top of pain. We believe that life should always be easy, that there is always a pill to take or a salve to rub.

Modern American life teaches people that struggle and discomfort are bad things. We have appliances that we use to make our lives as easy and comfortable as possible. Yet so much of what we hope to achieve in life takes a great deal of effort. Many of the men whom social workers see have faced years of pain, struggles, and setbacks. The path to healing and growth is often not an easy one. When clients believe that change is easy and will come without work and often hardship, failure is almost inevitable. Hard work and persistence are core hegemonic male values that, when balanced with other values, can be important strengths for men. Men's willingness to work hard for what they believe in, to suffer for their families or their "team," has often led to wonderful achievements. In practice, social workers can capitalize on this strength and help men use it in the service of meeting their needs.

This chapter has explored many core principles as they apply to men. Some of the principles are generic or atheoretical in nature; others are tied to specific theories. I hope you have been able to see the overlap of many of these principles and have developed a beginning understanding of their practice utility. In part 2 I apply these principles to important psychosocial dilemmas that men face and show how we can use these approaches to build on the existing strengths of men.

EXERCISE: THE STRENGTHS PERSPECTIVE: WHAT ARE OUR LIMITS?

In this exercise, use the Internet to explore the life histories of great men who overcame seemingly insurmountable obstacles. When you find a story to which you particularly relate, answer the following questions.

1. What strengths helped this man overcome his obstacles?
2. Why did he overcome his obstacles when others might have succumbed?
3. What would you have thought of this man's abilities to achieve success if you had encountered them at their "lowest"?
4. Think about people in the past who have underestimated you. In what ways were they wrong?

Men at Risk: Problems and Solutions

PART II

Men and Violence | SIX

Violence plays a central role in the lives of many men and is a significant factor in the disparity between male and female life expectancy (Kruger 2006). While men are the largest perpetrators of violence, they also are more frequently the victims of violence (Clatterbaugh 1990). In 2005 twenty-five out of one thousand men were the victims of violence, compared with eighteen out of one thousand women (U.S. Department of Health and Human Services 2006). Whether through crime, gangs, domestic violence, or war, the psychosocial costs of violence on the lives of men and their families are profound. This chapter explores the different types of violence in which men are involved, along with treatment issues and options. Men are both victims and perpetrators of many kinds of violence. As with many of the topics in this book, it is important for readers to develop an understanding of their own preconceived ideas and biases about men as victims and perpetrators of violence.

Even the most violent men deserve our respect, dignity, and empathy. Of course, they may also need to be imprisoned to protect others from their aggressive or dangerous behavior. Some practitioners have a difficult time reconciling the need to protect society from offenders with the values of the social work profession. But treating people according to social work values and protecting society from them are not mutually exclusive. Men can be incarcerated and also be afforded dignity, respect, and appropriate treatment by the professionals who provide for them (although certainly the justice system is not always known for these values). Working with violent men demands that we pay attention to many complex psychosocial factors. Many male perpetrators of violence have long histories of mental illness; in addition, many of these men have also been victims of violence. Social workers must learn how to be empathic and caring while setting appropriate boundaries and limits. A multitude of biopsychosocial factors must be assessed when deciding what types of supports and services these men need. It is also important for those working with men and violence to develop an understanding of the criminal justice system within their local area and know the strengths and weaknesses of that system. Some communities have been more been successful than others in developing preventative and treatment options for male offenders and victims of violence.

Men as Perpetrators of Violence

Men commit the vast majority of all violence. Sexual assault against women, rape of other men, general assault, and homicide are all behaviors that have profound personal and social costs. Providing services to male perpetrators is often controversial and requires careful attention to social work research, theory, and values. Exploring violence from the perspective of men and providing culturally appropriate services to them are important issues for the profession to take on in the coming decades.

Sexual Assault

Twenty-one percent of women report having been raped by a man during their lifetime (Tjaden and Thonnes 1998). Women who are sexually assaulted or raped may experience many physical and emotional traumas, including post-traumatic stress disorder, and are affected by the violation their entire lives.

Rape and sexual violence are often misunderstood. The rape of women is a crime not of passion, but of power, domination, and violence. On a social level, sexual violence is connected to oppression, dominance, patriarchy, and power. These factors are important when considering the risks and treatment needs of individual men, yet other psychosocial factors, such as depression, anxiety, and employment, must also be considered as part of a comprehensive assessment.

Sexual assault is sexual conduct and activity that is engaged in without the consent of the other person. This can include physical acts, such as fondling, groping, and forced sexual contact such as rape, or other behaviors such as voyeurism. Child molestation is also a form of sexual assault. Aside from child sexual abuse and molestation, rape is the most severe and damaging form of sexual assault. Rape may also be one of the most underreported crimes in the United States (Russell and Bolen 2000).

Women who have been raped often do not report the crime, for a number of reasons. Some fear that their perpetrator will harm them again if they do so. Women also fear not being believed by police and others, especially if they have a history of being sexually active or possess a criminal record. Society continues to stigmatize women who have more frequent, nonmonogamous sexual relationships, while men are often rewarded for such behavior. In many cultures, men who are highly sexually active are seen as "studs" or "Casanovas" while women are called "sluts" or, in Latino cultures, "putas." When working in the area of sexual violence, social workers must pay careful attention to the attitudes of their clients about women, sex, sexuality, and power. Individual treatment of men at risk for sexual violence should carefully assess and treat these attitudes. On a macro level, social workers should attend to how these messages are institutionalized within the criminal justice and other systems. Programs that challenge these beliefs in high schools or even in elementary schools are promising prevention methods that warrant further research. Social advertising campaigns should also help challenge the conceptions of women that help perpetuate violence against them.

Another reason that women who have been raped may not report their victimization is the shame and humiliation of the experience. Having internalized messages about the "dirtiness" of being a sexually active person, women often believe that they may have somehow caused their violation. Many violent men have also internalized these beliefs and blame women for their own violent and abusive behavior. These beliefs are ingrained not only within society, but often within professional helping communities, which may not be educated about the true nature of sexual assault. Men who hold that women are to blame for their behavior believe that women who may "tease" them "deserve it." They may believe that their own personal pains, frustrations, or failures are the responsibility of the women in their lives. Since rape is not a crime of passion, but of power, control, and dominance, some men seek revenge on a specific woman, or on women in general, through sexual dominance and control. Social workers must look for these signs of abusive power and work toward establishing safety contracts and other measures to ensure that men they work with find other methods of resolving their frustrations and pains.

The treatment of male perpetrators of rape has been controversial. The traditional feminist approach is to take a direct, confrontational approach with men who violate women sexually. It is certain that men who rape hold inappropriate and dysfunctional views about women, power, patriarchy, and sex. Men who rape must take ownership of their behavior and face punishment for their crime. Yet, some of the treatment issues of men may not be fully satisfied by this approach and may in fact not lead to desired outcomes. Both accountability and treatment are essential. Cull (1996:263) highlights the importance of providing men treatment and simultaneously setting behavioral limits and social consequences:

> Rarely do we hear loud expressions of "treat them," "help them to understand their behavior," "punish by all means, but provide constructive rehabilitation." Emotion takes over and rationality is lost. Rational argument will show that the truth is that rapists will one day be released from prison. They will return to the community and they will continue to present a risk of re-offense, unless they somehow come to understand their behaviour and, on release, return to society as a positively-changed and healthier individual. Furthermore, the rapist has used this form of behaviour as a weapon of power, of threat and of control for centuries. He will, unfortunately, continue to rape, and fear of the consequences will rarely act as a deterrent.

Research on treatment of the perpetrators is mixed—more research and the development of new treatment models are needed. Later in this chapter I discuss how cognitive behavioral therapies can be especially valuable in working with violent behaviors. CBT with sexually violent men must focus on helping them understand the cognitive roots of their violent behavior (often socially constructed and rooted within patriarchy and power) and the severe consequences for themselves of these beliefs: they must learn how their beliefs contribute to their own pain and loneliness. If men understand the personal costs of their cognitions and behaviors, they can become more invested in cognitive and behavioral change. While, for the profession of social work, social transformation is the ultimate goal of such interventions, individual men need to explore how change will benefit themselves.

In addition to micro-oriented practice, macro practice is an important aspect of social work practice in regard to sexual violence. Organizations have sought to change the political and cultural factors that perpetuate sexual violence against women. Macro-oriented social workers seeking to decrease violence against women have several potential options for intervention and affiliation. Advocacy groups work with various constituents of men and women to help educate communities about the impact of sexual violence. For instance, the Rape, Abuse and Incest National Network conducts community education programs and seeks to influence national policy related to sexual violence (RAINN 2007). Their toll-free number can be used by victims for support, as well as by professionals who seek to connect with others who are working for social change in this arena. Men Against Sexual Violence (2008) is another organization that is seeking to end sexual violence against women, working mainly in Pennsylvania. The group encourages men to be responsible for their own behavior and to challenge sexist and violent attitude and behaviors in others when they encounter them.

Intimate Partner Violence

Domestic violence, now more frequently referred to as intimate partner violence (IPV), is one of the most significant social problems throughout the world. So ubiquitous is the direct or indirect impact of IPV that it is difficult to imagine a social worker who will not frequently come into contact with victims, perpetrators, or witnesses of IPV. Social workers who work in substance abuse, the criminal justice system, family guidance clinics, and child welfare are often called upon to address IPV directly. Frequently they will be asked to address the impact of IPV on adult men who as children witnessed or were victims of IPV or domestic violence (Van Soest 1997).

Men frequently physically harm other men, women, and children. The statistics are frightening. One study found that 22.1 percent of women have been the victims of intimate partner violence during the course of their lifetime (Tjaden and Thoennes 2000). During the previous twelve months, 1.2 percent of women have been physically assaulted by their partners. Estimates of the number of women abused per year vary from two million (James and Gilliland 2004) to four million (Straus and Gelles 1986). Regardless of the actual number, intimate partner violence is a significant social problem that demands both micro and macro interventions.

Batterer intervention programs (BIPs) started in the 1970s, as women's rights activists sought to hold men accountable for violence against women and children. The Duluth model is the most popular treatment modality. Proponents assert that the model's main goal is to "transform men into nonthreatening, nonjudgmental listeners who are empathetic, honest, accountable, and egalitarian in their parenting, housework, and familial decision making. The internal goal is thus to change men from patriarchal authoritarians bent on controlling women into pro-feminist men. Doing so, the program philosophy assumes, will mitigate participants' violence" (Schrock and Padavic 2007:626).

While early studies claimed a decrease in the incidence of battery, Schrock and Padavic note methodological flaws in these studies. They cite the mixed success of this model and contend that meta analysis has not shown the programs to be effective. These findings are supported by a U.S. Department of Justice report (Jackson et al. 2003) that evaluated two traditional batterer intervention programs. These studies have important policy and practice implications, as some states have questioned the research and have begun to impose increased regulations on the structure and length of BIPs. Buttel and Carney (2005:22) state that "many states appear to be institutionalizing programs that either do not work or that are only marginally effective. The fear among treatment providers is that their effort to engage in alternative interventions or creative quality improvement of the existing programs will be hampered by legislation governing what they must do in terms of state standards."

Social workers who work with men should be aware of the current limits of BIPs and seek to design programs to meet the complex needs of clients who batter. Often substance abuse and mental health problems must be addressed for such programs to be effective. As noted, treatment programs must account for the needs, cultural differences, and strengths of men.

The World Health Organization (2007) has advocated a primary prevention approach to the problems of sexual and intimate partner violence. Such an approach seeks to lower the overall incidences of IPV by lowering risk factors and increasing protective factors throughout different populations. Such strategies include working with children in schools to develop nonsexist attitudes and behaviors, skills training for at-risk male populations, and programs targeted to educate men about the potential risks of IPV and the need to build relational skills. However, each community must undertake a thorough assessment of its risk and resiliencies and develop programming to reduce the potential risk of IPV. The World Health Organization suggests that the following factors be explored when looking at the risks for intimate partner and other types of violence: gender inequities; social norms supportive of rigid gender roles; poverty, economic stress, and unemployment; weak community sanctions; lack of institutional support from police and criminal justice; and dysfunctional and unhealthy relationships.

Violent Crime

Violent crime is an important issue in many communities, and one that social workers must find means of addressing. Statistics bear out the assertion that men are both frequently victims and frequently perpetrators of violent crime. For instance, 85 percent of all homicide victims ages 10–24 are male (U.S. Department of Health and Human Services 2006b). Substance abuse contributes to many crimes that men commit. Alcohol and other drugs affect a man's judgment and impulse control as well as the type of situations that men put themselves into.

Masculine ideals around risk taking, bravery, and the importance of physical prowess place men at significant risk of hurting others and being hurt themselves. Men often react to perceived affronts to their masculinity or other challenges by engaging in physical confrontations without thinking about their own safety or well-being. In fact, a man who might even consider the risk of being harmed in a physical confrontation would be considered less of a man in some social contexts. A man who disengages from a fight, or is unwilling to fight, is referred to by derogatory names for women or homosexuals. Many men have very old memories of being called "pussy" or "faggot"; we learn early that these are the worst things one can be. To avoid being less of a man, men are willing to threaten the use of violence, fight, or engage in other risky behavior to preserve their sense of masculinity. This willingness to engage in physical violence or put oneself senselessly in dangerous situations contributes to men's lower life expectancy. Once men confront each other in hostile and violent situations, they lose control of the situation and put their lives on the line. For instance, when I was a teenager I witnessed a flight at a dance club between two young men. Presumably, one man bumped into the other and crowded his space on the dance floor. The offended man confronted the other. They began to shove each other, and one of them slipped on a wet spot on the dance floor, hit his head, and died from the injury. The other man was charged and convicted of manslaughter.

Men who do not conform to hegemonic masculine ideals are at risk of violence at the hands of other men, and men who are less typically masculine and more feminine in their physical features are also at greater risk of physical violence. For instance, Uggen and Blackstone (2004) found evidence of sexual harassment in many work situations against men who do not conform to traditional masculine ideals. Men are more likely to be harassed if they seem more vulnerable and outwardly reject hegemonic male behaviors and attitudes. Uggen and Blackstone found that an increase in harassment correlated with an unwillingness to take part in conversations with sexual undertones, wearing "feminine" jewelry in the workplace, and lower financial status or perceived financial dependence. The perpetrators were generally men who adopted masculine ideals and behaviors over softer, more affective or collaborative workplace behaviors. The research also found that many teens and men who experienced harassment in the workplace did not report such occurrences, which put them at greater risk of further harassment. The effects of sexual harassment can be any number of physical and psychological complaints that, if left untreated, could lead to mental health issues in men. Low self-esteem, depression, and posttraumatic stress disorder may all be the result of violence.

Gay men have historically been subjected to violence at the hands of men who are threatened by alternative forms of masculine sexuality. This phenomenon was for a time known as "fag bashing" and was seen as an expression of true manhood. Being willing to commit violence upon one who "breaks the rules" of being a man is proof that one is a man himself. The case of Mathew Sheppard is a classic example. In 1998 two men pretending to be gay befriended Mathew, a 21-year-old gay college student, and offered him a ride. The men beat him with a pistol, tortured him, and killed him. The case gained national attention and became the impetus for strong antidiscrimination and antiviolence measures. Social workers and other advocates continue to fight for expanded views of what it means to be a man, and to help men who have been victims of homophobia and other forms of discrimination.

In addition to being perpetrators and victims of random violence, men are often victims of violence at the hands of other men, and at times women, with whom they share close relationships. Men who have been victims of violence must contend with physical, psychological, and social factors that make their healing complex. First, men who have been the victims of violence are less likely to seek help than women (Rowan 1997). The rugged individualism of men and myths of male invincibility make it hard for men to admit that they have been victimized. Men who have been victimized often believe that their victimization was an affront to their very manhood (Hamberger 1997). This is especially true for men who have been the victims of violence by women. Studies have shown an increase in intimate partner violence inflicted upon men by women (Henning, Jones, and Holdford 2005).

There is evidence that while intimate partner violence against men contributes to a small percentage of the arrests for intimate partner violence, women may actually physically abuse men at about the same rate that men abuse women. Straus (2005), in his analysis of the research on domestic violence incidence, found that the vast majority of research supports this notion. He also found that the majority of the large-sample research from self-reports of women actually demonstrates that most of this violence is not retaliatory or based on perceived threat. Eagly and Steffen (1986) also found similar domestic violence rates between men and women. Other research discovered that when violence is initiated by a woman, it is more likely to escalate to a severe incident (Feld and Straus 1989). While these findings may be controversial, it is important to look at the data objectively and to understand their implications. Given the prevalence of male victimization in domestic violence, viewing domestic violence as only a male-initiated problem serves to perpetuate family violence. Holding to stereotypes around violence contributes greatly to perpetuating the problem. For instance, many law enforcement officers still view any domestic violence incident as being male initiated. Also, not understanding the frequency of domestic violence perpetrated by women, men may tend to deny the problem or minimize its severity. It is also true that minor physical assaults by women may escalate into larger problems due to differentials in physical strength. That is, women may initiate physical violence with minimal force, yet a man may retaliate with greater force, thereby escalating the violence of the encounter. I must stress that presenting evidence of the near equal occurrence of domestic violence by women in no way excuses any domestic violence by men. Domestic violence by men remains a significant social problem that must be addressed. In addition to the psychological damage that intimate partner violence causes, Coker et al. (2002) found that men who were involved in intimate partner violence, whether as perpetrators, victims, or a combination of the two, had a significant increase in health-related problems. This evidence supports an ecological, biopsychosocial view of the psychosocial dilemmas of men.

Male Rape

The rape of men by other men goes back as far as ancient Greek society, when armies would rape their conquered enemies. Raping the vanquished was viewed as the ultimate act of domination, whereby the conquering soldiers would take the manhood of the defeated soldiers (National Center for Victims of Crime 2008). Then as now, rape was not a crime of passion or sexuality, but one of power, domination, anger, control, and humiliation (Groth and Birnbaum 1979). Men raping men is perhaps more prevalent than some might think. Studies show that 5–10 percent of all rape survivors are men (Lacey and Roberts 1991). Other research has suggested that 13 percent of reported victims of sexual assault and violence were men (U.S. Department of Justice 2003). It is probable that male victims of rape, like female victims, also under-report rapes because of similar experiences of shame, fear, and denial (Mezey and King 1987). Homophobia and the myth of male invincibility also prevent men from reporting and seeking services for their sexual victimization (Funk 1994). Men who are victimized fear that coming forward will be an admission of their weakness and evidence of their own sexual deficiencies.

Scarce (1997) explores the social contexts and reasons for male rape. As noted earlier, rape in all its forms is about power, control, and manipulation. For instance, imprisoned men who are targeted for gang rape are often (but not always) more effeminate, less muscular and dominant, and first time, non-violent offenders. Most perpetrators of prison rape do not view themselves as being homosexual and do not view sex with other men as such. While prisons are the largest context for male rape, men are also frequently sexually assaulted in the context of other mostly male or all-male institutions, such as fraternities, the military, and sports teams. Men are hesitant to report violations in these contexts, as these groups and their social contexts provide for many of men's psychosocial needs. A man who admits being raped by a fraternity brother, for example, may fear not being believed or being blamed for being "weak" or gay.

Men who are raped face multiple risks. First, they are at high risk of HIV/AIDS and other sexually transmitted diseases, given that they are unable to take sexual precautions. This is especially true since men who rape other men may have multiple problems, including criminality and substance abuse problems, which predispose them to numerous heath risks, including sexually transmitted diseases. Victims are also frequently physically harmed by the violent and forceful nature of the violation. Men who are raped may suffer from traumatic head traumas and other internal injuries that can be severe, even life threatening, and may lead to long-term health complications.

Additionally, men who are raped may face many adverse psychosocial consequences. The violation itself may lead to anxiety and posttraumatic stress reactions. Both men and women who are raped often experience extreme fear, hypervigilance, and reexperiencing of their trauma through painful day visions and nightmares (Itzin 2006). Men who are raped face the secondary trauma of experiencing a perceived violation to masculine identity (Chapleau, Oswald, and Russell 2008). Society teaches men that they should not allow others to take advantage of them, and that being the victim of a crime is a sign of personal weaknesses and frailty. Men who are raped have been made to feel dominated and conquered. They often feel weak and blame themselves for not being able to prevent the assault. The typical belief may be, "If I was more of a man, I would have prevented the rape. A real man would not have allowed this to happen to him." These negative and inaccurate cognitions become part of the target for intervention when working with such men; they must come to accept that they were not to blame, and that being a victim of violence does not speak to their masculinity. Men who are raped often are afraid to seek help, fearing mistreatment by those who are supposed to help. Law enforcement officers often treat male rape reports with distrust, disbelief, or with shaming responses (King and Woollett 1997). When men experience treatment such as this from law enforcement officers, who may be their first professional contact after the assault, they may be less likely to seek other type of assistance.

Gangs

Gangs have had a significant influence on the lives of American men and have influenced the well-being of many communities. The U.S. Department of Justice estimates that 800,000 gang members are part of an estimated 30,000 gangs in the United States and adversely influence over 2,500 communities. Gangs have been moving from their traditional strongholds of poor, inner-city neighborhoods to various other communities. As the Office of Community Oriented Policing Services of the Department of Justice (2005) noted, "Gangs are migrating nationwide and as they migrate they bring their culture of violence and fear to each new community. Many reasons could explain the modern migration factor such as expansion of gang territories and families moving because of jobs or incarceration" (http://www.cops.usdoj.gov/Default. asp?Item=1593). The Missouri State Highway Patrol (2000) provides a simple definition of a gang: "A gang is an ongoing, organized association of three or more persons—some are formal and others, informal, but most have a common name or common signs, colors, or symbols. Typically, members or associates individually or collectively engage."

Gang violence represents a significant problem not only in many American cities, but in rural environments as well. Incidences of gang violence have been on the rise (Trotten 2000). Gangs interfere in the lives of communities by controlling the movement of residents, increasing the incidence of violent crimes and drugs, and creating a sense of general unsafety. Gangs have become extremely seductive to young men from poor communities who have been historically disenfranchised. Changes in the urban landscape have led to an increase in the attractiveness of gangs for inner-city youth. For instance, as men from their communities become successful and move to the suburbs, few role models of affluence and success may exist. In this vacuum, gang members who deal drugs may represent a visible model of "success." Additionally, gangs provide young, disenfranchised men with a sense of belonging and community, a key developmental need for teenage boys. Those who work with gang members must understand the psychosocial reasons for gang affiliation.

Gang violence is also evidence of an international social welfare problem that has an impact on men transnationally. For instance, several youth gangs that started among Central American immigrants in Los Angeles have spread back to Central America. Estimates vary, but these brutal gangs may have up to 300,000 members (Barnes 2007). Barnes notes that members of youth gangs usually come from homes characterized by violence, poverty, and disintegration. Gangs provide young men a sense of structure, stability, belonging, and camaraderie.

In terms of prevention, Barnes notes four key areas for future development. First, young men should be given opportunities to find a meaningful place in society, including work. Second, helping men develop their social capital must be an integral component of any program. Third, vocational activities that help provide a sense of efficacy and self-determination should be provided. Finally, it is important that police and other law enforcement groups respect the human and civil rights of gang members so that these individuals become willing to invest in more traditional social institutions and do not see the police and other social institutions as the enemy. These four key areas dovetail well with the four approaches in this book, including existentialism's focus on meaning, CBT's focus on skill training and efficacy, and the strengths perspective's focus on developing resources. Additionally, the narrative approach may hold value for helping gang members understand the construction of narratives that support their violent behavior, including socially sanctioned narratives about the lack of choices for poor and minority men. In a very real sense, former gang members must engage in the reauthoring of their identities.

Prison

Over 90 percent of prisoners in the United States are men (Connell 2000), but not all men who are in prison are there for violent crimes or are dangerous to society. While violence among men certainly is a significant factor, 48 percent of men in prison are there for nonviolent offenses (Bureau of Justice Statistics, 2005b). Yet, being in prison increases the likelihood that men will use violence as a future coping strategy and increases men's risk of being a victim of violence (Garland 1985). Therefore, the imprisonment of men for nonviolent offenses continues to fuel the increase in violence.

Men of color are far more likely to be sentenced to prison than are white men. According to the Bureau of Justice Statistics (2005b), Latino men are two and a half times more likely to be in prison than are white men, while African American men are nearly seven times more likely. While prisons certainly serve the valuable social function of keeping people safe from those who do harm, it is impossible to ignore the social justice implications of men of color being overly represented in prisons: As Denborough (2002:75) notes, "to sincerely think about prisons involves trying to come to terms with the profound class and race-based injustices that our legal system creates and maintains. It is also to face the question of what to do with those whose acts seriously harm others, those who terrorize, assault and kill. During my years of working within prisons, I met with many men who had committed what I consider to be horrific crimes—callous, violent, cruel acts. I also met many lovely men brutalized by generational poverty, racism and/or ill-treatment."

Men in prison are an extremely at-risk population. James and Glaze (2006) present an extremely disturbing picture of the prison population. Over 56 percent of men in state prisons report problems with substance abuse, and nearly three quarters of men who have attended mental health programs in state prisons report substance abuse problems. In fact, prisons are often considered the largest de facto mental health facilities in the United States. For instance, 15 percent of the inmates in Polk County, Florida, are receiving psychotropic medication (Edwards 2006). Unfortunately, the violence that characterizes life in prison is not conducive to the treatment of most mental health disorders. Male offenders with mental health problems often regress while in prison and may be more likely to reoffend. Fortunately, some programs do provide services that help mentally ill men avoid prison. For example, mental health courts have been established to help divert mentally ill men from prisons (Black 2008). Steadman, Davidson, and Brown (2001) define mental health court as a specialty court that operates from the idea of "therapeutic jurisprudence." The mental health court "promotes psychological and physical well-being of a person in legal proceedings." The court personnel, judges, and attorneys embrace a therapeutic approach that focuses on the mental health and overall psychosocial needs of each person. A team approach is used for the accused perpetrator who suffers from mental illness, including supervision of treatment and "possible criminal sanctions for noncompliance." The team makes decisions from a holistic perspective and includes other services in the offender's treatment plan. Mental health courts are a positive step toward balancing society's need for safety and protection with the recognition that mental health problems are diseases, not moral issues. As of 2004 there were approximately seventy mental health courts in the United States, up from four in 1997 (Edwards 2006).

Other Practice Issues

All social workers must be able to assess the impact of violence in the lives of their clients. When assessing violence in the lives of men, it is important for social workers to find ways of asking clear and direct questions without making men feel defensive and judged. Social workers must carefully consider the language that they use. For instance, asking "have you ever committed abuse or domestic violence" may not elicit the desired response. "Tell me about any times you may have engaged in any physical behavior with another person" may be a nonthreatening way of beginning a conversation about violence. Asking "how has your life been influenced by violence" is one way of assessing the impact of violence. Workers can and should ask direct questions but must be careful not to ask them in a judgmental manner.

When the threat of violence is highly problem, it is extremely important that safety management becomes the most central intervention. A previous study by Harway and Hanson (1993) showed that only half of workers understood the importance of safety management in cases where the probably of lethality was high. Good crisis-intervention strategies are useful when safety management is indicated. In such situations, social workers must be patient in asking questions and should use collateral information from as many sources as possible in assessing the situation. It is also important to know that the most dangerous time for victims of domestic violence may often be when they leave the perpetrators. It is therefore important to handle such situations with a great care and regard for the safety of the victim.

The Four Theories and Violence

When responding to men who have been or are at risk of using violence, it is important not to minimize the intensity, depth, and complexity of violence-facilitating cognitions. Many are deeply rooted, core beliefs that are central to how a man has constructed his identity. A man who views his own self-schema as "tough guy" will not respond easily to simple cognitive disputation when these beliefs powerfully influence how he views himself. The work of reconstructing identity is complex and powerful; narrative methods in conjunction with CBT practices may be helpful. It is also important to help men focus on the behavioral consequences of these beliefs (e.g., jail, being apart from their children) as motivation to change.

CBT methods are valuable in helping explain some of the cognitions that contribute to domestic violence. It is important to understand the historical context of a man's beliefs that support violence. For instance, beliefs that support aggressive behavior may be functional in certain social environments, and at one time in a man's life they may have partially contributed to his survival. It is important to understand if a man views his aggressive and violent thoughts and behaviors as being functional before one attempts to change them. The first step of cognitive work with a man who views his violence as functional is to help him see that while his behaviors may have served a function at one time and in one context (in prison, for example), they are no longer meeting his needs and are leading to negative outcomes. He should be helped to carefully evaluate the current effects of his beliefs and behaviors, and how they negatively influence his life in the here and now. This type of "hedonic calculus" is often a prerequisite to cognitive change (Emery 1985).

Some cognitions rooted in the hegemonic masculine ideal may lead to violence when they are expressed in the extreme or exist in a man with a history of violence or other psychosocial risk factors. For instance, if a man believes that his wife "must listen to him" at all times, and "must behave" the way that he wants her to, he will feel extremely angry when she does not. If he has an extremely difficulty time tolerating difficult emotions, his anger may feel overwhelming. When a man experiences these thoughts and feelings within the context of a patriarchic structure that condones control of and violence against women, the potential for abuse is great. In using cognitive behavioral methods for treating domestic violence, there are several type of irrational beliefs that can be disputed. Most important are the beliefs that are associated with power and control. Working cognitively, workers must help a man uncover and deconstruct these beliefs and values and nonjudgmentally assist him to explore the negative, as well as the positive, effects of such beliefs. By focusing on both the positive and negative aspects, workers encourage men to find ways of thinking and behaving that are flexible and creative, while decreasing the risk of violence.

In chapter 5 I discussed the narrative therapy technique of externalization as an important technique when working with men. When it comes to men who have perpetrated violence, this method may be counterindicated. Henning, Jones, and Holding (2005:132) observed that "Male domestic violence offenders commonly utilize external attributions to excuse or justify their abusive behavior. More specifically, many abusive men attribute their aggression

to factors such as their partner's behavior, stress, substances, or financial difficulties." Therefore it is important that when using externalizing techniques,
the social worker makes certain that externalization not lead to a man abdicating responsibility for his actions. In other words, men must own their use of
violence without minimizing it or abdicating responsibility. An existential orientation—one that helps perpetrators focus on personal and social accountability and responsibility for their behavior—can guard against this potential-
ity and demonstrates the importance of choosing one's theoretical orientation
based on the presenting problems and needs of one's clients.

Still, narrative tools can be used with men who have been perpetrators
of violence. One particularly valuable technique is the empathy letter, in
which the client adopts the position of the victim. The client is helped to
place himself in the role by placing the words "Dear [his name]" on the top
line of the letter. The client is thus asked to write from his victim's perspective to himself, the perpetrator. This exercise is useful in helping perpetrators develop empathy for their victims. A therapist may also have the client
write a letter to the victim, either for the perpetrator's own therapeutic use
or, if appropriate, to give to the victim. Since many victims are family members who have daily contact with the perpetrator, the sharing of this letter
with the victim, usually within the safe confines of the therapist's office, can
often be therapeutic. It is important to assess how receptive the victim might
be, in order to prevent him or her feeling revictimized. This is congruent
with a restorative model of treatment, which helps the perpetrator take responsibility for his behavior (Van Ness and Strong 2006). It is important to
note, however, that couples counseling is usually not recommended until a
batterer has made significant progress in treatment and has learned to cope
with his own stresses and difficult emotions (Tolman and Bennett 1990). It is
important that the batterer and the therapist are confident that the batterer
will be able to handle hearing the pain and angry of his victim without the
risk of reperpetrating.

In developing skills for working with men around issues of violence, it is
essential to understand the meaning of different behaviors from a culturally
competent perspective. Each culture constructs the behaviors that are and are
not acceptable. Social workers should understand these cultural factors and
how they intersect with local, state, and natural laws, and with the values and
ethics of the profession. Unpacking the meaning and the cultural context of
human behavior is far from a simple task. It is important to remember that a
social worker's first responsibility is always to help maintain the safety of parties at risk of violence.

Case Example

This is a case study of a police officer who was abusive and committed a horrible crime. The case is provided not to present a typical pattern of behavior, but to demonstrate the tragic consequences of violence in the lives of men. The vast majority of law enforcement officers are law abiding and not abusive.

John Thompson was a 32-year-old police officer who killed himself in a double suicide homicide. Violence was a common thread running throughout John's social and personal life. His life ended when he shot himself and his wife by gunfire. John's case demonstrates the tragic and powerful confluence of unchecked, rigid, and overly extreme patriarchal values with low self-esteem. The personal factors were exacerbated by John being employed in an institutional context that often ignores interpersonal violence, and indeed at times mandates the use of violence.

John was married for three years before he began to physically abuse his wife, Carol, a former exotic dancer whom he met while attending the club in which she worked. He began visiting her there, and after several weeks they began dating. From the beginning, John struggled with trusting his new girlfriend's fidelity due to the nature of her job and John's own personal sense of inadequacies and beliefs about women. John's father had taught him that there were two types of women—those you had sex with and those you married. Even though Carol would not have sex with him for several months, John believed that she must be "a whore" since she was working as an exotic dancer. On some level, he found her unwillingness to have sex with him a challenge and frustration. It triggered painful feelings of inadequacy, the source of which I shall explore shortly. It also gave her, in the beginning, a great deal of power over John and compelled him to find a way of controlling some of his more aggressive impulses.

After six months of dating, John began to feel jealous of Carol's work situation. At first he felt proud that he was able to date a stripper. He bragged about it to his old friends and his friends on the police force and boasted about their sexual activities, even before they were having sex. In truth, John was very insecure about his sexuality and had been for much of his life.

Heavy as a boy, John never believed himself to be attractive to girls. In fact, one of his most painful memories was the repeated teasing of neighbor girls whom he had crushes on. They pretended to like him but made fun of him behind his back. When John got his first car at age 16, they used him for rides. One day he attempted to kiss one of the girls when they were drinking together in his car. When she refused to kiss him and even laughed at him, John felt enraged. He attempted to force himself on her sexually, but she fought him off. The girl never reported this incident. In his mind, John blamed her for being a tease and for using him. To him, it was "what she owed me." John bragged about having sex with the girl to his friends and received reinforcement for his angry feelings toward her.

John actually lost his virginity at the age of 17 while at a party. The girl with whom he had his first sexual experience was very drunk and the following day did not remember having sex with John. John's next several sexual experiences were with neighborhood prostitutes—something he never shared with anyone until several months before his death, when he told his therapist.

John was never able to admit his feelings of inadequacy to others. Privately, he felt ashamed and worthless a great deal of the time. However, he would not allow himself to experience these feelings for any length of time; he would usually drink, masturbate, or play sports as means of handling and expressing himself. Violence also provided John with a social means of demonstrating his worth to others. He learned to fight. On the football team, he was known as a player who was not afraid to play dirty and was willing to hurt opposing players in order to win. His violent tendencies were reinforced within this context, and he was frequently praised for his aggression.

Still, he felt inadequate. He learned to hide his sense of inadequacy with women by discounting their importance to him. When John went drinking with friends, women who did not express immediate interest were "just bitches." Over time, John learned to cover up most of his more vulnerable and difficult feelings with anger.

With his future wife, John was able to keep his anger mostly in check until the couple got married on a trip to Las Vegas. John immediately asked her to quit her job since she was now "his," and he would take care of her. Carol was ambivalent about quitting her job. On one hand, she really did not like the lifestyle that went with exotic dancing, yet on the other, she liked the independence that having her own work afforded her, and she had no other marketable skills.

Reluctantly, she agreed to quit. After several months of marriage, John started to become jealous of Carol for little reason. One day while at the supermarket, Carol said hi to a man who had been her neighbor as a child. John became extremely angry, stating that the man was actually a client of hers at the strip club. Within several more months, John began to physically prevent his wife from leaving the house. Predictably, his controlling and increasingly violent behavior had the opposite response to what he had hoped. Instead of keeping her at home, it led to her going away for several days at time. Carol attempted to control John's violent behavior by calling his station chief and threatening to file charges against John. She moved out of their home and asked John for a divorce. Filled with rage, John began to follow Carol in his squad car. One day he followed her to the club where she previously had worked and had begun to work again. Several evenings later Carol saw John following her, and she filed formal charges against him. John's station chief referred John to the department psychologist. After assessing John, he referred him to therapy.

John reluctantly made an appointment at the practice to which his chief referred him. His chief informed John that one of the therapists there saw other police officers. He also informed John that if he did not go to counseling he would be written up and disciplinary procedures would be initiated.

John's initial appoint was with Steve, a social worker who specialized in cognitive behavioral therapy with firefighters and police officers. Steve had worked with many traditional men and enjoyed working with this population. He saw their initial resistance to therapy not so much as a problem with either his clients or the therapeutic process, but as related to stereotypes about the nature of therapy. Steve believed that the goal of therapy was behavioral change—in particular, changes in how men behaved in moving toward their goals. From his experience, very few men had as their explicit life goals to abuse drugs or to be jealous and violent. He viewed these behaviors as interfering with the true desire and motivations of most men. To Steve, the goal of therapy was to help men see how their behaviors were interfering with their lives, and then to help them understand and change the thinking that supports their behaviors. Trained as a cognitive therapist, Steve's orientation was to help men develop new patterns of thinking that supported healthier behaviors.

John arrived for this appointment with Steve twenty minutes late. Steve welcomed John and did not comment on this tardiness. He knew that men often will try to sabotage therapy early on, and that pointing out John's tardiness prior to their establishing a therapeutic bond would not be useful. Steve offered John a seat and then made himself comfortable on his couch. Wanting to understand how John viewed coming here, and his motivations, he simply asked, "What brings you here today?" John informed him that his station chief asked him to come due to problems with his wife. Steve asked about the type of problems, and John mentioned that she had left him. Steve prompted John to expand, at which point he recanted the story. When doing so, his focus was mostly on his wife, on her behavior, and on what she was "making him do to her." While John had a vague sense of how out-of-control his behavior was, he blamed his wife for causing his feelings and behavior. If she just would come back to him, he would change and things would be all right. Beginning to intervene even during the assessment, a common practice in cognitively oriented approaches, Steve commented, "Your wife certainly has a great deal of power over your behavior, it seems." To this John smiled and responded, "It certainly seems that way, doesn't it?" Steve shrugged his shoulders, as if to say that he would not judge the situation but would allow John to come up with his own assessment. Steve's approach is to become progressively more directive as the helping relationship is established, and then to become progressively less directive as a client learns how to apply cognitive behavioral techniques to his or her life. As their session ended, Steve asked whether or not John wanted Steve to have contact with his station chief. He informed John that it was entirely up to him, and that he would have to fill out a consent form if he did. He also informed John that if a consent form was not filled out, he would not be able to tell his chief even that he had come. John said that he wanted his chief to know he attended, but not the specifics of what he said.

During their second session, John appeared agitated and less willing to talk. Now that he had told his story to Steve, he was uncomfortable about what would happen next. He felt better for "getting it out" but was unsure of what would happen next. John also admitted to Steve that he was not sure what to say and what not to say. He said that if he told Steve everything he was thinking about, he would "not be able to take it back, and it would change everything." Steve probed, but John was unwilling to say elaborate. This statement made Steve very nervous. He asked John if he was thinking about hurting himself or his wife. John looked down and said no, but Steve was not convinced. The session ended with John saying very little. Steve felt he had been placed in a difficult position during and after the session. He desperately wanted to establish a good working relationship with John, but he also believed that John was at risk of harming his wife. On the other hand, nothing that John said gave him any clear indication that he would harm his wife. Therefore, Steve had no grounds to attempt to involuntarily commit him for being a potential threat. Steve decided that the risks were too great and consulted with the psychiatrist and the director in group practice's. Both agreed that there was little that could be done but that Steve should discuss his concerns with John's supervisor, even if that meant damaging Steve's helping relationship with John. Steve called the chief and discussed his concerns.

John failed to show up for his third session. As agreed upon, and since Steve worried that John might be a threat to his wife, Steve called the station chief to say that John had missed their session. His chief informed Steve that John had failed to show up for work since their phone call, and that they were actively looking for him. Two days later, John was found dead, along with his wife, in her new apartment. He had shot them both.

Steve found out about the killing on the evening news. Shocked, he began to cry in disbelief. He wondered what he could have done differently.

FOR WRITING AND REFLECTION

1. What, if anything, could Steve have done differently?
2. What should Steve do now?
3. What systems seemed to fail both Steve and John?
4. Had John not killed himself, but continued with treatment, what CBT techniques could have been used?
5. What techniques could have been used from the other theories and perspectives discussed in this book?
6. What other lessons can we learn from this case with regard to practice with men?

Case Example

Kevin Sanchez is a 28-year-old mixed race Latino/African American man living in a rural community in the South. Kevin identifies primarily as Latino; his biological grandfather was African American, but the rest of his family came from Mexico two generations ago. Kevin is married to Sara, an African American woman. They have been married for five years. Kevin and Sara have two children, ages 5 and 2. Kevin works as a media consultant for a car manufacturer. The couple, originally from Chicago, moved to the South when Kevin was offered a position with his company. In many ways, the move has been a good opportunity for Kevin and his family. They were able to buy a house and live comfortably. In Chicago, they paid the same amount of money to rent a fairly small apartment as they do for their current mortgage on their home. However, they live over a thousand miles from their families, and both feel somewhat isolated. Sara, not a particularly social person and yet very close to her family of origin, has frequently experienced bouts of "the blues." When Sara feels bad, she tends to react with anger. She has a difficult time identifying and expressing her true feelings until after she explodes in anger and then calms down. Kevin and Sara have joked that in this regard Sara is like "a typical teenage boy."

The stress of family life and being away from her relatives has seemed to be getting to Sara, as she has begun to drink in order to relax. Sara's temper also has seemed to be getting progressively out of control.

During an argument about money, Sara threw an iron at Kevin, hitting him in the arm. Kevin was shocked and did not know how to respond. Sara stood there hollering at him. She screamed, "What are you going to do big man, you are just a pussy, you can't do anything." As Kevin stood in shock, Sara began to laugh at him. Kevin immediately left the house and went for a drive. He became angry that his wife treated him this way, and he started to think that perhaps he should have thrown the iron back. He did not like having these thoughts, and he realized that he and his wife needed help. Kevin had never been physically abusive to his wife and always prided himself on remaining calm during arguments. However, he realized that increasingly he is feeling less patient with Sara's outbursts and has thought about hitting her.

The following day, Kevin went to see his priest. It was the first time Kevin had been to church in several years. He explained to his priest what was happening and said that he was scared he would become violent with his wife if things escalated. In addition to discussing the issue from a spiritual perspective, his priest suggested that Kevin go see a social worker at the local family service agency. Kevin's priest, who sensed that Kevin was not enamored of the idea but, out of respect to the priest, might not voice his concern, told Kevin that he understood how hard it is for a man to admit that he cannot handle things on his own, especially when it comes to family. Kevin's priest knew that this is often particularly true of Mexican men. In Mexican culture, it is seen as a strength to be able to handle family problems within the family, and it is often perceived as a failure when one needs to go outside the extended family for help. Kevin's priest praised him for coming, saying that it was a sign of considerable strength, but firmly instructed Kevin that it was his obligation to his family to seek additional support. Kevin took the phone number of the family service agency and reluctantly promised to call.

Kevin drove away from church without knowing where he would go, or what he would do. He just drove, feeling numb, confused, and sad, wondering to himself, "Why is this happening to me?" He alternated between self-blame and anger at his wife. Kevin drove a few miles outside of town and pulled off onto a quiet country road. He began to scream at the top of his lungs and to violently beat his steering wheel. Soon Kevin found himself crying uncontrollably, more intensely than he can ever remember crying. Kevin cried for perhaps fifteen minutes and then sat silently with his eyes closed. He noticed that he felt better than he had in a long time, until he realized that he had some very difficult decisions to make.

When Kevin arrived home, he told his wife that he would be staying at a hotel for a few days, and that he wanted them to seek help for their problems. For the first time in a long time, he expressed sadness to his wife and his worry that the next time she was physical with him he would not be able to control his temper. He told her that he was scared their marriage would fall apart if they did not get help. Kevin had surprised Sara. She told him that he was blowing things out of proportion, and that since she did not hurt him, there really was not a problem. She said that she loved him and would work on her anger, but that she did not want to go see a therapist "because we're not crazy." Kevin told Sara about his conversation with the priest. Sara became angry, saying that he had no right to discuss her business with other people. She raised her voice and told Kevin that if he left the house, he would not be invited back. Kevin felt himself becoming angry, and he told his wife that while he loved her, she needed help. Sara began to scream and curse at Kevin, and he decided to leave immediately instead of packing his bags.

Kevin went to a local motel, checked in, and called Sara. Having calmed down, Sara was tearful and said that she wanted him to come home. He said that he would come home the following day if she agreed to either go see the priest with him or go directly to the counselor.

FOR WRITING AND REFLECTION

1. What strengths did Kevin exhibit in this situation?
2. What would your treatment plan be for the family?
3. How would you help Kevin and Sara keep each other safe?
4. What supports might their children need?
5. In what ways is Kevin typical and atypical of the hegemonic masculine ideal? What are the implications of your assessment for practice with Kevin and Sara?

Workers at Risk | SEVEN

Today we are experiencing a revolution in the workplace. Not only are institutions and huge conglomerates crumbling around us, our traditional ideas about work itself are dissolving. As a society we are undergoing a radical change in the way we think about work. We are starved for meaning and purpose in our lives, and with the breakdown in job security in the corporate world, we are no longer willing to separate our values from our work. There is a yearning to align life purpose with work to make it meaningful (Naiman 1998).

Along with family, work is one of the most central social institutions (Dudley 1994).Work and employment are not merely economic functions; within every society, work and the manner in which labor is organized define and are defined by social relationships (Schneider 1990). That is, the way in which society organizes the function of work is tied to how we treat each other and largely defines the roles that guide human relationships. Work also defines who we are. While many people criticize American society as relying too heavily on work for definitions of American identity, Americans are not alone in this attitude—work and employment contribute to the definition of identity within all societies. Rifkin (1994) notes that identity is greatly defined by work within a modern, technologically progressive, capitalist society. Men's social identities are largely constructed around work (Moberg 1997). What men do for work becomes an important part of how they see themselves, and how others view them. In the United States, one of the first questions men ask when they meet someone for the first time is "What do you do?" (implicitly, "do for a living"). (In contrast, in Latin America it is just as common to ask about family members prior to inquiring about one's occupation.) Work provides men with a context for developing social relationships and a key domain by which they may achieve meaning and worth. The contexts in which men work are varied. Work can be life enhancing, supportive, and growth oriented, or stifling, alienating, and degrading. A strength that many men possess is their willingness to take any available work in order to provide for their families, often to the detriment of their own health and well-being. For example, migrant laborers will often take any work at nearly any wage in order to send remittances home to their families (Chiquiar and Hanson 2005). Regardless of the role that work plays in the lives of a men, globalization and technological advances are changing the way men find, keep, and engage in work. The roles men play in work are also shifting as women become more central and influential in many sectors of the economy.

Social workers are called upon to help men resolve many work-related problems. Social workers help men who are unemployed, underemployed, or seeking job training. They provide counseling to men who are experiencing problems that negatively affect their work performance. Social workers help men improve their job-seeking skills and overall work performance, and they perform the undervalued yet essential task of case management. Employment-assistance social workers, hired by organizations to provide services for their employees, have provided services within various for-profit, nonprofit, and governmental organizations for over two decades.

Until the financial crisis and recession that began in 2008, unemployment rates in the United States were only approximately 3 percent, although they were significantly higher in some parts of the country. For instance, in 2006 Detroit had an unemployment rate of 5.9 percent, double the national average (Bureau of Labor Statistics 2007). Unemployment rates also vary according to race. The unemployment rates for African American men were 9.5 percent and for Latinos 5.9 percent. Additionally, poverty and unemployment have been significant among men in rural areas. The highest jobless rates in the United States in March 2007 were five agricultural areas, with El Centro, California, topping the list at 13.3 percent (Bureau of Labor Statistics 2007). National unemployment rates soared in 2008 and 2009, with the Bureau of Labor Statistics reporting a 10 percent jobless rate in 2009, equivalent to ten million unemployed workers.

In addition to unemployment, men have other work-related problems, such as alienating and meaningless work, stress, overreliance on work for meaning and self-worth, and having to work too many hours in order to provide for their families. This chapter explores many of these issues.

The Role of Work in Men's Lives

Work is arguably the primary pursuit for a vast majority of us. Yet, when asked what gives purpose and meaning to our lives, many of us tend to leave work off the list. In a culture in which many of us have lost control of our own work, work has become of merely instrumental value in the quest for other activities that give meaning to our lives (Dunn 2007).

Historically, work has been the context where men find their sense of connectedness to other men and their overall sense of belonging to other human beings. Work has provided men with a venue for developing a sense of who they are and understanding their wants and needs, through the very act of engaging in work itself.

So powerful is this notion of the capacity of work to define and shape consciousness that it became a core organizing principle for the theories of Karl Marx. The essence of Marx's theory rested on the centrality of work to the lives of human beings (Burghardt 1986). To Marx, one of the worst things that could happen to men was their disconnection from creative, engaging work (Fromm 1961). Men who work at jobs in which they are unable to fully engage their creative spirit suffer from a deep sense of alienation, dread, and depression (Mirowsky and Ross 1989; Ollman 1971). Even for men who view family as more important than work, most men view their most significant contribution to their families as earning a living. Work can provide men with a sense of competence, worth, and value.

While work has provided men with great satisfaction and a means of psychosocial support and development, men's overreliance on work as a source of meaning has great costs (Keen 1991). The pressure to succeed, indeed to be the best and most successful in one's profession, can be crushing. This is evidenced by the staggering rate of suicide in men: over 70 percent of all completed suicides are male (Horwitz and Scheid 1999). Many factors have made men's procurement of meaningful and/or sufficient employment increasingly difficult. As women have become more integrated into the workforce, men have found themselves in less protected and privileged positions (Timberlake, Farber, and Sabatino 2002). Men now have to compete with women for positions for which they previously only competed with other men. Men may at times be unprepared for this competition, as they may not have developed some of the affective skills that may be strengths for many women. While the profession should clearly support and champion the full participation and equality of women in all social institutions, we must also be cognizant of what these changes mean for many men, especially for poorest, most disenfranchised, and most at-risk men.

Additionally, numerous factors associated with globalization and postindustrialization have decreased the capacity of poor, uneducated, or semiskilled men to provide for their families (Holt and Thompson 2004). For instance, the North American Free Trade Agreement has led to an overall decrease in manufacturing jobs, especially those with union protections and benefits (Prigoff 2000). Traditional well-paid factory jobs have become less available to American men, who earn far more than factory workers in other countries. In a global economy, low- and semiskilled positions increasingly are moving east or south. When seismic economic forces separate men from their means of production, their sense of self, indeed their very sense of being, can be threatened.

For both men and women, the world of work in the United States has changed radically. Beneria and Santiago (2001) note that nearly one million experienced workers lost their jobs to layoffs and closures during the 1990s. Jobs that previously were viewed as secure are no longer seen as such. In the last two decades, many well-paying careers for working-class men have been automated or have moved abroad (Appelbaum and Batt 1994). An excellent example comes from a case study of the Cortland, New York, community and the impact of the Smith-Corona Corporation's decision to move its manufacturing operations to Mexico (Beneria and Santiago 2001). As relatively high-paying positions left the community, men were faced with few employment options and struggled with how to cope with the transition. Many men remained stuck, hoping that somehow the changes would be temporary in nature and not represent permanent shifts in America's economic and industrial reality.

The days of the "company man" who went to work for a firm in his early twenties, and retired from that same company after fifty years of service are largely gone. In fact, many men who expected to be with companies their whole lives have found themselves unemployed. Not only does the termination from long-term service lead to financial strains, it may also lead to feelings of abandonment and extreme loss and grief. A men who has placed considerable trust and faith in his employer can experience a deep blow to his sense of community and well-being when he is laid off or fired.

Conceptions of masculinity have been explored at several points in this book, in relation to how masculinity affects and is affected by various contexts or dilemmas. Work is central to the development of masculine identity. Early socialization about what it means to be a man often stresses men's capacity to produce, to work and endure work, and the importance of viewing work as our most important role and function. Ingham (1985) observed that men's sense of identity is often constructed by their work roles, and the social meanings attached to their sense as workers. Work provides the context by which men define their sense of masculinity (Telford 1996) and their very sense of worth (McLean 2003). In a real sense, to work is to be a man. To not work and not be able to provide for one's family is a blow to a man's sense of self and his very purpose. Holt and Thompson (2004) observed that "man as breadwinner" is one of the key roles that men adopt in their construction of their own masculine identity. They observed that men find meaning and value in this role yet often seek other roles, such as "man as action hero or rebel," in response to the sometimes limiting and confining aspects of the breadwinner role. The authors note the image of the American cowboy as the fantasy ideal, in that the cowboy is free to do his job without having to follow burdensome bureaucratic rules, and without having to report to supposedly oppressive superiors. In their qualitative interviews, they found that men "craft themselves as American heroes on a scale that is attainable in everyday life" (426). In other words, men construct identities that allow them to attain success in achieving a personally constructed sense of their own masculinity. Ehrenreich (1983) explored the notion of men as breadwinners in her presentation of the contradictions men feel in their search for masculinity and identity. She notes that as men have been progressively thwarted in their ability to achieve success in this domain, they seek liberation fantasies to help them contend with their socially constructed diminution.

As previously mentioned, the rise of feminism and the equality of women has also changed the context of work for men. While male power and privilege certainly are alive and well within most professions, women have made great inroads into professions that were traditionally dominated by men (Gibelman 2003). While many men may not publicly admit struggling with women's new roles in the workplace, some privately are distressed. Men are taught to view women as not possessing many of the skills and competencies that they view as essential to workplace success, including logic, drive, assertiveness or aggressiveness, willfulness, and toughness. However, women certainly do possess these skills, and men need to adapt to these important social changes, and to the multitude of other global transformations that the new millennium has brought.

Regardless of the reason, loss of employment or a career can be a debilitating event in a man's life. Men who have lost work have been shown to be at increased risk of a variety of emotional, psychiatric, and physical concerns, as well as other problems addressed in this book. Even when men are able to find work, some jobs present significant threats to their health and well-being, a topic covered in the following section.

Dangerous Work

Many of the jobs in which men have engaged have been detrimental to their health. That men are willing to take these positions is a sign of their dedication to their families and to their desire for self-sufficiency and financial independence. Some dangerous jobs have led to social advances that have benefited many members of society. Yet the long-term health consequences of some careers are profound. While social programs have been created to help those injured or disabled during dangerous work, society has not always exhibited sufficient gratitude for the dangerous work that some men do.

For instance, mining and industrial careers have been long known to have profound health consequences for men. Miners experience numerous respiratory illnesses in addition to the constant threat of explosions and collapse. It is also true that such work environments often are situated in poor, isolated rural areas with less access to quality health care and social work services (Ginsberg 1998), increasing the danger associated with such work. Some jobs that are not seen as classically dangerous may actually have serious health risks. Fishing is the most dangerous job for men in the United States. According to Drudi (1998), over the course of a forty-year career in fishing, a man has a 61 in 1,000 chance of suffering a fatal injury. Workers in this industry face threats from vessel casualties, falling into the water, and diving accidents. Due to deunionization and the push for lower wages and competition from globalization, many of these men do not have health care benefits. In total numbers of deaths, mining is the most hazardless occupation (Stephens & Ahern, 2001). Pilots of small aircraft also face significant and constant dangers. Pilots who spray pesticides on crops not only are placed at risk of future health problems from the chemicals but also often fly poorly maintained and outdated equipment. Between 1992 and 2001, nearly 150 men were killed in accidents involving such aircraft.

While women also engage in difficult and dangerous work, men disproportionately hold positions in some of the most difficult professions. Police and firefighters are expected to perform a valuable public service and respond perfectly under the most adverse circumstances. Police are often confronted with the most dangerous members of society, day after day, yet they receive strict public scrutiny and harsh criticism when things go wrong. Hypervigilance, hypercontrol, emotional detachment, and extreme emotional arousal have profound effects on these public servants (Miller 1995). The daily traumas that police, firefighters, and other crisis professionals experience may lead to posttraumatic stress disorder (McCafferty, McCafferty, and McCafferty 1992).

Practice Considerations

Being cognizant of the masculine scripts that shape men's attitudes about work may help social workers successfully work with men on the issues and concerns mentioned above. Social workers should never minimize the importance of work to many men. Practitioners should validate the prosocial, positive aspect of men's work. They should also have a good working knowledge of the local and national programs that can help men resolve their work-related problems. I will outline some of these programs after a discussion of how the four theories discussed in this book inform social work practice in this area.

The Four Theories and Work

Freud noted that success in love and work make for a meaningful life. Social workers often find themselves trying to help men figure out how to make their existing work more meaningful, and how to explore other work options. Of course, it is important to note that being able to choose between work options is usually the privilege of education and class. However, even men with relatively sophisticated training and education, such as computer programmers and engineers, can find themselves unemployed for long periods of time. Many men in the computer industry have found their function outsourced to other countries, where wages are much lower. Globalization is rapidly changing notions of work security and privilege and likely will continue to do so over the coming decades.

Still, helping men find and make meaning out of their work is an important task. Men are often socialized to work silently and not think about what their work means or how it feels. Clearly, a social worker helping men explore their work issues will not want to create problems where they do not exist. In addition, it is important for social workers to be careful of their own class biases in regard to work. For instance, I previously had a client who was a line cook in a hotel restaurant. He had many opportunities to "work his way up" and become the head chef or the maitre d'. However, he enjoyed the simplicity of his work, and the fact that he was able to work in relative peace and anonymity. He did not wish to discuss the meaning in his work and profession—he was content in his role and with what work meant for him. It would have been inappropriate to challenge his conception of the role of work in his life; social workers must always "start where the client is." Our own class and theoretical biases can greatly hinder our clients when we do not engage in sufficient self-reflection and attempt to apply a one-size-fits-all approach.

That said, many men do experience a sense of meaninglessness in their work, and social workers should help them explore these concerns. It is essential for social workers to truly understand that for many men, the loss of work means the loss of meaning, dignity, respect, power, and identity. Certainly we can critique the usefulness of investing so much of our emotional well-being in something that rests outside our control, and we can perhaps recognize that women have a healthier viewpoint when it comes to balancing work with other important domains of life. However, this does not negate the centrality of work in men's lives , and the realities that social workers must contend with.

Existential theory may be of value for working with men around work issues. In particular, the exploration of meaning, responsibility, and death are all valuable concepts. Practicing from an existential perspective, the social worker will seek to engage men in conversations about the meaning that work plays in the context of their lives. Axelrod (2001:117) explores some of the complex, often paradoxical issues that are involved for men in work.

> Compulsive activity, oscillations between fierce independence and need for approval, highly charged ideals and goals, precarious self-esteem, and preoccupation with proving one's manhood commonly color the work lives of male clients. As therapists, we strive to help our clients develop more emotionally authentic relationships with others and may presume to guide our male clients toward putting their work in perspective and paying more attention to their intimate bonds. However, if we do not seek to understand their passionate relationship to work on its own terms, we may neglect an important means of helping our male clients.

Axelrod speaks of the important balance that social workers must adopt with men around not only work, but also many of their deeply ingrained ideals and values. Social workers must validate the importance of work for men while helping them find a sense of balance. Making one's meaning in life and self-worth contingent on work alone may set men up for heartache and failure since employment and careers do not always last. By helping men find meaning in other life domains, social workers can enable them to increase their overall sense of meaning and purpose. Yet helping men find this balance is a difficult task requiring a great deal of patience. In engaging men in conversations around increasing the meaning of other aspects of their lives, and by implication decreasing the importance of work, social workers must never forget the central role that work plays, or they risk being either discounting or discounted. Social workers should explore with men how central work is in their lives and at times help them challenge the wisdom of placing so much of their sense of worth and identity on something that can be so easily taken way from them. Some of the questions that social workers can employ include:

- How does it affect you to have a great deal of the meaning of your life dependent upon your job?
- What would your life be like if work was taken away from you?
- How would you find meaning in your life if you could no longer work?
- If you had one month to live, would you continue with your job? If not, what would you do, and what would this say about how you construct meaning?

These questions may be good starting points for existentially oriented work. While some men place too much meaning on their jobs, others do not find meaning in their work. Some jobs, routine and monotonous in nature, may not easily lend themselves toward feelings of worth and meaning. However, all work has some important social function and can be used to nurture other parts of our lives. While some work may be inherently unexciting, a man can be helped to find meaning and pride in his capacity to do a good job, regardless of the context. By focusing on the quality of the job well done, and on things that are within a man's control, a social worker can improve a man's sense of meaning and purpose.

As previously explored, the therapeutic value of death lies in death's finality. That is, it reminds us that life is not infinite, that there is no dress rehearsal—this is all we have. The notion of death can help men who are stuck in difficult work situations develop a sense of urgency about decision making. This should not be confused with rash or irrational decisions made in the heat of passion. However, a man who is stuck in an unfulfilling career may be helped to think about his work in relationship to the finite nature of existence. In so doing, he may question whether or not he wishes to stay in his job for the rest of his life. Of course, this dilemma does not apply to all men at all times, as some men may have struggled with finding steady employment. However, even men who have not had stable careers may be helped to think about the finite nature of existence. Such discussions can motivate men to begin to take responsibility for that which they can control. As with other discussions of existential themes, it is important that dialogues about responsibility in the domain of work are carefully conducted so as to not shame a man for his work difficulties, regardless of their source.

Narrative therapy can be used in a variety of ways to help men with their work-related problems. If a man is overly aligned with the hegemonic norm of having work as his only source of meaning, a social worker can ask him to think of times in his life when he was able to construct a meaningful story that included other sources of meaning. For some men this is not possible, as they have always been overly attached to work and must construct a new story of a life with greater balance. This is not an easy task and will demand a great deal of creative exploration. Other potential sources of meaning can be family, friends, hobbies, spirituality, or other tasks or institutions. For some men, using narrative group work can be helpful. By hearing the stories of other men, they may begin to develop ideas for reauthoring their own lives. Some men hold narratives of themselves in which their main story is one of work failure. A social worker will want to help such a man explore previous examples that challenge this core narrative, a process that is referred to as exploring unique outcomes. The social may wish to work with collaborators who see the man in a more complex, nuanced light than he is able to see himself at present.

CBT is also a valuable tool for helping men deal with work-related issues. Many men have core irrational beliefs that may need to be challenged and disputed before they are able to live fuller lives and have work be in proper balance. One of the most common irrational beliefs that men hold can be stated as "I am not a man if I do not have a good, high-paying job." This belief is often also exaggerated. For instance, many men believe they are not good men if they are not wealthy and "totally successful" in their careers. The problem is that success is usually defined as an unattainable outcome and not a process-oriented goal that can be controlled. For example, an extremely competent and successful man may feel depressed and worthless if he is not "the best" at his job. Alternatively, a man may feel that he has failed as a father and a husband if he is not able to find work after losing his job, often for reasons totally outside his control. Helping men challenge these beliefs is essential and can be a first step in enabling them to combat the inertia that may be a symptom of post–job loss grief or depression. Experiencing a profound sense of loss and grief is normal after the loss of a job, particularly one that a man has held for a long time. However, this grief can easily become a more clinical syndrome if a man is not able to find positive ways of addressing the psychosocial and financial aspects of his loss.

In helping men cope with self-doubting feelings that may accompany loss, "rational role reverse," a technique from rational emotive therapy, may be helpful. Using this technique, the social worker asks the client to temporarily change roles with him or her. That is, the social worker adopts the role of client and asks the client to assume the role of helper. The social worker then asks the client for assistance with a problem, presenting a scenario that is analogous to the problem the client is struggling with. For instance, the social worker can tell the client that she feels worthless since he or she is not the best social worker in the world. He or she can describe feeling ashamed that a client may not get better. In addition, the social worker may mention feeling inadequate that he or she does not make a lot of money and is not wealthy. The social worker then asks the client to help the worker assess these cognitive and affective statements and provide some perspective. By helping the social worker explore and dispute some of these irrational beliefs, the client begins to develop cognitive disputational skills. Since the situation that the social worker presented is fairly analogous to the client's, the client will often begin to explore his own feelings and beliefs. The distance and detachment that this exercise provides can help the client learn to engage in the therapeutic process without a great deal of psychological threat. Exercises such as this are valuable for resistant clients, or those overwhelmed with their own difficult emotions.

Additional Practice Considerations

So central is work to men's identities and lives that all social workers who work with men will be called on to help with work concerns. However, several practice settings are specifically geared toward helping men with work. These include the unemployment system, job-training programs, and often substance abuse treatment, prison programs and postprobation and parole programs.

Job-training programs will become increasingly important over the next decade. As the pace of technological advancement accelerates, men will find themselves in need of increased skills training. It is hoped that the majority of this training can be provided while a man is employed. However, as more employers are outsourcing their work, retraining workers seems to be less and less a priority.

Helping men improve their functioning at work is the key task of social work practice in employment assistance programs (EAPs). EAP social workers are employed in the private sector (and sometimes in public or governmental agencies) to help workers with problems that interfere with their capacity to work. Such problems are varied but typically include substance abuse, work relationship issues, mental health issues, and the management of anger or other emotions. EAPs can provide support and resources to employees and administrators. Employees may seek the services of EAP social workers when they have personal concerns and may often seek therapy or referrals. Administrators can make referrals to EAPs but may also seek out EAP social workers for advice on how to resolve concerns about employees that are affecting the worker's performance. EAPs may also engage in wellness programs, in which preventative services are provided to help improve the physical and emotional health of employees. EAPs, at their best, function on the levels of both prevention and intervention and are able to work with the most at-risk and disadvantaged workers (Attridge, Herlihy, and Maiden 2005)

Job-Training Programs

Job-training programs are becoming increasingly necessary and must account for factors that make their design far more complex than even a generation ago. Many jobs demand specialized training. While it is true that the best-paying jobs demand considerable education and technical skill, many men may unfortunately need to work, at least initially, at less technically challenging service-sector jobs. Depending on the client, job-training programs may need to include an array of services in order to help them find and ultimately retain employment. This is particularly true of men who are homeless, have substance abuse problems, or struggle with mental illnesses. Proponents of comprehensive programs understand that the ability to obtain and sustain employment demands that many psychosocial needs be met. For example, Primavera in Tucson, Arizona, is an employment program that assists homeless and near-homeless adults learn job skills and find employment. The program incorporates case management principles and develops a comprehensive individual service plan to account for individualized needs of different clients, with particular attention paid to the creation of an employability development plan. The client's skills are assessed so the client can be matched with temporary employment while he is helped to search for a full-time job. This temporary employment helps him develop consistency, increase self-esteem and self-efficacy, and begin to learn or relearn employment-related skills. Primavera provides job-readiness classes that assist their clients in developing interviewing skills, understanding how to complete applications, do job search planning, and identify employment skills. Primavera also provides clients with bus passes, lunches, housing, and suitable clothing for work. The ultimate goal of the organization is to assist clients in obtaining full-time employment and the ability to live independently.

Another program, Career Gear (2008), is run by a nonprofit organization that helps "disadvantaged men" find and maintain employment and self-sufficiency. The program's motto is, "A Suit—A Second Chance." The program started in New York in 1989 and has expanded to other cities. At first, it simply provided clothes to men so they could attend job interviews, but quickly its services expanded to include job training and case management. The program seeks partnerships with other organizations that are sensitive to the needs of minority and poor men. Once a man is able to successfully find work, he is encouraged to stay connected through the alumni program, which provides peer support and networking, with a special focus on job retention and career advancement. Support groups and workshops help men develop skills such as managing budgets, parenting, and coping.

In Boston, Pine Street Inn (2008) has separate vocational and housing programs for men and women who have found themselves in difficult life circumstances. Its Working Men program provides shelter and job training. During their time in the program, men are helped to save money so they can find their own private housing. The program helps train men for several professions, including food services and building maintenance. The organization also operates the Support and Training Result in Valuable Employees (STRIVE) program, which teaches employment skills including interviewing, having a good attitude, and basic knowledge of computers.

What the best programs have in common is a recognition of the skills, risks, and needs of their clients. They each recognize that complex psychosocial factors are involved in finding and maintaining employment. They do not blame men for social factors that are beyond their control but help them be responsible in the here and now for their own lives.

Case Example

Fasad Mohammad is a 50-year-old man from Iran, living in New York. Fasad came to the United States in 1980, shortly after the start of the Iranian Revolution. At the time Fasad was finishing medical school, but he had to flee the country as some of his family members were politically active supporters of the disposed leader.

While a devout Muslim, Fasad was not in favor of the brand of fundamentalist Islam that was supported by the revolution. Still, he desperately wanted to remain in the country but realized that his life, and that of his wife, would have been in danger. For weeks Fasad struggled with the painful decision to leave the country. Iran was all he knew, and he loved his country and its people.

Fasad dreamed of becoming a physician and knew that were he to leave the country, this dream would be much harder, if not impossible, to achieve. Finally Fasad was able to arrange for transportation out of the country, and his family was smuggled through Iraq to Turkey. In Turkey he made plans to emigrate to the United States.

The majority of Iranians who Fasad knew went to Los Angeles. However, Fasad wanted to go somewhere else. He felt it would be too painful to be around so many of his countrymen, so he decided to move to New York. He reasoned that since so many immigrants started their lives there, he would follow in the footsteps of many great people. Fasad truly had the heart of a poet.

Needing to support himself and his wife, Fasad found work as a taxi driver. He had planned on driving a taxi for only several months, but shortly thereafter his wife developed breast cancer and died. Fasad was devastated. He loved his young wife dearly and could not imagine a life without her. They had planned to have children together and were hoping so start their family once Fasad found a way to go to medical school. Now Fasad was having, at age 25, to learn how to live life alone in a strange country in which he knew few people. Fortunately, his English was good, and he was able to get by. For two years Fasad's world was very small. He drove his taxi and largely kept to himself. He did attend his mosque several times a week, and he lived the life of a devout Muslim. He read the Koran daily, which gave him strength to go on. He prayed for guidance and direction, which never seemed to come. Still, he remained sure that one day some meaning and clarity would come into his life.

On a cold, rainy day, a young women flagged him down in his taxi. He recognized her accent as being Iranian, and they began to chat on the way to her destination. Fasad and the young woman found themselves enjoying each other's company a great deal. When Fasad dropped her off, he felt a deep need to see her again. Not knowing what to do, he decided to tell her just that. He asked if she would have coffee with him, she smiled, and they agreed to meet two days later. Within a short time, Fasad fell in love with Fatima, who turned out to be a physician herself. The couple married and had three children together. Fasad's wife, a surgeon, would often have to work long hours. The flexibility of his job allowed him to take care of the children while his wife worked. He loved being around his children—they provided him with a sense of meaning. His dream of being a doctor seemed to be less important to him for many years. He reasons that since his wife was a doctor and they were "partners," he was doing good in the world through helping her.

After many years Fasad began to feel some sadness and dissatisfaction with his life. He has very mixed feelings about his work, and how his occupation makes him feel about himself. Normally he enjoys his job, and he tells people that he actually likes it more than he would have liked being a physician. However, those close to him know that he privately feels as if he has failed in life because he did not reach his potential. While Fasad tries to put his career into perspective and to use the teachings of Islam to appreciate and enjoy his life, he has found this increasingly difficult to do. The start of his increased struggles with his work began after the bombings of the World Trade Center in 2001. Fasad was horrified at the bombings and believed that the bombers had violated the most basic tenets of his faith. Like many Americans, Fasad was horrified and depressed.

However, Fasad also felt that many of his clients were no longer as friendly and open as they had been in the past. Part of what had made his work meaningful was his ability to talk to other people, to listen to their problems, and to share a bit of himself. Fasad found that some people were no longer interested in having conversations with him. In fact, one day a man dressed in a suit informed him that he should "shut up and be thankful that he is allowed to stay in the country." Fasad did not know how to respond. For weeks after, he felt shocked and hurt and found it very hard to get to work in the morning. He began taking his taxi out later and later and returning earlier and earlier. His dispatcher, who had always admired Fasad as a person and as a worker, was understanding yet concerned. A Somali immigrant himself, he understood the heavy toll that discrimination could take on a man's sprit. He expressed his empathy to Fasad, who expressed gratitude but failed to discuss his own feelings.

Fasad continued to work at his job in this manner for three years. One day he woke up and decided not to go to work. He called his dispatcher and told him that he would not be driving a taxi anymore. Fasad's dispatcher told Fasad that instead of quitting, he would be able lay him off, which would allow him to collect unemployment benefits. At first Fasad expressed discomfort with his dispatcher's offer, as he did not want to accept "welfare." However, he also did not want to appear ungrateful and ungracious, so he thanked his friend and accepted. After consulting with his wife, Fasad decided to stay home with their now teenage children for a while and "figure out what was next." The family was doing fine financially and did not need his paycheck. Fasad had mixed feelings about this. On one hand, he was grateful that he did not have to rush out to find a new job immediately. On the other hand, the fact that his labor was "extra" made him feel somewhat useless.

Fasad filed for unemployment. The unemployment office had a contract with a program designed to help immigrant men and women seek jobs. While Fasad has been in the country many years, with his wife's urging, he decided he would see the social worker in the program who specializes on employment issues for immigrant men.

FOR WRITING AND SELF-REFLECTION

Imagining yourself to be the social worker designated to help Fasad, answer the following questions.

1. What methods would you use to work with Fasad?
2. Fasad informs you that he might want to become a doctor after all. What would you say to him?
3. What resources and services might be appropriate for Fasad at this time?
4. Using the Internet, explore a bit about Iranian and Islamic culture. What cultural factors might inform your work with Fasad?

Warriors at Risk | EIGHT

"The number of people who have suffered from mild
traumatic brain injury could be in the thousands, but
we just won't know about it unless we screen everybody
who comes back," said Paul Rieckhoff, executive
director of Iraq and Afghanistan Veterans of America.
"The system as it stands right now really depends on
[veterans] to self-diagnose and then navigate
the bureaucracy of red tape to get help.
—L. M. Colarusso, 2007

The protection of the community from outside invaders has been a primarily male role for many thousands of years (O'Connell 1989). Perhaps the greatest tragedy of the most recent wars in the Middle East has been the relative inattention to the needs of returning servicemen and women (American Psychological Association 2007). Frequent news reports have highlighted the lack of services for men injured in the war. National Public Radio reported on a Pentagon study that found an increasing number of officers discharged from the military for mental health concerns (Zwerdling 2007). According to this report, nearly 28,000 men have been discharged from the military for behavioral problems, many of which appear to be related to mental health. Additionally, many men have been removed from the military for "personality disorders," making them eligible to receive military benefits. The report suggests that many of these men did not have precombat mental health conditions but developed them during military duty. Military personnel have been facing longer and longer tours of duty, which has greatly affected the mental health and psychosocial well-being of many service personnel. This chapter discusses the experiences and needs of men who have put their lives on the line for their country. While many of us have negative feelings about some of the wars in which our country has engaged, it is essential that as social workers we separate the war from the warrior. Even men who have served in the armed forces may be highly critical of specific wars. However, the majority of men who join the armed forces do so for noble reasons, such as the protection of home and family or cherished American values (Cozza, Chun, and Polo 2005). Many view the military as their sole option for social and economic advancement. Military recruiters often promise a lifetime of benefits for men who serve their country. As fewer and fewer jobs provide health and retirement benefits, the military may be increasingly popular with poor and undereducated men.

The men and women who sign up for the armed forces deserve the best care that society can provide for them—they often face a mindboggling number of challenges upon their return from war that fall within the purview of social workers. Returning servicemen often need physical and mental health care, help with educational and career planning, family therapy, and other services.

The Experiences of Servicemen

It is impossible to understand the needs of current servicemen or veterans without understanding the horrors of war. While not all men who serve in the armed forces experience events similar to those that will be explored, many do. Additionally, the mere possibility that men may experience these events has a profound effect on their emotional well-being. The anticipation and fear of potentially catastrophic events can be highly traumatic. Even servicemen who have not faced combat may experience mental health concerns (Martin, Sparacino, and Belenky, 1996). In addition to the horrors of war and the difficulty of wartime stress, the culture and training of the military have a profound influence on men.

Even under the best of circumstances, war is an extremely stressful and traumatic event. Wars are unpredictable, and each war has emotional and physical consequences that are difficult, if not impossible, to predict. Each man has his own set of risks and resiliencies that account for a large portion of his reaction to stress and trauma (Kobasa 1979). For instance, some men who engage in close-contact killing experience emotional disturbance while others do not. What is clear is that all wars create numerous physical and mental health problems (Cronin 1998). As with many complex problems, a mix of biological, psychological, and social factors influence the eventual expression and outcome of problems. Even men in war who possess numerous protective factors may not be ready for the intensities and traumas of combat.

The stresses and traumas of war are too numerous to discuss in all their complexity in this kind of book. However, there are several salient experiences that must be explored. First, combat is inherently a violent and stressful situation. Soldiers are prepared for worst-case scenarios and are taught that even the smallest mistake may lead to the loss of their lives or the lives of those around them. This awareness can in and of itself lead to hypervigilance and extreme stress reactions. The army refers to this as combat stress, and it can often be a precursor to posttraumatic stress disorder (PTSD) (U.S. Army Medical Department 2007).

Men in combat, especially in counterinsurgency situations like those that characterize the wars in Iraq and Afghanistan, often engage in fighting at close range. These combat situations are chaotic, violent, and often very bloody. Soldiers in such situations will kill or be killed, and they will often watch other soldiers be injured or killed. They will need to care for fallen soldiers, and it is not uncommon for soldiers to witness the painful death of those to whom they have grown close. The sadness, loss, and trauma that such events create can last throughout a soldier's life, whether or not such events lead to diagnosable disorders. Soldiers in combat situations also experience loud noises and powerful explosions that can lead to physical and mental health concerns in and of themselves. Soldiers report hypervigilance and fear well after they return from combat because they have experienced shocking, unexpected, and deafening sounds.

Military training and experience in combat situations also encourage men to distance themselves from their own feelings. From the start of basic training, men are reinforced for anger and aggression. Admitting to feelings of vulnerability, sadness, loneliness, or other "softer" feelings is heavily frowned upon. Soldiers must also distance themselves from caring too much about others. Since soldiers are called upon to kill, they learn to view their enemies as being less than human. In short, soldier learn to distance themselves from their very humanity.

However, the need for detachment often contrasts with what soldiers actually experience on a day-to-day basis. Soldiers are far away from their families and experience isolation, loneliness, and sadness. They worry about themselves and wonder what will happen to those they love if they are killed. They also know that many marriages and other relationships do not survive the distance, time, and heartaches of deployment, and they may wonder about the solidity of their own marriage and other relationships. The boredom and monotony of war, along with the lack of personal space and privacy, are also extremely difficult for many servicemen. They interact with people on a daily basis who may or may not be friends or enemies. Mistrust therefore becomes a highly functional trait that increases the likelihood of survival. However, this lack of trust greatly affects their ability to feel a sense of connectedness and groundedness. In short, soldiers live in a world characterized by violence, stress, boredom, social disconnection, and fear.

While the conditions of warfare now may be somewhat different than those of the past, American men have always experienced the traumas of war. After World War II "the climate of postwar America did not favor communicating and sharing trauma and dislocation, in part because 'life disruption' was popularly believed to be the common condition. Everyone experienced this kind of disorder to some extent and felt compelled to reestablish a normal existence in family, work, and community. For many people impatiently trying to get on with their lives, the war and its human legacy became a repressed past. In this context, veterans learned to bury within their psyches the lingering stresses and emotions of war. The long-term costs of such behavioral inhibition result in a delay of working through war trauma" (Elder, Shanahan, and Clipp 1994:15).

The Current Context of Practice with American Soldiers and Veterans

Given the vast numbers of Americans currently engaged in combat, the majority of social workers practicing today will be involved in providing services to men who served during the wars in Iraq and Afghanistan. While many men will receive services from the Department of Veterans Affairs (to be discussed later in this chapter), many Iraq War veterans will be involved in health, mental health, and social service systems not affiliated with the military. In 2009, 140,000 American men were serving in Iraq. Over 200,000 others have served in Iraq—approximately the number of people living in Tacoma, Washington. Even social workers who do not directly provide services to these men will come into contact with the families of servicemen. It is likely that well over a million women, children, and men will be indirectly affected by the war, many of whom will need social work services of one kind or another.

Soldiers and veterans face many different types of mental health concerns and increased risk based on the compounding of various psychosocial risk factors. Soldiers and veterans are at an increased risk of depression, and, when combined with other psychosocial problems, this depression often has serious repercussions. The National Library of Medicine (2008) found that veterans, mostly men, who had been diagnosed with depression were 17 percent more likely to die than those who were not depressed. The study also found that depressed men had significantly more health problems than nondepressed veterans. It noted that in 2002 there were approximately 350 suicides among U.S. Army soldiers, but in 2007 the figure rose dramatically to 2,100. This increase is partly due to more accurate records, but that does not explain how the number increased by six times over a five-year period. In 2006 the army had a suicide rate of 17.5 per 100,000 soldiers compared to 9.9 per 100,000 civilians of the same age and gender.

Tanielian and Jaycox (2008) reported that 19–21 percent of soldiers who have returned from combat meet the criteria for posttraumatic stress disorder, depression, or anxiety. Of these men, 15–17 percent had symptoms of PTSD as early as three to twelve months after returning from combat. Veterans who were deployed for twelve months or more and experienced combat had the highest rates of PTSD.

The needs of these veterans are complex. PTSD and other mental health conditions may coexist with other problems, such as homelessness. Bernton (2008) conducted focus groups and community discussions in Seattle regarding the mental health needs of veterans. Bernton noted that the greater Seattle area has approximately 1,200 homeless veterans, and that many served in Iraq and Afghanistan and are in need of immediate mental health services that they cannot access. These issues would be manageable if treated quickly, but it was feared that they will go neglected. Without early detection and intervention, many of these men will develop long-term, compounding psychosocial problems. The longer a veteran with mental health disorders remains homeless, the more likely he will also remain unemployed, socially isolated, and at risk of developing significant health disorders. Without national efforts to reach these men, their problems will become increasingly difficult to treat.

Posttraumatic Stress Disorder

Posttraumatic stress disorder is one of the most prevalent and debilitating consequences of war for many soldiers. One study found that approximately 30 percent of Vietnam veterans experienced PTSD at some point after the war (Kulka et al. 1988). PTSD is an anxiety disorder caused by events that trigger intense responses of fear and horror (American Psychiatric Association 1994). Symptoms of PTSD include relationship problems, painful and recurring nightmares about the traumatic events, difficulty with controlling anger, impulsivity, and a numbing of other emotions. Prior to the identification and naming of PTSD, those who exhibited PTSD-type symptoms were often called "shell shocked" and were seen as weak and deficient in character. Prior to the creation of the diagnosis of PTSD, diagnosis was haphazard and treatments were few and ineffective.

Most research has demonstrated that while there certainly are risk factors that predispose someone to PTSD, the main cause of the disorder is the actual traumatic event (King et al. 1999). The diagnosis of PTSD increases the likelihood of several key psychosocial risks. For example, PTSD and reported experiences of atrocities are correlated with an elevated incidence of intimate partner violence (Taft et al. 2005).

The National Center for Post-Traumatic Stress Disorder (2006) lists six key points that family members of those experiencing PTSD should be aware. These serve as good, basic guidelines for social workers who need to understand the experiences of men with this disorder.

1. Stress reactions may interfere with a service member's ability to trust and be emotionally close to others. As a result, families may feel emotionally cut off from the service member.
2. A returning war veteran may feel irritable and have difficulty communicating, which may make it hard to get along with him or her.
3. A returning veteran may experience a loss of interest in family social activities.
4. Veterans with PTSD may lose interest in sex and feel distant from their spouses.
5. Traumatized war veterans often feel that something terrible may happen "out of the blue" and can become preoccupied with trying to keep themselves and family members safe.
6. Just as war veterans are often afraid to address what happened to them, family members are frequently fearful of examining the traumatic events as well. Family members may want to avoid talking about the trauma or related problems. They may avoid talking because they want to spare the survivor further pain or because they are afraid of his or her reaction.

Treating PTSD must be done holistically and ecologically. Currey (2007) suggests that medical practitioners are increasingly recognizing that interventions are needed that take into account multiple systems, including families, communities, care providers, and the military itself. This holistic approach seeks to include multidisciplinary teams of professionals that will attend to the various needs of veterans with PTSD. Social workers, acting as case managers, are at the center of this approach. Cognitive behavior therapy has been shown to be very useful in treating PTSD (Foa, Keanne, and Friedman 2000; Monson et al. 2006). CBT techniques are useful in treating PTSD by helping to control anxiety, rage, and impulsiveness and by helping to restructure belief systems that have been changed by the soldiers' reactions to the traumatic events (Foy 1992).

Physical Health Problems

While veterans face the same physical health problems that confront all men, many also have additional health problems stemming from their combat experiences. Studies have found, for example, that veterans of the Gulf War experience two to three times the amount of health-related symptoms as do other men (U.S. Department of Veterans Affairs 2003a). Combat soldiers are exposed to numerous environmental toxins and hazards that predispose them to a multitude of physical health conditions (U.S. Department of Veterans Affairs 2002). Some of these problems have received significant public attention. For instance, the health concerns of veterans exposed to Agent Orange during the Vietnam War have often been grave. Agent Orange, an herbicide used for deforestation and crop destruction during the war, contains a powerful toxin called dioxin (U.S. Department of Veteran's Affairs 2003b). Veterans advocacy groups believe that over forty different cancers and serious diseases are associated with this and other herbicides to which Vietnam veterans were exposed.

Traumatic brain injury (TBI) has recently been identified as a serious problem for veterans returning from Iraq and Afghanistan. TBI is not a new disorder, as it has long been recognized as a serious medical problem. According to the Centers for Disease Control (2006), a TBI is defined as a blow or jolt to the head or a penetrating head injury that disrupts the function of the brain. Not all blows or jolts to the head result in a TBI. The severity of such an injury may range from "mild," that is, a brief change in mental status or consciousness, to "severe," or an extended period of unconsciousness. Four million people sustain traumatic brain injuries each year. Men are two and a half times more likely to receive a TBI than women. Historically, TBIs have been caused by assaults, traffic accidents, and falls. As such, much of what pertains to TBIs in this section is relevant for practice with men who have not served in the military as well veterans (Langlois, Rutland-Brown, and Thomas 2006).

TBIs are often difficult to assess. Veterans returning home are currently not given a comprehensive screening to detect TBIs and other problems. Additionally, many of the symptoms of TBIs are common to other disorders. Some of these symptoms, such as difficulty with concentration, anger and impulse control, and depression, are often viewed from a psychological perspective. As such, TBI may also be misdiagnosed, or occur concurrently, with PTSD. Traumatic brain injury changes one's view of oneself. TBI often causes mild to severe physical, functional, and mental health disabilities. At times TBI leads to increased dependence on others. Dependence is difficult for many men, in particular for men returning from war. A warrior is supposed to be strong, independent, logical, and decisive. TBI often adversely affects these traits.

Hogan (1999:22) explores the relationship between disability and the hegemonic ideal: "Dominant cultural stories, from which all of us as individuals draw material for our individual stories, emphasize control, success, independence, physical prowess or beauty, speed, and other qualities that may seem lost or diminished after injury. Disabilities are viewed negatively, neurological injuries are not well understood even as a disability, and neurological disabilities often compromise people's abilities to communicate their experience."

Narrative therapy has been used with men suffering from brain injuries. Hogan (1999:21) explores the complex psychosocial factors that may often impede treatment of the physical impact of TBI: "Psychological and communication barriers often impede progress in rehabilitation after brain injury. Brain injuries may involve mental and physical limitations that occasion pain, anger, and sadness combined with decreased ability to communicate such emotions in ways that make it possible for other people to empathize and understand."

Narrative work can be valuable as a means of helping men come to terms with the impact of TBIs and other injuries. Narrative work may provide two different but equally important outcomes. First, it may help with the reconstruction of identity. Men need to learn how to revision themselves and their lives within the context of a new set of abilities, disabilities, and possibilities. Second, it may provide increased cognitive stimulation, which may help with recovery from the injury. More research on the effects of this and other psychologically based treatments of physical disorders is warranted. As previously noted, TBIs not only affect veterans but are a significant health risk for many men. For instance, Native American men are more than twice as likely as other men to suffer TBIs (Nelson et al. 2007) and should be carefully assessed for potential symptoms.

The U.S. Department of Veteran Affairs

The Department of Veterans Affairs (VA) is the most important provider of health and mental health services to former servicemen and women. Understanding the role and services that the VA provides is essential for social workers who will be working with veterans. The VA providers care for over five million veterans and their families (Congressional Budget Office 2007), with a variety of inpatient, outpatient, residential, and rehabilitative services. Historically, the VA provided care only for veterans (and their families) with service-connected disabilities, who were assigned priority rankings (1–8) that correspond to the level of their service-connected injury or disability. Now, however, the VA is open to all veterans and is frequently used by low-income veterans as a health care safety net. Not all veterans enroll, though, and many live too far VA hospitals and clinics to take advantage of the health care services they provide.

The VA is one of the largest providers of social work services in the United States and offers many employment and training opportunities for social workers. As of 2001, nearly four thousand social workers were employed by the VA (U.S. Department of Veterans Affairs 2007b).

Numerous social workers have received excellent training from the VA. I myself did my second-year MSW field placement at the VA medical center in Coatesville, Pennsylvania. During my internship I received outstanding individual and group supervision and went to many workshops and lectures. Assigned to an inpatient substance abuse treatment domiciliary, I was involved in all aspects of treatment. I provided individual therapy and group therapy and facilitated psychoeducational groups. I conducted intake assessments, engaged in case management, and developed discharge plans. I would strongly encourage social workers who have a desire to work with veterans, or who wish to gain experience with men in general, to consider the VA for training and employment.

The mission statement of the Miami VA Medical Center Social Work Service provides a sense of the aims and goals the VA has for veterans, and how social workers can meet these aims (Miami VA Healthcare System 2006): "The mission of Social Work Service at the Miami VA Medical Center is to provide all eligible veterans and their families with high quality psychosocial services that maximize community adjustment and social functioning. Social Work's holistic approach assists the Medical Center in providing timely and cost effective services focused on enhancing customer satisfaction. To accomplish our mission, social work is committed to:

- Working collaboratively with other disciplines as an integral part of the health care team
- Psychosocial assessments and treatment
- Providing comprehensive case management
- Providing patient and family education to enhance wellness
- Developing and coordinating VA and community resources and community partnering
- Identifying and engaging potential customers through community outreach

- Promoting staff development and training
- Participating in research and program evaluation
- Providing graduate training to social work interns through academic affiliates"

Secondary Traumatic Stress

Working with at-risk populations demands a great deal of emotional and physical energy. Social work is a demanding profession, and those working with clients with complex psychosocial concerns must develop their own healthy coping mechanisms. This is especially true for social workers who work with clients who have experienced trauma. Studies have found that social workers who work with those who have been traumatized may themselves be revictimized by the trauma (Bride et al. 2004). The name for this syndrome is Secondary Traumatic Stress (Figley 1999). Researchers have become increasingly aware of the effect that acute trauma, also referred to as Compassion Fatigue, has on helping professionals (Figley 2002). Symptoms of secondary traumatic stress closely mirror those of PTSD that were discussed previously.

Social workers who provide services to veterans and other traumatized populations must make sure they take good care of themselves. This is especially true for those who have been victims of trauma themselves. Secondary traumatic stress reactions are more common in those who have been exposed to trauma in the past (Rudolph, Stamm, and Stamm 1997). Prevention requires a holistic, biopsychosocial approach. Taking care of yourself physically, including proper diet and exercise, helps prepare the body for handling stress. Having a support system, including supervision and colleagues to discuss stressful work events with, is also valuable. It is important for social workers to communicate their needs to colleagues and ask for help. Relaxation techniques, such as meditation, should be utilized frequently to prevent emotional overload. It is essential that they learn to leave their work at work. All social workers must develop good boundaries around their work and personal life; this is especially true for those working with traumatized populations.

Social workers who work with traumatized populations or within contexts where trauma and loss are common are encouraged to use a self-assessment instrument to periodically assess themselves. The Compassion Fatigue Self-Test is one extremely valid and reliable measure (Figley and Stamm 1996). For social workers who find that they suffer from compassion fatigue, are overly involved in the lives of their clients, or know that they are experiencing "burn-out," seeking professional help is important. Social workers who are able to seek out and utilize the resources and services that they need will in all likelihood be increasingly empathetic to their clients and better able to provide services to men at risk. The cases that follow provide detail on how the strengths perspective, CBT, and existential theory apply to work with veterans.

Case Example

Keith Mitchell is a 31-year-old veteran from the first Gulf War. Keith was born and raised in Grand Rapids, Michigan, where he returned after the war. Keith did not see significant action during his time in the war but was emotionally impacted by the war in a significant way. As an infantry solder, Keith saw several dead Iraqi bodies. One in particular haunted him. He believed that the eyes of the dead solder were watching him. This was an image that would stay with him for many years. When Keith returned home, he found out that his wife had been having an affair. She stopped seeing the man, but their already shaky marriage began to deteriorate. Married for only two years married, Keith and his wife were not able to maintain their positive relationship given the difficulties brought on by separation, war, and an affair. While Keith did not admit it to his wife during the divorce, he had several one-night stands during their short relationship.

Shortly after his divorce, Keith was drinking with friends at a local bar when he met Mary, a local woman whom he had seen around town. They spent the night together and moved in with each other within several days. From the beginning, their relationship was filled with trauma and chaos. While Keith often complained about the erratic behavior of his new girlfriend, he also realized that her constant crises were comforting to him: they reminded him of the war. Since he had been home, Keith had found it very difficulty to relax. He would become very unsettled during quiet moments and found himself listening to the television or stereo at very loud volumes.

About two months after Keith moved in with Mary, he met a women at the supermarket. Later that night, Keith had sex with this woman in the back of his car. The day after Keith cheated on his girlfriend, he immediately told her of his affair. She slapped him in the face and told him to leave immediately. Keith complied. He grabbed a few of his belongings and left.

The following day his girlfriend, remembering that the manager of the bar where Keith worked had spoken to him about rumors of his stealing money, called and informed the manager that Keith told her he was indeed stealing money. When Keith reported to work the next day, Keith's manager fired him. Even though it was not true, Keith quietly left.

Without a job, a place to live, or his primary relationships, Keith began to feel increasingly anxious and depressed. Three days later he walked in front of a moving car on the highway. The car swerved and grazed Keith but still threw him off the highway. An ambulance was called, and Keith was taken to the hospital. He had a broken leg and numerous cuts on his face and arm. When the social worker met with Keith, Keith admitted to attempting to kill himself. The social worker informed the medical personnel, who decided to keep Keith in the intensive care unit for the night so he could be monitored physically and psychiatrically. The social worker met with Keith again and conducted a full psychosocial history. She found that Keith had been treated for both anxiety and depression for several years prior to his military service but had not received any therapy or medication during his enlisted time. As with many other enlisted men, Keith was afraid to admit to his mental health concerns to army personnel.

The following day the social worker returned to see how Keith was doing. He seemed less open and more distant. She wondered to herself if Keith was feeling vulnerable about having admitted some of his struggles to her; she understands that stoicism can often be a defensive reaction for men. She also wondered if some of Keith's issues about feeling abandoned by his girlfriend were impacting his current feelings toward her, his female social worker.

She tried to normalize the difficulty of talking to a social worker, especially after an event such as the one that transpired. She said that her goal was to provide the support that Keith needed, and she was open to helping him figure that out if he was unclear. She said that since different people had different needs, she would listen to him when he was ready.

FOR WRITING AND REFLECTION

1. Placing yourself in the social worker's shoes, how would you intervene with Keith?

2. Were you to see Keith for followup care, what services might you suggest to him?

3. If you were seeing Keith for long-term therapy, which of the four theories discussed in this book would you use (or what combination of them)? Why?

4. How do you explain Keith's nonmonogamous behavior? What are the treatment implications, if any?

Case Example

Jed Tucker is a 22-year-old man who recently received an honorable discharge from the army. Jed served for one year in Iraq, during which time he participated in significant combat. Jed was significantly injured when the armored car he was driving was struck by a roadside bomb. Jed's arm was severed by shrapnel, and he sustained a significant facial burn and internal injuries. When Jed was stabilized, he was taken to a military hospital in Germany for rehabilitation.

During Jed's time in the hospital, he became extremely anxious and depressed. Jed always had a difficult time sitting still; he was diagnosed as having Attention Deficient/Hyperactivity Disorder as a child. Consequently, he always struggled with school. Jed had hoped that he would have a lifelong career in the military. Now, facing discharge, Jed did not know what he was going to do. In addition to the loss of meaning that Jed was experiencing from the loss of his military career, Jed faced the adjustment to life with a disability. In addition to having lost his arm, Jed sustained significant stomach and bowel damage and will have to use a colostomy bag for the rest of his life. These two new challenges powerfully affected his sense of self as a man. Jed's main sources of self-esteem had all been connected to his body. He was very successful in sports during high school. He also was accomplished in martial arts and received accolades for this skill in the army. Jed also is an attractive man, who was known to have a body that was attractive to many women. Jed lost fifty pounds of muscle during his year of convalescence and did not recognize his own body. Now he experiences the decline in his physical abilities and functioning as an attack on his sense of being a worthwhile human being.

For the first six months of his treatment, Jed refused to talk to his doctors or hospital mental health staff about his feelings. He accepted medication for depression since he saw it as his duty to take medical orders. However, he felt that he did not have to talk about his personal problems. Jed felt ashamed and embarrassed to talk about his feelings. This second layer of shame complicated the already powerful feelings of shame that he was experiencing about his being "turned into a fucking gimp."

When Jed moved back home with his parents, his father, Sam, noticed a marked change in his son. No longer did he see a confident, hopeful young man, but a tortured and defeated man who looked far older than he was. Sam and Jed had a heart-to-heart talk in which Jed broke down in tears. This was the first time that Sam had ever seen Jed cry, and in fact it was the first time Jed had actually shed tears since his dog died nearly ten years before.

Jed agreed to ask his physical therapist at the VA center, Cal, for a referral to see one of the social workers. Knowing how resistant Jed has been to therapy, Cal picked up the phone and immediately called the outpatient counseling center. Cal asked if Andrew, a social worker whom he often works with, was available. Andrew has been a social worker associated with the VA for over twenty-five years. Cal likes to refer young men to Andrew because of his fatherly manner combined with a patient, nonthreatening, nonjudgmental approach. A gentle and small man, he exudes a strong sense of masculinity and power. Andrew is also a paraplegic, having lost his legs in a boating accident twenty years ago. Andrew is a man who is comfortable with his own limitations and his own masculinity and has a clear sense of mission and purpose in life.

Andrew used cognitive behavioral methods to help Cal deal with some of his PTSD-related symptoms. Andrew was very reluctant to talk about some of his war experiences and attempted to minimize the impact they had upon him. However, he had some classic systems of PTSD that were compounded by his other problems. Unwilling to directly address his experiences at first, Andrew decided that he would work on cognitive behavioral skill building that did not require direct exploration of what happened to Cal during combat. Cal agreed to have Andrew teach him a relaxation technique to help him relax and clear his mind. Andrew used a method that has been used frequently by cognitive behavioral practitioners and has roots in yogic practice. He had Cal relax in a chair with his eyes closed. He asked Cal to try to sit quietly and focus for a moment or two on his breath. He told him not to control his breathing, but just to pay attention to his breath as it left and then came back into his body. He then asked Cal to imagine that when he breathed in, relaxing energy was entering his body, and when he breathed out, stress and tension were leaving him. Andrew had Cal engage in this exercise for several minutes. When Andrew noticed that Cal became agitated, he asked him to open his eyes. He asked Cal how this felt, and he said that he felt relaxed, but that it was difficult to sit still for so long. Andrew praised Cal for his efforts and informed him that it often took months of practice to learn to relax. He stressed that one of the reasons that people often fail to learn and continue to use these methods is that they fail to appreciate how difficult it is to change their patterns and to become more relaxed.

The next time they worked together, Andrew had Cal engage in the same experience. After a couple of minutes, he taught Cal the second part of the exercise. Andrew instructed Cal to tighten and then relax each muscle group of his body. During the following session, he had Cal engage in the same sequence but then return to following his breath after the phase of progressive muscular relaxation.

Over the course of several months, Andrew had Cal practice this relaxation method at the beginning of each session and asked him to practice the technique outside his session, twice a week for five minutes. He gave Cal a chart to track how often he used the exercise. After approximately four months, Cal was able to do the relaxation exercise for fifteen minutes and was doing it at least four times a day at home. Andrew's consistent and graduated approach allowed Cal to integrate the technique into his life; it became a habit that Cal wanted to engage in, not something that he "had to do." Over time, Cal experienced increased periods without anxiety and hypervigilance. He began to feel accustomed to feeling relaxed and actively sought out the experience. The technique also made Cal more aware of how his body holds stress, and how he could listen to his body to learn about his moods. He began to pay attention to stress building in his body and to proactively use the relaxation technique and others skills he learned in therapy in a preventative manner.

FOR WRITING AND REFLECTION

Choosing one of the other cases in this book, adapt the methods that Andrew used with Cal for that client. Discuss how the process would be different. Explore what other techniques you can use to add to the overall effectiveness of the treatment process.

The Physical Health of Men | NINE

Perhaps the best metaphor for men's relationships with their bodies is the tie. Placed around the neck, the tie metaphorically (and in some ways literally) separates the head from the body. Breathing, the mind's way of regulating and paying attention to the body, is constricted, functionally separating the mind and the body. In many ways, the modern American man is disconnected from his body and from his physical health. Many of the values of hegemonic masculinity, including bravery, tolerance of pain, rugged individualism, and detachment from emotions and feelings, interfere with men's ability to maintain good health. For instance, being willing to tolerate pain and being brave and stoic lead men to underreport disease symptoms until illnesses reach acute states. Many disease processes that could be treated relatively easily become deadly as men "grit and bear" their symptoms, ignoring the signals their bodies are giving them. Some men are so disconnected from their bodies that they are not aware of signs of danger. Mahalik, Lagan, and Morrison (2006:192) explain that "one potential explanation of why men have less healthy lifestyles is that males are socialized to adopt masculine ideals that may put their health at risk. A gender role socialization framework posits that males are reinforced for adopting behaviors and attitudes consistent with traditional masculine norms (e.g., risk taking, self-reliance, and emotional control) and punished or shamed when they do not conform to traditional masculine norms."

This is made worse by men's reluctance to see doctors for wellness check-ups and routine physicals. This chapter looks at men's health and what social workers can do to help facilitate better health for men. I present aspects of the theories of health seeking, and the relationship between masculine values and ideals and health. I also discuss some of the most important health problems that men face. I explore why social workers may be reluctant to talk to men about their physical health and suggest strategies for engaging men in these conversations. Some social workers might even question why they need to understanding issues related to health. After all, isn't health the realm of other professions? If it were only that easy. As noted in previous chapters, psychosocial factors play an important role in biophysical processes. Hafen et al. (1996:12) ask: "Can emotions—the way we think, the way we feel—really be responsible, at least in part, for disease? A growing body of evidence indicates that they can. Some researchers in the field believe that as many has half of all patients who visit physicians have physical symptoms that are directly caused by emotions; other believe that the figure is as high as 90 to 95 percent. That's not to say that the symptoms are imaginary; it's just to say that their root is primarily mental more than organically physical."

In addition to these issues, this chapter highlights popular erroneous assumptions about men's health and disease. For example, some diseases that are typically considered "women's diseases" also infect many men. For example, two million men in the United States have osteoporosis (Jones 2004). While this is only one quarter the number of women who have the disease, men are less likely to be diagnosed and treated for this disease, placing them at high risk of complications, and perhaps leading to an underreporting of its incidence in men.

The chapter concludes with practice suggestions for helping men achieve better health.

Men, Masculinity, and Health

Many men are in extremely poor health. Poor lifestyle habits, an unwillingness to seek preventative and ameliorative treatment, feelings of invincibility, and general neglect for their well-being has lead to an increase in health problems for men. Heart disease, stroke, diabetes, cancer, and many other physical health conditions have become daily realities in the lives of millions of men.

Life expectancy is widely recognized as the best indicator of the overall health of groups or populations. While the life expectancy of men improved greatly during the twentieth century, the life expectancy gap between men and women has increased markedly (Centers for Disease Control 2004). It is ironic and paradoxical that as life expectancy has improved over the last century, the day-to-day health of many men has not. The greater life expectancy for both men and women has been attributed to improvements in biomedical technology, increased access to health care, preventative services, better nutrition, and healthier behavior. Men have benefited from some of these advances, yet less so from improved knowledge about self-care and prevention.

The widening male-female gap in life expectancy has several causes. Men engage in disproportionately more unhealthy behaviors and are less likely to engage in health-promoting activities (Courtenay 2000). Studies have shown that men go for routine physicals far less often than do women, and when they do go, they receive preventative health care advice from physicians far less frequently (Roter and Hall 1997). Men are less likely to ask about their bodies and their needs. They tend to see health in a highly mechanistic way: find the problem and replace the broken parts. When men visit doctors, they tend to report only symptoms they are currently experiencing, not other important information that could be valuable for preventing future disease.

Bravery and invincibility are hegemonic masculine values that have powerful effects on men's health-seeking behavior. These values, as lived personality traits, can be highly adaptive in certain situations. As previously noted, bravery is an essential trait for rescue workers trying to save victims of natural disasters. Feeling invincible and tuning out fear can actually increase the likelihood of survival in such acute, dangerous situations. However, the same feelings of invincibility do not support good self-care and health-maintenance practices. By not paying attention to their own mortality, many men neglect their physical health. From a CBT perspective, men can be viewed as holding irrational beliefs about their own health care and well-being. They irrationally believe that illnesses will not happen to them, and they frequently overestimate their well-being. It is not uncommon, for instance, for a man to overestimate the amount of exercise he is actually engaging in during the course of a week. From an existential perspective, men can be seen as engaging in "bad faith" by not being fully aware of the nature of their mortality and ultimate death. This denial of death is a powerful mechanism that inhibits men's health, and one that practitioners must thoroughly yet sensitively explore.

The Diseases of Men

Men have higher rates of mortality from the top ten leading causes of death than do women (U.S. Department of Health and Human Services 2006a).

According to the Centers for Disease Control, 28.4 percent of men's deaths are from heart disease, while 24.1 percent are from cancer (CDC 2002). Unintentional injuries make up 5.8 percent of men's deaths, followed by chronic respiratory disease, at 5.1 percent.

The *Harvard Medical School Guide to Men's Health* (Simon 2002) gives considerable attention to the three leading killers of American men: coronary artery disease, stroke, and cancer. This section describes the nature of these three diseases, but the behavioral and lifestyle solutions to these problems are addressed in the following section. This is because many of the problems related to men's physical health often have the same behavioral risk factors and solutions.

Coronary Artery Disease/Heart Disease

Coronary artery and heart disease is the number one killer of men. Coronary artery disease is characterized by a buildup of fatty tissues (called plaque) that blocks the normal flow of blood to the heart. The technical term for this phenomenon is arteriosclerosis. As arteries become clogged and flow is severely restricted, the heart does not receive enough oxygen—this is referred to as angina. When blood flow is completely blocked from an area of the heart, a heart attack occurs. In essence, a heart attack becomes the process of rapid muscular death of the heart. Without quick intervention, serious damage to the heart, and often death, will occur (National Heart, Lung, and Blood Institute 2008).

Smoking, high blood pressure, poor diet, and diabetes are particularly powerful risk factors in heart disease. Obesity is also considered a significant risk factor, and lack of exercise can compound or worsen all the risk factors. A family history of heart disease also predisposes men for increased risk. Stress and anger are psychosocial risk factors that are also considered to increase the likelihood or severity of coronary problems (Mayo Clinic 2006).

Stroke

Stoke is a form of cardiovascular disease that affects the blood vessels in the brain. Basically, a stroke occurs when a blood vessel in the brain bursts or when blood flow to the brain is inhibited, thereby causing damage to the brain. Technically there are two types of stroke. The first is called ischemic stroke and is a form of arteriosclerosis, where fatty tissues build up in the brain and cause obstructions. According to the American Stroke Association (2007), over 80 percent of strokes are of this variety. The other type of stroke is called hemorrhagic stroke. This type occurs when a weakened blood vessel leaks into the brain. Each type of stroke is broken down into subclassifications that refer to more specific types of dysfunction and disease processes. The brain is the most complex organ in the body, and strokes can create a complex constellation of symptoms and problems, including problems with speech, difficulties with muscular coordination, confusion or memory loss, perceptual difficulties, dizziness, and numbness or weakness of the face, arms, or legs, often on one side of the body. Heart disease and stroke have largely the same risk factors.

Cancer

Cancer is a highly misunderstood constellation of diseases. When people hear that someone has cancer, they often believe that the person is going to die. However, over the last two decades, as cancer treatments have become increasingly sophisticated, the majority of people who are diagnosed with cancer survive and recover to live normal lives.

Cancer occurs when cells grow out of control and attack normal body tissues. Cancers may spread throughout the body, a process known as metastasis. The specific cancer is named based on its place origin, not where it spreads to. For instance, lung cancer that spreads to the lymph nodes is referred to as metastatic lung cancer, not cancer of the lymph nodes.

Cancer is caused by damage or mutations to DNA. DNA may be likened to messengers that send instructions to cells about how to grow and behave. Cells often are damaged but have the ability to repair mutations in their DNA. When cells lose this ability because mutations occur, they may grow into cancerous tumors. While this may suggest that these processes are beyond a man's control, this is hardly the case.

The principles for all this are pretty straightforward: certain environmental and lifestyle activities are known to increase the chances of contracting cancer, and staying away from them markedly decreases such chances. The person who eats right, exercises properly, stays out of the sun, does not smoke, and does not have a family history that includes cancers has a relatively small chance of contracting most kinds of cancers (Ehlers and Miller 2002).

Cancer is a significant problem for men. The American Heart Association (2006) notes that half of all men, compared to one-third of women, will develop cancer at some point in their lives. According to the Centers for Disease Control (2006) the most common cancer among men is prostate cancer, at 140 cases per 100,000 men, followed by lung cancer and colorectal cancer. The leading cause of cancer deaths for men is lung cancer, followed by prostate cancer, colorectal cancer, and liver cancer. Incidence varies by race. For instance, overall cancer rates are highest among African Americans (611.0, 11 per 100,000), followed by whites (530.9), Hispanics (421.1), Asians/ Pacific Islanders (329.3), and American Indians/Alaska Natives (307.4). African Americans and whites are twice as likely to have lung cancer as Latinos, Asian Americans, or Native Americans, yet lung cancer remains the number one cause of cancer deaths across races. African Americans are twice as likely to die from prostate cancer as are men of other races.

Prostatectomy (the removal of the prostate gland) is the treatment that offers the best chance of survival for prostate cancer. Unfortunately, up to 90 percent of men who have prostatectomies become impotent. The use of medication, discussed below, has been shown to be effective in treating ED (Coleman 1998). However, as male identity is often constructed around a man's ability to perform intercourse, potentially complex and powerful emotional consequences can accompany prostatectomies (Oliffe 2005). It is therefore important for social workers and other health care professionals to carefully assess men who have been treated for prostate cancer for depression and other mental health concerns.

The earlier that most cancers are detected, the more likely that treatment will be successful (Cason 2008). Once a cancer metastasizes, treatment becomes far more difficult and complicated. Early diagnosis of cancer is predicated on two important factors, neither of which many men are good at. One is knowing one's body and being conscious of changes in it. This includes a regimen of self-examinations, for example, inspecting one's testicles for the presence of lumps. Second, frequent wellness examinations by a physician are essential to the prevention and early diagnosis of cancer, as they are for many other diseases.

Sexually Transmitted Diseases/HIV/AIDS

Sexually transmitted diseases (STDs) are infections that are transmitted through sexual contact, including oral, anal, and vaginal sex. The most common STDs are gonorrhea, chlamydia, syphilis, and HIV/AIDs. While HIV/ AIDS is also transmitted through intravenous drug use, it is important for men to remember that it is a sexually transmitted disease. STDs, like many of the topics explored in this section, are complex. As such, this discussion highlights only some of the most basic issues and concerns.

Gonorrhea and syphilis are more common in men, while chlamydia is more common in women. In 2006 more than 250,000 men contracted chlamydia, and nearly 180,000 gonorrhea. Over 8,000 men contracted syphilis (Centers for Disease Control 2007). Each of these diseases is now curable. At one point, syphilis was a deadly disease. Now it is easily treated with antibiotics, if it is detected. Without treatment, it can lead to a deterioration of the nervous system and death.

Different STDs have different implications for men's health and present different issues in regard to their identification and prevention. Many men still view HIV/AIDS as being transmitted only through gay sex. As such, homophobia prevents many men from taking appropriate precautions to prevent sexually transmitted diseases. However, it is possible for men to receive the HIV virus from heterosexual oral or vaginal sex. While the risks of spreading HIV/AIDS from oral sex may be smaller than from intercourse, risks still do exist.

While abstinence is the most effective way of preventing an STD, this is often not an option that fits with many men's value systems and desires. As such, it is important to help men make good choices about safer sexual behaviors. When used correctly, condoms are an effective means of reducing the likelihood of contracting or spreading sexually transmitted diseases. Condoms have not been shown to be 100% effective and must be used properly for risks to be reduced. It is often difficult for social workers, especially women, to ask their male clients about condom use. However, it is essential that practitioners begin to feel comfortable with this skill. The second exercise at the end of this chapter provides ideas on how to explore condom use with men.

Some of the characteristics of hegemonic masculinity make men susceptible to contacting STDs (Bowleg 2004). Men who view women as something to conquer, and sex as proof of masculinity, are more likely to engage in risky sex. Men's propensity toward feeling invincible regarding their health also make it less likely that they will practice safe sex. It is important when working with men to develop programs that use masculine concepts in the service of safe sex. For instance, in Brazil, lifestyle marketing campaigns that link safe sex practices with masculine images and notions of responsibility with machismo have been found to be successful in changing young men's views about safe sex practices (Guerriero 2002).

Erectile Dysfunction

Erectile dysfunction, the inability to sustain an erection during sex sufficient to complete intercourse or until satisfaction, has become increasingly recognized as both a medical and a psychosocial concern. Approximately 10 percent of healthy adult males age 55 have been shown to experience ED (Montorsi et al. 2003). By age 65, 25 percent of men have ED, increasing to more than 50 percent by age 75. As men become healthier in older adulthood and are living progressively more active lives, ED may be increasingly perceived as a significant limitation. Historically thought to be a purely psychological problem, ED is now known to often occur due to physical aliments or from the side effects of medication (such as some blood pressure medications). Psychosocial concerns can also lead to ED, such as stress, anxiety, pressure, problems in a key social domain (like family or work), or depression. Even when not caused by psychological factors, ED can pose powerful psychosocial consequences. Men with ED can develop feelings of inadequacy and low self-worth and can become depressed (Seidman et al. 2001). For men, potency and identity are closely connected with sexuality—not only a man's very sense of masculinity and self, but specifically his ability to perform penetration until climax. As Oliffe (2005:2250) observed, "Men who are unable to perform sexually are affected in deeply gendered ways, and embody marginalized, subordinated forms of masculinity that result in humiliation and despair."

Helping men explore their ED is therefore essential to their well-being. It is important to help normalize ED for men, and to encourage them to see their doctors in order to rule out medical problems. Exploring with men how their ED is affecting them is a difficult but important task for social workers and other health care providers to perform. Social workers should be prepared to contend with potential resistance, or with the intensity of an open exploration. It is useful to help men explore options for healthy sexuality that do not start and end with penetrative sex (Potts 2000). Suggesting that there are alternative ways of being sexually satisfied runs counter to the model of sexuality that men learn as boys. However, this model may not always serve them or their partners, who may wish for alternative models of physical intimacy.

A double-blind, placebo-controlled study by Althof et al. (2006) found that the use of Sildenafil (Viagra) for men with ED significantly improved not only sexual satisfaction in men, but self-esteem, confidence, relationship satisfaction, and overall well-being. The results were true across age cohorts in Mexico, Brazil, Australia, and Japan.

Additionally, many men seem to be taking drugs intended for erectile dysfunction to increase their capacity for sexual performance. Men who do not meet the classification of the disorder, but who wish to increase the number or duration of their erections, are using ED medications. This practice is controversial, as the long-term health effects of ED medications are not known; more research in this area is indicated.

Behavioral Strengths and Risks

This section looks at some of the significant risk factors that contribute to the health problems discussed in this chapter.

Smoking

According to the CDC, in 2003 some 23 percent of men smoked, compared with 19 percent of women (CDC 2004). Smoking is an important risk factor in numerous fatal conditions. In fact, the evidence against smoking is so clear, it can be said to actually cause, not merely contribute to, lung cancer, inflammatory lung diseases such as bronchitis, and the deadly disease emphysema. In fact, smoking contributes to 90 percent of the incidences of lung cancer in men (Inlander 1998). Smoking also increases the risk for heart disease, hardening of the arteries, and other cardiovascular problems. Nicotine, the most potent and prevalent of the many psychoactive substances contained in cigarettes, is a psychomotor stimulant that can increase stress. Also, since smoking reduces lung capacity and negatively affects health, it may be an important factor in hindering men's motivation to exercise.

Exercise

Most men are not taking care of their bodies. Moderate to vigorous exercise thirty minutes a day improves health. Most men are nowhere near achieving this goal. CDC statistics show that less than 12 percent of men engage in vigorous physical activity lasting more than ten minutes five times a week. Over half the men in the United States report that they never engage in vigorous physical exercise (CDC 2004).

Prevailing attitudes about exercise, health, and body image do not encourage a balanced view of exercise. Many men take an all-or-nothing approach, where they will exercise obsessively or not at all. Exercise is often seen only as something that can make the body look better. Men should be encouraged to integrate exercise into a healthy lifestyle. For instance, walking has been shown to be extremely valuable as a means of increasing overall health (Boarnet, Greenwald, and McMillan 2008), yet men often do not view it as exercise. What is important is that men begin to exercise and find exercise that they will continue with. Exercising at least thirty minutes a day, nearly every day, should be a goal, not a starting point. For sedentary men, beginning any exercise should be seen as an important step toward health. Walking up the stairs and taking walks during work breaks can be a good place to start. It is also important that men see their doctors before they begin an exercise regimen.

Diet

Diet is a significant risk or protective factor that contributes to many of the health risks of men, and it is often an important intervention in their prevention and resolution. Diet is also a risk factor in another risk factor, obesity. Like many health issues, diet is a difficult topic for social workers to address. Some may feel that it is outside their realm of responsibility. Others may question their capacity to provide good information, especially since so much conflicting advice about dieting seems to exist. However, there are some very basic dietary principles that are almost common sense, which could lead to significant change. For instance, a man who reports eating fast-food hamburgers, fries, and a diet soft drink every day for lunch is consuming very unhealthy food for at least a third of his meals per week. If the same man reports financial difficulties and is spending $7 per day on lunch and another $4 on donuts, coffee, and soft drinks for snacks, he is spending nearly $250 a month on unhealthy eating. His eating habits may be implicated in both his financial and physical health. If weight gain as a consequence of this habit is effecting how he feels about himself, his eating habits may have implications for each of his life domains. Over 40 percent of men report body mass index (BMI) scores in the overweight range, and nearly 23 percent have BMI scores that indicate obesity. Only 30 percent of men have BMI scores in the healthy range. A healthy diet and exercise are key factors in controlling weight (Payne 2006).

Researchers at the Harvard School of Public Health have created a new, modified food pyramid based upon the recent nutritional research (Willett 2005). The base of their pyramid, the foundation of their plan, is exercise. By stressing the importance of exercise in any eating plan, the healthy food pyramid promotes a holistic, integrated approach to food and wellness. The next level the pyramid, which should make up the largest selection of one's eating, comprises fruits and vegetables, healthy fats and oils, and whole grains. This is followed by nuts, seeds, beans, tofu, fish, poultry, and eggs. The next level consists of dairy, such as milk, cheese, and yogurt, of which one or two daily servings is recommended. At the top of the pyramid are red meats, butter, sugar, refined grains and starches, potatoes, and salt. These items should be eaten sparingly. Harvard researchers also suggest that counting grams of fat or other nutrients is not productive—the key is to eat good, healthy foods until you are satisfied. They view taking a multivitamin, and alcohol in moderation for those who can safely consume it, as valuable additions.

THE HEALTHY EATING PYRAMID

Department of Nutrition, Harvard School of Public Health

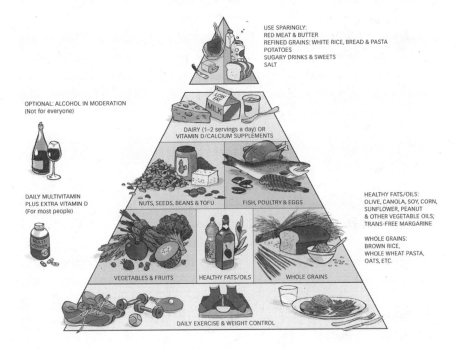

Figure 9.1. The healthy eating pyramid (Department of Nutrition, Harvard School of Public Health). © 2008 President and Fellows of Harvard College. Source: Adapted from *Eat, Drink, and Be Healthy* by Walter C. Willett, M.D., and Patrick J. Skerrett New York: Free Press/Simon & Schuster, 2005.

Stress

Stress is a ubiquitous part of modern life. Stress is also associated with health problems, such as heart disease, hypertension, obesity, and many other conditions, and therefore is a significant health risk (Lovallo 2005). Modern men work more and more and face increasing economic and family pressures. Men experience increasing stress as psychosocial pressures increase. The more pressures and demands that are experienced, the more likely they are to negatively experience these pressures. This is particularly true for men from historically disadvantaged groups who must deal with multiple stressors, including significant institutional barriers. For instance, an undocumented Mexican construction worker may face the daily stress of fear of deportation, survival in a country in which he is unfamiliar with the language, rules, and norms, accessing health care when he is sick, and the burden of sending money to family still in Mexico.

Our other lifestyle patterns and habits do not insulate us from feeling stress. Many men have little time to relax and do not know how to do so when they do have the time. While some stress does help motivate us, men must learn to reduce the external sources of stress in their life, when possible, and find ways of increasing their coping strategies.

Practice Guidelines

Men's views of heath prevention and maintenance are extremely important for social workers to consider. Beliefs such as autonomy, independence, and invincibility as well as many men's sense of being disconnected from their own bodies are important to consider when devising strategies to help men improve their health.

Since autonomy and control are extremely important to many men, it is important for practitioners to emphasize the role that individual and personal choice has in the development of good health practices. Rarely should social workers and other professionals present only one option to men. It is best to present men with multiple options for their treatment and health prevention, and to present facts and statistics about the efficacy of these approaches. While men may often choose health and treatment options based on their values, they also frequently respond to evidence-based options. Again, professionals should make sure that a man knows that treatment decisions are his to make.

Blood pressure control is a good example. Many treatments exist for treating hypertension. Yet some of these options may increase the likelihood of erectile dysfunction. Merely prescribing medications without understanding the role of sexuality in a man's life may lead to lack of compliance or trigger emotional and/or behavioral concerns. It is important to help men explore the impact that medication and style changes may have on their lives. Men should also be helped to explore various treatment options when more than one exists. For instance, mild cases of hypertension may be treated through diet and exercise. Too often, medical professionals spend too little time with men explaining potential treatment options and negative side effects. While social workers do not have the medical training to make medical decisions for or with clients, they can help men process the information that doctors are providing for them. Social workers also may help men learn to talk to their physicians in a way that leads to outcomes that are more beneficial for them. Role plays and other in vivo practice methods can be useful in this regard.

While social workers must integrate the psychological, social, and biological realms of human behavior into practice, many social workers may feel less comfortable when exploring the biological domain (Furman, Jackson, Downey, and Seiz 2004). Talking about health demands knowledge of many subjects that are often not taught during the education of social workers. However, even more important than information is having worked through one's own issues and concerns around a lifestyle that supports physical health. Social workers who have not been able to come to terms with their own healthy eating, exercise, or other health-related lifestyle considerations may feel self-conscious talking with men about their health. However, it is essential that they become comfortable exploring these issues with men. Many of the psychosocial factors that bring men to treatment, including depression and self-image (related to other concerns such as violence and substance abuse), have biophysical components related to health and health behavior. Also, social workers may be the only helping professional that many men encounter. The exercise at the end of the chapter is designed to help practitioners explore these issues.

Social workers may also take important lessons from cognitive therapy when helping men explore their health issues. There are several key beliefs that interfere with their seeking and obtaining health care. One of the key beliefs has to do with men's sense of invincibility: "It won't happen to me." Men learn to believe that they can overcome anything, and that the outside world will not affect them. Men do not pay attention to their own pain and therefore are not sensitive to their own needs. Stoicism can be particularly deadly, as men ignore warning signs. Men also have many cognitive distortions in regard to their perceptions for needing health care. Men will minimize their health concerns and believe they can handle these concerns on their own. At times men may have cognitions that do not serve them yet are culturally accepted norms and beliefs that fall outside classical definitions of irrationality. It is important that social workers work slowly and carefully on helping men deconstruct and challenge beliefs that are congruent with the hegemonic masculine ideal as well as with various cultural traditions yet may be harmful to themselves. Taking an overly directive approach in regard to such beliefs may place a social worker at odds with his or her client's culture, thereby producing alienation.

For example, social workers working with Latino men should be aware of the notion of *fatalismo*, which has been shown to be one factor that contributes to health disparities for this group (Huerta 2003). *Fatalismo*, or fatalism, is the belief that what actually occurs in life is what is supposed to happen. According to this belief, if a man becomes ill, it is God's will that he is sick. It is important that social workers do not treat this as an irrational belief, as is deeply embedded in the context of many Latino cultures (Delgado, Jones, and Rohani 2005). Native Americans are known to hold a very similar set of beliefs, which at times can make it difficult to implement prevention programs in their communities. When social workers find evidence of fatalism impacting the help-seeking or receiving behaviors of their male clients, it is important to carefully listen to and validate the client's cultural belief. The social worker must adopt an attitude of learning, not teaching. In culturally competent practice, we want to adopt the attitude that it is our job to learn from the client about their culture and what it means to them. The REBT method of Socratic dialogue can be valuable in this situation—not to label beliefs as rationale or irrational, but to present to clients potential discrepancies and disparities between how they are applying their cultural beliefs. For instance, it is logical to assume that if God created disease, God also had a hand in creating doctors and medicine. The following questions help create this dialogue: If God created disease, then did he also create doctors? Did he create doctor's capacity to cure? How about medicine? Helping clients explore alternative explanations and expressions of their own cultural norms allows them to maintain dignity and control while helping them to question the utility of some of their health-hindering beliefs.

Using the narrative approach may also be of value when working with men's health issues. Carlick and Biley (2003) found narrative therapy useful when helping clients deal with the stresses and burdens of cancer care. They explore how current and changing narratives may help clients adjust to their illnesses. Clients may be helped to explore how the diagnosis of cancer creates an all-or-nothing narrative in which the cancer becomes the totality of their story. This is true for many health-related concerns, where illness and disease become dominant metaphors and themes that pervasively redefine identity. Through writing exercises or other restorying techniques, men can be helped to reauthor a narrative in which they develop an acceptance of their health problems but contextualize these problems within the context of their entire lives. Men can also be encouraged to develop a relationship with their illnesses through writing directly to their disease. This helps them externalize their conditions, thereby viewing themselves as separate from and greater than their illness. For instance, a man can write to his diabetes, exploring his anger at it having such a negative impact on his life. The feelings of anger and rage directed toward the disease and not the self can then be used as a source of energy. This contrasts to the inertia that men may feel when they experience the debilitating self-incrimination they feel when they equate their illness to their identity.

Case Example

Ron grew up in a conservative Jewish household in the West, raised by his mother and his stepfather, a retired military officer. Family life was chaotic; his stepfather was authoritarian and angry. His mother was in and out of psychiatric hospitals and suffered from prescription drug addiction. As a child Ron engaged in many difficult behaviors. He once was found sitting in a closet at school, having sat there for fifteen hours. When the janitor found him, Ron said he had "lost track of time." A loving and sweet boy, Ron was easily distracted in school and was told he was hyperactive. Due to his family chaos, Ron was never brought into treatment for his condition. He was also largely ignored due to his mother's focus on his sister, with whom the mother primarily identified. In high school Ron was largely an outsider due to learning disabilities and behavior problems. But his sweet nature and his ability at soccer enabled him to make friends despite his strange behavior.

Ron enlisted in the Army at the age of 18. There he found the stability and structure he needed. He trained to be a medic and found that the army's clear expectations allowed him to, in his words, "grow into himself." While he struggled in school, Ron was very bright and was able to easily grasp his work. He became an outstanding medic and over the years was afforded increasing responsibilities. He soon married his high school sweetheart and had children. The army was good to Ron. While at times he would get into trouble for "being stupid and not thinking," his basic good nature and willingness to accept responsibility for his mistakes allowed him to be successful.

Ron's home life was stable initially, but at times troubling even early on. His wife was a fairly cold and unemotional woman, while Ron was far more emotionally expressive. He wanted more physical closeness with his wife but accepted that she was not "a giving person." Ron also was frustrated that he worked extremely hard but his wife seemed to do very little. Not only did she work only periodically, she did little housework. The couple had three children—two boys and a girl. All three were hyperactive. As his wife did not set limits with the children, Ron found himself having to be the disciplinarian for three hyperactive children. When the boys were very young the family moved from the midwestern United States to a base in Germany, on orders from the army.

At the age of 33, Ron began to experience problems with his coordination and speech. He found himself not being able to play soccer as well as he had (he had been playing competitively in the service) and wondered if his thinking was not as clear as it once had been. For months Ron kept his symptoms to himself, hiding them from his family. Finally one of the soldiers under his command expressed his concern. He informed Ron that he had noticed that he was walking oddly would repeat himself frequently.

At this point Ron was forced to admit that something was wrong. He sought medical care and was referred for a neurological examination. Ron was soon diagnosed with multiple sclerosis. For several months he struggled to make sense of the diagnosis and how it would impact his life in the army—a life that had served him well for over fifteen years. His disease progressed quickly, and he was forced to quit playing soccer. Ron was eventually flown to the United States for treatment. He stayed in the hospital for several weeks, after which he applied for a discharge from the military. Upon his return to Germany, his discharge was granted, along with a settlement for a disability income that would allow him and his family to live reasonably well. However, his discharge was an extremely painful event for Ron. Not only was his physical health in decline, but he truly loved his work. He loved being responsible for his team and for mentoring younger medics. To Ron, being an army medic was the one thing in his life that he did well and that gave him a sense of validation. His wife was always critical of him. Given that he also struggled with hyperactivity, he largely blamed himself for this children's problems. At the end of his early adulthood, Ron was having to contend with many complex changes in addition to the normal developmental shifts that a man encounters at this time. Ron's sense of self and identity were seriously challenged. However, he kept these powerful feelings largely to himself. He learned to be a good soldier, to follow orders, to accept what was given to him, and to not complain.

Ron decided to move his family back to the Midwest to be nearer to his mother, his oldest sister, and her family. His family bought a house in a rural community forty minutes from a VA hospital and from his sister and mother. The next year proved challenging for Ron. His health declined markedly, and he was no longer able to swallow. His children did not adjust well to their new life in the United States. His daughter began to act out. Ron struggled to control his now 15-year-old daughter's rebellious behavior and school difficulties. Not knowing how to respond, he informed his daughter that if she did not get better grades, he would come to her class and sit with her. The day after her report card came, he informed her that he would be coming to class the next day. Shortly after, his daughter said that she was sad and asked her father to "comfort her." When Ron tried to give her a hug, she grabbed him and began to choke him. Weakened by his MS and having a hard time swallowing, Ron struggled to get his daughter off him. He finally managed to pull her off but was having difficulty breathing. Ron's wife called the paramedics and Ron was taken to the hospital. Ron's sister pleaded with Ron to seek family counseling, but he rationalized that he was all right and could handle his daughter.

Several months later Ron's mother was found in the a supermarket parking lot passed out in her car. Moments before, she had been observed wandering around the supermarket, confused and speaking incoherently. She was taken to the hospital, where tests revealed she had taken large quantities of prescription pain killers, tranquilizers, and muscle relaxants. Ron's sister attempted to intervene and asked Ron to support her in doing an "intervention" for their mother. Ron stated that he did not want to get involved, and that she and his mom would have to work things out between themselves. Not having been compelled to confront her addiction, Ron's mother was released from the hospital. Three months later, Ron became worried about his mother when she had not returned his calls for two days. He went to her house and found her dead on the couch from an apparent drug overdose. Months after his mother's death, Ron is haunted by the images of his mother's decomposing body. He continues to struggle with his physical decline, and with periodic difficulties with his children. His wife remains critical and disengaged. To this date, Ron has refused to seek help, which his sister frequently suggests to him.

FOR WRITING AND REFLECTION

1. To date, Ron has been unwilling to seek help. When you read about a case such as this, what do you experience?

2. Were Ron's sister to speak with you, as her social worker, about her brother, what suggestions would you give to her?

3. What have you learned about masculinity and the treatment of men that is applicable in this case?

Case Example

Jeff Lewis is a 55-year-old man who was recently hospitalized after a massive heart attack. Jeff's family and friends were hardly surprised by Jeff's hospitalization, as he is a morbidly obese man with uncontrolled high blood pressure. As with many obese men, in particular African American men, Jeff also has diabetes. While speaking to the doctor about Jeff's care, his wife Valerie expressed concern that someone had to "talk some sense" into her 350-pound husband, who after three days in the hospital was already asking family members to bring him cigarettes and fast food. It was clear to the doctor that Valerie was scared and frustrated with her husband; her hands were shaking and she was clearly fighting back tears. Jeff's doctor, being fairly blunt, informed Jeff that if he did not change his habits, he would not live very long. Jeff responded angrily, telling the doctor that he had been fine until this point, and that he was as strong as an ox. Recognizing how entrenched Jeff's beliefs were, and seeing how upset Valerie and other members of the family were, the doctor informed Jeff that he was going to have the social worker come talk to him. Jeff angrily proclaimed that he did not need a social worker. Valerie and Jeff's oldest daughter, Lashondra, insisted that Jeff talk to the social worker. Through tears, she said that if he did not do so she would do it herself, since watching her daddy kill himself was going to make her crazy, and when he died they would all need social workers. Lashondra's tears and fear seemed to soften Jeff's resistance, and he agreed to speak to the social worker.

Jeff Lewis was always a heavy boy. Growing up with a single mother who had little time or money to cook healthy food (nor knowledge about health), Jeff was "raised on TV dinners and cheap whatever." Jeff also learned form his mother that eating could be a source of comfort. Jeff's mother was a very religious women who did not drink, smoke, or go out. She worked hard at two jobs as a housekeeper and "did the best that she could." She also was very overweight and suffered from arthritis. At times, late at night, Jeff would see his mother in tears, crying and rubbing her arthritic hands. Raising three boys alone and working sixteen hours a day took their toll. As a means of self-soothing, Jeff's mother would bake and eat pieces of cake, often consuming a whole cake. She died of heart disease at the age of 58.

As a boy, Jeff was never good at sports. He was never physically challenged to a fight, as he was always much larger than other boys his age, and he put on an air of angry confidence and toughness. He began to lie about his physical prowess and would tell stories about the fights he was in. Jeff felt protected by his size. He learned to rationalize that he was "big boned" and was just naturally heavy. Jeff never thought much about exercise, healthy eating, or health in general. In school he paid little attention during health class, and he saw messages about health as "for other people."

When Jeff got married, at the age of 22, he weighed about 260 pounds. He was borderline obese but carried his weight fairly well. His wife, a slightly heavy woman, was not bothered by her husband's size. Over the years he continued to put on weight. Throughout his twenties Jeff worked as a plumber. In his thirties he started his own plumbing company and did well. He raised good children, was happily married, and never thought much about his body or health, until his heart attack.

When the social worker came to talk to Jeff, his wife and daughter were in the room. After the social worker introduced herself, she asked Jeff if this would be a good time to speak, or if he wanted to speak in private. His wife declared, "It's a good time, and we're are staying here, because he will smooth talk you to death!" Everyone laughed, and the social worker waited for Jeff to respond. Knowing the intensity of his wife's and daughter's wishes, and feeling as if he had surrendered to their better judgment, he smiled and said that now would be fine. The family talked about their concerns about Jeff and his habits. They spoke about having no experience with healthy eating or exercise, and how they all needed to learn. Jeff's wife and daughter did a good job of not blaming him, instead seeing his health as a family issue. Jeff appreciated this and was able to listen and engage his family on this level. The social worker talked about the various services that were available to Jeff, and by extension the family, while he was in the hospital. She discussed the role of a nutritionist in helping teach about healthy eating, and the physical therapy program that was designed to help people learn how to exercise. Both were considered part of his cardiac aftercare. The social worker also discussed a program to help him quit smoking, which would be essential to his recovery and health. Jeff was less than thrilled about this but found his family very persuasive.

As they agreed upon, the social worker visited again while the nutritionist came to speak to Jeff and his family. The nutritionist was well versed in culturally sensitive practice, knowing how to discuss healthy eating as it pertains to African American diet and culture. The nutritionist asked Jeff to describe his typical day's food intake. Jeff usually left home early in the day and stopped off for coffee and donuts. When asked how many donuts, Jeff hesitated and said that he usually ate three or four. When asked about his coffee, he stated that he put in two or three artificial creamers and usually two or three sugars. For dinner, Jeff's wife admitted that she usually cooks fried food, often in lard. She said that Jeff's favorite meal was fried chicken—he would usually eat three pieces. The nutritionist began to discuss ways of cooking African American foods in a more heart-healthy way and was able to provide a couple of pamphlets on the subject. She also recommended a good cookbook that adopted traditional African American dishes to a more heart-healthy diet. The nutritionist met with the family several other times over the next week and explored with them the fundamentals of a heart-healthy diet.

The physical therapist also met with Jeff and his family. Under his doctor's supervision, they began to devise a plan to help Jeff get into better physical condition. These meetings were part of a comprehensive strategy that constituted Jeff's cardiac rehabilitation. One of the key factors, besides diet, would be to help Jeff develop a habit of exercise. Given his weight and lack of exercise history, he would have to start very slowly. Walking and mild weight training using very small dumbbells became the core of his program, along with stretching. Jeff started by walking on the treadmill for five minutes, his heart carefully monitored during the exercise. Over the course of this two weeks in the hospital, Jeff began walking for twelve minutes at a slightly faster pace. Upon Jeff's discharge, his social worker helped him and the family develop a comprehensive biopsychosocial plan to help him improve and maintain his health. During the social worker's final visit with Jeff alone, they explored his ambivalence toward making lifestyle change. The social worker appreciated how far he had come, both in his lifestyle changes and in his honesty about his feelings.

FOR WRITING AND REFLECTION

Think of how the family dynamics and intervention might have been different for families from different backgrounds. Write about how you would approach this work differently were you a social worker working with a Latino, Asian, or Native American family.

EXERCISE—BECOMING COMFORTABLE WITH DISCUSSING HEALTH

To become comfortable discussing health issues with men, you will need to explore your feelings and beliefs about your own health. For five minutes, write about your feelings about your own body and your own health.

EXERCISE—EXPLORING CONDOM USE WITH MEN

For the following exercise, pick two cases from the proceeding chapters. In the space below, write a narrative of how you would use the concepts you have learned so far in this book to explore the issue of condom use and safe sex. Afterwards, answer the questions that follow.

1. What obstacles can get in the way of your having this conversation?
2. How might your gender and ethnicity impact the conversation?
3. What theories might inform your discussion? How can you use these theories?

Men and Mental Illness | TEN

Men may feel more threatened than women do by
rapid social, political and economic change. When
such change affects traditional male roles in the home
and workplace, men may experience a profound loss of
identity, status and dignity, which increases their risk of
depression and other mental illnesses.
—Mayo Clinic, 2004

Explorations of mental health are often really discussions of mental illness, not mental "health." That is, we tend to discuss what is wrong with people psychologically, and not what is well about them. This pathology focus is the function of many factors, most recently the medicalization of mental health and social services. Since the early days of the development of psychology and psychiatry, however, the focus has been on human pathology. In the United States today, and to a large extent in social work practice with the U.S. context, the prevailing discourse on mental health is one steeped in biomedical terminology, concepts, and treatment. This is not to say that viewing mental illness through the lens of modern science is all wrong; since the 1950s, medical science has come a long way in treating severe and persistent mental illnesses.

Yet the medical model is only one lens through which to view mental illness. Even conditions that are biological in etiology often require more ecologically based interventions (Bachrach 1992). Such approaches take into account the biopsychosocial realities of how mental illnesses are experienced, viewing the whole life context of the person. This chapter discusses some of the common mental illnesses of men. Because social workers must understand the conceptualizations that dominate the mental health field (the *Diagnostic and Statistical Manual* [DSM] and the medical model), I explore ways in which social workers can use and modify these models to better serve their clients. The chapter begins with discussion of conceptions of mental illness and a way to contextualize current medical model practices. It goes on to explore various important diagnoses and how social workers can use the four theories outlined in this book in working with men who have mental health disorders.

Mental Illness: An Overview

It is being called a silent crisis, a sleeper issue. But there are signs that this sleeper is at last awakening. Around the world studies, surveys, Internet networks, journals, and newspaper articles are shedding light on the shadowy subject of men's mental health. Among the findings is the revelation that new fathers are vulnerable to postpartum depression. In Canada, young and middle-aged men are being hospitalized for schizophrenia in increasing numbers. The gender gap among people with mental illness is much narrower than might be suspected (Canadian Mental Health Association 2007).

While the diagnostic categories discussed in this section appear to be scientific and certainly are based on evidence, psychiatric diagnoses change across cultural contexts and across time. In early iterations of the *Diagnostic and Statistical Manual of Mental Disorders* (Spitzer 1981), homosexuality was viewed as a mental illness. Therefore, classifications should be seen as approximations to help us understand the nature of disorders, and to help treat those who experience them. Jackson (2001) suggests four uses of diagnosis: (1) to provide a shorthand abbreviation for a constellation of symptoms; (2) to help form the basis of intake and admissions to appropriate services; (3) to help qualify an individual for payment from insurance or some other source; and (4) for decisions about potential medication management. Jackson provides excellent advice when he warns that "professionals have the responsibility to use diagnoses and diagnostic information, as with all treatment information concerning clients, with great care. . . . The formal classification and naming of mental illness and the assignment of diagnoses are perceived by some people as having great, almost magical significance. It is important that the worker remember the symptoms are not the illness nor is the person 'the diagnosis'" (21).

Mental illnesses and their diagnoses are socially constructed and differ across populations. That is, the manner in which even biologically based conditions express themselves will vary across cultures (Bodley 1994). Incidences of mental illnesses vary greatly between countries and cultures (Kaelber, Moul, and Farmer 1995). Geertz (1973) observed that even the most basic forms of human experience, such as simple emotions, are culturally constructed. The strong cultural base of mental illness has important implications for this discussion. That is, while we can make some generalizations about mental illness, the mental illnesses of men differ from those of women. The World Health Organization has noted that "research shows that socially constructed differences between women and men in roles and responsibilities, status and power, interact with biological differences between the sexes to contribute to differences in the nature of mental health problems suffered, health seeking behavior or those affected and responses to the health sector of society as a whole" (World Health Organization 2002). In general, however, mental illnesses can be broken down into several classifications: thought disorders, mood disorders, behavioral disorders, and personality disorders.

The DSM-IV, the fourth edition of the American Psychiatric Association's *Diagnostic and Statistical Manual*, has many detractors, not because of the multiaxial diagnostic system itself, but because of the manner in which it is used. The DSM-IV is the most widely used classification system of mental illness in the United States, and throughout much of the world. Typically, when someone refers to a client's diagnosis, the reference is to Axis I of the system. However, the DSM-IV actually consists of five axes, which address many domains of human behavior. The authors of the manual note:

> The use of the multiaxial system facilitates comprehensive and systematic evaluation with attention to the various mental disorders and general medical conditions, psychosocial and environmental problems, and level of functioning that might be overlooked if the focus were on assessing a single presenting problem. A multiaxial system provides a convenient formula for organizing and communicating clinical information, for capturing the complexity of clinical situations, and for describing the heterogeneity of individuals with the same diagnosis. In addition, the multiaxial system promotes the application of the biopsychosocial model in clinical, educational, and research settings. (APA 2000:25)

The authors allude to the risks of focusing only on a narrow band of data in describing a client's problems and concerns. When each of the axes is given equal weight (which in practice is very rare), the system can have great value as a tool in organizing a compressive assessment.

Axis I syndromes are the clinical disorders of childhood and adulthood, ranging from persistent and chronic to more temporary adjustment disorders. There are fourteen categories of disorders, including many that are discussed in detail in this chapter.

Axis II consists of personality disorders and mental retardation. Personality disorders are entrenched patterns of feeling, behaviors, and thoughts that interfere with psychological, physical, and social well-being. While many of us at times exhibit personality traits such as paranoia, the person diagnosed with paranoid personality disorder has a rigid, inflexible, and dysfunctional pattern of behavior that is resistant to change by outside stimuli (i.e., consequences from the environment or feedback from others). As with Axis I disorders, the DSM provides decision-making checklists to help in diagnoses for Axis II disorders. The diagnosis of a personality disorder should not be given casually or cavalierly. In fact, research has shown that some personality disorders are frequently overdiagnosed. For example, antisocial personality disorder was significantly misdiagnosed and overdiagnosed in a sample of prison inmates with substance abuse disorders (Darke, Kaye, and Finlay-Jones 1997). Diagnosing personality disorders is often difficult. What may at times appear to be evidence of a personality disorder may actually be due to other problems and diagnoses.

Developmental disabilities are also listed under Axis II. Mental retardation and other developmental disorders are important to consider, as they provide guidance to the cognitive capacities of those with those conditions. When a social worker encounters a man who has been diagnosed with mental retardation or another developmental disability, it is important to gather as much information as possible from various collateral sources in order to develop a good, comprehensive treatment plan.

Axis III is where general medical conditions are reported. Reporting general medical conditions in the multiaxial system is useful to help other professionals understand the complete diagnostic picture. This may be particularly true of men, who are less likely to report physical problems. However, physical conditions often play a large role in the expression and severity of mental health disorders. For example, a former athlete in his early forties may have strong negative self-appraisals related to symptoms of early onset arthritis. The negative influence this may have on his identity can exacerbate many mental health disorders, such as depression.

Axis IV, psychosocial and environmental problems, calls for including such important problems as those related to primary support groups, the social environment, occupational issues, housing, economic issues, access to health care services, interaction with the legal system/crime, and other environmental factors. In other words, the DSM calls for the inclusion of the type of assessments that social workers typically do. While this axis consists only of a listing or very short description of psychosocial and environmental problems, social workers should include them when they use the DSM system. By doing so, they encourage other mental health practitioners who may be less inclined to view clients problems and contexts more holistically, not merely as biomedical conditions. For example, poverty, unemployment, and living in an area without public transportation can influence a man's ability to access his mental health care. Helping medical personnel understand these real problems can enable them to view their clients as having multiple barriers and not merely as being "treatment resistant."

Axis V is the Global Assessment of Functioning (GAF). The GAF is a numerical report of a worker's judgment about the overall functioning of a client. The scale, which is broken down into ten-point increments, begins with the score of 90–100, describing someone functioning at a superior or high level in a wide range of lifespan domains. A man with superior functioning experiences no current symptoms and is successful in each of his social domains. Additional scale categories include minimal symptoms and high functioning, moderate symptoms with some psychosocial disruptions, and more severe symptoms with major disturbance in psychosocial well-being. A decision tree has been developed to help increase the reliability of the GAF as a diagnostic tool (Yamauchi et al. 2001). However, caution should be taken when using the GAF. In their conclusions to a study of the GAF of nearly ten thousand clients of the Department of Veterans Affairs, Moos, Nichol, and Moos (2002) question the accuracy of clinicians' use of the GAF and its utility in resource allocation or in predicting mental health outcomes.

The GAF, as with each axis of the DSM, should be used as a component of a comprehensive assessment. Social workers should use their clients' past diagnoses as one component of their assessment. Diagnoses change over time and are highly contingent on context. For instance, GAF scores can change radically based on the time of assessment. Each of us experiences times of crisis in our lives, and during those times our GAF scores would be far lower than where they typically may be. As such, it is important to contextualize the GAF score with historical information.

Mood Disorders

Mood pertains to the manner in which feelings and emotional states are experienced and expressed. Mood disorders are psychiatric conditions that negatively affect mood. The most common forms of mood disorder are depression and bipolar disorder Social workers working in mental health settings will want to familiarize themselves with other mood disorders that are not considered here.

Depression

While women are nearly twice as likely as men to be depressed, nearly 7 percent of men (more than six million) are depressed at any given time during a one-year period (NIMH 2005). When discussing their own mental health, men are unaware that many of the somatic symptoms associated with depression, such as chronic pain, digestive problems, and headaches, might be playing a part in their down mood (NIMH 2005). Because men are more likely than women to ignore physical problems, they often downplay these concerns, making them less likely to seek treatment.

Men have other misconceptions about depression, often stemming from traditional or hegemonic male values of autonomy, self-determination, and individuality. Men traditionally see being depressed in terms of character and morality. Being depressed is viewed as a sign of weakness: a real man is able to transcend his feelings and "do what he has to do." These beliefs often compound the problem of male depression. Since depression is often a biomedical problem, or at least a biopsychosocial concern with a large biological component, men who are not able to transcend their depressed mood on their own tend to feel a great deal of shame, self-blame, and loathing (Real 1998). These feelings and thoughts further exacerbate depression in men.

Depression in men often manifests itself differently than in women (Goodwin and Guze 1996; Kaplan and Sadock 1998). Men are more likely to report (or at least admit to) irritability, loss of interest in work, fatigue, or disturbances in sleep than more "feminine" emotions such as sadness, guilt, and worthlessness (NIMH 2005). Men seek treatment less frequently than women, but they have developed methods of coping with depression, however harmful they may be. Men may become increasingly obsessed with and preoccupied with work. They may also engage in substance abuse or other addictive disorders. Men will also frequently engage in reckless or self-destructive behavior, such as provoking fights or driving too fast. Also, while men make fewer suicide attempts than do women, more than four times as many men die by suicide (Moscicki 2001). Men are also less likely to experience bouts of crying than are women, making clinical measures that rely on this emotional expression problematic (Love and Love 2006).

As with other mental health concerns, different races experience depression differently, and they may experience different social forces that contribute to the development and manifestation of depression (Kessler and Cleary, 1980: Foster 1993). Baker and Bell (1999) posit that depression may be underdiagnosed in African American men. In a study of older African American men in Harlem, Love and Love (2006) found that 28 percent of their community sample and nearly half their clinical sample had measurable signs of depression.

The Real Men, Real Depression campaign represents a significant effort at incorporating gender-sensitive health promotion material into a comprehensive public awareness program geared at men and depression. Developed by the National Institute of Mental Health, the campaign is designed to help men recognize, acknowledge, and seek treatment for their depression (NIMH 2003). The campaign has used video, audio, textual, and Internet-based promotional methods to provide men and their primary care and mental health practitioners information about how depression manifests itself in men. The campaign has sought to normalize depression, talking about "real men" for whom depression is a normal part of their lives. Perhaps more important, the men it portrays are not shown as diminished by virtue of being depressed. Thus the campaign encourages men with traditional male values to recognize and seek treatment for their depression (Rochlen, McKelley, and Pituch 2006).

Bipolar Disorder

Bipolar disorder is a mood disorder that is more common than some people may believe. Approximately two million people have bipolar disorder, which occurs equally in men and women (NIMH 2007b). People usually develop bipolar disorder during late adolescence or early adulthood, with the vast majority developing the condition prior to age 35. According to Spearing (2007:3), "Bipolar disorder causes dramatic mood-swings—from overly "high" and/or irritable to sad and hopeless, and then back again, often with periods of normal mood in between. Severe changes in energy and behavior go along with these changes in mood. The periods of highs and lows are called episodes of mania and depression."

Symptoms of manic episodes include racing thoughts, excessive energy and activity, euphoria, irritability, compulsive behaviors, poor judgment, overestimation of one's abilities, and rapid speech. In a depressive episode, people with bipolar disorder exhibit typical depressive systems. During periods of severe mania, some people experience psychotic systems such as hallucinations, delusions, paranoia, and grandiosity. It is important that men experiencing these symptoms have a good psychiatric examination, as people with bipolar disorder exhibiting psychotic symptoms may be misdiagnosed as having schizophrenia.

Bipolar disorder is often poorly understood. Many people with bipolar disorder are able to function at extremely high levels, hold professional jobs, and lead fulfilling and productive family lives (Miklowitz 2008). Additionally, pharmacological treatments for bipolar disorder are much improved from the past. I have had clients who have worried about medication robbing them of their personalities and turning them into "zombies." While side effects of medications are certainly prevalent, treatments are now far more sophisticated than even a decade ago. Still, evidence suggests that in spite of new pharmacological treatments, a comprehensive treatment approach that helps people prepare for relapses is essential. In fact, a two-year study of people receiving a comprehensive evidence-based approach for bipolar disorder found that half of the research participants had at least one relapse (DePaulo 2006).

Anxiety Disorders

Modern life creates a great deal of stress. The human mind and body are programmed for a far simpler existence yet have to contend with highly complicated and often overwhelming stimuli (Mirowsky and Ross 1989). In addition, many men are working more hours in more stressful positions yet finding that their incomes are buying less and less. The pressures that men face are often enormous, and even under the best of circumstances they can lead to a good deal of stress. When we speak of men's problems with anxiety, we can refer to "normal" and clinical problems. That is, clinical forms of anxiety can be classified in accepted categories, discussed below, and are considered actual forms of mental illnesses. Nonclinical forms of anxiety are "normal" reactions to life stress. However, just because a man's anxiety does not meet the diagnostic criteria does not mean it is not a problem. Men's reactions to stress may be normal in the sense that they are typical, but that does not mean that they are healthy. For men with anxiety disorders, these normal life stresses are more central in their lives. Anxiety disorders make men more susceptible to difficulty in handling normal life stresses and can lead to feelings of being overwhelmed and out of control.

According to the National Institute of Mental Health (2007a), there are five clinical classifications of anxiety disorders: generalized anxiety disorder, obsessive-compulsive disorder, panic disorder, posttraumatic stress disorder, and social phobia. Each of these conditions is a relatively common form of mental illness that can be effectively treated, typically with a combination of medication and psychotherapy. While the prevalence of anxiety disorder is somewhat higher in women than in men, it still has a great impact on men. For example, nearly one million men suffer from obsessive compulsive disorder, roughly the same number as women (Kessler et al. 2005). Posttraumatic stress disorder has recently reached nearly epidemic proportions in men who have served in the military, as was discussed in chapter 8. Masculinity and stressors over men's roles also influence the anxiety levels of men. Eisler, Skidmore, and Ward (1988) found that men who experience higher levels of stress over their masculine identity and gender roles have an increased level of general anxiety and increased anger.

How do we know when a man has moved from a more normative anxiety response to an anxiety disorder that should be treated? Typically, normal anxiety will dissipate within six months without professional intervention (NIMH 2007a). When a social worker identifies a man who may need help with anxiety, it is important to help him normalize the problem. Research has shown that while anxiety disorders are complex, biopsychosocial phenomena and biological predispositions seem to play a large role in their expression (NIMH Genetics Workgroup 1998)

Schizophrenia

Schizophrenia is a chronic condition of the brain for which there is no clear cause. It is believed that the disorder has multiple genetic influences. Historically conceptualized as a thought disorder, it is now seen as having clear biological components. Studies have found that the brains of people who have the disorder are markedly different from those who do not (Greenstein et al. 2006). Symptoms include disorganized thinking and delusions, hallucinations, extreme fluctuations in mood, flat affect, distorted perceptions of self-worth, social withdraw, and other social and behavioral dysfunctions.

According to the National Institute of Mental Health, nearly 1 percent of all people are affected by schizophrenia (NIMH, 2007b:1).

[It] is a chronic, severe, and disabling brain disorder that has been recognized throughout recorded history. A person with schizophrenia may hear voices other people don't hear or they may believe that others are reading their minds, controlling their thoughts, or plotting to harm them. These experiences are terrifying and can cause fearfulness, withdrawal, or extreme agitation. People with schizophrenia may not make sense when they talk, may sit for hours without moving or talking much, or may seem perfectly fine until they talk about what they are really thinking. Because many people with schizophrenia have difficulty holding a job or caring for themselves, the burden on their families and society is significant as well.

The institute also notes that while women develop symptoms in their late twenties to early thirties, men tend to develop symptoms in their late teens and early twenties. This has profound implications for treatment and the course of the disorder. Since people are less socially and financially stable in late adolescence and early adulthood, men who develop schizophrenia may be less likely to have the nurturing, stable social support mechanisms needed to help them achieve the most positive outcomes. Developing severe mental illness earlier makes it harder for men to find lasting and secure employment options and may predispose these men to a lifetime of dependency. Other research has shown that this disorder has a more severe course in men than in women (Castle and Murray 1991). For instance, the hallucinations of men with the disorder tend to be more resistant to medication than the hallucinations of women. Research has shown that men with schizophrenia actually have far greater brain abnormalities than do women (Frederikse et al. 2000).

Historically, people with the disorder were shunned or persecuted. Typical treatment of those with persistent mentally illness throughout much of history has been incarceration or isolation as "evil." It is likely that the majority of people who found their way into asylums had either schizophrenia, another psychotic disorder, or bipolar disorder. The earliest signs of treating schizophrenia as a disease can be found in the development of a general hospital in France in the 1600s (Foucault 1965). The mentally ill were provided asylum, yet the intent of hospitalization was to treat them. In the early development of the American colonies, asylums treated the problem as a moral issue and sought to help the mentally ill person to internalize normal social rules and behaviors (Grob 1994). The moral treatment of schizophrenia became the norm in well-established asylums and hospitals in the eighteenth and nineteenth centuries. During the 1920s American hospitals and asylums were overwhelmed and underfunded, merely warehousing their most ill patients (Karger and Stoez 1998). Soon, American hospitals began to experiment with invasive surgeries, and the lobotomy became a standard procedure through the 1940s (Mechanic 1969). Beginning in the 1950s the advent of the early antipsychotic medications ushered in the modern era of treatment of schizophrenia. The ability to medicate those who are persistently mentally ill made it possible for many people with schizophrenia to live in their communities. Since that time, significant research has been dedicated to finding increasingly effective treatments with less severe side effects. In 1963 the Community Mental Health Act started the community mental health movement.

While the goal of having people live full and healthy lives as part of their communities was a significant step forward in the care and treatment of people with persistent mental illness, community mental health centers and supportive services were underfunded. Additionally, early antipsychotic medications had particularly difficult side effects, resulting in many patients not continuing on their medication. The poorest of the mentally ill, and those without community resources or families, were often forced to live in substandard boarding homes—a problem that continues for many people who have this disease.

Today, while the advent of managed care often makes it increasingly difficult for the persistently mentally ill to pay for nonmedical care, partial hospitalization programs and psychosocial rehabilitation programs help provide meaningful structures and a sense of community to men with schizophrenia. Medications are now far more effective than they have been historically, with fewer side effects. Perhaps the most important nonpharmacological service for the persistently mentally ill has been intensive case management (ICM). ICM services are

> a key part of the continuum of mental health services and supports for people with serious mental illness. Intensive case management promotes independence and quality of life through the coordination of appropriate services and the provision of constant and on-going support as needed by the consumer. The direct involvement of the consumer and the development of a caring, supportive relationship between the case manager and the consumer are integral components of the intensive case management process. Intensive case management is responsive to consumers' multiple and changing needs, and plays a pivotal role in coordinating required services from across the mental health system as well as other service systems (i.e., criminal justice, developmental services, and addictions). Case managers fulfill a vital function for consumers by working with them to realize personal recovery goals. Case managers work to build a trusting and productive relationship with the consumer and to provide the support and resources that the consumer needs to achieve goals, stabilize his/her life and improve his/her quality of life. (Ontario Ministry of Health and Long Term Care 2005:2)

This explanation of ICM is particularly strengths-based and represents the state of the art in thinking about ICM. However, not all ICM services are focused on strengths: some are more focused on symptom alleviation and management of the "patient." It is also true that in many ICM programs caseloads are far too large for the work to truly be intensive. Case workers also may not have BSWs or MSWs and may not have the values, skills, and knowledge necessary to provide be truly effective (Gibelman and Furman 2008).

Antisocial Personality Disorders

Certain personality disorders are more prevalent in one sex or the other. While biological predispositions are evident in some personality disorders, it is likely that gender identity and development also plays as significant role (Golomb et al. 1995). This is clear when exploring antisocial personality and its prevalence in men (3 percent of the population) and women (1 percent). Personality disorders also seem to differ in their prevalence across different socioeconomic backgrounds, cross-culturally, and cross-nationally (Torgersen, Kringlen, and Cramer 2001). The DSM-IVR (APA 2000:701) notes that the prevalence of personality disorders in clinical settings may be up to 30 percent of the population. The main feature of antisocial personality disorder is a "pervasive pattern of disregard for, and violation of, the right of others that begins in childhood or early adulthood and continues into adulthood."

Moeller and Dougherty (2001) noted that the name and exact criteria of the disorder have shifted over the last century, with terms such as sociopathy and moral insanity, having been previously used. Each of these conceptualizations has stressed the lack of emotional attachment to others, and the willingness or even joy associated with causing others harm.

The DSM-IV (2000) lists seven criteria that constitute this pattern of disregard for others; to be diagnosed with antisocial personality disorder, an individual needs to have three pertain to them, since the age of 15: repeated criminal behavior, deceitfulness, impulsiveness, irritability and aggressiveness, reckless disregard the safety of others, irresponsibility, and lack of remorse. It is also noted that these behaviors are not due primarily to a psychotic disorder. When children exhibit these symptoms, the diagnosis is conduct disorder. Antisocial personality disorder is considered very difficult to treat, as it is viewed as a pervasive system of behaviors, thoughts, and feelings deeply engrained into personality structures. Antisocial personality disorder is also often not treated as a mental health condition, as the diagnosis so frequently corresponds with criminality, and is therefore handled more as an issue of social control by the criminal justice system (Hart and Hare 1996; Hirose 2001).

There is evidence that treatment can help people with antisocial personality disorder live more socially responsible lives. In one study, a therapeutic community treatment was found to reduce arrests, incarceration rates, and drug use in the sample of people who also carried the diagnosis of antisocial personality disorder. The therapeutic community treatment consisted of six to ten months of community-based, in-patient residential treatment and two months of outpatient follow-up. Also, some evidence exists for the potential of medication in reducing aggressive and impulsive behaviors of men with antisocial personality disorder, although additional research is needed (Hirose 2001).

The Strengths Perspective

Charles Rapp of the University of Kansas has done innovative and ground-breaking work using the strengths perspective with people who have severe and persistent mental illnesses (Rapp and Wintersteen 1989). Using an approach that stresses the importance of case management, Rapp and Wintersteen advocate for engaging clients in a discussion of how social conceptions about mental illness serve to place artificial limits and constraints on those with mental health disorders. When people internalize these notions, they construct identities of themselves as more limited than they really are. Their own personal failures, and the failures of systems that are desired to serve them, reinforce these self-defeating conceptions. A strengths approach begins not with the person as being mentally ill, but as a human being having goals, hopes, and dreams. People with severe and persistent mental illness may not have thought about their aspirations in some time, and treatment providers tend to view them in terms of their problems. Additionally, the actual nature of mental illnesses may have harmed the individual's capacity to view his or her own strengths and resources. The worker adopting this model helps a person look at his or her strengths historically, seeking to uncover abilities and talents that may not have been accessed for many years. These uncovered skills and dreams are then utilized to help the person develop and work toward goals that will lead to an enriching and meaningful existence. The approach also focuses on the resources and capacities of the community in helping people reach their goals and dreams, and in helping them establish meaningful and engaged community involvement.

In their systematic study of the efficacy of various case management approaches, Rapp and Goscha (2006) found ten factors that are strongly correlated with positive client outcomes (including hospitalization, housing, self-esteem, social contacts, and satisfaction with life).

1. The case manager delivers as much of the help or services as possible. The authors note that while making referrals is valuable, case management approaches that rely too heavily on referrals have been found to be ineffective.

2. Natural community resources are the primary partners. The strengths model emphasizes finding strengths and resources in one's own community and helps people to make natural and sustained connections in their social work.

3. Work is in the community. Workers should be working with clients out of the office, in the settings in which the clients live, work, and play. By

so doing, case managers can help clients develop complicated systems and skills by providing direct feedback.

4. Individual and team case management works. Some approaches rely on a team of individuals, while others utilize one primary case manager. Both approaches have been found to be effective.

5. Case managers have primary responsibility for a person's services. This helps avoid fragmentation and client disengagement.

6. Case managers can be paraprofessionals. Supervisors should be experienced and fully credentialized.

7. Case loads should be small enough to allow for a relatively high frequency of contact.

8. Case management service should be time unlimited.

9. People need access to familiar persons twenty-four hours a day, seven days a week.-

10. Case managers should foster choice.

The Four Theories and Mental Illness

Since severe and persistent mental illnesses are viewed as biological brain disorders, some practitioners have erroneously concluded that cognitive therapy should not be used with this population. However, by adopting a strengths perspective, social workers come to view people with mental illness as having the capacity to work toward meaningful and fulfilling lives. CBT can be used to help a man illuminate some of the blocks and limitations that he possesses, in service of meeting his goals. Some of these may be related to his mental illness, yet others can stem from other problems of living that many people face.

CBT has also been used with some of the actual symptoms of severe mental illness. For instance, cognitive therapy can be used to help persons who have mental illness test the veracity of their thoughts and learn how to not listen to their hallucinations. Tower et al. (2004) found that cognitive therapy can decrease a mentally ill person's perceptions of the power and authority of his or her command hallucination and can lead to increased treatment compliance. Research has shown that for some clients, cognitive therapy may be as effective as psychiatric medication (Kingdon et al. 2008). In working with clients with bipolar disorder, cognitive therapy can be used to help people identify the thoughts and behaviors associated with episodes of mania or depression and to plan mechanisms for helping them prevent a serious relapse.

To assist the client to pay close attention to these symptoms, a list of these thoughts and behaviors should be made and reviewed daily. An action plan should be clearly explicated, with easy-to-follow action steps that the client takes when he, or those close to him, encounter the listed items. In a twelve-month study of cognitive therapy group treatment for individuals with bipolar disorder, Lam et al. (2003) found that group treatment decreased the number of episodes of the disorder, the number of hospital admissions, and improved overall mood. They conclude that cognitive therapy can be a useful tool in conjunction with a mood stabilizer.

While not typically used with persistent mental illness, existential therapy is certainly an important intervention with mood disorders. Nonbiologically based depression may often occur when a man finds himself not living his life according to his own dreams, desires, and passions. Since men are taught to be good warriors and not pay attention to their feelings and desires, they may "stuff" their needs and wants and become depressed about the manner in which they live their lives. Existentially oriented practitioners, or the social worker adopting the existential perspective eclectically, will help a man discover his forgotten desires. Existentially oriented practitioners would not encourage a man to abandon his current responsibilities to peruse his dreams but would help him develop a sense of purpose and a life mission that is consonant with his current life course, or help him make responsible, meaning focused, decisions. Perhaps on a more fundamental level, working existentially with depressed men calls on the worker to help them pay attention to the small joys in life in the here and now and find meaningful, enjoyable activities to incorporate into their life.

People with mental illnesses are frequently stigmatized and subjected to prejudice and discrimination. All too often they learn to see themselves as being fundamentally flawed and defective. This self-definition, supported by socially constructed stereotypes is reinforced by social workers and other helping professions. Narrative therapy calls on us to separate the person from the problem and help men see themselves as persons who have a problem called mental illness, not as a mentally ill, defective person. Helping people suffering from these disorders make this separation can lift some of the shame and depression that can greatly compound their conditions. In a very real sense, the disabling condition is not merely the mental health disorder itself, but the internalization of the notions of "mentally ill" and "disabled." Researchers and practitioners have found that helping families and community members focus on nonpathology-based language can greatly improve outcomes for people with mental illness (Lysaker, Lancaster, and Lysaker 2003). As with existential theory, narrative work helps expand what is possible for people by focusing on their dreams, hopes, and desires (Holma and Aaltonen 1995). By so doing, men with persistent mental illnesses develop new narratives about themselves that reflect the complexity of what it means to be human (Holma and Aaltonen 2007).

Case Example

Nick Rotoni is an Italian American firefighter living in a large urban area in the northeastern United States. Nick was referred to therapy by his station chief for difficulty controlling his anger in work situations. During the first meeting, Nick told his therapist that he did not like "touchy feely stuff" and that since he was not "crazy" he did not need therapy. His therapist understood the cultural variables involved in these statements: traditional men often believe that displays of emotions are a sign of weakness, and therapy is something only for the ill. The social worker sought to normalize the experience, telling Nick that therapy is not only about feelings, but about learning concrete skills and tools to help fix real concerns. He also told Nick that therapy is not only for people who are "crazy" (using Nick's language), but for normal people who want to "make a change or two." Given that Nick had a keychain that said Chevy, the social worker decided to use an automotive metaphor. He told Nick that therapy was like taking your car for a tune-up. Even when your car is fine, sometimes you need to get your carburetor or timing belt adjusted. By fine-tuning things and replacing parts before they are broken, you can prevent future problems. Also, sometimes you just want to upgrade parts, like putting in a high-performance exhaust system to give you a little extra power.

Nick related to this metaphor. Sensing that he would not be compelled to admit to weakness or failure, Nick began to relax. He actually continued with the metaphor, stating, "You know Doc, sometimes you do have parts that need to be fixed." The social worker responded that this was true, and that it was a sign of strength for someone to be willing to admit this and work toward change. To the social worker's surprise, Nick began to discuss his problems with anger, anxiety, and depression. Focusing on listening nonjudgmentally and empathically, the social worker was very careful to reflect the content and context of the interview more than the emotion. It would be important at a later date to help Nick own and work on his emotional control, and therefore identify and explore his feelings, but this had to be on Nick's timeframe. Besides, Nick was choosing to be very open, very quickly. After he shared his story, Nick was clearly feeling vulnerable. He stated, "You probably think I'm something of a lunatic or a little girl for blabbing like this, huh?" The social worker responded that just the opposite was true, that he was impressed that Nick took control of the session by telling his story, and that it took a "real man" to be able to be honest and responsible for himself. The social worker used the language of hegemonic masculinity to help Nick feel comfortable with sharing his feelings. He reframed what is traditionally not seen as "masculine" behavior to be included in a new vision of potential forms of masculinity, which Nick could use to improve his affective repertoire (i.e., that other feelings besides anger would be appropriate to express). During the first several sessions, the social worker and Nick identified his primary problems as anxiety and depression, and that his anger was to a large degree a symptom of both. Also, Nick identified that growing up angry was the only feeling he was allowed to have without being labeled "a skirt" by his father.

Once the problems were identified, the social worker and Nick discussed treatment options, including medication and individual therapy, with individual therapy focusing on cognitive behavioral work. The social worker explained that the purpose of cognitive behavioral therapy was to help Nick develop the tools to be his "own therapist." Nick liked this idea and expressed reticence to taking medication. He said that he thought he could work on the problem without medication. The worker told Nick that it would be Nick's decision, and that they would evaluate Nick's progress periodically. Down the road, if Nick decided he wanted to try medication, he would be given a referral to the psychiatrist. The therapist also asked Nick to agree that if his anger or depression did not decrease within the first two or three months, or if at any time it worsened, he would see the psychiatrist to be evaluated for medication. He stressed that this would only be an evaluation, and that no one would compel Nick to go on medication. Nick agreed that this was a good plan.

Nick's therapist began their second session by explaining the cognitive-behavioral model of emotions. Nick seemed to have a difficult time following a more theoretical discussion, so his therapist told him that it meant that thinking caused feelings. The social worker decided to present a teaching metaphor to Nick. He asked Nick to imagine the social worker coming home and saying to himself that he was going to train his dog to shake hands today. As a matter of fact, his dog must shake hands, must obey him, and the dog had better learn how to do it fast! The social worker asked Nick to imagine the dog not being able to quickly learn this new behavior the social worker continuing to say to himself and then out loud, "You better learn this now. You must learn this immediately! How dare you not do it the right way?" The social worker then asked Nick to explain how the social worker would feel if these were the thoughts that entered his mind. Nick stated that he must be feeling pretty pissed off. The social worker then asked Nick to imagine him dealing with the situation in a slightly different manner. He asked him to imagine that the social worker was not anger, but just slightly disappointed and annoyed. He asked Nick what he would say to himself so he would feel those feelings. Nick thought about it and responded, "Well, you could just tell yourself that it's a dog, and a dog is not always going to do what you want it to do—that you have to be patient with a dog, and these things take time." The social worker praised Nick and said that he was already doing the kind of work that he needed to do to learn to deal with his own anger. He explained that the type of exaggerated, demanding thoughts that the social worker was presenting in the situation with his dog were just the kind of thoughts that made people angry. He explained that the goal was to move extreme anger to mild anger or annoyance, and to have more rational thoughts that were more in touch with reality. He explained that Nick helped him change his demand to a preference—that while it would be nice to train his dog, he could not "make" it happen, and certainly not in such a short period of time.

He then asked Nick to explain to him situations in which he became angry, and suggested that perhaps they could look at the thinking that made caused him to become angry. Nick began to discuss how he believed that people had to do things his way because he knew what was best. When that did not happen, he would become very upset. The worker reflected that "people just do what Nick wants them to do." Nick laughed and said that while it sounded ridiculous, that was what he believed. For the next several sessions, the worker used various methods to help Nick change his demanding, anger-producing beliefs. He used rational role reversal, in which Nick adopted the role of the therapist. He used an empty chair method, having Nick play the roles of the "rational" and the "ir-rational" Nick. He used logs between sessions to help Nick learn to stop himself when he started to become angry, and to begin to use his new disputation tech-niques on his own. These methods help Nick reduce his overall level of anger. At this point, Nick and his worker began to work on his depression and anxiety, also using cognitive behavioral methods.

Over time, as Nick began to trust his social worker, he become clearer about his needs for direct feedback and advice. In week eight he asked his social worker if he thought he needed medication. The therapist chose to give Nick his direct opinion instead of reflecting it back to him; Nick asking for direct feedback was an important development in the therapeutic relationship. The therapist said that he thought Nick could use something to help him improve his anxiety and depression, and that they would continue to work on helping Nick work on his issues. He praised Nick for his willingness to be open to something different and said that he knew it was hard for Nick to even think about taking medication. After seeing the psychiatrist, Nick was placed on an SSRI, a medication that has been shown to be effective for both anxiety and depression. Nick continued to improve. As he continued in therapy, he began to explore more affective-related topics and became interested in exploring some of some more existentially re-lated themes.

FOR WRITING AND REFLECTION

1. How might have the therapist used the other methods to work with Nick?
2. What strengths and limitations might you have in working with Nick?
3. What macro social work issues does this case bring to mind? How might you work toward change in this area?

Case Example

Vernon Cuaswell is a 51-year-old African American man living in Baltimore. Vernon attends a community mental health day program and lives in a boarding home. He has had schizophrenia for over twenty years. He grew up in a working/middle-class African American neighborhood. His father worked at a local shipyard as a union foreman, and his mother was a schoolteacher. He and his brother and sister were "spoiled rotten." The family cared for their children extremely well—they frequently went on vacations, and the children nearly always had tutors for the subjects in which they did not excel. Vernon had saxophone lessons for many years and frequently went to camp during the summer. He was a happy and well-adjusted boy who did well at school. Throughout high school and college, he was a model of success. He majored in history and decided he wanted to go to graduate school in African American studies and ultimately be a writer or a college professor. He graduated from college magna cum lade. His parents and family were extremely proud of him. After he graduated, he used the money he received from graduation to backpack through Africa, spending six months there and finding volunteer opportunities in orphanages along the way. He did whatever was needed and felt grateful to do so. Traveling and getting in touch with his history made him feel alive, vital, and energized. The experience galvanized his desire to return to graduate school.

Vernon first began to develop symptoms of schizophrenia when he was in graduate school. While he was working on his master's degree in African American studies, he began to hear voices. His family noticed that he was becoming more moody. They attributed this change in mood to the stress of school, and perhaps him coming into his own has a person. He was becoming, they reasoned, more of a man. Over time, however, he began to worry his family more. He became paranoid and angry and blamed them for his "oppression."

The once periodic voices soon became constant. Vernon also began to have problems with sleeping. Within several months he because extremely paranoid and withdrew from others nearly completely. He stopped visiting his family and did not return their calls.

Vernon was living in graduate housing at the time. The staff became worried that this once cheerful man who was always there to help others was becoming difficulty and angry. One day, Vernon left his room with a small backpack and did not return.

What happened next is a bit of a blur to him. He knows that for several years he lived under bridges and ate food from behind fast-food restaurants. He moved around from city to city, spending his days in libraries reading history, politics, and conspiracy theories. For several years he remained large invisible to others, having learned how to live on the streets without being found. He periodically sent angry letter to his family, blaming them for forcing him to go to college, for his "indoctrination." Vernon believes his first hospitalization was during this period. He only recalled being medicated and strapped down "for a few weeks or so."

Vernon finally retuned home after nearly three and a half years of living on the streets. He was tired, depressed, and beaten down. He told his family that people from outer space had given him drug therapy, and that he was better now. His father informed him that he could only stay in their home if he went to the doctor and followed through on the doctor's orders. His father said that he and his mother were actually scared of him, and that they were not sure what to think about their son. They told him that they loved him and wanted him to get help. Vernon agreed and went to see the doctor, who placed him on Thorzine, an early antipsychotic medication. The medication made him extremely sleepy, made his tongue very dry, and had other powerful side effects. He did not feel like himself, but he agreed to stay on the medication. For the first several months, Vernon worked on rebuilding his life. He started taking classes at a local community college, with the idea of returning to gradate school. He found a part-time job in a library and began dating one of his coworkers. However, believing that he did not need his medication any longer and disliking its side effects, Vernon stopped taking it. His mood began to change rapidly. He again become sullen, hostile, and paranoid. Several days later, he was arrested at the library after screaming at patrons. The police did not immediately recognize him as someone who was mentally ill, or they did not have the training needed to care for the mentally ill, and they badly mishandled the situation. Never violent, Vernon wound up being shot by a police officer in the shoulder. He was hospitalized for his injury and placed on medication again. While he was psychiatrically stable, he became extremely depressed, finally realizing the depths of his illness. Upon being released, he attempted to kill himself and was rehospitalized. At this point, Vernon was committed to the state psychiatric hospital, where he lived for the next fifteen years.

By the time Vernon had become my client, he had been attending the community mental health center for the last seven years. Vernon was assigned to me when I was an intern in the center's psychosocial rehabilitation program. My supervisor said that Vernon had not had a therapist for individual therapy for many years but stated that he wanted to try to "talk about things." My supervisor said that during our first few weeks of group work, Vernon had become comfortable with me and told her he would like to work with me. True to his wonderful sense of humor, he told my supervisor that at the very least "I might be able to learn something." Vernon was the first person I had ever worked with in individual therapy who was persistently mentally ill. I was afraid, and I was not sure how to proceed. In truth, I was not sure what my role with Vernon would be. Clearly, I would not be helping him "fix" his mental illness. The social work maxim "start where you client is" felt like all that I knew in terms of beginning my work with Vernon. Since I would be with Vernon all year, I saw it as my first task to understand who he was, beyond his diagnosis.

During our first session, I told Vernon I was grateful that he asked to see me for one-on-one sessions. I asked him what he hoped to gain, and why he wanted to start these sessions at this time. He explained that he related to my use of poetry in one of our group sessions, and that he had written a great deal of poetry when he was in college. He said that he liked to write poetry and somehow hoped I could use poetry with him, and perhaps talk to him about things that bothered him. Vernon began to discuss his current life context. He said that while he felt comfortable with the day program, it was painful for him that his life had not amounted to much. He said that he had largely accepted that he would not work again, and that he may always have hallucinations. He wanted life to have some meaning, and to find a way of "engaging" the world. He said that it was painful for him that he had lost so much of his "intellectual strength" and that he was living "life on the edge." He did not really want to talk about the past a lot but really wanted to write about his life now, and his future.

Given that Vernon wanted to work on creating meaning in the here and now, and given his desire to write, I expressed to him that perhaps we could use writing as a vehicle for creating meaning and value. I explained that writing was actually one of the ways that I created meaning in my own life, and that I would be glad to be a partner with him on his journey.

During the time between our session, I reread several articles and parts of books on poetry therapy (Bump 1987; Goldstein 1990; Leedy 1987; Lerner 1981). During our second session, I brought several poems for Vernon and me to read, and I also developed a writing exercise. I realized that I had to balance being prepared and facilitative of his writing, with the need to have him take ownership for our sessions. I started our session by asking how he was feeling. I then told him that we could do several things that day: we could continue our discussion, we could read some poems that I brought, or we could try a poetry-writing exercise. He responded that he would like to do all three. I affirmed that we certainly could do that, and we could plan our time accordingly.

For the next year, Vernon and I read and wrote poetry together. After we read poetry, we discussed what it meant. I attempted to keep the sessions focused on Vernon, and on his responses to the poetry and what they meant to his life. Frequently, however, Vernon asked me what the poem meant to me. Given the nature of our sessions, and after exploring the issue of self-disclosure in great depth with supervisors and teachers, I would periodically self-disclose. I tried to use my self-disclosure in ways that would be helpful to Vernon, but at times I merely shared with him—he often needed to see me as an authentic human being. Given Vernon's social isolation, the depth of our sharing provided him with a source of connectedness. Vernon was a well-educated man who had lost so much. During our time together, he wrote poems that helped him clarify who he was in the past and present, and who he wanted to be in the future. For the first time in many years, he began to have dreams about the future.

FOR WRITING AND REFLECTION

In a few paragraphs, explore how you might work with Vernon at different points in his developmental path.

Older Men at Risk | ELEVEN

Kosberg (2002) notes that media representations and social views present a bimodal view of older men, who are depicted as either privileged and trouble-free or frail, weak, and incompetent. Older men with financial resources, in particular white men, are seen as the cause of social problems. For instance, older privileged men are viewed as being responsible for war and poverty. That men who have had financial success in their lives should need services may appear unlikely to those who view them stereotypically. They are viewed as vigorous, dominating, and powerful, with the ability to live and do as they please. On the other extreme, older men without resources are viewed as weak and frail, possessing neither strengths nor resources nor the capacity to contribute to society. They may be viewed as drains on society, expending tax revenues needed for their care. Older men without power and status are viewed as bumbling, pitiable, and almost ridiculous.

These stereotypes mask the real needs, strengths, and limitations of older men, thereby rendering them as dehumanized others (Kosberg and Kay 1997). Older men are actually a diverse group. Each older man possesses his own biopsychosocial strengths and limitations. Older men have social-, psychological-, and spiritually based developmental strivings and needs. They have the need to create meaningful, fulfilling lives, just as do younger men. Some older men have nonnormative problems that are dismissed by a society that has by and large neglected its entire older adult population, and by professions that have focused more on the needs of older women (Kosberg and Mangum 2002).

This chapter discusses the general needs of older men, the social contexts in which they live, and suggestions for social workers. It is important to remember that older men may struggle with all the other concerns that are addressed in this book. Reaching older adulthood does not absolve men from struggling with sexual identity, their relationships with others, mental health problems, substance abuse, or any other problem that men can face throughout their lifespan. These problems express themselves differently in older adulthood, as they do in each life stage. A man must meet these challenges within the context of the developmental milestones and dilemmas that are a normal part of adult development. As seen in chapter 3, the degree to which a man has successfully met his developmental challenges, personal goals, and dreams and handled his social relationships will set a powerful context for the last stage of his journey.

Conceptions of Aging

Developing conceptions of aging are related to our valuation of the aging process and to the manner in which human beings are valued as they make this developmental journey. Arras, Ogletree and Welshimer (2006:66), in their exploration of male development, describe the relationship between men's development in middle age and their movement toward older adulthood:

> Little attention has been paid to health-promoting practices as men make the transition from the middle to the later years of their life. Middle age represents a time when individuals start to acknowledge their own aging, may face health problems for the first time, and begin to feel vulnerable. This developmental period can pose a crisis, with the potential for opportunity and threat. Healthy behaviors in middle age, carried through to later years, have a profound impact on psychological, social, and physical well-being, potentially extending and improving quality of life.

While I explored some of the developmental issues of aging in a previous chapter, in order to understand the issues of older men it will be helpful to look at some conceptions of aging. Exploring their own biases about the aging process also helps practitioners understand the internalized messages they carry that may affect their work with men. Negative conceptions about aging have actually been correlated with a decreased life expectancy. Levy et al. (2002) found that people who had a positive conception about the aging process lived 7.5 years longer than those who did not. Positive conceptions about aging had a more powerful effect on longevity than physiological factors such as blood pressure and body mass index. Therefore, exploring and altering, as needed, our own conceptions of aging can actually help us live longer! The exercise at the end of the chapter will help you explore your own conceptions of aging and should be done before reading on.

Conceptions of aging vary from culture to culture. Within the mainstream of American society, older adults are not viewed with the same regard as they are in other societies. For example, the age of a presidential candidate who is older than 70 is viewed as a potential problem, whereas in China the top government officials serve well into their eighties. Asian cultures revere older adults: aging is associated with wisdom, strength, and insight. Confucian philosophy obliges Chinese to take care of and honor older adults. However, in China, and for Chinese Americans in the United States, the traditional structures that support this reverence may slowly be changing. Fuligni and Zhang (2004) contend that as Chinese families become smaller, and as China's economic power and industrialization have lead to social policy that encourages nuclear, nonextended families, the elevated status of older Chinese people has begun to diminish. This diminution may also be accelerated and exacerbated by acculturation and the adoption of more Western, capitalistic ideals.

An important aspect of how aging is socially constructed is related to the phenomenon of ageism. The Canadian Network for the Prevention of Elder Abuse (2007) notes that ageism is a social attitude. It is a way of looking at older people that stereotypes them, just as people of particular races are stereotyped as being "smart," "industrious," "thrifty," "lazy," or "easygoing," or men and women are stereotyped as being "strong," "nurturing," or "sensitive" because of their gender. Ageism is also manifested in attitudes whereby people believe that older adults can be treated in demeaning ways. Many people note that as they grow older and as reach certain age milestones (age 65 being one of them), others begin to treat them differently. Their attitudes change. In many cases, being treated differently means being treated as "less"—less valued, less capable, and so on. Or they are stereotyped. Ageism is also reflected when younger people implicitly or explicitly act as if they are more entitled to family or social resources than older adults are.

Ageism is significant and often subtle. Research has shown a difference exists between younger adults' feelings toward older adults in general and their feelings toward their own grandparents (Striker and Hillman 1996). In general, younger adults feel more positively about their own grandparents and have more negative feelings about older adults in general. Striker and Hillman conclude that the role of grandparent mitigates overall negative feelings that younger adults have about older adults. In other words, younger adults have significant bias about the abilities, resources, and value of older adults. While the findings are alarming, it also points to the value that younger adults place in specific relationships with older grandparents, a factor that can be used by social workers in various kinds of intergenerational programs.

Examples of ageism abound, but they are frequently connected to the world of work. Especially during difficult economic times, older men may not be treated well in their workplaces. This is ironic, as older men may typically have the experience and skills needed to mentor younger adults in difficult times. Workplace ageism is harmful not only to older men but also to society as a whole. Given that older men are now living longer, having them maintain employment will help insure that they will need significant levels of care for shorter periods of time.

Zalman Schachter-Shalomi has been a leading advocate of a movement called "spiritual eldering." Spiritual eldering seeks to reenvision the role of older adults in American society. He affirms that older adults are seen as burdens on society yet should be viewed as being part of the potential healing of the world—as sources of social transformation. He notes: "The model that I'm proposing does more than respect the elder to a position of honor and dignity based on age and long life experience. It envisions the elder as an agent of evolution, attracted as much by the future of humanity's expanded brain-mind potential as by the wisdom of the past. With an increased life span and the psychotechnologies to expand the mind's frontiers, the spiritual elder heralds the next phase of the human and global development" (Schachter-Shalomi and Miller 2001:3).

Physical changes associated with the aging process are important to our understanding of conceptions of masculinity. While society has shifted toward strongly valuing intellectual and economic power, physical prowess and abilities have long been important aspects of masculine identity. Men tend to reach their physical peak at some point in their early thirties (depending upon the measure that is used, e.g., endurance or strength). Physical changes often begin as early as age 35, when levels of testosterone begin to decrease. These changes have been referred to as Aging Male Syndrome, and they affect some men more than others (Jones 2008). For many men, physical decline is a slow and gradual process; for others, it is far more rapid. Physical changes can include weight gain, sleep issues, erectile problems, muscle loss, an increase in urination, loss of bone density, and loss of hair. Psychological effects that can accompany these changes include feeling heavy or overweight, depression, irritability or anger, and a loss of perceived energy. It is difficult to tell precisely when these changes represent a normal part of the aging process versus a clinical syndrome. It is important that men who are experiencing some of these problems see a medical doctor, in particular a urologist or another medical doctor specializing in the concerns of men. Some authors have noted that the syndrome may also be related to heart disease (Alexandersen and Christiansen 2004). Men experiencing these problems can have their testosterone levels checked and in some cases be treated with testosterone injections or androgen replacement therapy.

The Social World of Older Men

As previously noted, men have profound needs for social and emotional support that are often not recognized nor met (Blieszner and Adams 1992; Lang and Carstensen 1994). This is especially true for older men. Research has shown that older men have fewer friendships than women and report their friendships as being of less importance (Antonucci and Akiyama 1997; Elkins and Peterson 1993; Fox, Gibbs, and Auerbach 1985). What is not known is if the devaluation of friendship is developmental or related to the adoption of masculine schemas that affect the maintenance and development of relationships. Given that many men have also not learned the skills of negotiating intimate relationships and their emotional complexities, some older men may hold a lifetime of unresolved social conflicts that have led them to be distant from and mistrusting of others. Regardless of the reasons, which vary from man to man and necessitate a thorough assessment, older men often suffer from insufficient social support. The consequences of this are profound. Men without social support are at far greater risk of physical and mental health concerns, even death, than those with such support (Shye et al. 1995).

Men, and older men in particular, learn to rely on women for the majority of their emotional support. Marriage lowers the likelihood of death for younger and older men alike (Kotler and Wingard 1989). While statistically men die younger than women, many men do find themselves widowers and alone. This often presents serious psychosocial difficulties for men, as expressed in this passage: "The socialization of men to not express their emotions and to be dependent on women for many aspects of domestic life may contribute to high levels of distress among them when faced with situations such as bereavement. Many studies from the US and UK report that a greater proportion of widowers experienced mental and physical health problems than did widows, although both women and men were vulnerable to illnesses and ailments on losing a spouse" (World Health Organization 2002).

Social workers must therefore work at helping men, particularly men who are isolated, to develop meaningful social networks. Certainly, this is not an easy task. Social workers must contend not only with individual men's own personal relationship barriers, but also with social ideas about the value of older men, and social and structural barriers.

Retirement

Socially viewed as a reward for a lifetime of work, retirement is not easy for many men. Men know that they are supposed to be happy about the end of their work lives, but this often makes the adjustment to retirement all the more difficult. For many men who strongly identified with their jobs, work was their primary source of identity, social support, and connectedness. For many men, the loss of work is the loss of life. This loss may often manifest itself in more than symbolic ways; suicide is more common in older men than in nearly any other segment of society (Conwell 2001).

Social security, or old-age, survivors, and disability insurance, as it is technically named, is the main source of retirement income for many men who were unable to save during the middle of their life. Contrary to popular belief, this is not an entitlement program, but the federal insurance program that the vast majority of American workers pay into throughout their work careers. The age at which a man can retire and receive full social security benefits depends on the year in which he was born, with a maximum age for receiving full benefits being 67 years old for men born after 1960. In 2008 the current maximum benefit, based on full contribution into the system, was $2,185 per month (Social Security Administration 2008). For men with continued family responsibilities and health concerns, or for those who live in expensive cities, social security may not be enough.

Men frequently hold misconceptions about planning for retirement. A study by New York Life Insurance company found several key flaws in men's thinking about their retirement (Updegrave 2006). First, men tend to grossly underestimate the amount of years they will need to cover with retirement savings. About 50 percent of 65-year-old men are estimated to live to 85 years old. However, few men plan on having twenty years of income at retirement age. Additionally, the study found that women are more likely than men to ask for retirement planning help.

Depression

While depression may be a common occurrence in older men, it is not a normal or natural part of the aging process. As with other conditions that older men struggle with, stereotypes about the nature of the aging process influence how helpers see the possibilities for older men. Laidlaw et al. (2003) demonstrate how CBT is useful for helping older adults with their depression. They observe that it is important to help older adults face the socially constructed stereotypes that they may have internalized—for instance, that they are worthless, decrepit, and useless, and that their lives have no meaning. It is especially important to help older men who have retired evaluate the beliefs they hold about themselves regarding work and productivity.

Alzheimer's Disorder and Dementia

The National Institute on Aging (2007) estimates that approximately 4.5 million Americans have Alzheimer's disorder. Approximately 5 percent of men and women between 65 and 75 years old have the disorder, with the disease becoming increasingly more common with increased age. Those who suffer from the disorder typically survive eight to ten years postdiagnosis, although some have Alzheimer's for considerably longer.

According to the Alzheimer's Association (2007), "Alzheimer's (AHLZ-high-merz) disease is a progressive brain disorder that gradually destroys a person's memory and ability to learn, reason, make judgments, communicate and carry out daily activities. As Alzheimer's progresses, individuals may also experience changes in personality and behavior, such as anxiety, suspiciousness or agitation, as well as delusions or hallucinations."

Many people believe that Alzheimer's disease is a natural part of the aging process, something that all people will struggle with. However, Alzheimer's disease is not a normal part of aging but an actual neurological disorder that leads to marked deterioration in health and functioning over time. Alzheimer's disease is always progressive and nearly always leads to severe cognitive impairment. At some point, should they survive long enough, all men with Alzheimer's lose the ability to care for themselves and appear to be entirely different people from who they once were. While the exact causes and processes of the disease are not totally known, new research has increased our understanding of it. Those with Alzheimer's disease possess deposits of plaque in their brains (amyloidal plaques) and tangled bundles of fibers (neurofibrillary tangles).

Some genetic markers have been identified (National Institute of Neurological Disorders and Stroke 2007). Other explanations that are currently being explored include the impact of environmental factors, such as lead or aluminum, dietary deficiencies, and the slowing of the capacity for creating neurotransmitters. Other theories include the oxidation of neurons as a key factor. As such, some clinical trials have looked at the use of dietary supplements that prevent the oxidation of cells (Markesbery, Schmitt, and Kryscio 2007). At the present time there are no cures or research-supported ways of slowing the progression of the disease itself. However, medications currently exist that may effectively treat some of the symptoms of the disorder in some patients, although this is disputed by some researchers (Brenner 2007).

Perhaps more than any other disease, men have a profound fear of Alzheimer's disorder. By virtue of the fact that it destroys cognition, rationality, autonomy, and personal freedom and control, the disease impacts many of the capacities that men hold dear. Ongoing research on the disorder is therefore critical.

Older Men in Care

When a man is no longer able to care for himself, and when there are no family members to care for him or his family is unable or unwilling to do so, he may find himself living in a care facility. Different ethnic and cultural groups have different values about caring for older adults. For instance, African Americans are more likely to care for their older parents than are whites (Hooyman and Kiyak 2002). Asian Americans, who tend to see the family as the unit of analysis more than the individual, also are far more likely to care for their older adults parents (Pinquart and Sorensen 2005).

Fennell and Davidson (2003) observed that men are often unlikely to choose supported living situations voluntarily, and paradoxically the services that may prevent them from having to be placed. They found that men's valuation of independence and autonomy and their difficulties accepting help are important reasons for their resistance. However, they also found that older men typically perceive social services as not being designed with them in mind. This contention is supported by Kosberg (2005), who urges providers to design services that take into account the desires and needs of older men, from their personal and cultural perspectives.

There are several levels of assisted living arrangements. The least restrictive option is independent living with in-home care, which may be provided by family members. As Alzheimer's disease progresses, the emotional and physical resources of families are often taxed. Men possessing Alzheimer's disorder and other forms of dementia who no longer have family to care for them will often end up in residential care. This is also true for men whose dementia has progressed to the stage where they will need round-the-clock supervision. According to Jones (2002), more than 230,000 people with Alzheimer's disease live in residential care. Men facing the prospect of having to move from their homes to residential care face many difficulties.

While dynamics of nursing homes and other care settings are complex for all older men, this may be particularly true for men from diverse communities. For instance, in the mid-1970s, no nursing homes existed on the geographically huge Apache reservation in north central Arizona. Therefore, older adults who were in need of nursing care would be placed in homes in Phoenix, often several hours away. Being distanced from their communities and frequently not being able to speak in their native language greatly contributed to the isolation of many Apache men. Cooley, Ostendorf, and Bickerton (1979) presented a program that led to improved well-being and connectedness for this population. A simple transportation program was created to enable family members to visit their relatives living in the facility, bring them traditional Apache food, and help them maintain cultural connections. Apache mental health workers would spend time with these older men and women, informally proving them with caring, support, gossip, and companionship. The authors note that programs that connect older adults to their culture and provide them meaningful ways of continuing in the cultural life of their communities may be valuable for other populations.

Elder Abuse

According to the American Psychological Association (2009), over 2 million older Americans are the victims of physical, psychological, or emotional abuse or significant neglect. Older adults who have been victimized often have an increased risk of death or serious health problems. Elder abuse is the infliction of physical or psychological harm on older persons. Physical abuse can take the form of slapping, hitting, or assault with objects, or the use of physical restraints.

Emotional abuse is perhaps more difficulty to define. According to the APA (2007), "Emotional or psychological abuse can range from name-calling or giving the 'silent treatment' to intimidating and threatening the individual.

When a family member, a caregiver, or other person behaves in a way that causes fear, mental anguish, and emotional pain or distress, the behavior can be regarded as abusive. Emotional and psychological abuse can include insults and threats. It can also include treating the older person like a child and isolating the person from family, friends, and regular activities—either by force or threats or through manipulation."

Elder neglect is related to the failure to provide proper and needed care to older adults. Elder neglect may actually account for nearly half of all cases of elder abuse. Examples of elder neglect are not providing older people with sufficient medical care, food, water, or shelter, or not helping them meet a myriad of psychosocial or physical needs. Social workers working with older men are faced with the complexities of having to sort out various degrees and levels of neglect, and they must work with many systems and caregivers in its resolution. Elder abuse and neglect occurs within many contexts and is committed by many different people. Elders may be abused or neglected within nursing homes or other care facilities, but the majority of such abuse is committed by family members at home. Elder neglect in nursing homes and other care situations is often not clear cut. For example, an older man with early onset Alzheimer's disease began to experience a good deal of depression. He also was fairly difficulty to deal with; he was often angry and hostile to nursing home staff and his doctor. Consequently, when he stated he did not want help for his depression, they did not follow up, in spite of his suffering. A social worker identified his anger as a symptom of his Alzheimer's disorder and his depression and was more patient with him, willing to not take his hostility personally. After repeated meetings with him, she assisted him in getting medication, which greatly reduced his emotional suffering. Did the behavior of the care staff and doctor constitute neglect? Legally, no, yet some of the man's needs were clearly ignored—it was easier to do so than to deal with his anger. As noted, social workers need to look beneath men's affect in order to help understand their needs and concerns.

Older Men in the Community

When the spouse of an older person dies, it is important to reconsider living arrangements for the surviving spouse. Many older men find these deliberations difficult. On one hand, they have learned that a real man does not need others—he should be independent. On the other hand, given that many men rely on their spouses for a large portion of their emotional needs, older men who lose their spouses may wind up feeling extremely lonely. One of the ways that older women have increasingly dealt with this dilemma is through living with other women friends. The prohibitions against men doing this are great. Men who are seen living together often have their sexuality questioned; this can be difficult for older men. Also, as discussed earlier, many older men do not have the requisite skills for forming new friendships. However, in spite of these difficulties, some men have found that living with a friend can become an important part of their staying connected and may lead to a new, healthy life structure. A recent example was presented in a newspaper article in the *Charlotte Observer* (Kelley 2007). The article describes two men who met at a senior center and soon developed a close friendship. They began taking classes together at a local community college. In spite of different personalities, both men, in their mid-eighties, found their friendship enriching. Soon one of them moved into the other's home. They began to divide household chores and developed rituals of living together. Both men felt that living together has heightened their independence, as they have been able to achieve things they were not able to achieve on their own. For instance, the men enjoy cross-country travel, and they work out together.

There are several types of community organizations and groups that meet the social needs of men. Veterans of Foreign Wars clubs are popular with older male veterans. Civic associations such as the Lions Club are also popular with men. In a neighborhood in which I lived in San Francisco, older working-class Italian men met at the local bar and spent the day talking over drinks (usually one beer that was nursed very slowly) and playing pool. The neighborhood bar served as a social club for these men, many of whom did not drink alcohol. There was never any pressure from the bartender for the men to purchase drinks (alcoholic or other). Everyone seemed to understand the importance of the bar not only as a business, but as a social institution as well. Other communities have social institutions that function as a means of helping older men. For instance, in the Puerto Rican community of Philadelphia, older men would meet and socialize at the park, where they play dominos, or at the local bodega (store), where they play cards.

Cooper, Groce, and Thomas (2003) advocate for the use of Afrocentric, intergenerational programs designed for African American men. They present the Maturing Africans Learning from Each Other (MALE) project, designed to provide for the spiritual, social, and developmental needs of African American male youth and older adults. The program consists of an intergenerational mentoring program designed to teach and reacquaint men with Afrocentric values. Through didactic training, discussion, and mentoring experiences, older African American men experience a sense of social connectedness and are afforded the opportunity to contribute to the development of younger men. Preliminary data showed that the program holds great potential for meeting the social needs of the participants. By helping different generations of men connect to their cultural heritage, the program works simultaneously toward personal and social transformation. The authors note that the program's focus on helping explore death as an integral life stage, a concept that is congruent with an Afrocentric viewpoint, helps these men begin to find meaning in older adulthood. They found that some participants began to discuss with their loved ones their mortality and their hopes and dreams regarding the aging process for the first time.

Aspects of narrative therapy are particularly useful with older men. One of the key tasks with many older men is to help them view the successes in their lives, and to help them view their struggles and problems within a narrative of strength and resilience (Fast and Chapin 2000).

Reviewing one's life is a life-long, natural human process that helps people understand the stories of their lives (Staudinger 2001). As such, practitioners and scholars have developed an approach called life review or reminiscence therapy (Butler 1963). A great deal has been written about the use of reminiscence in therapy with older adults (Harris 1997). Research has shown the use of reminiscence to be effective in working with adults, and that it can be part of an integrated, eclectic approach to practice (Birren and Deutchman 1991; Hillman and Stricker 2002). Harris (1997) found the approach to be appropriate for work with culturally and linguistically diverse men. This method fits in nicely within a narrative framework, as it helps men verbalize stories about the best and most important experiences in their lives. In reminiscence, the worker encourages men to recall significant events from their life that provide them with meaning and pleasure (Burnside and Haight 1994). The goal of this type of work is to help men feel good about their lives and place their pasts in order (Cook 1991). At times, men will have negative evaluations about aspects of their lives that they will need to come to grips with. At times, the goal will be to help them accept these aspects of their story and place their failures in perspective. At other times, the narratives of some older men may be full of harsh judgments based on socially imposed expectations about how they should have lived their lives. This may be particularly true of men whose lives have not aligned closely to the hegemonic male ideal, or who have engaged in violent, destructive, or other injurious behaviors. Or men may have more subtle or pervasive senses of their own failings; for example, men who were not able to build successful careers or families. They may have come to understand that they have not lived their lives as "real men should." Men in these situations are often plagued by self-doubts, regrets, and depression.

In situations such as this, cognitive and narrative techniques may be valuable in helping men alter the current story of their life. From a narrative perspective, having men "thicken the story" by discussing the context of the events and their own evaluations is valuable. The goal is to help the man place his perceived failures within the context of his social situation, personal or social constraints, or other factors that can help him view his story in a different light. For instance, one older man was preoccupied with not spending more time with his children or not developing a career that felt meaningful. Through elaborating on the context, by telling his story in great detail, it became clear that he held a factory job during the day and worked as a bartender at night to support his family. His wife, who struggled with anxiety and depression, was not able to work outside the home. She felt overwhelmed with raising their children. As such, he did the best he could do. As a therapeutic aid, the therapist solicited two letters from his children (with the client's permission) in which they both said they respected their father greatly. This approach is also congruent with CBT and has been used with depressed older adults.

The main method used is a systematic examination of recollections in order to reframe thoughts and attitudes and focus on past coping and positive views of oneself. In the context of depression, fostering integrative and instrumental reminiscences is particularly salient. Integrative reminiscences refers to distanciated and contextualized reappraisal of losses, shortcomings, and difficulties; review of development of personal values, commitments, and life objectives; and reappraisal of negative events in terms of personal meaning. Instrumental reminiscence refers to recall of episodes of problem solving and positive adaptation, review of adequacy of past and present life objectives, and reactivation of a competent self-concept (Cappeliez 2004).

Relating this work to previous discussions of CBT, the approach may be used to help challenge beliefs that are self-downing and self-injurious. Generalizations about one's life are considered a core irrational belief and can be helped by eliciting evidence that runs counter to these generalizations and helping a man see how he is not clearly viewing the whole context of the story.

Reminiscence can be used both individually and in groups. In groups the therapist facilitates sharing among members and validates support and encouragement. The therapist can take a supportive, facilitative posture or a more directive approach, depending on the group members' cognitive capacities and their ability to help each other in the reframing/reauthoring process.

Creative props, such as photographs, video or audio recordings, and related objects can be used to help trigger memories. Music, especially important songs taken from key developmental periods of clients' lives, can be a particularly valuable method. Olfactory and tactical methods can also be used to help stimulate memories. Friends and relatives may be used individually or in groups to help trigger memories or facilitate discussion about specific life-course events. Utilizing family members and others in this manner can help decrease social isolation and bring people into the care of their older adult friends or relatives in a positive manner.

Several gerontologists have utilized narrative-inspired approaches in their work with people with Alzheimer's disorder. Using reminiscence work with these men can provide a sense of personal integration and connections in their lives, social bonding and support in the context of group work, and even assistance in maintaining their cognitive capacities. In one study, using an experimental design showed that reminiscence groups have positive impact on cognitive functioning and social withdrawal for persons with Alzheimer's disorder and other types of dementia immediately following treatment as well as six months after (Tadaka and Kanagawa 2007). However, the authors recommend that due to the nature of the disorders, treatment groups should be continued, or offered periodically, for gains to be maximized. Other research has led practitioners and researchers to support the use of these and other psychosocial methods in treating Alzheimer's disorder and other types of dementia (Head, Portnoy, and Woods 2004).

When facilitating discussions, it is important to take into account the cognitive capacities of clients. Reminiscence and other therapeutic groups for older adults with dementia work best when the groups are homogenous in terms of cognitive capacity and, to the degree possible, age.

Spiritual eldering, discussed previously, is congruent with an existential approach. The approach is part of an overall movement in gerontological studies, positive aging. Positive aging and the age-ing to sage-ing movements seek to help older adults reclaim positions of meaning and moral authority in their communities. Age-ing to sage-ing groups encourage older adults to meet together to explore their potential for continued growth. Writing exercises and reflective discussion focus on how people can use their life experiences to bring healing and repairing to the world, and to further the development of their communities. This movement seeks to incorporate spirituality in the lives of older adults. Many older adults reengage their traditional religions or develop new ways of engaging in spirituality. Even the negative consequences of aging can help lead to a deepening of spirituality. Dass (2001), a longtime leader in

interreligious spiritual development, explored how his stroke, or what he refers to as "stroke yoga," helped him develop spiritually. He noted that having to
shift from being a caretaker to being taken care afforded him the opportunity
to learn to appreciate love and connectedness in a new way. For him, one of
the greatest spiritual realizations is the connectedness of human beings to each
other, to our communities, and to our planet. By being less invested in worldly
achievements, the older adult can develop a new, less egocentric way of being.

Not everyone explores these issues of meaning through a theistic frame.
Existentialism teaches us that older adults may visit these larger issues of
meaning without being "religious." It is the role of the social worker to accept the older adult's belief system and help him or her use these beliefs as
strengths, and as a potential mechanism for healing and change. Common
to each of these approaches is a focus on the strengths of older men. Finding
ways of helping older men maximize their current strengths and resources
should be part of all social work practice with men.

Creative and artistic approaches have often been advocated as an important tool in helping older adults achieve a sense of wholeness, integration,
meaning, and pleasure. Beck (2000:1) explores the notion of a creative elderhood as a valuable model for aging, and also as a description of the value of
artistic media.

> Creative elderhood approaches aging by exploring the wellness potential of artistic
> self-expression and creativity, vital nutrients to our personality development and
> overall health. Art and creativity fuel playful curiosity and more of the body/mind's
> potential to breed wellness. Actively creative people generally possess a broader
> range of responses and a more encompassing vision. Creation and expression em-
> power individuals to move beyond mere thought, to make concrete the experi-
> ences of their lives. This act of translation fosters growth and well-being—transfor-
> mation—emotionally, intellectually, physically, socially, and spiritually.

Art has been used in a variety of settings to help older adults with reminiscence and to be vital and alive. Poetry is one artistic medium that has frequently been used with older adults. However, those who use creative arts
methods must be sensitive to the desires of men with whom they work. To
help older men achieve maximum autonomy, social workers should not compel them to engage in artistic explorations if they do not want to. Those who
try to engage older men in the arts walk a fine line between exposing them
to media and ideas to which they may not be accustomed and forcing these
methods upon them.

Several years ago I conducted a poetry group for nursing home residents with Alzheimer's disorder. One of the men who was asked to join the group was clearly ambivalent about participation. He would sit at the edge of the group and sometimes appear to listen, and other times he would not. Each time I asked him to sit where he would be comfortable and said that if he ever wanted to sit in the group, in particular next to me, I would be delighted. Learning that up until several years ago he loved to shoot pool, I found poems to read in the group related to the topic. Within several sessions, he began to sit with the group and would request poems about playing pool. No longer able to write, he soon told me about what he liked about shooting pool. I used his words to form a poem and brought it to him before the group. I asked him if he would like for me to read it to the group, which he was very happy for me to do.

The existential approach to therapy pays special attention to end-of-life issues. Death is a core therapeutic reality for existential practitioners. An existential approach focuses on helping people end their lives with dignity, hope, and meaning. Death is a difficult concept for many social workers to contend with, but it is essential that social workers develop the capacity to discuss these issues. One of the ways to become more comfortable exploring death with others is to do some personal work around one's own death, as called for in the second exercise below. It is important to note that some people have had painful experiences around the death of love ones and have avoided looking at death. If this applies to you, you will want to proceed with caution engaging in this exercise.

The National Association of Social Workers (2004:4), in its development of standards for palliative and end-of-life care, dedicates one of its standards to the attitude and self-awareness of social workers who confront end-of-life issues: "Social workers in palliative and end of life care shall demonstrate an attitude of compassion and sensitivity to clients, respecting clients' rights to self-determination and dignity. Social workers shall be aware of their own beliefs, values, and feelings and how their personal self may influence their practice."

Many types of social workers will work with clients who must prepare to face the prospect of dying. The importance of social workers helping to prepare older men for dying was also confirmed by Vig and Pearlman (2003:1598) in their qualitative study of older men who are dying:

Participants believed that their actions could help ensure good deaths. A sense of completing one's preparations for death assured some participants that the burdens on loved ones would be minimized after their deaths. The belief that dying with unfinished business would lead to a bad death, for example, motivated some participants' preparations in the present. One participant responded that the most important thing in his life was to "see that everything is taken care of, so that everything can be in the hands of my wife, and it'll be an easy transition when I'm gone." By organizing his finances and preparing his funeral, this man felt that he could soften the blow of his death on his wife.

Participants valued their independence. They expressed concerns about becoming dependent and burdening loved ones during the process of active dying and death. One individual described the emotional burden on his loved ones if he died in a debilitated state, "Well, the only one that bothers me would be to wind up, you know, incapacitated and lying in a hospital bed indefinitely. . . . That would be the worst scenario that I could imagine . . . just not being able to take care of yourself even as far as going to the bathroom . . . I wouldn't want my children to remember me that way; I wouldn't want S. to remember me that way."

Hospice and palliative social work are important social work specialties that often involve older men. Hospice social workers engage in a variety of roles. Palliative care and hospice care differ but may be provided by the same social worker (Christ and Sormanti 1999). Palliative care refers to care that focuses on the reduction of pain and discomfort and can be provided at any point during a serious illness. Hospice care refers to providing services to clients who are no longer actively seeking a cure for their illness, and who are expected to live for less than six months. Both these types of care serve as a critical link between a dying man's family and his medical team. Hospice social workers are able to help family members understand the complex medical issues involved and make informed chooses about their loved one's care. Hospice social workers provide case management services for families also will help family members through the complex feelings of grief, sadness, stress, and anger that they may struggle with.

Case Example

Willy is an 85-year-old man who lives in the same midwestern city in which he was born. In many ways, his life has been typical of men born in the early 1920s. His early childhood was happy and fairly easy; his father worked as a foreman in a meat-packing plant and was able to support his family well during Willy's early childhood. They lived in a medium-sized home around the corner from the school Willy attended. His mother cared for Willy and his two younger brothers. Willy was 8 years old when the Great Depression began and his father lost his job. For the next decade, his father went from odd job to odd job; his mother was rumored to have sold her body for money. At age 13 Willy dropped out of school to beg for money for his family. These were difficult years. Willy frequently found himself in violent situations, and he was beaten and even once raped. He has spoken about this experience with very few people in his life. He still feels a great deal of shame for "letting" the man take advantage of him instead of being able to fight him off. In his late teens, Willy was able to find odd jobs fixing small machines; he was handy and was able to learn to be a mechanic from a neighbor. This was a skill that would serve him well throughout his life.

When World War II began, Willy was drafted. He quickly learned to be an airplane mechanic and was sent to the South Pacific. Willy was lucky and made it through the war physically and mentally unscathed. Upon his return, he got a job as a mechanic for the United States Postal Service. It was just the kind of job he was looking for, something that would be stable and secure and would allow him to continue to use his skills. Willy constantly worked at being the best mechanic he could. His fear of economic insecurity drove him to learn as much as he could.

Since the 1950s Willy's main form of socialization has been through bowling leagues. Willy loves to bowl. On some level, bowling teams remind Willy of the war: no matter what you feel about your teammates, they are your teammates and you support them. Loyalty and teamwork are important values that he cherishes. Willy enjoyed the stability of the bowling league; it contrasted greatly to the instability he experienced during the Depression, the defining event of his life.

An added benefit of bowling leagues was that he was able to meet women. Within a year of his return from the war, Willy met Karen, who also worked for the post office, as a letter sorter. After a year of dating, Willy and Karen married. Their life was fairly "basic," in Willy's words. Karen quit her job within several years, and they had three children. They enjoyed their family life. Willy provided his children with a stable environment. He is not a particularly demonstrative men, but neither is he cold or distant. While he rarely hugs his children or tells them that he loves them, each of them feels loved and cared for. They understand that their dad is an "old-fashioned, working-class guy." Willy prides himself on being a responsible man, and on following through with his obligations. The purpose of life is to "do a good job, and raise your family right," in his words.

Willy retired from his job at the age of 70. He was ambivalent about retirement but had to admit to himself that he was not able to do the work any longer. Willy began to struggle with several health problems. He was diagnosed with arthritis in his early sixties. For nearly a decade, his hands hurt while he worked, and they hurt a great deal during his bowling leagues, which he and his wife participated in three times a week, though he was unwilling to give them up.

About the time of his retirement, Willy also had begun to develop mild trem- ors in his hands; his doctor feared that he was developing Parkinson's disease or some other neurological condition. Further testing from specialists revealed that he does indeed have the disorder—he was diagnosed at age 71. However, Willy was fortunate in that the disease did not progress as rapidly as it often does, and he was able to maintain his bowling ritual and his quality of life. How- ever, this began to change. He has recently been experiencing both intense pain and tremors in his hands. For the first time in fifty years, he has had to miss time from his bowling league. One day he was feeling too tired to leave the house. Another time his hands hurt too much to bowl. To Willy, missing bowling was emotionally painful. Willy is currently struggling with what his changing health status means for his sense of self. He has been increasingly moody and irritable with his wife and children. He has a hard time remembering things. Willy has not sought out the care that would help him for several reasons. First, since he has not been comfortable talking about his feelings, those around him do not know how bad these changes in his health status make him feel. His family at- tributes his change in mood solely to the progression of his Parkinson's disease, not to his feelings of sadness and loss about his vitality. In fact, like many men of his generation, Willy did not develop the emotional vocabulary to talk about the "softer" emotions. At this point, Willy remains stuck between an old self that he is not able to access and a new self that he cannot envision.

FOR WRITING AND REFLECTION

1. What are Willy's current psychosocial needs?
2. How can Willy be helped to move toward a new vision of his future?
3. How can Willy's bowling league be used as a source of strength?
4. How can Willy's family be helped in this situation?

EXERCISE 1

Please do the following free-writing exercise. Write a paragraph using each of the fol- lowing prompts.

When I think of older men I think of:

Older men can contribute:

Older men are capable of:

The problem with older men is:

EXERCISE 2

The purpose of this exercise is to help you explore your own beliefs about death, in particular your own death. Begin this exercise by relaxing with your eyes closed for several minutes. Once you are relaxed, visualize your own funeral. Spend time doing this. Imagine the setting. See who is there. Listen to what people are saying about you, about your life. Spend about ten minutes meditating on this exercise.

FOR WRITING AND REFLECTION

1. What was this exercise like for you?
2. What did you learn about your own conceptions of death from this exercise?
3. Based on these conceptions, how might your beliefs about death influence your work with older men?

Diverse Men at Risk | TWELVE

In spite of many similarities, men are not a monolithic group. Social workers work with men from many racial, ethnic, cultural, and religious groups. Being able to understand how diversity affects social work practice with men is an essential skill. As with other groups, there are often as many intragroup differences as there are intergroup differences. This chapter discusses some of these key cultural differences and attributes of men from diverse backgrounds and their implications for social work practice. It should be noted that any proper discussion of the complex concerns and needs of diverse groups of men would warrant an entire book. The aim here is merely to sensitize social workers to some of the issues pertaining to diverse groups of men that are not explicitly or sufficiently covered in other sections of the book. Before discussing the specific cultural variables related to different groups of men, a comment about culturally sensitive practice is warranted.

Culturally Sensitive Practice

Many wonderful books have been written on the topic of culturally competent practice, and all social workers should familiarize themselves with these works (Devore and Schlesinger 1991). However, in a very real sense, all good social work practice must be culturally competent. Throughout this book I have treated men as a culturally distinctive group. Culturally specific factors not only affect how problems are manifest but provide a context for possible solutions to those problems.

Racism, Oppression, and Discrimination

One of the misunderstandings of micro social work practice is that it focuses merely on "personal issues." It is true that contemporary American social work practice has centered on the individual as the locus of problem identification and alleviation. Yet, individual and social factors are profoundly linked. This book has explored the impact of socialization, for instance, the impact of hegemonic masculinity, on the cognitive content, processes, and structures of men. It has examined how micro methods can be used to help men evaluate and change their often rigid and unhelpful conceptions of masculinity. The same process can occur with oppression, discrimination, and racism.

Much debate exists as to what constitutes culturally sensitive social work practice, the degree to which relevant content is currently infused into social work curriculum, and the effectiveness of such methods (Hopps 1988). Colon (1996) emphasizes the need for a "generalized sensitivity" to cultural factors in working with diverse populations. Williams (1988) presents a policy-based approach. He suggests that a policy course on racism and oppression should act as the "integrating mechanism" for cultural content throughout the curriculum. In this model, theories of power and oppression are seen as the main organizing principles, equipping students with the analytical tools necessary for culturally sensitive practice. Williams suggests that this organizing principle can be used with other themes, such as the effects of culture on human development, distribution of social resources, cross-cultural practice, distribution of welfare provisions to certain groups, ethical issues in research with minorities, social and distributive justice in social welfare, and the effectiveness and relevance of practice theories with various cultural and minority groups. While this model of culturally sensitive practice has value as an analytical tool, it does not lend itself to direct practice situations. Knowledge concerning the etiology of social problems does not necessarily lead to clear practice prescriptions.

Harper and Lantz (1996) take a different approach to culturally sensitive social work. Instead of focusing on factors that differentiate social work practice between groups, they have posited curative factors that transcend cultural boundaries. They have identified seven factors that are useful in solving "emotional" problems across cultural contexts: respect for the client's worldview; the importance of hope; helper attractiveness, i.e., warmth, genuineness, and compassion; techniques designed to give clients more control of their lives and environment; rites of initiation, defined as rituals designed to cope with life stage transitions; cleansing experiences, rituals designed to let go of unwanted emotions; and existential realization, or helping a client search for meaning. The authors note that while these factors are curative within all cultures, the manner in which they are expressed and experienced differ markedly. In addition, these factors must take into account the realities of minority status, including the experience of being unwanted and shunned by dominant groups.

Such theorists focus on clinical skills and knowledge needed for culturally sensitive practice across ethnic groups. That is, they seek to identify domains that a practitioner must understand in order to work with a given population. They do not focus on the specifics of given client groups but provide insight into what factors need to be explored by those seeking to work with minority populations. Leininger (1987) posits that helpers must learn to identify what helping behaviors are accepted within a given community before services can be provided.

While focus on cross-cultural curative factors or on the nature of the minority experience itself is an important component of culturally sensitive social work practice, there are several limitations that such a focus has as an organizing principle. For instance, it does not allow helpers to understand the discrepancy between their own values and those of their clients. Lau (1986) observed that helpers may not possess the same worldview and value system as their clients and therefore may be unaware of what behaviors and beliefs are sanctioned by the group, and which are idiosyncratic to the individual. Further, Goldenberg and Goldenberg (2002) remind us that there is a danger in generalizing about norms of minority cultures: such generalizations may easily calcify into ethnic stereotypes. They suggest that the purpose of learning about cultural differences is to assist the helper in recognizing lifestyle patterns and behavior as normal for the given group. Without such knowledge the helper may label unfamiliar behavior as deviant or dysfunctional. With this warning in mind, the sections that follow explore some of the important issues to consider when working with different groups of men.

Gay Men

Homosexuality has become increasingly accepted in American life. Recently, John Amicci, a former professional basketball player, expressed surprise at the acceptance and warmth he felt after announcing to the public that he is gay. However, while gay men have become more accepted in American society, being homosexuality clearly is still stigmatized within many segments of American culture. Gains that were made during the 1980s and 1990s have been somewhat threatened by more conservative shifts within the American political landscape. It has become more common and accepted for some religious conservatives to say that they accept gays and lesbians, but not "their behavior." This linguistic twist, when critically examined, is little more than a more subtle form of homophobia and prejudice.

Social cues such as this make the discovery and expression of one's sexuality as a gay person complex. Hughes (2003:262) explores this complex relationship between the social and individual constructions of identity for gay men.

> While the term "gay" seems commonplace and generally accepted by most people, it is important to note that the meaning a man gives his own sexuality may differ from that which society gives it. Some men may place less emphasis than others on their same-sex attraction and more emphasis on other aspects of their sexuality, such as the emotional dimensions of their relationship or their particular sexual fantasies. Others may feel constrained by the label "gay" and the images it conjures. Regardless of whether or not we agree with people "staying in the closet" or "passing" as heterosexual, many men who are attracted to other men and who engage in same-sex behaviour do not openly—and sometimes not inwardly—identify as gay. It seems that social workers need to be sensitive to the meaning different people give to their sexual identity and how it is expressed in their lives. Encouraging people to provide their own labels, whether its gay, bisexual, queer or something else, might be one strategy.

Homophobia and heterosexism were briefly explored previously, but they demand increased attention in this section, as they are terms that describe oppressive conditions that have a deep impact on the lives of all men. They are so pervasive in the lives and psyches of men that they warrant their own discussion.

Homophobia refers to the hatred and fear of gay men. It locks all people into rigid and gendered ways of being that inhibit creativity and self-expression. It compromises the integrity and humanity of heterosexual people by pressuring them to treat others badly. Homophobia inhibits one's ability to form close, intimate relationships with members of the same sex. Societal homophobia adds to the pressure to marry, which in turn places undue stress and often trauma on heterosexual spouses and children. Homophobia may encourage premature sexual involvement to prove that one is normal, which increases the chances of teen pregnancy and the spread of sexually transmitted diseases. Homophobia combined with sexphobia (fear and repulsion of sex) results in the elimination of any discussion of the lives and sexuality of people who are lesbian, gay, bisexual, or transgendered (LGBT) as part of school-based sex education, keeping vital information from all students. Such a lack of information can kill people in the age of AIDS. Homophobia can be used to stigmatize, silence, and, on occasion, target people who are perceived or defined by others as gay, lesbian, or bisexual but who are in fact heterosexual. Homophobia prevents heterosexuals from accepting the benefits and gifts offered by LGBTs, contributions that are social, theoretical, political, artistic, familial, religious, and so on (Flood 1997).

Political advocacy is an important social work intervention when working with gay men. Most gay couples are still not afforded the right to marry or the same legal protections that married, heterosexual men have. Social work ethics require social workers to work for equal rights of all their clients (National Association of Social Workers 1999).

Transgendered Men

Transgender refers to a diverse group of people who do not identify with the sex to which they were born. Other transgendered people were born with aspects of sex traits from both men and women (intersex). Transgender differs from sexual orientation. People who are transgendered may or may not identify themselves as being transgendered, some believing that the term does not carefully depict their individual gender- and sex-related identity. Trangendered persons are not necessarily gay, lesbian, or bisexual—many identify as being heterosexual. Regardless, transgendered persons who are viewed by the outside world as men face significant stigma and are not well understood.

Social acceptance of transgendered individuals, whether they started life as men or as women, remains low. The incidence of transgendered men has been estimated to be between 1 in 10,000 and 1 in 30,000 (Harry Benjamin International Gender Dysphoria Association 2001). Transgendered people are often viewed as deviant or degenerate in many communities. However, some Native American communities are far more tolerant of transgendered persons. In these communities, the term two-spirit is used to describe those in whom both the masculine and feminine spirit live within the same body (Lang 1998). Depending on the community, two-spirit refers not only to transgendered people, but to gays and lesbians as well. While the term has been used as such in English for only about two decades, many Native American languages contain words with the same meaning.

The needs of transgendered persons remain unmet. While part of this can be blamed on the society as a whole, the mental health profession in general may be part of the problem (Brown and Rounsley 1996). Transgendered men are typically diagnosed as having "gender identity disorder," which pathologizes their gender identity. Social work has responded positively to this problem with formal statements of acceptance of sexual identity diversity in its code of ethics (National Association of Social Workers 1999).

While programs in some of the larger American cities serve the needs of this population, the majority of cities and small towns do not. Social workers in smaller communities who provide services to a wide variety of men should become familiar with the issues of transgendered men. As transgendered expressions of sexuality are extremely diverse, social workers should humbly seek to understand how each person expresses his or her sexuality and seeks affirmative, affectual relationships.

Latino Men

Latinos are now the largest minority population in the United States, constituting over 13 percent of the population. It is estimated by the year 2025, one quarter of the U.S. population will be Latino (U.S. Census Bureau 2006). Latinos, also referred to as Hispanics, are not a monolithic group. Latinos originate from Mexico, the Caribbean, South America, or Central America. While the primary language in most Latin American countries is Spanish, Portuguese is spoken in Brazil, and indigenous languages are often the first languages in Peru and Guatemala. In the United States, Mexican Americans are the largest Latino group, followed by Cubans, Puerto Ricans, and those from Central America. Many Mexican American families never left their ancestral homelands but became residents of the United States when the country annexed parts of Mexico.

Latinos are generally misunderstood, and this may be especially true of Latino men, who are often thought to be lazy and abusive (Gonzalez 1996) and seen as having little interest in adapting to "American" customs (Delgado 2006). The Latino male is seen as "macho" and aggressive; the protective, positive aspects of the cultural norm of "machismo" are too often unrecognized in Latino men throughout the world (Gutman 1996; Willis 2005).

The reality of Latino men is very different from the stereotypes. For instance, many employers actually view Latino men as better and harder workers (Aponte 1996; Kim 1999). Those who are not documented citizens often must work multiple jobs; many send a great deal of their earnings to their country of origin to support their families.

Latinos in general, and men in particular, underutilize social and physical health services (Fiscella et al. 2002; Padilla, Ruiz, and Alvarez 1989). Services are too frequently not provided with sensitivity to the cultural, political, social, and linguistic realities of Latinos. Many agencies struggle with finding trained social workers who can provide services in Spanish. Agencies who are not able to find such personnel can help bridge this gap by establishing partnerships with indigenous helpers and healers, an important part of providing culturally competent services.

Both the narrative approach and the strengths perspective may have special utility when working with Latino men. Zuniga (1992) explored the importance and utility of *dichos*, or wise sayings, in working with Latinos. Latinos have a profound respect for history, culture, and the oral tradition. As such, helping Latino men find valuable dichos that they can use as metaphors for personal growth and transformation can be useful. For instance, when I traveled to Nicaragua in the 1980s, the whole nation rallied around the dicho "Aqui no se rinde nadie," nobody gives up here. I have found this expression helpful in working with Latino men who are trying to overcome addiction or health-related concerns. The strengths perspective is also very important with Latino men who adhere to the masculine norm of machismo. By focusing on their strengths and what they have done well for their families and themselves, social workers can engage Latino men in the most prosocial aspects of machismo and can help them develop a positive helping relationship. Helping Latino men feel a sense of *orgullo*, or pride in what they have achieved, often in difficult circumstances, is a valuable part of helping them fortify their own internal and external resources.

While dominant models of masculinity change conceptions of what it means to be a man in other parts of the world, other social forces affect what it means to be male in the United States. Migration and transmigration have rapidly changed the face of the United States, and thus who and what is an American man. Many of the Latinos in the United States live what is now being referred to as a transnational pattern of migration (Furman and Negi 2007). Transmigrants differ from traditional migrants in that they maintain lives and identities in both their sending and receiving countries. Historically, studies of migration have used the concept of assimilation as its central organizing principle: migrants to the United States were expected to find ways of adapting to the dominant culture. However, this was a mischaracterization of the relationship between host country and migrant: they both had an impact on each other in complex and powerful ways. Yet, there was an expectation that migrants would find a way to meet the demands of their host countries and over time would find ways of adapting their behavior to their new cultural context. Yet, transnational migrants live in two worlds. For instance, Mexican day labors may work in the United States for several months, often in isolation from traditional social structures, and return to Mexico for months to spend with their families. Such transmigrants find themselves in the middle of two worlds, between differing notions of what it means to be a man.

Asian American Men

Asian Americans are also an extremely diverse group. This diversity and its history is often not well understood by the American public. Chinese men began arriving in large numbers in the United States in the middle of the nineteenth century to work in the California gold rush and as laborers on the transcontinental railroad. In the 1880s the largely male Chinese population of workers were discouraged from immigration by the Chinese Exclusion Act. This act also affected Chinese American men, who had an increasingly difficult time traveling to China and returning to the United States.

Japanese Americans arrived in the United States in the late 1880s to work in the agricultural industries of Hawaii and California. Originally welcomed, over 100,000 were impressed in internment camps during World War II, one of the lowest points in the history of human rights in the United States (Zinn 2005). Through this experience Japanese American men, who viewed themselves as Americans, first and foremost, often lost their careers, property, and many sources of meaning in their lives. While it is perhaps difficult to imagine this happening today, it demonstrates the depths of relatively recent racism to which Asian American men have been subjected.

Other significant Asian American populations include men from the Philippines, India, Pakistan, Korea, Vietnam, and Cambodia, among others. The Immigration Act of 1990 increased the number of middle- and upper-class Asians immigrating to the United States by giving immigration preference to those in the medical and technological fields.

Stereotypes of Asian males portray them as weak and submission. Media representations of subservient Chinese men have permeated Western television and movies. A recent film, *The Slanted Screen* (2006), explored the evolution of stereotypes of Asians in cinema. The film shows how Asian men have been portrayed at times as devious, diabolical, and deceptive, silent and subversive, bumbling, effeminate, or masters of martial arts. Rarely are Asian Americans portrayed as real humans with depth, substance, strengths, and vulnerabilities. Although the Asian population is growing rapidly and Asian Americans can now be found in communities throughout the United States, currently they comprise only 3 percent of the population and have historically lived mostly on the East and West Coasts. Thus many Americans, even social workers, may buy into these stereotypes.

The majority of Asian American men do not conform to the hegemonic masculine ideal, either physically, socially, or emotionally. Asian American men tend to be less mesomorphic than other racial groups. Additionally, while there is huge diversity in Asian cultures, expressions of dominance and aggression in the public realm are generally discouraged. Again, these differences should be seen only as cultural tendencies; they vary based on the degree of assimilation and adherence to middle-class cultural norms. As with each population discussed in this chapter, social workers must use cultural tendencies as hypotheses for understanding individual men.

African American Men

Elsewhere in this book I have noted that African American men have higher rates of several psychosocial and health concerns than some other populations. It is important when discussing these health and psychosocial issues that we place them within the proper context and not engage in the pathologizing of African American masculinity. Hunter and Davis (1994) present a cogent discussion of how African American masculinity has been described in the theoretical and empirical literature. In the early part of the twentieth century, research and scholarship portrayed African American men as incompetent and psychologically damaged. Early scholarship focused on the maladaptive behaviors of black men. When this research was contextualized, it connected African American men's behaviors to a legacy of racism. However, the problem was still seen to reside within African American men themselves. It was not until the 1960s that the discourse shifted. New research and scholarship found that African American men did in fact ascribe to values congruent with mainstream American life yet encountered structural and institutional barriers that impeded their ability to participate in many institutions. However, according to Hunter and Davis, the literature was slow to shift to a discussion the strengths and resiliencies of African American men. They note:

> Studies of Black women emphasize how out of oppression a unique definition of womanhood was forged, one in which adversity gave rise to strengths. However, the discourse around men and oppression focuses on the stripping away of manhood. It is a perspective that castes Black men as victims and ignores their capacity to define themselves under difficult circumstances. Clearly, Black males have had to be men in a historical and cultural context that varied radically from White males', however, emasculation and pathology were not the inevitable consequences of this variation. (21)

In other words, black men (and other minority men as well) have developed considerable strengths from having to meet the challenges presented to them. These strengths coexist with risks. Masculinity and its expression are complex and are not the only factors that are involved in the creation of human risk. Many biopsychosocial factors intersect to create the magnification of many behaviors.

Masculinity, and its expression, is still an extremely important variable. Several studies have explored varying conceptions of African American masculinity.

Cool pose behaviors often interfere with authentic heterosexual relationships. Cool pose behaviors impede men's attempts to develop open, expressive emotional relationships with women. In addition, not being able to regulate the cool pose behaviors, black males often have difficulty disclosing or expressing feelings in a meaningful way to those with whom they wish to be close. The toll is more evident in the mistreatment of self and other African Americans. Black men unable to express their feelings, fears, or worries are constantly under pressure to prove their manhood. Their emotions often can result in assault, accidents, homicide, suicide, alcoholism, or substance abuse. In addition, in order to be "cool," African American men may distance themselves from uncool activities like achieving success in school (Pierre, Mahalik, and Woodland 2002).

In chapter 10 I discussed the problem of depression in men in general, and how the stigma that men experience inhibits their ability to recognize, admit to, and ultimately seek treatment for depression. In his courageous autobiography, which includes statistics and discussions with mental health professionals, John Head (2004) explores how this is particularly salient for African American men. He notes that racism and social stigma compound depressed African American men's overwhelming feelings of worthlessness and shame. He cites findings that physical health disparities (such as high rates of diabetes and hypertension) are part of what leads to the severity of depression in African American men.

Cultural factors influence the expression and willingness to seek treatment.

> We call depression "the blues" in the black community. We're taught to shrug off this mental state. For many of us, it is not just a fact of life; it is a way of life. When bluesmen wail, "Every day I have the blues" or "It ain't nothing but the blues" or similar words from a thousand songs, they do more than mouth lyrics. They voice a cultural attitude. They state the accepted truth at the heart of their music: Having the blues goes along with being black in America. In addition, from the time we are young boys, black males have ingrained into us an idea of manhood that requires a silence about feelings, a withholding of emotion, an ability to bear burdens alone, and a refusal to appear weak. The internal pressure to adhere to this concept of masculinity only increases as we confront a society that historically has sought to deny us our manhood. (Head 2007:3)

In additional to therapy and medication, Head explores the need for black men to stay connected to their families and social systems, get exercise, eat well, and in general live a positive and healthy lifestyle. He notes the importance of men focusing on their whole selves, which includes their social selves, spiritual selves, and psychological selves.

Native American Men

To speak of Native American men as one group is problematic. The diversity that exists within Native communities in the United States is staggering. As with other groups, social workers who have been born and raised within the dominant culture may apply an individualistic worldview in their work with Native men. I do not want to underestimate how difficult it is for those of us brought up to see the world through our own cultural lenses to truly transcend this perspective. Each of us must constantly engage in in-depth and continued self-reflection to guard against our own cultural biases.

Weaver (1999) conducted a qualitative study of Native American social workers and social work students. Her study explored what factors respondents believed were needed for culturally competent practice with Native Americans. She divided responses into requisite skills, values, and knowledge, which form the core of culturally competent practice. Respondents noted four areas of knowledge: diversity, history, culture, and contemporary realities. Diversity refers to the importance of understanding that Native Americans are an extremely diverse group. History refers to the importance of understanding the history of Native nations/tribes within the area in which social workers practice, along with a general knowledge of the relationship between the United States government and Native American people. Culture refers to the general cultural traits shared by most Native people, such as reverence for older people and different cultural ways of relating to death and loss. Lastly, the contemporary realities of life of Native American people on and off reservations, including health disparities and disproportionalities, must be understood. The study found the need for two areas of skills: general skills and containment skills. General skills refers to good, solid social work practice competencies. Containment skills refers to the need for social workers to develop the capacity to restrain themselves in practice. Weaver notes that containment skills involve "patience, the ability to tolerate silence, and listening—all skills that require social workers to be less verbally active than they might be with clients from other cultures. Containment skills require social workers to refrain from speaking" (221).

These skills may be hard for social workers from cultural background in which silence and verbal restraint are less a part of their cultural traditions. I found in teaching practice classes that developing the capacity to use silence therapeutically is an important social work skill for working with all clients, as silence provides people with the space to think and do their own work. This is true for Native people as well. Operating from a strengths perspective, social workers should allow Native American men the space to explore their own solutions.

In terms of values, Weaver's study found helper wellness and self-awareness, humility and willingness to learn, respect and open-mindedness, and social justice to be important in working with Native American clients. I have previously mentioned how critical self-awareness is, along with the ability to understand one's own biases. The study also suggested that being emotionally grounded and in touch with one's own spiritual tradition may be of value. Humility is key in working not only with Native Americans, but with all culturally diverse clients, as workers must learn from them about their own interpretations and personal constructions of their cultural. Respect and open mindedness call social workers to value the perspectives of their clients and seek to understand how their clients' worldviews lead them to conclusions that may differ from their own. In such situations, social workers would do well to employ the skills of patience and listening, thereby seeking to fully and deeply understand the realities of their clients. Finally, social workers working with Native American men must understand the importance of social justice and macro practice. They must understand the impact of colonization and social policies and must advocate for the empowerment and self-determination of Native men.

Krech (2002) explores multiple methods that are appropriate for working with Native American men. He recommends programs that integrate traditional, Native American values and structures within the context of the modern world. "This calls for a blend of old and new methods; a combination of processes that have worked in the past connected with those that are working now" (92). Krech warns helpers to find easy ways of respecting the beliefs and cultures of diverse populations without romanticizing them. He observes that glorifying cultural traditions separates them from the difficult realities of actual living and may lead to a fear of questioning how effective they may be for different problems at different times. He advocates for several methods to be used in this flexible, contextually driven, culturally competent manner. These include the use of mentoring programs that educate men about traditional teachings and ways, the development of community wellness activities, drumming and singing, community-based celebrations, storytelling and narrative, and the integration of twelve-step programs as a vehicle for storytelling about recovery and renaissance. He posits that these and other methods that are based on more communal and community-based practice are more relevant and effective for Native American men than those that center on the individual.

Case Example

Dat Ngyuen is a 25-year-old Vietnamese man who lives in San Francisco. Dat was born in Vietnam, and his family fled the turmoil of postwar Vietnam when he was 3 years old. Dat's family lived in a relocation camp until he was 5 years old. He does not remember living in the camp, yet his sister says she still has nightmares about the crowded conditions, the lack of food, and the fighting that transpired there. The oldest child in the family, Dat is close to his two sisters and his younger brother. He now works as an accountant for a large Silicon Valley computer company and mostly enjoys his job. He finds his tasks a bit monotonous at times but enjoys his coworkers, is treated well, and is happy with his income.

However, Dat is currently experiencing a great deal of stress in his life. His father was recently attacked while walking home late at night. His father was intoxicated at the time, having participated in the Vietnamese ritual of Nhau, a socially sanctioned form of male binge drinking. His father has consistently attended his Nhau group for many years. The Nhau serves several functions in the life of Vietnamese men. Men use their Nhau as a form or personal and professional support. In Vietnamese culture, men do not share their feelings freely, but they are permitted to bring up difficult situations in this group context. Nhaus are highly controversial for more assimilated Vietnamese and outsiders, as they are at times viewed as supporting alcoholism.

Since the family arrived in Vietnam, his father has struggled greatly with the process of assimilation. In Vietnam his father was the owner of a small store and was fairly successful. Typical of traditional Vietnamese families, Dat's father was the head of the household and had absolute authority in his home and with his family. He was grounded, respected, and a good provider. He gave good advice and, while not very affectionate, was kind and supportive. However, he never was able to consistently find work once he moved to the United States. Also, his experiences in the war made him anxious and depressed, although he rarely discussed them except in his Nhau group. These experiences, his feeling diminished self-worth, and his socially accepted drinking patterns have led to a long history of alcohol abuse.

Dat is extremely disturbed about this father's situation. Dat has always had mixed feelings about his father. While Dat loves his father very much, he also feels a lack of respect for how his father has lived since arriving in the United States. These feelings are particularly difficult for Dat, as in Vietnamese culture respect for one's father is a core, almost sacred value. This conflict points to Dat's historical struggles with the process of assimilation and acculturation, and how that intersects with his own personal identity.

Dat was visiting his father in the hospital when the social worker was called to meet with the family. The hospital staff was concerned that Dat's father seemed very depressed and withdrawn and was unwilling to share much information with the doctors. Sally, the social worker, had some experience with Southeast Asian clients; she shared with the family that she understood that such feelings were not readily expressed to strangers. Sally asked if the family had any concerns that they wanted to share. Dat felt conflicted in that it was considered shameful in Vietnamese culture to talk about problems outside the family. Yet, he also recognized that this was a potentially opportune situation to get help for his father. Besides, Dat's perspective on help seeking was fairly modern—fairly "white," in his words.

Case Example

Rodolfo Burgos is an 18-year-old Puerto Rican man living in a group home for teens and young adults with behavioral and emotional diagnoses who cannot be maintained in their own homes. Rodolfo has lived in group homes for nearly ten years. He was originally placed in care due to his mother's addiction to crack cocaine. Rodolfo lived with both his mother and his father for the first several years of his life, but his father did not like life in the mainland United States and returned to Puerto Rico. Rodolfo's father kept in touch with him weekly, but when Rodolfo was 8 years old his father stopped calling. His mother would tell Rodolfo that his father probably did not love him any more, and that Rodolfo needed to move on. It was only several years later that Rodolfo found out from relatives that his father, a fisherman, was killed in a boating accident. However, as a young boy, Rodolfo wondered what he did to cause his father to leave in the first place, and what he did to make his father stop calling. He believed that it was probably because he was mentally retarded, or an "idiot" as his mother frequently called him, or because he had a hard time controlling his anger.

Prior to living in residential treatment facilities and group homes, Rodolfo and his mother were frequently involved in child protective services. His mother had been accused of neglect several times by neighbors, which led to investigations. In spite of there being evidence of neglect and often extreme verbal abuse, the child welfare system in their city was overwhelmed with too many cases and too few workers. Consequently, Rodolfo never received the protection he needed, and his mother did not receive help or consequences for her neglect and abuse.

Rodolfo is a young man who has much to overcome. He has been tested as being moderately mentally retarded. He also has an extremely difficult time controlling his anger and other feelings; he has been diagnosed as having intermittent explosive disorder. Rodolfo is also legally blind—he can see things between two and six feet from him but does not see up close well and cannot see details more than six feet away. Rodolfo has had dozens of pairs of glasses over the years, frequently destroying them in fits of anger. He is easily frustrated and angered. Over the years he has learned that he can get his way by becoming angry. This realization has been a dangerous combination for a young man who struggles with controlling his feelings, is over three hundred pounds, and does not see very well. While Rodolfo is very large and physically powerful, he is not mobile enough to defend himself against many boys his age who have lived in the group homes with him. Consequently, Rodolfo has been beaten up frequently. Due to his victimization at the hands of others and his own feelings of inadequacy and limitations, Rodolfo also has the habit of picking on younger and less physically able boys. In fact, this problem has led to significant problems for Rodolfo at his school. For the past year he has been attending special education classes in a public high school. Being mainstreamed after many years of attending school in partial hospitalization programs has been very important to Rodolfo's sense of himself as a "normal" person.

Rodolfo was suspended for throwing his desk at a smaller, younger boy who called him stupid. The security guard at school responded to the situation with excessive force, and he and Rodolfo became engaged in a physical confrontation. The police were subsequently called, and Rodolfo was taken to jail. While in his communal jail cell, Rodolfo began to scream and bang on the walls. Two of the men in his cell, who were hardened criminals, beat him until he was unconscious.

Rodolfo has many strengths. He loves to draw, and he has created some very powerful cartoons. He spends a great deal of time drawing, and he takes great pleasure and solace in his works of art. He frequently shares his drawings with the staff in his group home and with people in the neighborhood. When he is in control of his emotions, he enjoys people's company and has a wonderful sense of humor. When feeling good about himself and his environment, he is easy to be around. He likes to laugh and playful teases the group home staff. Rodolfo can be warm and good and has a desire to learn. He has many professional staff who care for him. Over the years he has endeared himself to many day staff as well as his therapists. In fact, Rodolfo has become something of an institution within each of the systems that he has been involved in. He is loved, and feared, by many.

Rodolfo's funding for residential treatment will cover him until he is 21 years old. At that point, he will need to move to independent living, semi-independent living, a group home or residential treatment facilitated for mentally retarded adults or for mentally ill adults. Rodolfo has never fit easily and neatly within any care system. His complex problems and abilities mandated interdisciplinary and cross-system collaborative relationships that demanded careful case management.

Rodolfo's most recent case management is provided by the clinical social worker for his group home. Bob, recently out of graduate school, provides individual therapy and develops the therapeutic plan in collaboration with the other professionals and para-professionals. Bob also provides that he calls "hang-out therapy," recognizing that a good deal of the therapeutic interaction that occurs in a milieu such as this happens spontaneous while spending time with the clients, outside the traditional therapeutic hour. Bob schedules his work hours so he can have dinner at least every other week at each group home (he is responsible for several homes) and periodically stops by at other times. Bob and Rodolfo have developed several goals: (1) to help Rodolfo maintain his "cool" and not act violently; (2) to help him develop a long-term plan for "what to do when I am grown up"; (3) to plan for future living arrangements ; (4) to develop more friendships and social contacts; and (5) to spend more time doing art and less time "watching TV and doing dumb stuff."

Bob was careful that the goals for treatment were developed in collaboration with Rodolfo, as he tries to use his clients' words in the formulation of their goals. He finds that when working with young men, it helps to use their own language as a means of reminding them that the goals are their own, and to help them take ownership for them.

In their sessions together, Bob tries to balance a sense of informality and "fatherliness" with a sense of focus. He lets Rodolfo lead sessions at the start but is careful each session to help him explore at least two of his stated goals, and to assess their progress. To do this, Rodolfo has a journal in which he and Bob write together about Rodolfo's progress and action steps that they both will take. Bob is also conscious of not being overly behaviorally focused. He believes that Rodolfo must, in his own way, contend with the larger developmental and existential issues of a young man his age. In all likelihood, Rodolfo will spend most of his life living in some type of structured care. Bob believes that the best long-term situation for Rodolfo would be a semi-independent living situation.

Regardless, Rodolfo needs to develop a sense of identity that is not contingent on traditional measures of success. It is for this reason that Bob is strongly supportive of Rodolfo's art and his sense of himself as an artist. He believes that through his art Rodolfo can find a sense of meaning and purpose and can connect to others. However, while displaying some talent, Rodolfo would have to improve greatly to ever have a possibility of doing something professionally with art. Also, his other issues would make it very difficult for him to be able to support himself in such a competitive profession. As such, Bob feels responsible for both strongly encouraging Rodolfo's art and helping Rodolfo engage in reality testing. For example, Rodolfo frequently talks about selling his drawings for "thousands of dollars." He reasons that if painters like Picasso can sell their work for millions of dollars, so could he.

FOR WRITING AND REFLECTION

1. How would you assess Rodolfo's goals? To what degree are they realistic? How might they be modified?
2. How would you proceed with Rodolfo at this time?
3. What systems of care should be engaged?
4. How might you facilitate social relationships for Rodolfo?
5. How might various concepts related to masculinity affect this treatment?

Men, Compulsive Disorders, and Addictions

Compulsive behavior and addictions have had immeasurable costs in the lives of many men, and in the lives of those who love them. Substance abuse, sexual compulsivity, and compulsive gambling are well known to have damaged the lives of many men and their families. However, compulsive behaviors that have historically been thought to be problems of women, such as compulsive overeating and shopping, have also had a major impact on men's psychosocial health. This chapter explores the role that compulsive behaviors and addictions have played in men's lives.

Whether compulsive sexual behavior or gambling meet classic definitions of addiction, described below, may largely be an academic debate. Some authors have argued that repetitive and destructive engagement in these behaviors should be classified as compulsive disorders, not addictions (Koob et al. 1998). While these distinctions may have some currency, their utility to working clinicians may not be as relevant. What is important is that these problems are significant in the lives of at-risk men and lead to important personal and social consequences. For the purpose of simplicity, I use the terms addiction and compulsive behavior fairly interchangeably. I encourage you, while reading this chapter and in practice with men, to be less concerned with definitional issues than with how we can use our current knowledge base to improve the lives of men. Understanding the nature of addictions and compulsive disorders is important but should not be overemphasized.

Defining Addictions and Compulsive Behaviors

Classic definitions of addiction are based on a chemical dependency model and the physiological responses of the body (Goodman 2006). More modern conceptualizations of substance abuse explore the relationship between bodily responses and the behavioral/psychosocial responses of the addicted person. The two key concepts in the classical conceptualizations of addictions are withdrawal and tolerance. For a person to meet the definition of dependence or addiction, both withdrawal and tolerance must occur. When a substance on which someone is dependent is suddenly removed, physiological symptoms of withdrawal are present (Wise 1996). Withdrawal symptoms range greatly, depending on the type of substance. For example, mild withdrawal symptoms from alcohol dependence include anxiety, irritability, depression, and rapid changes in emotions. Severe withdrawal symptoms from alcohol can include hallucinations (known as delirium tremens, or DTs), extreme agitation, high fever, and convulsions. Withdrawal symptoms from methamphetamine can include extreme fatigue, irritability, intense hunger, and psychotic reactions. Tolerance occurs when the addicted person needs increasingly more drugs to achieve the desired effect. The alcoholic who once was able to get drunk on several drinks may soon drink a case of beer and a bottle of hard liquor every day. When withdrawal symptoms are extreme and tolerance has been built up over time, treatment usually will include some type of medication (Mayo-Smith 1997). For extreme alcoholism and opiate abuse, inpatient hospitalization is usually indicated (Kosten and O'Conner 2003).

Carnes (2001) presents a model of sexual addiction that has great utility for understanding addictions in general. His portrayal of the addictive cycle explains a good deal of the power of addictions. According to Carnes, the addictive cycle starts with preoccupation, where the addict begins to think obsessively about engaging in his addictive behavior. This preoccupation can occur for a variety of reasons, such as the experience of strong emotions, stress, or environmental stimulus. The preoccupation is overwhelming and pushes the addict into engaging in the rituals that move him behaviorally toward his addiction. Ritualization occurs when the addict begins to engage in actions that are associated with and supportive of compulsive behavior. For instance, a compulsive gambler may begin to hold a good-luck charm in his hand, put on a certain outfit, and or begin to search the Internet for new gaming sites. After spending time engaging in the addictive ritual, the addict will then engage in the compulsive behavior itself. Depending on the actual addiction, the engagement in the behavior may not represent the longest period in the addictive cycle. For example, a cocaine addict may spend days in a state of preoccupation, hours in a state of ritualization, yet only a few minutes smoking cocaine. When finished engaging in the addictive behavior or consuming the drug, the addict will feel a sense despair and related feelings of hopelessness, powerlessness, and self-loathing. Often not having the skills to handle this final stage and its powerful emotions in a life-affirming way, the addict will begin the cycle again, with preoccupations helping the addict deny the painful feelings.

Substance Abuse

Substance abuse is both a cause and an effect of numerous psychosocial problems. Men are both more likely to have substance abuse problems and more likely to experience their deleterious effects than are women. Conell and Weisner (2006) found the one-year prevalence of substance abuse disorders for men to be 7 percent. Doyle (1996) reports that men are three times more likely than women to die from alcohol abuse and related health problems. There are many drugs and substances that can be abused, each with its own constellation of problems and issues. For instance, some drugs, such as cocaine, are illegal. The use of illegal drugs places men at high risk of involvement in the criminal justice system and may place them in situations where violence is likely to occur. Prescription drug abuse may present the potential of involvement in the criminal justice system (e.g., through driving while under the influence) yet does not represent the same type of risk for such involvement as does illegal drug use. However, many prescription drugs are highly addictive. Abusers are easily able to rationalize their addictions since their drugs are prescribed by physicians for real (at least at one time) physical conditions. However, prescription drug abuse, as with other types of substance abuse disorders, can be debilitating and even fatal.

Research has also found that men are more likely than women to relapse after participating in substance abuse programs (Fiorentine et al. 1996). Fiorentine and colleagues found that increased participation in group therapy may be one of the key factors that help women to be more successful in treatment. Relating these results to previous explorations in this book on masculinity and treatment, it may be that these groups did not taken into account the different needs of men and women vis-à-vis treatment. This research presents yet another reminder of the need to tailor treatment to realities of working with men.

Other research supports the need to take into account gender differences when designing services. McKay et al. (1996) found that men in treatment for cocaine addiction are less likely to report negative feelings and more likely to believe that they can control negative emotions and addictive impulses. Men are less likely to believe they are at risk of relapse when they are feeling good. Consequently, men may benefit from CBT training that helps them identify the thoughts, beliefs, behaviors, and environmental stimuli that are associated with their own relapse. As men are less likely than women to discuss their feelings, helping them focus on the behavioral and environmental risk factors may be of use. This can be done not only in talk therapy, but through behavioral logs and writing exercises. What is important is that men are helped to find treatment options that meet their individual and cultural needs.

Alcohol Abuse

Alcohol is by far the most widely used and abused substance. Alcohol use differs from many other drugs in that certain aspects of alcohol use are socially sanctioned, and alcohol use is legal. Indeed, social rules and norms influence what is viewed as acceptable versus not acceptable. A glass of wine over a business lunch is considered perfectly acceptable while having a shot of whisky in one's office is certainly not, in spite of the fact that both have roughly the same amount of alcohol. Alcohol use that falls within the norms and rituals of a culture tends not to lead to problematic behavior. It is when alcohol use falls outside of socially acceptable rituals and norms, or when it is used by those with a predisposition toward alcoholism (based on a history of familiar alcoholism, a personal history of alcohol abuse, or other risk factors), that problems can occur. It is important to remember that longitudinal research has linked alcohol abuse with heredity (Cloniger, Bohram, and Sigvardsson 1981). However, not all alcohol use is problematic. In fact, moderate alcohol use has been shown to decrease one's risk for heart disease (Mukamal, Chiuve, and Rimm 2006), even for men with significant risk factors such as hypertension (Beulens et al. 2007). Still, alcohol is a powerful psychoactive drug the use of which should be taken seriously.

Misunderstandings regarding alcohol abuse increase the problems of abuse and lead to poor treatment outcomes. For instance, alcohol is often seen as a party drug, but it is actually a central nervous system depressant. Alcohol use is also often viewed in black-and-white terms. Many people in the addiction treatment community view any alcohol use that leads to any problems as an addiction. Those holding this view often take very confrontational approaches with clients in order to help clients understand that the root problems lies in the fact that they are an addict. This may be counterproductive, as clients whose drinking represents part of a larger problem but has not taken on the hallmarks of addiction or compulsive behavior may be put off by exaggerations of the consequences of alcohol in a person's life. This should not be confused with denial, in which a person denies or minimizes the severity of drinking or its consequences. As with other behavioral problems, what is called for is a comprehensive, biopsychosocial assessment that explores the true nature and severity of the problem.

Men are more likely to drink than women. Over 30 percent of women are lifetime abstainers from alcohol use, compared with 17.8 percent of men. Some 56.7 percent of men are regular drinkers, compared with 38 percent of women. Men are also disproportionately represented in heavy drinkers. Of those who are current drinkers, more than 20 percent of men have reported drinking more then five drinks in one session more than twelve days per year, compared with 6 percent of female drinkers.

Cultural factors play a significant role in alcohol abuse. Such cultural issues present challenges for social workers since one of the most important values of the profession is to respect cultural differences. However, when cultural traditions support an individual's self-defeating behavior, it is incumbent on the social worker to find ways of gently challenging such cultural norms as they manifest in individual behavior. For instance, in many working-class communities drinking at a neighborhood bar is an important social ritual. Indeed, in some communities the neighborhood bar is a significant place of social support for working-class men (Courtney 2003). For many men, having a drink or two after work does not lead to debilitating life consequences. For a man with alcoholism, engaging in this social ritual might be life threatening. For social workers, it is important to help such a man understand the core psychosocial needs that he is attempting to fill and find new, life-enhancing ways of meeting these important needs.

Sexual Addiction

Wolfe (2000) estimates that 7 to 10 percent of the U.S. population is afflicted with some form of sexually compulsive behavior. The National Council on Sexual Addiction Compulsivity confirms these findings and reports an estimated 16–21.5 million Americans are sexual addicts (Cooper et al. 1999).

Sexual addition or sexually compulsive behavior may not meet the classic characteristics of addiction, yet some men's lives clearly become out of control due to compulsive sexual behavior. While no clear research has demonstrated that compulsive sexual behavior involves physiological responses similar to substance abuse, sex addicts have noted that they have experienced effects similar to those who struggle with amphetamine addiction (Augustine Fellowship 1986). Additionally, sexual addiction experts have observed the phenomenon of withdrawal (Carnes 2001; Earle and Crow 1989). Men who engage in sexual addiction may engage in one or more of a constellation of sexual behaviors. Some men compulsively masturbate to pornography. Others engage in risky, anonymous sex. Some compulsively frequent prostitutes. The last two behaviors place men at risk of sexually transmitted diseases, involvement in the criminal justice system, or physical harm.

The line between compulsive sexual behavior or addiction and hypersexuality may not always be clear. In one of the most comprehensive reviews of the literature on sexual addiction, Gold and Heffner (1998) note that the field of sexual addiction is still based too much on theory and anecdotal data. They suggest the need for empirical studies to test some of the key concepts and definitions. Some authors believe that the construct of sexual addiction itself is a means of controlling sexual behavior that falls outside of social norms (Levine and Troiden 1988). They note that behaviors that are viewed as healthy and normal in one context may be viewed as pathological in another. However, other authors note that the differences between hypersexuality and sexual addiction are clear. Addictive behaviors are those that in which men place themselves in significant harm in spite of the consequences (Coleman 1992). Other areas of a person's life become compromised as a result of the addictive behavior.

The Internet has provided a context for sexual addiction that makes it extremely reinforcing and difficult to treat. Men with sexual addictions to pornography can find an endless supply of images and video online. Easy access to the Internet twenty-four hours a day makes it easily for total isolation (Cooper et al. 1999). Davis (2001) explores the cognitive roots of what he refers as specific pathological intent use (with a focus on sexual addiction). The cognitive factors include a tendency toward black-and-white thinking, a propensity toward a ruminative/obsessive cognitive style, negative beliefs about one's capacity to meet one's needs outside of an online context, and cognitions associated with poor self-image. Davis stresses the cognitive behavioral connection, in that the cognitive distortions and maladaptive thinking will become more pronounced in the presence of the behavioral stimuli (pornography or other sexual stimuli). It is theorized that excessive pornography use may increase sexual violence in some men. It is posited that men already predisposed to sexual violence will experience a decrease in inhibition, a normalization of the behavior based on the viewing of dominant and aggressive materials, and an increase in arousal, thus increasing the likelihood of sexual violence (Itzin 1992). Bergen and Bogle (2000) interviewed one hundred women victims of sexual abuse who received services from a rape crisis center. They found that nearly 30 percent of the perpetrators used pornography, and 14 percent of the abusive situations in some ways imitated pornographic scenes. While not all men who watch pornography become sexually violent, there are other effects of consuming pornography compulsively. For instance, men who watch pornography may have a decreased sex drive toward "real women," as they compare pornographic images and scenes to the real-life women. Excessive pornography use may also have an impact on men's ability or desire for intimate relationships with women or adversely affect their level of intimacy with their partners (Zimmerman et al. 2002).

Gambling

Compulsive gambling is a significant social and personal problem for men. Numerous stories in the media describe men who lose families and careers to compulsive gambling. Perhaps most famous is Pete Rose, the baseball legend who was banned from baseball for life for betting on the game. Yet, stories such as this may obscure the actual nature of men's gambling addictions. Very few men with gambling problems lead glamorous lives; indeed, distortions and fantasies regarding wealth, fame, and glory are part of what makes the addiction so insidious (Joukhador, Maccallum, and Blaszczynski 2003). Many gambling addicts engage in solitary, compulsive behaviors that lead them toward feelings of hopelessness and despair (Spanier 1994). Gambling in America has powerful consequences. While casinos and gaming have increased the revenues of and benefited Native American tribes, they have also led to an increasing problem with gambling, which has led to problems in parenting and child behavior (Momper and Jackson 2007).

The addiction cycle of gambling is similar to sexual addiction. Like sexually compulsive behavior, the high provided by gambling is an action or behavior. Action is an appropriate term because for men the action or thrill is one of the key addictive ingredients. When a man moves from more social to compulsive or pathological gambling, he finds himself spending more time thinking about placing bets (or playing cards). The high he gets is real; compulsive gambling produces changes in neurotransmitters similar to some forms of substance abuse (Abbott 2007). Over time the gambler develops "tolerance" and needs to make increasingly larger bets to experience the same high. As the gambler becomes more addicted, he find that his self-esteem, in addition to his finances, becomes highly influenced by the gambling. When he is going well in his bets, he believes himself to be especially smart, skilled, and lucky. When he does poorly, he may alternate between blaming himself, thereby feeling depressed and self-loathing, and blaming others.

Over time, men deep in the throws of compulsive gambling begin to lie about their behavior and to increasingly take risks with their financial life. They may take out loans that others do not know about, take out retirement money if they have any, or sell family heirlooms or jewelry. All the while they rationalize these behaviors in their mind, believing that they are close to winning it all back.

Gambling addiction is also highly associated with criminality. In one study, Ladd and Petry (2002:302) found that 19 percent of male "pathological gamblers" had spent time in prison, and that these men were five times more likely than the women in their sample to report being involved in current criminal behavior. In referring to the entire population of compulsive gamblers, the authors note that "a myriad of negative health, psychosocial, and economic consequences accompany pathological gambling. For the individual pathological gambler, physical and emotional health comorbidities are often involved, including substance abuse, circulatory and digestive disease, sexual dysfunction, anxiety disorders, depression, and suicide. Broad societal consequences include family or community disruption, financial loss, and legal and employment problems."

When looking at theoretical frameworks and models of treatment, perhaps the wisest advice comes from James and Gilliland (2001), who stress that each theory or perspective contains an element of truth, and that no model is able to serve all populations. Men are a diverse group with diverse needs; social workers will want to consider various approaches to treatment. This is an important notion to keep in mind as we begin to explore some of the most popular treatment models for substance abuse and other compulsive behavioral problems.

Treatment Approaches

Prior to alcoholism being viewed in medical and biological terms, treating addictions was predicated on a moral view of the problem. Substance abuse and other behavioral problems were viewed as being the result of bad education, poor moral upbringing, and lack of character. Treatment often was based on moral education, reeducation, and/or religious experiences. Less gentle approaches to substance abuse treatment were also based on the idea that the addict was at fault for his addiction and would need to be confronted about the nature of his problem. According to this approach, addicts are deep in denial about their own problems and need to be shaken up, shocked if you will, into admitting to their problems. Those who take this approach have been known to yell at clients and say demeaning things. That this approach is usually not effective is just one reason not to adopt it; it is also ethically problematic for professional social workers. Dignity and respect are two fundamental social work values that are important to uphold for ethical and instrumental reasons. Overly coercive behavior usually harms the helping relationship. When confrontation is utilized, it should be done by firmly and respectfully presenting the discrepancies between a client's behavior, feelings, and beliefs. Confrontations should always be done with respect and dignity (Ivey and Ivey 2007).

Twelve-Step Programs

Twelve-step self-help programs are the most popular form of treatment for addictive and compulsive behaviors (Humphreys 1999; McCrady and Miller 1993). It is estimated that over 90 percent of inpatient treatment programs are at least in part based on twelve-step programs (Roman and Blum 1997). Twelve-step support groups are designed to help people with a variety of addictive problems. The names of the groups clearly illustrate the problems they are geared toward: Overeaters Anonymous, Alcoholics Anonymous, Narcotics Anonymous, Marijuana Anonymous, Gamblers Anonymous, Sex and Love Addicts Anonymous, Sex Addicts Anonymous, and so on. The original twelve-step program was Alcoholics Anonymous (AA) (2007b). According to the organization itself, there are over 100,000 meetings of AA word wide, with an estimated two million members in 150 countries.

Twelve-step programs are participant-led and based on spiritual and religious principles designed to help the addict face the full effect of the addiction, as illustrated by the twelve steps of AA listed below (Alcoholics Anonymous 2007b).

THE TWELVE STEPS OF ALCOHOLICS ANONYMOUS

1. We admitted we were powerless over alcohol—that our lives had become unmanageable.
2. Came to believe that a Power greater than ourselves could restore us to sanity.

3. Made a decision to turn our will and our lives over to the care of God as we understood Him.

4. Made a searching and fearless moral inventory of ourselves.

5. Admitted to God, to ourselves, and to another human beings the exact nature of our wrongs.

6. Were entirely ready to have God remove all these defects of character.

7. Humbly asked Him to remove our shortcomings.

8. Made a list of all persons we had harmed and became willing to make amends to them all.

9. Made direct amends to such people wherever possible, except when to do so would injure them or others.

10. Continued to take personal inventory and when we were wrong promptly admitted it.

11. Sought through prayer and meditation to improve our conscious contact with God, as we understood Him, praying only for knowledge of His will for us and the power to carry that out.

12. Having had a spiritual awakening as the result of these steps, we tried to carry this message to alcoholics, and to practice these principles in all our affairs.

One of the great advantages of such programs is that they are free to all. While the program is financially supported by its members, there is no obligation to provide donations. Typically, members place a dollar in a collection basket that is passed out at the beginning of the meeting. While twelve-step meetings vary in format, they tend to follow a typical structure. Meetings often begin with a prayer, typically the serenity prayer, followed by a reading of the twelve steps. Subsequent activities depend on the individual format of the meeting but may include a reading from one of the twelve-step-oriented books, a speaker who shares his or her experiences with addiction and recovery, open sharing by attendees, or a combination of these. Meetings are usually ended with another prayer.

Another great strength of twelve-step programs is the support that is provided to people in pain. Newcomers are encouraged to identify themselves and are usually approached by more experienced members offering support after the meeting. A phone list is available for newcomers and those struggling with their compulsive behavior. Members are encouraged to call one another for support, especially when they are thinking of engaging in their addictive behavior. Members are also encouraged to choose sponsors who provide them with additional support and help guide them in applying the principles.

Why twelve-step programs are successful for some is a matter of debate. One of the factors, however, appears to be that members are encouraged to develop new behavioral patterns that alter their engagement in the addictive cycle. For instance, when someone begins to engage in the obsessive thinking characteristic of the preoccupation stage, he or she may break the cycle by reading a passage from the recovery-oriented literature, calling someone on the telephone, or some other recovery activity.

While twelve-step programs have been extremely valuable, they are not for everyone. The dilemma is that many substance abuse treatment programs are firmly rooted in the twelve-step tradition. This may work well for men from Christian backgrounds, as the twelve steps are based on Christian principles, and twelve-step groups typically incorporate Christian prayers. When a man is an atheist or from another religious tradition, he may find such programs uncomfortable at best, and against his core values at worst.

Cognitive Behavioral Approaches

While the twelve-step model may be the most popular approach to treatment of addiction, it is not the only one. Cognitive behaviorally based models have been shown to be effective in treating addictive disorders (Holder et al. 1991; Oei and Jackson 1982). Cognitively based approaches are not only implemented by professionals; several cognitively oriented support groups have also been developed (Knaus 1998).

Cognitive behavioral approaches vary by focus. However, each includes the connection between an individuals' belief systems and the behaviors that lead to addictive behavior. For instance, some approaches focus mostly upon irrational beliefs (Ellis et al. · 1988), others focus on increasing motivation (Holder et al. 1991), while others emphasize the development of social skills (Roth and Fonagy 1996) They also may be the treatment of choice for those men who are turned off by twelve-step programs (Ellis and Velten 1992). Further, cognitively based models are congruent with many of the cultural values that are important to men. In contrast to twelve-step programs that focus on men's powerlessness over their addiction, cognitively based approaches concentrate on what men have power over, and what aspects of their thinking and behavior they can control.

The Self Management and Recovery Training (SMART) program is a self-help discussion group that provides an alternative to twelve-step programs. SMART groups are based on what their literature refers to as scientifically supported concepts and methods. The program largely is a mix of cognitive behavioral methods designed to help people with compulsive disorders stop using drugs. Hovarth (2000) describes SMART meetings as being ninety minutes in length and led by a nonprofessional meeting coordinator. Unlike in twelve-step programs, coordinators may or may not be in recovery themselves but are familiar with the cognitive behavioral methods used for helping people control their compulsive behaviors. SMART meetings tend to be more dialogical than twelve-step programs, where one person speaks and then another for a set length of time. The SMART program is based on teaching participants recovery training and self-management. Recovery training helps group members work on their motivation for recovery and on their ability to contend with urges. Members also learn to engage in self-management training, which helps them alter irrational beliefs that support their addiction. Members are encouraged to work toward understanding the reasons for their compulsive behaviors and finding alternative means of fulfilling their needs. For instance, if a man drinks as a means of helping himself deal with his shyness, he is encouraged to seek assertiveness training or psychotherapy to help him become more socially competent.

The National Institute of Drug Abuse (Carroll 1998) presents an evidence-based CBT model for cocaine dependency. Key to the program is conducting what the author terms a functional analysis. A functional analysis consists of an assessment of the environmental context, emotions and their associated cognitions, skills and strengths, and cognitive behavioral triggers. When clients relapse in their addiction, the therapists help them carefully explore the thoughts, feelings and behaviors that precipitated their relapse. Carroll suggests a comprehensive assessment focusing on the use of assessment tools such as the Addiction Severity Index, Treatment Attitudes and Expectation forms, as well as more open-ended questions. Key interventions include motivation, the presentation of the CBT treatment model, functional analysis, and skills training. While it is important to help clients not return to social contexts that reinforce their addictions, at times this is difficult to achieve. Therefore, one of the most important skill sets is refusal and assertiveness skills, which help the client refuse substances. Carroll suggests using within-session role-play as a means of helping clients develop these skills. In this model, the client picks a specific problematic situation from their past. The therapist adopts the role of the person attempting to sell the addictive substance or entice the client to use it, and the client practices resisting. Clients should be encouraged to discuss the potential effect of their responses, and to learn to find ways of responding that will lead to the best outcome. At times, passive/avoidant responses (e.g., I have a really bad cold and my nose is all messed up, I am going to pass today, or I have to take a urine sample later today to my parole officer) may be equally effective when compared with more assertive responses (Hey man, don't mess with me, I don't use anymore). These methods are particularly effective in group settings where members can provide each other with realistic feedback about the likely responses to their efforts.

Other Treatment Approaches

Narrative methods may also be useful in treating addictions and compulsive behavior. Twelve-step groups and treatment programs frequently use writing exercises, which are congruent with some narrative principles. Tubman, Montgomery, and Wagner (2001) used letter writing as a tool in substance abuse treatment. Clients were encouraged to write letters saying goodbye to their drug of choice. This technique helps externalize the problem and facilitates the process of grieving for one's old lifestyle and drug. This approach is typically conducted in a group setting, where clients have fifteen minutes to write their letters, with the last forty-five minutes used for sharing and feedback.

Some authors have noted that for many, substance abuse and other compulsive disorders are ways of coping with existential problems (Greaves 1974; Trujillo 2004). As Cook (2007) notes: "It is generally well-recognized among professionals that people in the throes of addiction got that way looking for some sort of meaning in life. A pharmacological blindfold is used to deal with the emptiness that accompanies this lack of meaning." Meaninglessness, dread, existential anxiety, and fear of accepting personal responsibility are themes that many recovering people explore with therapists and in their support groups.

Case Example

Charles Smith is a 35-year-old African American man living in North Philadelphia. He was sent to his local community mental health center's program by his parole officer for substance abuse. Substance abuse treatment and job training were two of Charles's conditions for parole. Charles recently spent nine months in prison for selling crack cocaine. This was the third time he was incarcerated for selling drugs. Charles was placed on parole for five years, and his parole officer and the court have assured him that if he goes back to selling drugs, he will complete his entire sentence.

During Charles's intake interview, he professed discomfort with expressing his feelings but said that he believed that depression and sexually compulsive behavior were two of the things that often contributed to his selling drugs. Charles reported that he was trained as a chef. For two years he worked as a line cook in an upscale restaurant. While the job was at a prestigious restaurant, it did not pay well. The long, late hours were stressful for him, and the lack of money weighed heavily on him. He was consistently broke, spending a good deal of his money on prostitutes.

When he was in high school he sold crack cocaine on the street. He quit when he went to cooking school, and he stayed away from drugs and from dealing for many years. However, during one particularly stressful night, he found himself fanaticizing about how much money he made while dealing, and how he could afford all the sex he wanted if he sold drugs "once in a while." Soon thereafter, while cruising for prostitutes in his car, he saw some-one he knew from his old neighborhood, who had become a well-known drug dealer. His old acquaintance offered to help him begin to sell drugs once again. Within a few weeks, Charles had quit his job and soon returned to selling drugs as a means of attracting and affording prostitutes. For the next several years, Charles was consumed with drugs and prostitutes who would provide him with sex for small amounts of cocaine, or the promise of cocaine in the future. Charles said that he had sex with prostitutes at least three times a day, every day, for many years. He said that he practices what he termed "semisafe sex," which to him meant that he used condoms for intercourse but not when receiving oral sex. Much to his own surprise, he never had any venereal disease.

By the time Charles found himself in therapy, he was ready to change. He desperately wanted to build a meaningful life for himself but admitted to equally powerful desires for drugs and sex. Charles's therapist John, a clinical social worker, helped support him in exploring his motivation for staying clean and for building a new life. He adopted a strengths-based approach, recogniz-ing that Charles had many assets. He was intelligent, reflective, and had previ-ous success as a chef. Not only did he possess this training and experience, but he had a profound passion for cooking. Charles's eyes would light up when he spoke about his culinary creations, and he felt a deep sense of loss that he had not developed his skills further. John wondered out loud to Charles if it would be a valuable goal for him to become as obsessed with creating food as he had been with sex and drugs. Charles's eyes welled up with tears, and he silently nodded. Under his breath he repeated, "Become obsessed with creating." John sat silently, looking slightly down to give Charles time and space to be with his emotions. After a few minutes, John said, "Pretty honest and real for a guy who says he does not like to express his feelings. Thanks Charles for trusting me enough. Thanks."

John also began to slowly and gently challenge Charles on some of his irra-tional thinking. For instance, Charles stated that his goal was to "never have sex again" and to learn that "money was the root of all evil." Charles's therapist won-dered how realistic these views were, and if they were not setting Charles up for disappointment and failure. He educated Charles about the cognitive distortion of "black-and-white thinking" and explored how creating standards that were neither realistic or possible to achieve could be dangerous. Charles was able to recognize his black-and-white thinking and to come up with more realistic and less dogmatic beliefs. His therapist suggested that he use his twelve-step meetings to deal with the issues of developing a healthy sexuality apart from his compulsive behavior, but he said he was not ready to look at sex as anything other than a drug. He recognized that this would have to change over time, but he did not believe the time had come. John pressed Charles to openly and honestly explore these issues. Charles was doing well in therapy and seemed to be feeling more hopeful in his life.

During his eighth session, Charles broke down in tears. He admitted that while returning from a Narcotics Anonymous meeting, he began cursing for prostitutes. As soon as he turned the corner to look at the first woman, Charles felt the addictive rush that was triggered by the ritual of his cursing. Quickly he found himself deep inside the addictive cycle, in a crack house using cocaine with a prostitute. Charles was extremely worried that he would fail his urine test and wondered if he could skip the test that week. He feared that if he came up "hot" he would be sent back to prison. After discussing the situation, Charles and his therapist agreed that the best strategy would be for Charles to talk directly to his parole officer and admit what had happened. Charles's therapist agreed to speak to the parole officer as well and to highlight Charles's willingness to engage in treatment and his honesty about his relapse.

Charles called his parole office with John present. The parole officer was understanding. He agreed to meet with Charles and John the following day in order to support Charles in his recovery. John asked Charles and his parole officer who could also be involved in the meeting as a means of helping create a supportive network for Charles. Charles suggested his new Narcotics Anonymous sponsor, as well as his job-training coach, who was helping him look for a job as a cook. Both agreed to attend the meeting the following day.

Charles and his therapist spent the rest of their session preparing for the meeting. They discussed that the main goals would be for Charles to take responsibility for his mistake, to seek additional support and accountability, and to become increasingly empowered in his treatment process. John also probed Charles about the risks of a continued relapse. Charles admitted that he did have thoughts about using drugs, but that he was not planning on it. John asked Charles if he planned to use the day before his relapse, to which he replied he did not. Charles was able to realize on his own that perhaps he was not safe from relapse. After some discussion and weighing of his options, Charles decided to call his brother and see if he could spend night with him and his family. Charles called from his therapist's office, and his brother agreed to come pick him up and take him to his home. In the last few minutes of the session John validated all the positive work that Charles had done. He assured Charles that relapses are often part of the recovery process, and that all the steps that Charles was currently taking were positive.

The following day Charles met with his therapist, his counselor, and his Narcotics Anonymous sponsor. John asked him how he was feeling. Charles admitted to being afraid that he would be sent back to prison. He turned to his parole officer and asked him if there was any way he could avoid going back to prison. His parole officer assured him that given the way he was handling his relapse, he would not be sent back at this time. His parole office did stress that staying away from drugs was a condition of his parole, and that if this happened again he could not guarantee that his parole would not be revoked. John asked Charles what help he needed at this point. He said that he really wanted to "get on which his career." He was working in a fast-food restaurant as a cook, not the type of job that he wanted. His sponsor and job coach stressed the importance of patience. His sponsor noted that Charles had spent many years tearing his life apart, and that it would take more then a couple of months to build it back. Charles nodded in agreement and said that he believed he had been stressing himself out by thinking he had to achieve everything "now." His sponsor said that this was typical addictive thinking, and that he would have to work on achieving balance if he wanted to stay clean.

John decided to bring up Charles's sexually compulsive behavior as an important issue to discuss. He wondered if this needed treatment in and of itself, or if it was something that Charles could work on in given his current supports. John brought up the possibility of Charles adding one meeting a week, a twelve-step program for people struggling with sexually compulsive behavior. All the members of Charles's support team thought it was a good idea. Each of them saw that Charles's substance abuse was largely triggered by his sexually compulsive behavior, and that he would need to address this more directly. Charles agreed and admitted that while he did not want to face this issue, he would trust everyone's judgment. The meeting concluded with John summarizing what had occurred and thanking Charles's support team for their caring and guidance.

Over the next year that John and Charles worked together, Charles's life changed considerably. Coincidently, the day after the meeting he was asked to interview as a line cook in an upscale restaurant that was known to be an excellent training ground that rewarded creativity. He attended meetings of Sex and Love Addicts Anonymous and became very involved in service. He had one slip with a prostitute several months later but did not use any drugs. He immediately called his probation officer, sponsor, and therapist to inform them, and he came in the following day for an unrequested drug test. He was proud of how far he had come and wanted to be open about his slip. John and Charles ended their work together after fifteen months. Before termination, they moved from a more cognitive, systems-oriented, skills-focused approach to a more client-directed, humanistic approach. As Charles put behind him his addictive behavior, he was able to spend more time in therapy visioning a future for himself. Throughout the process, John continued his strengths-based orientation, helping Charles recognize and build his existing strengths and develop new sources of power, hope, and resiliency.

QUESTIONS FOR WRITING AND REFLECTION

1. How might a narrative therapy approach have been used with Charles?
2. What other cognitive distortions/irrational beliefs might Charles have held that reinforced his addiction?
3. Describe the strengths of using community support in the treatment of men.
4. How might the notion of hegemonic masculinity inform this case?
5. What types of culturally relevant interventions might have been utilized in this case that were not addressed?

Case Example

Luis Rodriquez is a 54-year-old man struggling with an addiction to heroin. Within the last six months, Luis learned that he is HIV positive. Luis's diagnosis of HIV has led to his being extremely depressed. He admits to having thought about killing himself "before this damn disease turns me into a drooling cripple." Luis has been in a crisis for the last several weeks as he has resumed injecting heroin after eight months of being clean and sober. While using heroin, Luis does not take good physical care of himself. He rarely eats, sleeps too much or too little, and has had many colds and rashes.

Luis has come in for counseling at a community mental health center's drug and alcohol program. The program is located in the Puerto Rican community in a large northeastern U.S. city. Luis himself is Puerto Rican. He was born on the island and moved to New York with his parents when he was in his teens. Luis speaks good English but is self-conscious about his accent and is not entirely fluent. He prefers to speak in Spanish with other Latinos but in English with whites and African Americans. Luis is proud of his heritage and is quick to point out to the unknowing that Puerto Rico is indeed part of the United States.

Luis has asked to see the one white clinical social worker in the agency. This social worker also happens to be the only staff member with a master's degree. To Luis and many other Latinos, advanced degrees and training are a sign of quality. Besides, one of Luis's friends is a client of the social worker. This type of personal referral is extremely important in the Latino community. Luis's friend told him that he trusted his therapist, and that since he was not part of the community it was more likely for his "business to stay private." Given Luis's fear of being stigmatized and shamed, this was an important factor in his decision.

The clinical social worker, Ed, a 28-year-old man who had graduated with his MSW degree only six months before, is close to bilingual in English and Spanish. During their intake interview, Ed informed Luis that they could work together in English, Spanish, or a combination of both. Ed told Luis that he understand how sometimes people felt more comfortable talking about certain subjects in one language and others in the other. Luis appreciated this sensitivity and said that he mostly wanted to speak in English, but that he might want to go back and forth and use Spanish words when did not know a particular English word.

During the intake session, Luis admitted to having used heroin the night before. He said that he was very "real" and "straight up"; he would tell his therapist the truth. Luis prides himself on his honesty. He believes that no matter how far a man has fallen, he must always carry himself with dignity. Dignity, or *dignidad*, is an important value in the Latino community and honestly was a key part of how Luis had chosen to express this dignity. He said that part of his personality is to be honest, sometimes brutally honest. Living with integrity is "what men have to do to be men."

It became clear to Ed that Luis's sense of his own masculinity was extremely important to his identity, and core to how he saw his value as a human being. Luis noted that having to use condoms now with his girlfriend of six years, who has remained HIV negative, makes him feel like less of a man. Also, he admitted that since his diagnosis, it is difficult for him to achieve an erection, as he says "I just don't feel sexual any more." When asked how he felt about his decreased sex drive, he said, "I feel like a eunuch, like someone had cut it off. I am almost not a man anymore."

Luis was having to confront the implications of an extremely painful health diagnosis and his drug addiction. It was clear to Ed that Luis truly was dealing with profound existential struggles, and that this approach would provide the basic framework for their work together. Since existentially oriented work is predicated on an authentic and open helping relationship, Ed explained to Luis how he saw Luis's current problem, and what their work together might be. Ed stated that Luis seemed to be struggling with finding meaning and purpose in a life that seemed far more tenuous than it once did. Luis agreed and stated that living with a "death sentence" has sapped his desire to really live. Luis admitted to at times feeling as if his life is actually over, and that he is just "buying time" until he dies. Ed listened intently and through his nonverbal communication expressed a deep understanding for Luis's pain. Tentatively, Ed said that perhaps there was another way to see it, and wondered if Luis wanted to hear what Ed was thinking. By giving Luis the option of hearing an alternative interpretation, Ed was doing two things: empowering Luis to take ownership for his therapy and the potential construction of his own meaning, and decreasing the likelihood that Luis would respond defensively. Luis said he very much wanted to hear what Ed had to say. Ed explained that, first, he did not believe that Luis's diagnosis was a death sentence, and that new medications make the disease fairly manageable. Ed than said that in his opinion, being aware of one's own potential death is essential for full and authentic living. When a man lives his life as if were his last day, or perhaps last year, then he truly appreciates life and lives it to its fullest. Ed suggested that while HIV was not something he would wish on anyone, perhaps Luis could find a way of using it to create a life full of meaning.

Since existential therapy encourages the therapist to be more open and self-revealing, Ed shared an exercise that a teacher of his had his classes do in graduate school. Every morning for a month, Ed woke up and consciously imagined his own grave plot. He imagined that his life would soon be over, and that his job for the day was to live as fully as possible. Ed said that this exercise made him realize how precious life was. After Ed told this story, he sat with Luis in silence for a few minutes. Realizing that his goal was not to "fix" Luis but to engage him in conversations about creating meaning and living fully, he felt no need to break the silence. Ed was learning that silence is an important therapeutic tool.

After a while, Luis began to speak in a philosophically, contemplative tone He said that he once heard that we are all born to die. Maybe he was looking at his life in a "backwards" manner and had always been a positive person, even during difficult times. Luis wondered out loud if he could find a way to view his life positively again. Ed told Luis that it would be a challenge to be that positive person now, and he wondered what Luis would have to do to get that part of himself back. Infusing some cognitive therapy into his session, he asked Luis what he would have to believe about himself and his life to start to think more positively, more hopefully. Luis explained that he would have to stop blaming himself for having the disease, and that he would have to see himself as a survivor and get out of the "depression crap." Ed and Luis spent most of the last part of their session talking about Luis's depression and about his heroin use. Based on the amount of heroin that Luis had been using over the last several months, a medically supervised, inpatient detoxification program would be needed. Luis agreed, and Ed called a local hospital with a particularly good program to ascertain if they had openings. The social worker, with whom Ed had worked many times, informed him that they would have an official opening the next morning, but that if Luis came and "hung out with him" and could do without a room, they would figure something out. This informal arrangement was possible based on the relationship that Ed had cultivated with the detox social worker. He knew that when Ed said a client desperately needed to go to rehab now, he meant it. Ed felt this was the case with Luis, given his depression, the amount of heroin he was using, and his HIV status.

Before Luis was released from detox, the detox social worker called Ed to help them coordinate services. Ed, who had spoken to Luis twice during his stay, agreed to attend a meeting the day before Luis's release. Luis, Ed, the detox social work, and Luis's girlfriend were present at the meeting. Luis looked healthy. In two weeks he had put on several pounds and begun to take his medication as it was prescribed. The group treatment and intensive meetings had helped give him an increased sense of focus. While in treatment, Luis had met several other HIV-positive men. From these men, Luis had become to view his health status as a personal challenge.

FOR WRITING AND SELF-REFLECTION

1. What might be some next steps in Luis's treatment?
2. Which of the four theories would you use at this point? How would they be applied?
3. What factors are effecting Luis's sense of his own masculinity? How would you help him address these factors?
4. What factors may impede Luis's recovery?
5. How would you help Luis and his girlfriend work on their sexual relationship together?

EXERCISE

As with many of the other issues in this book, many social workers have biases about addictions. Respond to the following prompts as a means of exploring your biases. When you have finished, write a paragraph where you challenge your own thinking.

When I think about men who are alcoholics, I think that they:

When I think of drugs addicts, I think that they:

When I think about men who are compulsive gamblers, I think that they:

When I think about men who are sex addicts, I think that they:

Self-reflection: Critique and challenge the statements you wrote above.

Self-reflection: Write about your own experiences with addiction (your own behavior, or that of those you care about). How may these experiences impact your work with men who struggle with compulsive behavior?

Conclusion: What Is Right About Men?

FOURTEEN

> Aquí, no se rinde nadie. Nobody gives up here.
> —Augusto César Sandino

For the past thirty years, masculinity and men have taken a beating in the popular media. To some degree, the same can be said for how men have been conceptualized and treated by the helping professions. For instance, as previously discussed, machismo has been a poorly understood cultural attribute that characterizes Latino men's behavior. Popularly characterized by an inappropriate abuse of power within the family, machismo also centers on the obligations of the Latino male to support his family, and the lengths they will go to achieve these aims. Decontextualized and viewed without an insider's perspective of the social realities of Latino life and history, many misinterpret machismo and other Latino cultural traits (Hardin 2002).

Perhaps more influential than how men have been portrayed through these stereotypes and biases is that the history of the human sciences has been far more concerned with human pathology than with human strength (Strumpfer 2006). Even within the profession of social work, which tends to view people in terms of hopes and possibilities, few of our theories have pointed us toward a strengths orientation. We tend to look for the problems in people and situations. This has not been helped by the recent evidence-based practice movement, which tends to focus on human pathology and easily quantifying variables. Sadly, less attention has been given to harder to measure attributes, such character, strength, and will. However, within the last decade, positive psychology has began to change this focus on pathology by applying scientific methods and research to positive human attributes. Social work and the evidence-based practice movement would do well to explore this research and take lessons from it.

Existential psychology and social work (Krill 1978; Van Deurzen-Smith 1997; Willis 1994; Yalom 1980), positive psychology (Bohart and Greening 2001; Gable and Haidt 2005; Snyder and Lopez 2002), and the strengths perspective of social work (De Jong and Miller 1995; Maluccio 1981; Weick et al. 1989) view human beings as possessing far more strengths than weakness. Their proponents have observed men's capacity to survive, transcend, and even thrive within the context of difficult, painful, and oppressive circumstances. Throughout this book I have explored how the strengths perspective can frame our work with men. This chapter looks at other issues related to the strengths of men that are not necessarily tied to overcoming a specific problem area or were not appropriate for other chapters. It also examines the future of social work and several key social trends, transformations, and shifts in the profession itself.

The Resiliency of Men

Resiliency is the ability to adapt to and bounce back from adverse circumstances (Luther and Ziegler 1991; Norman 2000). Without the occurrence of adverse or difficult conditions, there is no need to be resilient. As such, resiliency is the synthesis of risk and protective factors and the capacity to overcome obstacles. Traditional resiliency research looks to personality traits or environmental factors as contributing to resilience (Cowen et al. 1990; Gamezy and Masten 1986; Werner 1990). In his exploration of the resiliency of men who have transcended extreme adversity, Fox (2000) discusses the "will" of men and its relationship to overcoming obstacles. Ultimately, resiliency is about how one responds to the normative and exceptional traumas and tragedies that men face in their lives.

Sheehy (1999) observed the lives of men who thrived well into older adulthood. She noted the cases of extraordinary men, such as the astronaut John Glen, who each year passed the physical and mental examinations needed to remain available for potential spaceflight. She noted that men who continue to thrive and excel later in life are not exempt from losses. George Burns, for instance, began his solo career at the age of 80, after his wife and lifelong partner died. Sheehy notes that "what stands out most strikingly in this enviable robust population is their personal resilience and self-reliance. They do not easily accept others' authority. They prize autonomy. They tend to be their own bosses and do not retire early. All have suffered losses and major setbacks. But whatever is taken from them, they find ways to adapt and to maintain their independent spirit" (25).

Courage

Courage and bravery are important ideals that many men strive to achieve. Previous chapters explored the personal consequences of risk taking, yet it is difficult to imagine the history of the world without great acts of courage by men. It is perhaps equally true that each of us have known men in our own lives whose lesser-known but no less courageous acts have left a powerful mark on our own lives. Influenced by the work of Gilmore (1990), Axelrod (2001:118) notes that "in most societies the three male imperatives required for cultural replication—impregnating women, protecting dependents from danger, and providing for kin—are either dangerous or highly competitive. The rituals and ideals comprising real manhood develop in conjunction with one or a combination of these three imperatives, inspiring men to deal with these risks rather than fearfully withdrawing. These rituals and ideals must by nature be dramatic challenges to the man's strength, courage, and very maleness."

Acts of courage also come in forms that may not align with current hegemonic ideals yet are profoundly courageous nonetheless. Perhaps the best example was Mahatma Gandhi. Gandhi's courageous use of nonviolent, civil disobedience won independence for India. He believed in humility, truth, and living a simple life. He had the courage to live according to his own convictions and model the type of peaceful interactions that he wished others would adopt. In the face of great violence and deprivation, he had the courage to live a life of peace and nonviolence. Countless men involved in the American civil rights movement acted with similar courage in the face of overwhelming institutional barriers and systematic violence. This kind of courage, a stubborn persistence to "do the right thing," is a powerful hegemonic masculine trait that has led to social and personal transformation throughout history.

Stoicism

In preceding chapters I presented many negative consequences of the lack of emotional expressiveness of men. Yet, stoicism may also be a strength in many situations. For instance, crisis workers understand that to be most effective in the most traumatic situations, they must not allow themselves to experience many emotions, including fear. Rescue workers who saved people during Hurricane Katrina and in the twin towers during the tragedy of September 11, 2001, would not have been able to function and save lives had they allowed themselves to feel the full spectrum of emotions that would be normal in such a situation.

In fact, a major philosophical movement was predicated on and provided the name for stoicism. Stoic philosophers believed that rationality and emotional control were key human virtues. They believed that negative emotions such as envy or rage should be controlled. The stoics were not against emotion but warned of living one's life according to unexamined feelings.

This approach to feelings is an important strength that many men possess. Not being overly emotionally reactive enables one to think through potential reactions to situations and allows for measured and reasoned responses. Many men have learned to take a balanced approach to emotional expressiveness. This balanced approach consists of recognizing the importance of being emotionally available to those they love. It also includes honoring their own feelings of sadness, loss, grief, and pain while keeping their anger in check. It honors emotional control as an important tool that can serve them well in some social situations.

Hobbies

As the maxim says, boys like their toys, and big boys may like bigger toys. Not typically discussed as strengths, hobbies can often be healthy outlets that help men find balance and social connections in their lives. One study found that men who enjoyed their retirement were over twice as likely to find satisfaction in a hobby as men who were not satisfied with their retirement (Valliant, DiRago, and Mukamal 2006). Overall, having a hobby may be an important part of well-being for many men. Albert Ellis (2004) referred to hobbies as an absorbing life interest and believed that they were key to life satisfaction.

It is through hobbies that men may find increased social connectedness with those who have similar interests. My hobby is collecting and drinking (very small amounts) of single malt scotch. For the last several years, I have participated in a single malt scotch Internet forum and have made friends through this involvement. Periodically I talk to my "scotch buddies," as my wife appropriately refers to them, on the phone and online. I have met several while traveling, and I enjoy trading samples with several. It is through this hobby that I am able to make new friends and social connections outside of work. This is important—when work becomes the only source of social connection, it can at times take on a part in life that is too large. Lately I have begun to play ping pong, a hobby that has allowed me to connect to a diverse group of men and women.

Nonhegemonic Strengths

Throughout this book I have noted ways in which men do not live and perform according to the hegemonic idea. This is a type of courage in and of itself. So ingrained are these ideals that to define ourselves in other ways is perhaps more than an act of courage, it is an act of transcendence. It would be impossible to list here the innumerable ways men break with these powerful social norms for the betterment of self and society. How poorer the world would be without the artist who would not conform to social rules about work and responsibility. Vincent Van Gogh painted through poverty and mental illness to provide the world his own unique portrayal of beauty. Some of the most memorable moments of my life were spend at the Museum of Modern Art in New York, being spellbound by his masterpiece *Starry Night*.

Practice and You

> In the faces of men and women, I see God.
>
> —Walt Whitman

It is my hope that during the previous chapters of this book you developed an appreciation of the complexity of the problems of men. I also hope that you have gained an appreciation for the many strengths that men possess and have developed an understanding of how to facilitate the use of these strengths in service of helping men meet their goals, dreams, and aspirations. It is also possible that by this time you are feeling a bit confused at how to work with such a diverse population. You may be wondering how you will ever be able to effectively work with men given the multitude of theories, skills, approaches, problems, and programs that this book has addressed. If this is the case, congratulations! You truly have come to appreciate how difficult it is to know everything about providing services to such a diverse group. Social work practice is neither simple nor easy. We can never learn everything, and we never stop working to perfect our skills. While cultural competence is often discussed as if it were an endpoint, it is actually a process and a journey. Developing your skills as a social worker, if you choose, can be a lifetime adventure of growth and exploration. Perhaps total competence as an endpoint is an unrealistic goal. I would suggest that it is more realistic for each of us to strive to become better people and better social workers little by little, day by day. Just as clients cannot tackle all their problems at one time, social workers cannot learn everything all at once. We must strike a delicate balance between being self-reflective and self-responsible, while being gentle with and accepting of our foibles.

An important concept to help you put all that you have learned into its proper place is practice wisdom. Goldstein (1990a) conceptualized practice wisdom as the integration of life experiences, theories one has learned, education, and emotional reactions. In a very real sense, social work practice is an art form. As with other arts, we master techniques so they become second nature. That is, once we have learned techniques so well that they become second nature, we are able to be creative, spontaneous, and alive. In a very real sense we study hard and practice our "chops" so we can forget what we studied when we are in front of real clients with real pains, needs, and joys. We must stay in the moment and be present for the men that we encounter. I understand that this may sound unattainable when you first begin to practice, but I can assure you that over time much of what you have learned will almost seem intuitive. In fact, after a while you will become so comfortable with your skill set that you will have to challenge yourself to learn new tools and methods, to stay abreast of the new research and innovations. Early in one's career competence is a concern; after a while the main enemy becomes complacency.

When exploring the needs of any group, it is important that we use information creatively and flexibly and strive to make judgments based on a good, careful assessment and avoid stereotypes. All knowledge and theory in social work practice should be regarded as hypotheses that you will test through your developing understanding of your client. Yalom (2002) contends that it is far easier to diagnose a client after fifteen minutes than after fifteen weeks, months, or years. Men, as all human beings, are complex and evolving. The most important source of knowledge about a man will be that man himself. It may take a while for him to open up; many men have preconceived ideas about the helping process and often view opening up to a social worker as a sign of weakness. Patience and openness are keys to good practice. Each man will be the expert on his own life, on his own truths. You will find that a man who may appear to fit many of the traits of hegemonic masculinity may have important differences. For instance, a former supervisor of mine was extremely competitive, assertive, and achievement oriented. A muscular man, he had the air of someone who would be classified as classically macho. Yet, he had a profound love of the opera, was extremely patient and caring, and easily spoke of his more vulnerable, "softer" emotions.

The Future of Social Work Practice with Men

It is difficult to attempt to see into the future and anticipate what social work services may look like at some distant point. This section explores several potential trends and movements that have been briefly discussed in prior sections and what these trends may mean for the future of social work practice with men. These issues are the increasing influence of the Internet and hypertechnologies, the continued movement toward the equality of the sexes, globalization and transnationalism in the context of an increase in diversity, and the future of social work practice in general.

Internet and Hypertechnologies

The Internet holds some interesting possibilities for social work practice and for practice with men in particular. While some authors, including myself, question the impact that the Internet may have on family and community relationships, it is also true that very few men actually spend a great deal of time in the community outside of work. For example, it is well known that the average adult spends approximately 4.5 hours a day watching television (Williams, Raynor, and Ciccolo 2008); such significant time spent in such isolated, sedentary activities makes it less likely that men will engage in more physical or community based-activities.

As new technologies make human contact via computers feel more "real," the possibilities exist for men to develop increased participation in online communities that meet their psychosocial needs. Even older technologies can be valuable tools for helping men with a variety of problems. For example, one study showed that telephone counseling using a CBT model decreased depression and increased medication treatment compliance for people suffering from multiple sclerosis (Mohr et al. 2000). Telephone group therapy was found to be successful in helping depressed, disabled older adults (Evans et al. 1986) and disabled adults across the lifespan (Evans et al. 1984). As Internet and telephone technologies become more integrated, social workers and other helping professionals will continue to have new techniques and methods at their disposal.

Equality of Sexes

It is clear that women in the United States and around the world still suffer from large economic, social, and political disparities. Patriarchy still exists, and it is far easier for a men to succeed than it is for women. However, it is also clear that women in the United States have far greater access to the fruits of society than they did fifty years ago. For example, in the 2008 election, Hillary Clinton was a serious contender for the U.S. presidency, something that would not have seemed possible only a few decades ago.

Throughout this book I have examined the paradox between accepting men for who they are and helping them explore often negative consequences for rigid adherence to hegemonic masculine ideals vis-à-vis their presenting problems. However, some practitioners advocate challenging patriarchy as a key aim of all social work practice. Male and female scholars have challenged the rigid notions of masculinity that oppress women and harm men and have sought to actively engage men in giving up their power and privilege and their negative means of expressing their masculinity. This type of practice is not designed to assist men with self-defined presenting problems, but with social change and transformation through challenging hegemonic conceptions of masculinity. Referred to as antihegemonic practice, this approach seeks to alter the power relationships between men and women and work toward a more egalitarian, just society. While social workers working with individual men must never elevate a political agenda over a client's individual needs, all social workers should help men evaluate the costs to themselves, their families, and their communities of rigid adherence to hegemonic masculine ideals. However, macro-oriented social workers may take a far more assertive stand and are strongly encouraged to work toward gender equality for the betterment of both men and women.

Nylund and Nylund (2003:387) demonstrate how narrative therapy can be a powerful tool in achieving this aim.

> The narrative approach takes into account the effects of discursive practices in shaping one's identity, particularly gender discourse. This approach to therapy does not see men as the problem, but rather views "the problem" as the internalization of patriarchal discourses that circulate in the culture. From this lens, therapy becomes a process of examining dominant discourse and inviting clients

to step into alternative and/or preferred stories of the self. By bringing together the personal and the political, narrative therapists resist hegemonic masculinity and invite men into alternative ways of thinking and being.

It is important to note that the Nylunds used the verb "invite." Men are invited into exploring how language, institutional structures, power dynamics, and their relationships are influenced by gender ideals that may be implicated in many of the problems they face. The narrative therapist who adopts an antihegemonic, profeminist stance sees hegemonic masculinity as being enslaving of both men and women. This is a wonderful bridge, as the authors point out, between micro and macro practice, provided that the needs of the client are always placed before the goal of social change. Workers who are uncomfortable with this ordering are encouraged to work in more macro settings, with women, or with men who are perhaps farther along the road to gender equality.

I am aware that this last statement may be taken out of context and may appear reactionary and antifeminist, but I do not believe this to be the case. It merely places the value of client self-determination above a social change agenda within the context of micro practice. Social work practice is impossible without value and ethical conflicts, in which one cherished set of ideals is pitted against another (Furman 2003b). Through discussion with colleagues and supervisors and dedicated self-reflection, each social worker must find his or her own answers to this complex practice dilemma (Furman, Downey, and Jackson 2004).

Diversity and Globalization

The fact that the United Sates is becoming increasingly diverse has important implications for men. One of the powerful changes brought by globalization is that conceptions of masculinity are slowly becoming more diverse. This increasing diversity in thinking about masculinity makes it increasingly likely that alternative conceptualizations of masculinity will be accepted. This diversity is welcomed, but it does mean that men may not be able to rely on clearly articulated norms of behavior. Role confusion is one of the costs of social change and transformation, and it is why some argue for preserving more traditional masculine and feminine roles. While I firmly believe that societies must work toward more egalitarian relationships and social structures, it is also important not to deny the difficulties men have faced due to these seismic shifts in social arrangements.

Globalization is likely to have some similar effects as notions of what it means to be a man are influenced by changing transnational organizations and institutions. As men representing various conceptions of masculinity come into increasing contact, they will have new opportunities and challenges. And as social work becomes increasingly global and transnational, social workers will be called on to understand how masculinity is expressed and explored within various social contexts. The profession's capacity to develop services and organizational structures to meet these challenges will be a key task during the decades to come.

The Future of Social Work

Social work in the twenty-first century will encounter many challenges. The professional will be called on to examine its values, aims, and mission in the context of a rapidly changing, globalized world. From its beginnings, social work has been the profession that has advocated for the poorest of the poor, the most oppressed and disadvantaged, and those at most risk of harm. The primary roles of social workers in the early decades of the profession were advocacy and social justice. This remains the primary mission of the profession in many parts of the world (Estes 1992; Healy 2001; Link, Ramanathan, and Asamoah 1999). Yet, as social work in the United States has attempted to become more accepted and professional and has increased its reliance on science as its primary source of knowledge, the profession has moved away from these more social or macro aims (Furman, Langer, and Anderson 2006). The majority of social workers with master's degrees in social work find themselves in roles very similar to those of counselors and psychologists, providing psychotherapy and engaging in individual behavioral change. Some have argued that the "social" in social work has been diminished as the unit of analysis and intervention has shifted increasingly away from communities and toward the individual.

I do not mean to disparage the profession. Indeed, this book has largely relied on more micro-practice theories and their utility in working with men. My purpose in presenting this assessment is to alert social work students and social workers to the trends that are occurring and their potential implications. One of the potential implications of viewing social problems solely from an individual or medical model lens is that social structures and problems may go unchallenged and unresolved. It is important that social workers continue to challenge oppression in all its forms and advocate for the most vulnerable.

As we have come to see, many men are vulnerable and have experienced a great deal of oppression and discrimination. Simultaneously, men have maintained a relative position of power when compared with women. Social workers in the future will need to continually grapple with this dual reality in their practice with men and women alike. Similarly, they will need to advocate with their agencies to have the freedom to fight social injustice when they see it, not merely provide billable hours for specified services. Social workers should remain the conscience of agencies and society alike.

As social work has become more individually and micro-oriented, the importance of developing new structures for macro practice has increased. As noted, globalization and transmigration have made the boundaries of the United States far more diffuse. Energies, resources, and lives transcend international borders. Business, advocacy groups, migrant populations, and families are increasingly moving across and between national boundaries, physically as well as in cyber space.

While international corporations and many groups of people have been quick to recognize this movement toward transnationality, the same cannot be said of social work (Furman and Negi 2007). The profession has not created the structures needed to provide services to people across national boundaries. Furman et al. (2008) provide one of the first discussions of the need for social work to develop organizations capable of operating transnationally. They posit the potential of using a wrap-around model, using new Internet-based and telephonic communication tools such as Skype in working with geographically dispersed families. They demonstrate how interdisciplinary treatment planning meetings, adapted from child-centered, family-focused wraparound services, can coordinate services for complex transnational groups. The authors recognize the need for organizations to conceptualize and test models of transnational practice. Our current understand of what an agency is will need to be expanded and shifted to account for new developments in technologies and the service realities of culturally different groups that exist within countries with different values and laws. Such developments will necessitate that social workers develop new skills and competencies in terms of building complex organizations.

Social work must also conduct more research on the positive aspects of men and masculinity and explore treatments that focus on what is right about men. By so doing, it will create long-term social capital for men and women alike. In an analogous exploration of the field of psychology, Gable and Haidt (2005:106) observe that we have invested greatly in identifying proximal causes of mental illness and creating effective therapies for those who are already suffering from disorders, but we have fallen short of identifying distal buffers to mental illness, such as personal strengths and social connections and prevention aimed at the larger population. Ironically, then, one of the costs of focusing resources solely on the treatment of those who are already ill may be the prevention of these very same illnesses in those who are not ill through research on the strengths and circumstances that contribute to resilience and wellness.

This does not imply that social work, psychology, and the other helping professions should ignore the problems and concerns of men. It merely points out that we should explore the positive as a way of preventing and ameliorating problems and achieve greater balance between exploring risks and strengths in our research, education, and practice.

Case Example

Each of these two case examples explores the life of a man who has transcended great obstacles to contribute a great deal to others. In truth, each of the men discussed in the previous chapters could have their life explored here. A key lesson of the strengths perspective is that even those who engage in difficult behaviors, whose lives may not have turned out the way they had hoped, or who have profound limitations do possess more strengths than weaknesses. This assertion is not merely based on an optimistic view of people but, this book has explored, has powerful implications for social work practice. In his presentation of case studies of the lives of men who have battled suicide, Fox (2000) notes that courage is often expressed as the willingness to choose life in spite of numerous, painful obstacles. The man who is the subject of the following case example is the embodiment of this type of courage.

Walter Levin is a 55-year-old Jewish man living in the San Francisco Bay area. Walter's story is one of resiliency. In spite of numerous familial, interpersonal, and physical wounds, Walter has worked hard at making the best out of his life. Despite struggles with depression and suicidal feelings, he has chosen to live and seeks to make the most out of his existence.

Growing up, Walter never felt like he fit in. He had a hard time in school, specifically with understanding sequential directions and with math. This was before the notion of learning disabilities was readily accepted, and Walter began to think of himself as merely stupid. His father, a high-powered academic, was critical and judgmental of Walter. He frequently told Walter that if he did not work harder to overcome his "barely average intelligence" he would wind up a failure. Walter's mother, also being fairly judgmental, did not understand her son either. School was therefore a painful place for Walter, and home provided little refuge. His two brothers, who were both more than ten years his senior, achieved well in sports and in academics. They teased Walter, who did not care for competitive sports, and he became increasingly sullen and depressed.

Walter left home when he was 15 years old and spent the next decade traveling the country working odd jobs. One of these jobs was as a cook in a small restaurant in Hawaii. While in Hawaii he began to practice yoga and developed a spiritual discipline. He spent his free time in his practice, as well as exploring the island on his bicycle. While Walter dated women on and off, his relationships often did not last long. They often were undone by his lack of self-confidence. He would begin to behave in an insecure manner and would feel that he did not deserve to be in the relationship. Women would often find those feelings too difficult to deal with, and his depression and poor self-image therefore lead to a self-fulfilling prophesy characterized by abandonment.

His lack of self-confidence and near paranoia about how others felt about him was lamentable, as Walter possesses many strengths. First, he is kind and generous. Walter truly cares not only for the individuals who come into his life, but also about the world in general. Walter was always involved in political advocacy and worked at making the world a better place. He is also funny and engaging. Especially in his early to middle adulthood, Walter's playful spirit made him easy to be around. He is also deeply insightful. In spite of his own beliefs of about his lack of intelligence, he is a deep thinker who is able to develop powerful insights. He also possesses excellent problem-solving skills, which have served as an asset.

During his mid-thirties Walter started a tree-trimming business in the San Francisco Bay Area. He did reasonably well and was able to support himself fully. During this time Walker began to study photography. Art and creativity have always been important to Walter. In many ways, he is happiest when he is able to appreciate the inherent artistic beauty in life, events, and objects. The study of photography seemed to help Water live out his lifelong desire to be an artist. As a student, Walter became friends with a group of other young photographers and artists. This group of friends would spend many hours roaming the city taking photographs and enjoying each other's company. For the first time in many years, Walter felt as if he belonged.

Just as his life was coming together, Walter experienced a life-changing tragedy. Walking a female friend home late at night, a man pulled a gun on Walter and his companion. The man asked the woman to take off her clothes, and Walter instinctively placed himself in front of her. The man pulled the trigger and shot him in the abdomen. Walter was rushed to the hospital, where, true to his resilient nature, he survived in spite of losing a great deal of blood. He needed six hours of surgery for the doctors to repair the damage to multiple organs. While he survived, Walter would need three more surgeries to further repair the damaged caused by the bullet. For six months he was forced to have a colostomy bag, as his intestines were not functioning.

This event, which occurred at the age of 48, was a major setback in Walter's life. Since he was unable to work, his tree-trimming business soon failed. Walter was forced to give up his apartment and for the next year stayed with friends. He felt useless and hopeless. Suicidal feelings, which he had struggled with as a symptom of his depression for years, began to intensify. However, soon Walter was able to find work again as a cook and began to take psychiatric medication. For several years his life was went through many ups and downs. He had periods of unemployment mixed in with months of work. He become increasingly angry, and at times his perceptions of others bordered on paranoid. Still, ever resilient, Walter began to take control of his life. He found a good job as a chef and a small apartment, and he entered a period of stability.

Paradoxically, as Walter's life become more stable, he found himself increasingly depressed and disoriented. Not forced to deal with survival and crisis, Walter found himself facing some of his developmental and social realities. He was a 55-year-old man who had no family and had few friends or social connections. While his job was stable, he was not sure how many years he would be able to continue the intense work of being a chef. This realization produced a great deal of worry, as Walter had no retirement savings. Without constant crisis, he realized he had many regrets about the past, and many fears and doubts about the future. He also found himself profoundly lonely and felt a void in his life. For the first time in many years, Walter had health insurance and decided to seek therapy, and perhaps medication. He determined that he wanted to have a woman for a therapist. He reasoned that he wanted the perspective of a woman, who might help him find some insights into why he pushed women away. Being honest with himself, he also felt lonely for female company. This realization was difficult for Walter, as it made him feel like "a loser."

FOR WRITING AND REFLECTION

1. Think of a man in your life who, like Walter, has been a survivor. What strengths does he possess?
2. How does society feel about men like Walter and the man you identified?
3. How do you evaluate such men?
4. How would you work with Walter in therapy?
5. What principles and concepts in this book would be most applicable for working with him?

Case Example

In each of the cases in this book, the majority of men either were the recipients of social work services or were in need of services for some significant psychosocial problem. While it can easily be argued that each of us will need social work services at some point in our life, many people are able to transcend life's obstacles without professional intervention. It is also true that many individuals not only transcend but thrive. Research in positive psychology and resiliency has begun to explore exceptional individuals who are able to achieve amazing accomplishments (Duckworth, Steen, and Seligman 2005). This last case presents the life of one person who is just such a man. While his life certainly has not been free of problems and pain (he was divorced early in his twenties), it has been characterized by a series of successful developmental transitions and triumphs. A man of many graces, he has lived well and inspired many with his gentle example.

Skip Jackson is a 62-year-old man who has recently retired from his fifteen-year career as university professor. Skip came to the professorate and academia later than many. He was a successful advertising executive for a decade before, which followed a successful career as a jazz trumpet player. Throughout his life, Skip had learned to trust his inner voice. When he believed it was time for a change, he embraced that change. He never saw moving from one career to another as a failure, but as a new opportunity to excel. A man of many talents and interests, Skip believed that each season of life would lead to different adventures. He believed in riding the wave of life, not fighting it.

Skip was raised in a working-class neighborhood of a city in the Pacific Northwest. He describes his childhood as "groovy," a term he frequently used to describe life. Skip developed musical interests early on. His mother sang in their church choir, and she taught Skip to play the piano. He remembers the first time he really heard the trumpet. He was driving in the car with his parents and heard the jazz great Sonny Rollins playing on the radio. His mother began to speak to his father, and Skip blurted out, "Shut up a second, Mom." It was the only time he talked like that to his mother. He was spellbound by the sound, and his shocked parents recognized that something powerful was happening to their son. He was 8 years old.

Within days, Skip began taking trumpet lessons. He fell in love with his first trumpet, a "real hunk of junk" that he still plays from time to time. In high school, he began to play in various jazz bands. Older musicians in the community started to pay attention to him, and soon they invited him to sit in with them at shows. He was 16 at the time. Upon graduating from high school, he was invited by several prominent jazz bands to join them. However, Skip had promised his dad that he would attend college, so he did. He continued to play music, was invited to join a successful jazz band, and spent the next several years touring during the summers and holiday breaks. While he loved playing, he did not like the life of a traveling musician. In his sophomore year he decided that while music would be a lifetime love, he was not sure if it would be a lifetime career. He changed his major from music to business administration so he would have something "practical to fall back on." When Skip graduated, he toured for three years with a nationally recognized band, recorded a solo album, and was frequently asked to play on the albums of others. While he continued to love music and his horn, he quickly tired of the life of a musician and began to look for other work opportunities. Several months later, at the age of 26, Skip took a job writing ads for a large advertising company. His musician friends were shocked. They could not understand how he "gave up." So many people tried to earn their living as a musician, and he was one of the few who was able to do so. He assured them that he had made the right decision, and that he was going on another path. He was so quietly and gently self-assured that his friends soon accepted his change. He continued to go to their shows, and he showed no signs of remorse or regret. They admired him for his acceptance of his inner truths.

Part of the impetus for leaving his career was his desire for a stable and loving relationship. At the age of 24 he met and quickly married a young jazz singer. Their marriage ended within a year. The young woman, prone to bouts of depression, was having serious manic episodes and would disappear for many days at time. Skip tired of this behavior and realized that he had made a mistake. The two divorced after six months of marriage.

Skip was devastated at the loss of his marriage. For the first time in his life, he took something as a personal failure. After work each day for several months, he wrote in a journal as a means of sorting out his feelings. He sorted out in his mind the things that he did that contributed to his relationship problems and the things that were caused by his former wife's mental illness. He was able to accept his part without feeling blame or guilt, and he used it as a learning experience.

Skip stayed with his new company for over ten years. During that time he quickly was promoted. He moved up the corporate ladder and within two years was vice president. His creativity, trustworthiness, and steady personality were a good match for the hectic world of advertising. People experienced him as a stabilizing force, as their rock. At that point he decided to get his MBA degree. He enrolled in a program that allowed him to attend one evening a week. During his first semester he met Kathy, a student in one of his courses. Kathy, who worked in finance, was in many ways the perfect match for Skip. Also a stable, solid person, she greatly enjoyed the arts. Kathy received her undergraduate degree in art and was a fine painter. She was far more emotionally expressive than Skip, and emotionally they balanced each other well. They appreciated each other's emotional style and wished to be more like the other. After a six-month courtship, Skip asked Kathy to marry him during a romantic weekend getaway. The two remain married nearly forty years later. Skip and Kathy raised three children together. After finishing her MBA, Kathy started her own consulting company, which allowed her to work part-time throughout their marriage. It also afforded her the time and space to paint, which she continued to do.

After ten years, Skip decided to accept a position as a faculty member in a local university. Skip and Kathy invested well, and money become less of a concern. Skip loved the opportunity to teach and was viewed as a great colleague and resource during his career. While he never was an academic superstar and was not as successful as he had been in the world of business, Skip was happy and enjoyed his life.

Skip developed a complicated health concern in the form of a rare autoimmune disease. For two years he struggled with frequent viral infections. Several times he wound up hospitalized. After this difficult period he was placed on a medicine regime that helped him stabilize.

Once his health was stable, Skip began playing a great deal more music. He found great pleasure in returning to his old passion and loved playing, especially now that the expectations were not so intense. He could just "blow the horn and let it go." He was asked to play with many of his old musician friends and had far more opportunities than he could accept. At about the same time, the climate within his business school began to deteriorate. The dean fought constantly with the faculty, who were divided into factions. Skip found many of the issues that people were fighting over petty and refused to take sides. Ironically, many people therefore experienced Skip as being fair and impartial, which led to their talking to him about their concerns. By not being involved in the college's drama, he became the calm eye in the hurricane. After a year of this, he decided that he had enough money to retire from full-time employment and announced his decision to leave.

Since Skip's retirement he has spent most of his time gardening or playing music. An old musician friend asked him if he wishes he had remained a working musician his whole life. He replied, "Not for a minute. If I did, I never would have missed it so much and would not be having so much fun with it now!" Skip remains actively engaged with those he most cares about, and with the activities that currently bring him the most pleasure.

FOR WRITING AND REFLECTION

1. Is it hard for you to believe that Skip was truly so happy all these years? If so, why?

2. What does your response tell you about how you perceive men, and about your conceptualization of human behavior and existence?

3. What are the dominant themes and metaphors within Skip's life?

4. Assume that Skip became suddenly depressed over having left his position as a college professor. What approach would you use in working with him?

5. What characteristic that Skip possesses do you wish you had more of? Why? How can you develop this attribute in yourself?

EXERCISE

Think of a man who you have respect for, who you value, who you believe has many strengths. Explore and describe his strengths. How do they define who he is? How do they help him achieve this goals and dreams? Do these strengths help him overcome key limitations?

EXERCISE—THE STRENGTHS AND RESILIENCY OF MEN

For this exercise, interview a man about his strengths and how he has used his strengths and resources to overcome adversity. During your interview, try not to ask about any problems, issues, or concerns. If the man you are interviewing brings them up on his own, ask him what skills and resources he used to overcome these issues. Ask him how he has grown from his own trials and tribulations. Ask him what he likes about himself, and what others like about him. Instead of giving you a script of questions that you must ask, see it as your job to mine for strengths, to find out everything possible you can about the man you are interviewing.

Resources APPENDIX

The following section contains many resources for and about men. I am providing these resources as a means of gathering more information, and for social workers to assess in terms of appropriateness for their own male clients. I in no way advocate the views expressed by some of these resources.

INTRODUCTION: General Resources About Men

Changing Men Collections: Text, video, and audio collections at Michigan State University pertaining to men, masculinities, and the men's movement.
  http://www.lib.msu.edu/coll/main/spec_col/radicalism/men/
Health Institute, Men's Health: A list of wellness-related resources for and about men, from the Australian national government.
  http://www.healthinsite.gov.au/topics/Men_s_Health
Men's Center: Described as "the male affirmative resource center," the Men's Center is a web site that seeks to provide resources to help men live positive, productive, and healthy lives.
  http://www.themenscenter.com/index.htm
Men's Studies and Men's Movement: Internet gateway—a list of academic and nonacademic sources about men from Carnegie Mellon University Libraries.
  http://www.library.cmu.edu/Research/SocialSciences/Gender/ms_internet.html

Men's Web: An Internet journal with articles, discussion, and links to various issues related to men.

http://www.menweb.org/

2. Men's Psychosocial Health in a Global Era

Men's Resources International: The goal of this organization is to help men around the globe practice healthy and compassionate forms of masculinity. With a special focus and history in Africa, the group engages in organizing and training men around issues of violence, gender, and masculinity.

http://www.mensresourcesinternational.org/template.php?page=aboutus

A New Role for Men—United Nations Population Fund: This branch of the United Nations focuses on development- and population-related issues in developing countries. The website explores the role of men and masculinity in the process of development and the empowerment of women.

http://www.unfpa.org/intercenter/role4men/

3. Conceptions of Masculinity and the Development of Men

American Men's Studies Association: This organization encourages teaching, research, and clinical practice on men and masculinities. It supports the development of academic programs in men's studies, encourages interdisciplinary study and practice, and sponsors an annual conference on men and masculinities.

http://mensstudies.org/

Division 51: Society for the Psychological Study of Men and Masculinity: This is the group within the American Psychological Association that focuses on the study of men and masculinity. It encompasses research, treatment, and education.

http://www.apa.org/about/division/div51.html

National Organization for Men Against Sexism: A profeminist, gay-affirmative, antiracist organization, this group seeks to enhance the lives of all men. It holds a national conference and has chapters in several cities throughout the United States.

http://www.nomas.org/

Hard Hat Brotherhood: The website states that the organization is founded on the premise that men sometimes just want to "hang out and be one of the guys." The organization bills itself as encouraging men's relationships with each other through "doing guy stuff," and its members are from diverse socioeconomic groups. While international, most Hard Hat groups are located in California and Michigan.

http://www.hardhatbrotherhood.com/

Men's Leadership Alliance: This nonprofit organization is dedicated to men living authentic, joyful, "soulful lives." It seeks to inspire men to live authentically in the service of a sustainable world. The website states: "We hold a vision of authentic manhood. The cultural motif of modern manhood strikes us as shallow. So often, emptiness results from a life lived in service of superficial manhood devoted to competitive achievement, sexual conquest, empty, escapist pleasures and spiritual poverty." The organization sponsors men's leadership and development retreats in a wilderness setting, and personal coaching.

http://www.mensleadershipalliance.org/

4. The Relationships of Men

Dads and Daughters: The mission of the organization is to help maximize the father–daughter relationship, regardless of the type of involvement of the father. Stepfathers and nonresidential fathers are valued. The organization is committed to promoting supportive and fulfilling relationships and advocacy for fathers.

http://www.dadsanddaughters.org/our-work/topics-for-research.aspx

National Fatherhood Initiative: The organization seeks to improve the well-being of children by increasing the proportion of those growing up with involved, responsible fathers. The group seeks to educate fathers, develop national leadership, develop curricula and training, and encourage alliances.

http://www.objector.org/

5. Theoretical and Practice Guidelines

Beck Institute for Cognitive Therapy and Research: Founded by Aaron T. Beck, one of the developers of cognitive therapy, the institute serves as a training ground and research center on cognitive therapy. It also provides direct services from a cognitive perspective. Professional resources include books and information about the assessment tools, such as the well-researched Beck Depression Inventory.

http://www.beckinstitute.org

Center for Narrative Practice: A narrative therapy training center located in Manchester, England.

http://www.narrativepractice.com/

Dulwich Center: This group engages in training, research, collaboration, and cohosting of international conferences in narrative therapy and community work. The center's work represents the new movement in narrative therapy, which is to move the work from an individual to a community-based model. The center's link to articles is particularly useful, as it provides some excellent introductory and advanced readings on many narrative related topics.

http://www.dulwichcentre.com.au/intcourse2007–2008.htm

Albert Ellis Institute: Formerly the Institute for Rational Emotive Therapy, this institute is dedicated to providing training and services in rational emotive behavior therapy. Social workers can receive several levels of training, which include day-long intensives, certificate programs, and fellowships. The institute also provides resources related to REBT.

http://www.albertellisinstitute.org/aei/index.html

International Society for Existential Psychotherapy and Counseling: Founded in 2006, the organization was created to advance the study and practice of existential psychotherapy. The society sponsors training and is developing its network and infrastructure. The organization is evolving and encourages those who are interested to contact it.

http://www.existentialpsychotherapy.net/ICECAP/icecaphome.php

International Society for Existential Psychology and Psychotherapy: A division of the International Network on Personal Meaning, this group's mission is to advance existential psychotherapy. It supports dialogue and sponsors the professional journal *International Journal of Existential Psychology and Psychotherapy*.

http://www.existentialpsychology.org/

Narrative Therapy Library: A resource that lists many books, articles, and workshops on narrative therapy. The site includes free articles on narrative therapy.

http://www.narrativetherapylibrary.com/default.asp?ID=1

Narrativeapproaches.com: This website was developed by Jennifer Freeman, David Epston, and Dean Labovits, three of the key developers of narrative therapy. The site provides links to training, professional resources, books, and articles about the approach.

www.narrativeapproaches.com

University of Kansas, School of Social Work, What Is the Strengths Perspective: This website is maintained by the school of social work that was instrumental in developing the strengths perspective. The site includes a discussion of the history, knowledge base, key principles, assessment strategies, and relationships to other approaches.

http://www.socwel.ku.edu/Strengths/about.shtml

PART 2: Problems and Solutions

Male Development and Empowerment Center: Located on the campus of Medgar Evers College in New York, this center's mission is to assist males in the community to become more self-aware, develop leadership skills, and support and encourage educational and personal goals. It offers seminars on subjects such as how to enhance male-to-male communication, increasing one's financial position, specific industries, and accessing resources to assist in protecting parental rights. www.mec.cuny.edu

6. Men and Violence

Gang Resistance Education and Training Program: This website offers a curriculum for youth, delivered by law enforcement officers, to help prevent youth gang activities.
http://www.great-online.org/

Men's Anti-Violence Network: A group of community and business leaders dedicated to stopping domestic violence.
http://www.themangroup.org/aboutman.shtml

Men's Resource Center for Change: The organization's website states that its mission "is to support men, challenge men's violence, and develop men's leadership in ending oppression in ourselves, our families, and our communities. Our programs support men to overcome the damaging effects of rigid and stereotyped masculinity, and simultaneously confront men's patterns of personal and societal violence and abuse toward women, children, and other men." The organization provides training, anger management, and antiviolence programs in Massachusetts, and advocacy and education via political and social action. It provides links to many good resources related to men.
http://www.mrcforchange.org/

National Latino Alliance for the Elimination of Domestic Violence: An organization of Latino and Latina advocates dedicated to the elimination of domestic violence. It stresses the strengths within the Latino community and the role of racism, discrimination, and other oppression in the perpetuation of domestic violence.
http://www.dvalianza.org/Templates/index.htm

National Youth Gang Center: This federal agency falls under the Office of Juvenile Justice and Delinquency Prevention. The purpose of the organization is to help policy makers, researchers, and practitioners reduce youth involvement in gang-related activity. The website provides up-to-date research on the nature of gangs, their prevention, and intervention.

http://www.iir.com/nygc/

Rape, Abuse and Incest National Network: The largest anti–sexual assault organization in the country. It conducts workshops and programs on sexual assault and operates the national Sexual Assault Hotline.

http://www.rainn.org/

Toolkit to End Violence, from the National Advisory Council on Violence Against Women Office: The goal of the toolkit is to provide guidance and resources to communities, policy makers, and individuals to end violence against women.

http://toolkit.ncjrs.org/

United States Army Sexual Assault Prevention and Response Program: The army program designed to eliminate sexual assault in the military. It focuses on prevention, education, policy formation, advocacy, and treatment.

http://www.sexualassault.army.mil/

White Ribbon Campaign: An Canadian organization with a global focus, the campaign has been fighting violence against women since 1991. It encourages men to join in solidarity against violence by wearing a white ribbon at a specific time during the year and to join community-based antiviolence activities.

7. Workers at Risk

Department of Veterans Affairs Vocational Rehabilitation and Employment Services. The office that seeks to assist veterans in regard to employment and job training issues.

http://www.vba.va.gov/bln/vre/

Employee Assistance Program: An excellent resource with links to many other EAP-related and government resources.

http://www.eapmanager.com/links/links.htm

Employee Assistance Professional Association: As the name suggests, the website for the organization of employee assistance professionals. The organization has five thousand members from various professions, including social workers.

http://www.eapassn.org/public/pages/index.cfm?pageid=1

Everything Must Change—Philadelphia, PA. This is a faith-based program that provides job training and job placement to persons who were unskilled and unemployed. Some of the job-training skills are in construction and commercial building trades industries. This organization also partners with other organizations to provide services for substance abuse treatment and prevention of addiction.

http://www.phillyfuture.org/node/5836

e-VETS Resource Advisor: This group is available for veterans who are looking for employment. It provides job search assistance, job listings, additional training and assessment, and other services specific to veterans. It also advises veterans of their legal rights and responsibilities under federal laws.

www.dol.gov/elaws/evets.htm

Job Corps: A federally funded program that offers job-skills training for young people. It gives them a chance to learn a trade and get a high school diploma or GED and provides assistance in finding employment. Job Corps provides residential and nonresidential programs. Some of the vocational offerings are business, sales, culinary arts, nurse's aid, carpentry, painting, construction, landscaping, and welding.

http://www.jobcorps.dol.gov

Primavera Foundation—Tucson, AZ: The Primavera employment programs assist homeless and near homeless adults in learning job skills and finding employment. Participants are enrolled in an Individual Service Plan that involves a case plan and an Employability Development Plan. The client's skills are assessed to match them with temporary employment while searching for full-time jobs. Primavera provides job readiness classes that assist its clients in developing interviewing skills, understanding how to complete applications, job search planning, and identifying employment skills. Primavera also supports clients with bus passes, lunches, housing, and suitable clothing for work. Its ultimate goal is to assist clients in obtaining full-time employment and the ability to live independently. Primavera also partners with the Jackson Employment Center, which is a one-stop career center that provides job training for the homeless, continuum of care to working men, women, and families, and support services after clients secure employment, to ensure employment success and advancement.

http://www.primavera.org

United States Department of Labor, Employment and Training Administration: The federal agency that oversees job training programs and provides states with grants for state-administered unemployment and vocational services. Of particular note is the administration's web page, Advancing Your Career. On this page are links to information on career development, an analysis of high-growth jobs, programs for youth, and advising on how to deal with the loss of a job.

http://www.doleta.gov/etainfo/

http://www.doleta.gov/jobseekers/

8. Warriors at Risk

Central Committee for Conscientious Objectors: The nonprofit organization that helps men and women make choices about disengaging from military service. It also seeks to educate people about the realities of military service and war. It operates the GI Hotline, which provides information to servicepeople about their general military rights and their rights regarding discharges.
http://www.objector.org/

DefenseLink/The United States Department of Defense (DOD): DefenseLink is the official website of the DOD. The mission of the DOD is to provide military resources to secure the United States. The website provides links to many issues related to U.S. service members, including information on current conflicts and research.
http://www.defenselink.mil/

Disabled American Veterans (DAV): The DAV is a nonprofit organization with over a million members. Its mission is improve the lives of disabled veterans and their families through advocacy and referral to services. The DAV directly lobbies the federal government on behalf of disabled veterans. Its largest program, the National Service Program, works directly with the government on helping veterans receive the benefits.
http://www.dav.org/

U.S. Department of Veterans Affairs (VA): The government agency that is responsible for the health and well-being of all veterans of the United States Armed Services. VA medical centers and clinics are located throughout the United States. The VA provides comprehensive physical and mental health care. Since the vast majority of members of the armed forces are men, the VA provides many services that are focused on the psychosocial needs of men.
http://www.va.gov/

VA Social Work: The VA Department of Social Work is the largest provider of social work services in the world. The website provides a wealth of information about veterans and services to them.
http://www1.va.gov/socialwork/

Veterans of Foreign Wars of the United States of America: Community-based service organization.

Veterans Resources: An Internet site that provides links to news stories pertaining to veterans and those that serve them. This site also includes a free Internet forum, in which veterans and other interested persons can discuss topics including disability benefits, medical services, educational benefits, and other topics of interest to social workers.
http://www.veteransresources.org/

9. The Physical Health of Men

American Academy of Anti-Ageing Medicine—Men's Health resource page: A list of more than fifty articles that explore various men's health related issues.
http://www.worldhealth.net/p/mens-health.html

American Cancer Society: A nonprofit organization dedicated to finding cures for cancer, helping people find the medical resources they need to manage their disease, and helping people live successfully lives with cancer. Its mission is to engage in collaboration with other organizations to eliminate suffering from cancer through research, education, advocacy, and service.
http://www.cancer.org/docroot/home/index.asp

American Diabetes Association: This organization provides important information about how to prevent and treat diabetes, a significant problem with men, in particular African American men.
http://www.diabetes.org

American Heart Association: The mission of the organization is simple: to build better lives through cardiovascular health. The organization promotes education and treatment of heart-related diseases.
http://www.americanheart.org

American Urological Association: This organization maintains a website for a patient education. Good discussions of urological-based disorders and referrals to urologists are provided.
http://www.urologyhealth.org/

Centers for Disease Control (CDC): The CDC provides a comprehensive list of topics around men's health. The website includes a valuable quiz that tests your knowledge of men's health issues. "Tips for a healthy lifestyle" provide men with guidelines for behaviors that will increase the likelihood of their improving their health or remaining in good health.
http://www.cdc.gov/men/

Everyman: A British nonprofit organization dedicated to raising funds and education for the prevention and treatment of testicular and prostate cancer. The site contains valuable information on testicular self-checks and on prostate health.
http://www.icr.ac.uk/everyman/

International Society for Men's Health: A multidisciplinary international organization dedicated to gender-specific medical services. The organization has a strong focus on the prevention of men's health risks. Publishes the *Journal of Men's Health*.
http://www.ismh.org/en/ismh-home/ismh-home.html

Mayo Clinic Tools for Healthy Lives, Men's Health Center: This website provides information, treatment options, and resources on men's health issues, such as prostate health, sexual health, STDs, and fertility. Its A–Z list of men's health conditions includes psychological and psychosocial concerns as well as physical health issues.

http://www.mayoclinic.com/health/mens-health/MC99999

Men's Health Network: A network of health care providers, nonprofit organizations, and businesses dedicated to improving men's health through education campaigns and networking. Its goals include reducing men's premature mortality, increasing physical and mental well-being, and reducing the impact of violence on the lives of men.

http://www.menshealthnetwork.org/

National Kidney and Urologic Diseases Information Clearinghouse, National Institute of Health: This website provides a wealth of information and resources about a variety of diseases affecting men. The site contains an A–Z list of each of the major urological diseases, including an excellent set of links on erectile dysfunction. The site is known to be based on up-to-date, evidenced-based medical practice and research.

http://kidney.niddk.nih.gov/index.htm

University of Texas, Houston, Men's Health Issues: A website that discusses some of the key men's health issues.

http://medic.med.uth.tmc.edu/ptnt/00000391.htm

10. Men and Mental Illness

Depression and Bipolar Support Alliance: An Internet-based resource that provides information about bipolar disorder and depression. The site links contains links to support groups and other valuable resources.

http://www.dbsalliance.org

Men and Mental Illness, A Silent Crisis, Canadian Mental Health Association: An Internet-based resource that helps men and providers understand the often ignored issues related to men and mental illness.

http://www.cmha.ca/bins/content_page.asp?cid=3-726

National Alliance for the Mental Illness (NAMI): NAMI is the largest grassroots organization dedicated to improving the lives of the mentally ill and their families. The organization engages in political advocacy and education on issues that pertain to people with mental illness. It also operates a twenty-four-hour-a-day helpline that receives more than four thousand callers a month. The website provides a wealth of information on issues pertaining to men with mental illness.

http://www.nami.org/

Real Men/ Real Depression, National Institute of Mental Health: The Real Men, Real Depression project seeks to help educate men about depression. The website presents the story of real men talking about their own depression as it relates to their sense of self as men. Diverse men's stories are presented. The focus of the campaign is to help men understand that depression is not a sigh of weakness, but a treatable disorder. The site also provides information on symptoms, treatments, and sources of support.

http://menanddepression.nimh.nih.gov/

World Health Organization (WHO)/Mental Illness: The WHO provides a great deal of information about mental illness, its prevention, and its treatment. Much information is provided on mental illness from an international perspective, as well as the impact of social and environmental catastrophes on mental health. The WHO developed the ICD-10, a classification system of mental disorders that provides an alternative to the DSM-IV.

http://www.who.int/mental_health/emergencies/en/

11. Older Men at Risk

Administration on Aging: A division of the Department of Health and Human Services, the branch of the federal government that funds programs under the Older Americans Act. Home health care, community-based care, visiting nurses, and meals programs are some of the many services that administration has funded for thirty-five years.

http://www.aoa.org

Alzheimer's Association: The national organization with the mission to cure Alzheimer's disease through research, and to improve the care and support for people with the disorder.

http://www.alz.org/

American Association of Retired Persons (AARP): The membership organization of thirty-seven million older Americans. The AARP advocates for the physical, financial, and social well-being of older Americans.

http://www.aarp.org/

International Association for Hospice and Palliative Care: An international advocacy organization that seeks to have palliative care viewed as a human right, thereby increasing access to services worldwide.

http://www.hospicecare.com/Organisation/

John A. Hartford Foundation: The foundation states that its overall goal is to increase the capacity of the nation to provide effective and affordable care for older adults.

Since 1929 the Hartford Foundation has been providing grants to improve training to gerontological specialists, provide social services, and conduct research for
the issues of older adults.

http://www.jhartfound.org/

National Hospice and Palliative Care Organization: An organization dedicated to excellence in palliative and hospice care. The organization stresses holistic care, the
development of palliative care standards, the training of professionals, and the
integration of palliative and hospice care throughout the health care system.

http://www.nhpco.org/templates/1/homepage.cfm

National Institute on Aging: Federal government agency that coordinators and funds
research on aging. The website provides valuable links to research grant opportunities and health information.

http://www.nia.nih.gov/

12. Diverse Men at Risk

Gay Men of African Descent: Based in New York, this organization seeks to support
gay black men through advocacy and programming. It conducts street outreach
in New York, distributing condoms and providing sexual health information. It
also provides HIV support groups and HIV testing.

http://www.gmad.org/index.html

National Black Gay Men's Advocacy Coalition: This group is committed to improving
the health and well-being of black gay men through research, policy, training,
and advocacy. The website lists its core values as honesty/integrity, love/caring,
trust, respect, independence, and commitment to excellence. The website provides daily links to news stories around the world that address the rights and lives
of gay men.

http://www.nbgmac.org/

100 Black Men of America: The mission of this organization is to improve the quality
of life in the African American community by enhancing economic and educational opportunities. The group seeks to develop youth leaders and is based on
values of respect for the family, spirituality, justice, integrity, and empowerment.
It conducts training programs, leadership forums, and conferences.

http://www.100blackmen.org/

Parents, Families and Friends of Lesbians and Gays (PFLAG):- An organization whose
mission is to promote the well-being of people from diverse sexual orientations
and gender identities through advocacy and education.

http://www.pflag.org/

World Professional Association of Transgender Health: A professional organization devoted to the health and well-being of transgendered people. Members represent professionals in social work, counseling, other mental health fields, medical professions, voice and speech therapies, and other professions. It publishes standard-of-care guidelines for working with transgendered individuals.

13. Men, Compulsive Disorders, and Addictions

Al-anon: The twelve-step support group for family members who have problems with alcohol. Al-anon helps its members share their experiences, hopes, and strengths with each other so they can set limits with the problem drinkers in their lives and heal from negative effects that alcohol abuse has had on their lives.
http://www.al-anon.alateen.org/english.html

Alcoholics Anonymous (AA): AA is the largest self-help organization in the world. It is based on the twelve steps, a spiritually/religiously based program that focuses on concepts such as powerlessness over one's addiction and the importance of peer support.
http://www.alcoholics-anonymous.org/?Media=PlayFlash

Co-dependents Anonymous: While the phenomenon of codependency has typically been applied to women, this twelve-step self-help group is open to both men and women who have been affected by the addictions or problematic behavior of others.
http://www.codependents.org/

Gamblers Anonymous: A twelve-step support group for compulsive gamblers. The website contains a twenty-question quiz to help people determine if they have a problem with compulsive gambling. As with the websites of many twelve-step programs, a comprehensive list of meetings is linked to the homepage.
http://www.gamblersanonymous.org/

Overeaters Anonymous: A twelve-step support group for compulsive overeaters. While the majority of members are women, many men do attend and are welcome.
http://www.oa.org/index.htm

Rational Recover: Self-help program for compulsive behaviors that is truly self-help in nature. The is work is done individually and not with support groups.
http://www.rational.org/html_public_area/rrsn.html

Sexual Compulsives Anonymous: A twelve-step support group for sexually compulsive behavior. While open to all, the group is predominantly composed of gay men. This program focuses less on abstaining from all sexual behavior and more on men developing their own sexual recovery plans. It seeks to help people express their sexuality in ways that are physically, emotionally, and spiritually healthy.
http://www.sca-recovery.org/

Sex Addicts Anonymous: A twelve-step support group for people who engage in sexually compulsive behavior. The website contains a self-assessment to help people determine if they have a problem with sexual addiction.
http://www.saa-recovery.org/

Sex and Love Addicts Anonymous: A twelve-step program that seeks to help members stop engaging in destructive sexual or romantic entanglements. The organization recognizes that sexual, social, and emotional anorexia, in addition to compulsive behavior, may negatively impact people's lives.
http://www.slaafws.org/

SMART Recovery: Face-to-face and online support groups for all addictive behaviors. The program is based upon cognitive behavioral principles and is appropriate for men for whom the twelve-step programs are not.
http://www.smartrecovery.org/

Workaholics Anonymous: A twelve-step program for those who wish to stop working compulsively. A "big book" is now available to those interested in this relatively new program. The website also has links to PDF files that contain valuable information on the topic.
http://www.workaholics-anonymous.org/

References

Abbott, A. (2007). Neuroscience: The molecular wake-up call. *Nature* 447: 368–370.

Abbott, F. (ed.). (1990). *Men and intimacy: Personal accounts exploring the dilemmas of modern male sexuality.* Berkeley: Crossing Press.

Act Up. (2007). "Act Up oral history project." http://www.actuporalhistory.org/ interviews/index.html.

Addis, M. E., and Mahalik, J. R. (2003). Men, masculinity, and the context of help seeking. *American Psychologist*, 58, no. 1: 5–14.

Alcoholics Anonymous. (2007). "AA at a glance." http://anonymous.org/en_information _aa.cfm?PageID=10.

——— (2007b). *Alcoholics Anonymous.* (4th ed). New York: Alcoholics Anonymous.

Alexandersen, P., and Christiansen, C. (2004). The ageing male: Testosterone deficiency and testosterone replacement. *Arthrosclerosis*, 173, no. 2: 157–169.

Althof, S. E., O'Leary, M. P., Cappelleri, J. D., Hvidsten, K., Stecher, V. J., Glina, S., King, R., and Siegel, R. L. (2006). Sildenafil Citrate improves self-esteem, confidence and relationships in men with erectile dysfunction: Results from an international, multi-center, double-blind, placebo-controlled trial. *Journal of Sexual Medicine*, 3, no. 3: 521–529.

Altman, D. (2004). Sexuality and globalization. *Sexuality Research and Social Policy*, 1, no. 1: 63–65.

Alzheimer's Association. (2007). Fact sheet. http://www.alz.org/national/documents/ PR_FFfactsheet.pdf.

American Cancer Society. (2006). Detailed guide: What is cancer? *Cancer Reference Information*.www.cancer.org/docroot/CRI/content/CRI_2_4_1x_What_Is_Cancer .asp?sitearea=.

American Psychiatric Association. (1994). *Diagnostic and statistical manual of mental disorders.* 4th ed. Washington, D.C.: American Psychiatric Association.

———. (2000). *Diagnostic and statistical manual of mental disorders.* (4th ed). Washington, D.C.: American Psychiatric Association.

American Psychological Association. (2007). Elder abuse and neglect: In search of solutions. *Public Interest.* http://www.apa.org/pi/aging/eldabuse.html.

———. (2009). Elder abuse and neglect: In search of solutions. http://www.apa.org/pi/ aging/eldabuse.html.

———. Presidential Task Force on Military Deployment Services for Youth, Families and Service Members. (2007). *The psychological needs of U.S. military service members and their families: A preliminary report.* Washington, D.C.: American Psychological Association.

American Stroke Association (2007). *Types of stokes.* http://www.strokeassociation. org/presenter.jhtml?identifier=1014.

Andersen, A. E. (1995). Eating disorders in males. In K. D. Brownell and C. G. Fairburn (eds.), *Eating disorders and obesity: A comprehensive handbook,* 177–187. New York: Guilford.

Andersen, M. L. (ed.). (2007). *Race, class and gender.* Belmont, Calif.: Thomson/ Wadsworth.

Antonucci, T. C., and Akiyama, H. (1997). An examination of sex differences in social support among older men and women. *Sex Roles,* 17, nos. 11–12: 737–749.

Aponte, R. (1996.) Urban employment and the mismatch dilemma: Accounting for the immigration exception. *Social Problems,* 43, no. 3: 268–283.

Appelbaum, E., and Batt R. (1994). *The new American workplace: Transforming work systems in the United States.* Ithaca: Cornell University Press.

Arras, R. E., Ogletree, R. J., and Welshimer, K. J. (2006). Health-promoting behaviors in men age 45 and above. *International Journal of Men's Health,* 5, no. 1: 65–70.

Ashford, J. B., Lecroy, C., and Lortie, K. L. (2005). *Human behavior in the social environment: A multidimensional perspective.* (3rd ed.) New York: Wadsworth.

Attridge, M., Herlihy, P. A., and Maiden, R. P. (eds). (2005). *The integration of employee assistance, work/life and wellness services.* Binghamton, N.Y.: Hayworth.

Augustine Fellowship (1986). *Sex and love addicts anonymous.* Boston: Augustine Fellowship.

Austrian, S. G. (2002). *Developmental theories throughout the life cycle.* New York: Columbia University Press.

Axelrod, S. D. (2001). The vital relationship between work and masculinity. A psycho-analytic perspective. *Psychology of Men and Masculinities*, 2, no. 2: 117–223.

Bachrach, L. L. (1992). Psychosocial rehabilitation and psychiatry in the care of long-term patients. *American Journal of Psychiatry*, 149, no. 11: 1455–1463.

Baker, F., and Bell, C. C. (1999). Issues in psychiatric treatment of blacks. *Psychiatric Services*, 50, no. 4: 362–368.

Balswick, J. (1988). *The inexpressive male*. Lexington, Mass.: Lexington Books.

Bannon, I., and Correia, M. C. (eds.). (2006). *The other half of gender*. Washington, D.C.: World Bank.

Barnes, N. (2007). *Executive summary: Transnational study on gangs*. Washington Office on Latin America. http://www.wola.org/index.php?option=com_content&task=viewp&id=272&Itemid=2.

Baum, N. (2004). On helping divorced men to mourn their losses. *American Journal of Psychotherapy*, 58, no. 2: 174–185.

Baumeister, R. F., and Sommer, K. L. (1997). What do men want? Gender differences and two spheres of belongingness: Comment on Cross and Madison. *Psychological Bulletin*, 122, no. 11: 38–44.

Beck, A. T. (1976). *Cognitive therapy and the emotional disorders*. New York: International University Press.

Beck, A. T., and Emery, G. (1985). *Anxiety disorders and phobias*. New York: Basic Books.

Beck, C. (2000). Creative elderhood: What's art got to do with it? Ms.

Beck, J. (1995). *Basics and beyond*. New York: Guilford.

Beck, R., and Fernandez, E. (1998). Cognitive-behavioral therapy in the treatment of anger: A meta-analysis. *Cognitive Therapy and Research*, 22, no. 1: 63–74.

Becker, E. (1971). *Denial of death*. (2nd ed.) New York: Free Press.

Behan, C. (1999). Linking lives around shared themes: Narrative group therapy with gay men. *Gecko*, 2: 18–34.

Benda, B. B. (2006). Survival analysis of social support and trauma among homeless male and female veterans who abuse substances. *American Journal of Orthopsychiatry*, 76, no. 1: 70–79.

Beneria, L., and Santiago, L. E. (2001). The impact of industrial relocation on displaced workers: A case study of Cortland, New York. *Economic Development Quarterly*, 15, no. 1: 78–89.

Bergen, R. K., and Bogle, K. (2000). Exploring the connection between pornography and sexual violence. *Violence and Victims*, 15, no. 3: 227–234.

Berlant, L. (ed.) (2000). *Intimacy*. Chicago: University of Chicago Press.

Berlin, S. B. (2001). *Clinical social work practice: A cognitive-integrative perspective*. New York: Oxford University Press.

Bernard, M. E., and Joyce, M. R. (1984). *Rational emotive therapy with children and adolescents.* New York: Wiley.

Bernton, H. (2008). Sen. Murray to do more for vets on streets. *Seattle Times,* February 22. http://seattletimes.nwsource.com/html/politics/2004195019_veterans22m.html.

Beulens, J. W. J.., Rimm, E. B.., Ascherio, A., Spiegelman, D., Hendriks, H. F. J., and Mukamal, K. J. (2007). Alcohol consumption and risk for coronary heart disease among men with hypertension. *Annals of Internal Medicine,* 146, no. 1: 1–35.

Birren, J. E., and Deutchman, D. E. (1991). *Guiding autobiography groups for older adults: Exploring the fabric of life.* Baltimore: Johns Hopkins University Press.

Black, L. 2008. "Mental health court" turns 1 year old. *Chicago Tribune,* February 20. http://www.chicagotribune.com.

Blackburn, I., and Twaddle, V. (1996). *Cognitive therapy in action: A practitioner's casebook.* London: Souvenir Press.

Blechman, E. A., and Brownell, K. D. (Eds.). (1998). *Behavioral medicine and women.* New York: Guilford Press.

Blieszner, R., and Adams, R. G. (1992). *Adult friendship.* Newbury Park, Calif.: Sage.

Bly, R. (1990). *Iron John: A book about men.* Reading, Mass.: Addison-Wesley.

Blyth, D. A., and Foster-Clark, F. S. (1987) Gender differences in perceived intimacy with different members of adolescents' social networks. *Sex Roles,* 17: 689–718.

Boarnet, M. G., Greenwald, M., and McMillan, T. E. (2008). Walking, urban design, and health. *Journal of Planning and research,* 27, no. 3: 342–358.

Bodley, J. H. (1994). *Cultural anthropology: Tribes, states, and the global system.* Mountain View, Calif.: Mayfield.

Bohart, A. C., and Greening, T. (2001). Humanistic psychology and positive psychology. *American Psychologist,* 56, no. 2: 81–82.

Böhnisch, L. (2008). The current discussion on men and masculinities. Social Work and Society: *International Online-only Journal,* 6, no. 1. http://www.socwork.net/2007/festschrift/esw/boehnisch

Bowleg, L (2004). Love, sex and masculinity in sociocultural context. *Men and Masculinities,* 7, no. 2: 166–186.

Brenner, S. (2007). Currently used medications for Alzheimer's disease are not very effective. *American Journal of Medicine,* 120, no. 12: 388–397.

Bride, B. E., Robinson, M. M., Yegidis, B., and Figley, C. R. (2004). Development and validation of the Secondary Traumatic Stress Scale. *Research on Social Work Practice,* 12, no. 1: 27–35.

Brindis, C. D., Barenbaum, M., Sanchez-Flores, H., McCarter, V., and Chand, R. (2005). Let's hear it for the guys: California's male involvement program. *International Journal of Men's Health,* 4, no. 1: 29–53.

Brokaw, T. (1998). *The greatest generation*. New York: Random House.

Brooks, G. R. (1998). *A new psychotherapy for traditional men*. San Francisco: Jossey-Bass.

Brooks, G. R., and Silverstein, L. B. (1995). Understanding the dark side of masculinity. In R. F. Levant and W. S. Pollack (eds.), *A new psychology of men*, 280–333. New York: Basic Books.

Brown, M. L., and Rounsley, C. A. (1996) *True selves: Understanding transsexualism—for families, friends, coworkers, and helping professionals*. San Francisco: Jossey-Bass.

Buber, M. (1955). *Between man and man*. Boston: Beacon.

Bump, J. (1990). Innovative bibliotherapy approaches to substance abuse. *The Arts in Psychotherapy*, 17: 335–362.

Bureau of Justice Statistics. (2005a). Victims' statistics. Office of Justice Programs, U.S. Department of Justice, http://www.ojp.usdoj.gov/bjs/cvict_v.htm.

———. (2005b). Prison statistics: Summary findings. Office of Justice Programs, U.S. Department of Justice, http://www.ojp.usdoj.gov/bjs/prisons.htm.

———. (2006). *Criminal victimizations, 2005*. Department of Justice. Washington, D.C.: Bureau of Justice Statistics.

Bureau of Labor Statistics. (2007). Metropolitan area employment and unemployment summary. http://www.bls.gov/news.release/metro.nro.htm.

———. (2008). Employment situation summary. http://www.bls.gov/news.release/empsit.nro.htm

Burghardt, S. (1986). Marxist theory and social work. In F. J. Turner (ed.), *Social Work Treatment*, 590–617. New York: Free Press.

Burns, D. (1989). *The feeling good handbook*. New York: Morrow.

Burnside, I., and Haight, B. (1994). Reminiscence and life review: Therapeutic interventions for older people. *Nurse Practitioner*, 19, no. 4: 55–61.

Butler, R. N. (1963). The life review: An interpretation of reminiscence in the aged. *Psychiatry*, 26: 65–76.

Buttell, F. P., and Carney, M. M. (2005). Do batterer intervention programs serve African American and Caucasian batterers equally well? An investigation of a 26-week program. *Research on Social Work Practice*, 15, no. 1: 19–28.

Camarota, S. A. (2007). Immigrants in the United States, 2007: A profile of American's foreign-born population. Washington, D.C.: Center for Immigration Studies. http://www.cis.org/articles/2007/back1007.html.

Camus, A. (1942). *The stranger*. New York: Knopf.

Canadian Mental Health Association. (2007). Men's mental illness: A silent crisis. http://www.cmha.ca/bins/content_page.asp?cid=3-726.

Canadian Network for the Prevention of Elder Abuse (2007). *Promising approaches in theprevention of abuse and neglect of older adults in community settings in Canada*. http://www.cnpea.ca/Promising%20Approaches%20Final%20%202007.pdf

Canda, E. (ed.) (1998). *Spirituality in social work: New directions*. Binghamton, N.Y.: Haworth.

Cappeliez, P. (2004). Cognitive reminiscence therapy for depressed older adults. Nanaimo, Canada: Seniors' Psychological Interest Group. http://www.seniorsmentalhealth.ca/cognitive%20reminisence.pdf.

Capra, F. (1983). *The turning point*. New York: Bantam.

Career Gear (2008). http://www.careergear.org.

Carlick, A., and Biley, F. C. (2004). Thoughts on the therapeutic use of narrative in the promotion of coping with cancer care. *European Journal of Cancer Care*, 13, no. 3: 308–317.

Carnes, P. (2001). *Out of the shadows*. (3rd ed.). Minneapolis: Hazelden.

Carr, A. (1998). Michael White's narrative therapy. *Contemporary Family Therapy*, 20, no. 4: 485–503.

Carroll, K. M. (1998). *A cognitive behavioral approach: Treating cocaine addiction*. National Institute on Drug Abuse, NIH Publication Number 98–4308.

Carter, B., and McGoldrick, M. (1989). *The changing family life cycle: A framework for family therapy*. Boston: Allyn and Bacon.

Cason, F. (2008). Colorectal cancer: Early detection increases survival rates. University of Toledo Medical Center. http://www.universityhealthmatters.com/articles .php?artid=58.

Castle, D. J., and Murray, R. M. (1991). The neurodevelopmental basis of sex differences in schizophrenia. *Psychological Medicine*, 21, no. 3: 565–575.

Cavanaugh, K., and Cree, V. E. (eds.). (1996). *Working with men: Feminism and social work*. London: Routledge.

Centers for Disease Control. (2002). Leading causes of death: Males—United States, 2002. http://www.cdc.gov/men/lcod.htm.

——. (2004). Summary health statistics for U.S. Adults: National health interview survey, 2004. Vital and health statistics, Series 10, No. 228. Washington, D.C.: Government Printing Office.

——. (2006). United States cancer statistics: 2003 incidence and mortality. United States Department of Health and Human Services. http://www.cdc.gov/cancer/npcr/npcrpdfs/US_Cancer_Statistics_2003_Incidence_and_Mortality.pdf.

——. (2007). Sexually transmitted disease surveillance. Atlanta: U.S. Department of Health and Human Services.

——. (2008). Physical exercise for everyone. http://www.cdc.gov/nccdphp/dnpa/physical/everyone/recommendations/index.htm.

Chapleau, K. M., Oswald, D. L., and Russell, B. L. (2008). Male rape myths: The role of gender, violence, and sexism. *Journal of Interpersonal Violence*, 23, no. 5: 600–615.

Chatterbaugh, K. C. (1990). *Contemporary perspectives on masculinity: Men, women, and politics in modern society.* Boulder: Westview.

Chiquiar, D., and Hanson, G. (2005). International migration, self-selection, and the distribution of wages: Evidence from Mexico and the United States. *Journal of Political Economy*, 113, no. 2: 239–281.

Christ, G. H., and Sormanti, M. (1999). Advancing social work practice in end of life care. *Social Work in Healthcare*, 30, no. 2: 81–99.

Clark, M. L., and Ayers, M. (1991). Friendship similarity during adolescence: Gender and racial patters. *Journal of Psychology*, 126, no. 4: 393–405.

Clatterbaugh, K. (1990). *Contemporary perspectives on masculinity: Men, women, and politics in modern society.* Boulder: Westview.

Cloniger, C. R., Bohram, M., and Sigvardsson, S. (1981). Inheritance of alcohol abuse cross-fostering analysis of adopted men. *Archives of General Psychiatry*, 38, no. 8: 861–868.

Cochran, S. V., and Rabinowitz, F. E. (2000). *Men and depression: Clinical and empirical perspectives.* San Diego: Academic Press.

Coker, A. L., Davis, K. E., Arias, I., Desai, S., Sanderson, M., Brandt, H. M., and Smith, P. H. (2002). Missed opportunities: Intimate partner violence in family practice settings. *American Journal of Preventative Medicine*, 23, no. 4: 260–268.

Colarusso, C. A., and Nemiroff, R. A. (1987). Clinical implications of adult developmental theory. *American Journal of Psychiatry*, 144, no. 10: 1263–1270.

Colarusso, L. M. (2007). Concerns grow about war veterans' misdiagnoses: Brain injuries can defy easy detection. *Boston Globe*, June 10. http://www.boston.com/news/nation/articles/2007/06/10/concerns_grow_about_war_veterans_misdiagnoses?mode=PF.

Coleman, E. (1992). Is your patient suffering from compulsive sexual behavior? *Psychiatric Annals*, 22, no. 6: 320–325.

——. (1998). Erectile dysfunction: A review of current treatments. *Canadian Journal of Health Sexuality*, 7, no. 3: 231.

Colon, E. (1996). Program design and planning strategies in the delivery of culturally competent health and mental health services to Latino communities. In. Y. Asamoah (ed.), *Innovations in delivering culturally sensitive social work services*, 164–182. New York: Haworth.

Commonwealth Fund. 1999. *Health concerns across a woman's lifespan: 1998 survey of women's health.* New York: Commonwealth Fund.

Compas, B., Haaga, D., Keefe, F., Leitenberg, H., and Williams, D. (1998). Sampling of empirically supported psychological treatments from health psychology: Smoking, chronic pain, cancer, and bulimia nervosa. *Journal of Consulting and Clinical Psychology*, 66, no. 1: 66–112.

Conell, C., and Weisner, C. (2006).The prevalence of substance abuse disorders: Capture-recapture using medical information. Paper presented at the annual meeting of the American Sociological Association, Montreal.

Congressional Budget Office. (2007). The health care system for veterans: An interim report. Washington, D.C.: Congressional Budget Office.

Connell, R. W. (1990). An iron man: The body and some contradictions of hegemonic masculinity. In M. A. Messner and D. F. Sabo (eds.), *Sport, men and the gender order*, 83–95. Champaign, Ill.: Human Kinetics Books.

——. (1998). Masculinities and globalization. *Men and Masculinity*, 1, no. 1: 3–23.

——. (2000). Masculinity and violence in world perspective. In A. Godenzi (ed.), *Frieden, kultur und geschlecht*, 65–83. Freiburg: Freiburg University Press.

——. (2003). Masculinities and masculinity politics in world society. Lecture on November 25, 2003, at Rutgers University Institute for Research on Women, Distinguished Lecture Series. http://irw.rutgers.edu/lectures/connelllecture.pdf.

——. (2005). Change among the gatekeepers: Men, masculinities, and gender equality in the global arena. *Journal of Women in Culture and Society*, 30, no. 3: 1801–1825.

Connell, R. W., and Messerschmidt, J. W. (2005). Hegemonic masculinity: Rethinking the concept. *Gender and Society*, 19, no. 6: 829–859.

Conwell, Y. (2001). Suicide in later life: A review and recommendations for prevention. *Suicide and Life Threatening Behavior*, 31, supplement: 32–47.

Cook, D. D. (2007). Existential therapy can work for youths. *Addiction Professional* September/October. http://www.addictionpro.com/ME2/dirmod.asp?sid=&nm=&type=Publishing&mod=Publications%3A%3AArticle&mid=8F3A702742184197 8F18BE895F87F791&tier=4&id=11A83BF53D9C4D4D9A7784E5E095E409.

Cook, E. A. (1991). The effects of reminiscence on psychological measures of ego integrity in elderly nursing home residents. *Archives of Psychiatric Nursing*, 5, no. 5: 292–298.

Cooley, R. C., Ostendorf, D., and Bickerton, D. (1979). Outreach services for elderly Native Americans. *Social Work*, 24, no. 2: 151–153.

Cooper, A., Putnam, D., Planchon, L, and Boies, S. (1999). Online sexual compulsivity: Getting tangled in the Net. *Sexual addiction and compulsivity*, 6: 79–104.

Cooper, R., Groce, J., and Thomas, D. (2003). Changing directions: Rites of passage programs for African American older men. *Journal of African American Studies*, 7, no. 3: 3–14.

Corcoran, J. (2006). *Cognitive-behavioral methods for social workers: A workbook*. Boston: Allyn and Bacon.

Correia, M. C., and Bannon, I. (2006). Gender and its discontents: Moving to menstreaming development. In I. Bannon and M. C. Correia (eds.), *The other half of gender*, 245–260. Washington, DC: World Bank.

Courtenay, W. H. (2000). Engendering health: A social constructionist examination of men's health beliefs and behaviors. *Psychology of Men and Masculinity*, 1, no. 1: 4–15.

———. (2003). Key determinants of the health and well-being of men and boys. *International Journal of Men's Health*, 2, no. 1: 1–30.

Courtney, J. C. (2003). *The social construction of atmosphere in a neighborhood bar.* Paper presented at the annual meeting of the American Sociological Association, Atlanta. http://www.allacademic.com/meta/p107447_index.html.

Cowen, E., Wyman, P., Work, W., and Parker, G. (1990). The Rochester Child Resilience Project: Overview and summary of first year findings. *Development and Psychopathology*, 2, no. 2: 262–268.

Cozza, S. J., Chun, R. S., and Polo, J. A. (2005). Military families and children during operation Iraqi Freedom. *Psychiatric Quarterly*, 76, no. 4: 371–378.

Crokett, L. J., and Silbereisen, R. K. (2000). *Negotiating adolescence in times of social change.* New York: Cambridge University Press.

Cronin, C. (ed.). (1998). *Military psychology: An introduction.* Needham Heights, Mass.: Simon and Schuster.

Cross, S. E., and Madison, L. (1997). Models of the self: Self-construals and gender. *Psychological Bulletin*, 122, no. 11: 5–37.

Cull, D. (1996). The treatment of rapists: A measure of prevention. *Proceedings of the Australian Institute of Criminology.* Canberra, Australia. http://www.aic.gov.au/publications/proceedings/20/cull.pdf.

Currey, R. (2007). Wounded warriors: Lost in a labyrinth of care. *Social Work Today*, 7, no. 5. http://www.socialworktoday.com/archive/septoct2007p32.shtml.

Cusack, J., Deane, F. P., Wilson, J., and Ciarrochi, J. (2006). Emotional expression, perceptions of therapy, and help-seeking intentions in men attending therapy services. *Psychology of Men and Masculinity*, 7, no. 2: 69–82.

Darke, S., Kaye, S., and Finlay-Jones, R. (1998). Antisocial personality disorder, psychopathy and injecting heroin use. *Drug and Alcohol Dependence*, 52, no. 1: 63–69.

Dass, R. (2001). *Still here: Embracing aging, changing and dying.* New York. Penguin.

Davis, R. A. (2001). A cognitive-behavioral model of pathological Internet use. *Computers in Human Services*, 17, no. 2: 187–195.

De Cecco, J. (1987). *New York: Gay relationships.* New York: Routledge.

De Jong, P., and Miller, S. D. (1995). How to interview for client strengths. *Social Work*, 40, no. 6: 729–736.

Delgado, M. (2006). *Social work with Latinos: A cultural assets paradigm.* New York: Oxford University Press.

Delgado, M., Jones, K., and Rohani, M. (2005). *Social work practice with refugee and immigrant youth in the United States.* Boston: Allyn and Bacon.

DeNavas-Walt, Carmen, Bernadette D. Proctor, and Cheryl Hill Lee. (2005). U.S. Census Bureau, Current Population Reports, P60-229, Income, Poverty, and Health Insurance Coverage in the United States: 2004. Washington, D.C.: U.S. Government Printing Office. http://www.census.gov/prod/2005pubs/p60-229.pdf.

Denborough, D. (2002). Prisons and the question of forgiveness. *International Journal of Narrative Therapy and Community Work*, 1, no. 1: 7–5.

DePaulo, J. R. (2006). Bipolar disorder treatment: An evidence-based reality check. *American Journal of Psychiatry*, 163, no. 2: 175–176.

Devore, W., and Schlesinger, E. G. (1991). *Ethnic-sensitive social work practice*. New York: Macmillan.

DiGiuseppe, R. (1981). *Using rational-emotive therapy effectively*. New York: Plenum.

Dobson, K. (ed.) (2002) *Handbook of cognitive-behavioral therapies*. (2nd ed.) New York: Guildford.

Doherty, W. J., Kouneski, E. F., and Erickson, M. F. (1998). Responsible fathering: An overview and conceptual framework. *Journal of Marriage and Family*, 60, no. 2: 277–292.

Doyle, R. (1996). Deaths caused by alcohol. *Scientific American*, 275: 30–31.

Drudi, D. (1998). Fishing for a living is dangerous work. *Compensation and Working Conditions*.

Dryden, W., and DiGiuseppe, R. (1990). *A primer on rational-emotive therapy*. Champaign, Ill.: Research Press.

Dryden, W., and Neenan, M. (2004). *The rational emotive behavioral approach to therapeutic change*. London: Sage.

Duckworth, A. L., Steen, T. A., and Seligman, E. P. (2005). Positive psychology in clinical practice. *Annual Review of Clinical Psychology*, 1: 629–651.

Dudley, J. R., and Stone, G. (2001). *Fathering at risk: Helping nonresidential fathers*. New York: Springer.

Dudley, K. S. (1994). *The end of the line: Lost jobs, new lives in postindustrial America*. Chicago: University of Chicago Press.

Dunn, C. P. (2007). The meaning of work (course description). Masters of Arts and Liberal Studies Program, San Diego State University. http://www.meaningofwork.com/.

Dutton, D. B., and Browning, J. J. (1988). Concern for power, fear of intimacy, and aversive stimuli for wife assault. In G. Hotaling, D. Finkelhor, J. T. Kirkpatrick, and M. A. Straus (eds.), *Family abuse and its consciences: New directions in research*, 163–175. Newbury Park, Calif.: Sage.

Eagly, A. H., and Steffen, V. J. (1996). Gender and aggressive behavior: A metanalytic review of the social psychological literature. *Psychological Bulletin*, 100, no. 3: 309–330.

Earle, R., and Crowe, G. (1989). *Lonely all the time.* New York: Pocket Books.

Edwards, A. (2006). Polk mental-health court aims to treat inmates' ills. *Orlando Sentinel* October 1. http://www.orlandosentinel.com.

Egan, G. (2004). *The skilled helper.* (8th ed.) Pacific Grove, Calif.: Brooks/Cole.

Ehlers, G., and Miller, J. (2002). *Facing your fifties: A man's reference guide to mid-life health.* New York: M. Evans.

Ehrenreich, B. (1983). *The hearts of men: American dreams and the flight from commitment.* New York: Anchor/Doubleday.

Eisler, R. M., Skidmore, J. R., and Ward, C. H. (1988). Masculine gender-role stress: Predictor of anger, anxiety and health-related behaviors. *Journal of Personality Assessment,* 52, no. 1: 133–141.

Elder, G. H., Jr., Shanahan, M. J., and Clipp, E. C. (1994). When war comes to men's lives: Life course patterns in family, work and health. *Psychology and Aging,* 19, no. 1: 5–16.

Elkins, L. E., and Peterson, C. (1993). Gender differences in best friendships. *Sex Roles,* 29, no. 7/8: 497–508.

Ellis, A. (1958). Rational psychotherapy. *Journal of General Psychology,* 59: 37–47.

———. (1973). My philosophy of psychotherapy. *Journal of Contemporary Psychotherapy,* 6, no. 1: 13–18.

———. (1979). Rational-emotive therapy as a new theory of personality and therapy. In A. Ellis and J. M. Whiteley (eds.), *Theoretical and empirical foundations of rational-emotive therapy,* 1–99. Monterey: Brooks/Cole.

———. (1985). *Overcoming resistance.* New York: Springer.

———. (1994). *The essence of rational emotive therapy.* New York: Institute for Rational Emotive Therapy.

———. (1997). *The practice of rational emotive behavior therapy.* New York: Springer.

———. (2004). *Rational emotive therapy: It works for me—it can work for you.* New York: Prometheus.

Ellis, A., Abrams, M., and Abrams, L. D. (2009). *Personality theories: Critical perspectives.* Thousand Oaks, Calif.: Sage.

Ellis, A., McInerney, J. F., DiGiuseppe, R., and Yeager, R. J. (1988). *Rational emotive therapy with alcoholics and substance abuses.* Needham Heights, Mass.: Allyn and Bacon.

Ellis, A., and Velten, E. (1992). *When AA doesn't work for you: Rational steps to quitting alcohol.* New York: Barricade Books.

Emery, G. (1985). Cognitive therapy: Techniques and applications. In A. T. Beck and G. Emery (eds.), *Anxiety disorders and phobias: A cognitive perspective,* 167–313. New York: Basic Books.

Ephross, P. H. (2005). Social work with groups: Practice principles. In G. L. Greif and P. H. Ephross (eds.), *Group work with populations at risk,* 1–14. (2nd ed.) New York: Oxford University Press.

Erikson, E. H. (1959) *Identity and the life cycle.* New York: International Universities Press.

Estes, R. J. (1992). *Internationalizing social work education.* Philadelphia: University of Pennsylvania Press.

Evans, R. L., Fox, H. R., Pritzl, D. O., and Halar, E. M (1984). Group treatment of physically disabled adults by telephone. *Social Work in Health Care*, 9, no. 3: 77–84.

Evans, R. L., Smith, K. M., Werkhoven, W. S., Fox, H. R., and Pritzl, D. O. (1986). *Gerontologist*, 26, no. 1: 8–11.

Fallows, D. (2005). How women and men use the Internet. *Pew Internet and American Life Project.* http://www.pewinternet.org/PPF/r/171/report_display.asp.

Faludi, S. (1999). *Stiffed: The betrayal of the American man.* New York: HarperCollins.

Fast, B., and Chapin, R. (2000). *Strengths-based care management for older adults.* Baltimore: Health Professions Press.

Feld, S. L., and Straus, M. A. (1989). Escalation and desistance of wife assault in marriage. *Criminology*, 27, no. 1: 141–161.

Fennell, G., and Davidson, K. "The invisible man?": Older men in modern society. *Ageing International*, 28, no. 4: 315–325.

Feske, U., and Chambless, D. (1995). Cognitive behavioral versus exposure only treatment for social phobia: A meta-analysis. *Behavior Therapy*, 26, no. 4: 695–720.

Figley, C. R. (1999). Compassion fatigue: Toward a new understanding of the cost of caring. In B. H. Stamm (ed.), *Secondary traumatic stress: Self-care issues for clinicians, researchers and educators*, 3–28. (2nd ed.) Lutherville, Md.: Sidran.

——— (ed.). (2002). *Treating compassion fatigue.* New York: Brunner-Routledge.

Figley, C. R., and Stamm, B. H. (1996). Psychometric review of compassion fatigue self test. In B. H. Stamm (ed.), *Measurement of stress, trauma and adaptation.* Lutherville, Md: Sidran.

Fiorentine, R., Anglin, M.D., Gil-Rivas, V., and Taylor, E. (1997). Drug treatment: Explaining the gender paradox. *Substance Use and Misuse*, 32, no. 6: 653–678.

Fiscella, K., Franks, P., Doescher, M. P., and Saver, B. G. (2002). Disparities in health care by race, ethnicity, and language among the uninsured. *Medical Care*, 40, no. 1: 52–59.

Flaxman, E., Ascher, C., and Harrington, C. (1992). *Evaluating mentoring programs.* New York: Institute for Urban and Minority Education, Teachers College, Columbia University.

Flood, M. (1997). Homophobia and masculinities among young men (lessons in becoming a straight man). Lecture presented to teachers, O'Connell Education Center, Canberra, Australia, April 15. http://www.xyonline.net/misc/homophobia.html.

———. (2005/2006). Changing men: Best practices in sexual violence education. *Women Against Violence*, 18: 26–36.

Foa, E. B., Keane, T. M., and Friedman, M. J. (eds.). (2000). *Effective treatments for PTSD: Practice guidelines from the International Society for Traumatic Stress Studies*. New York: Guilford.

Foster, D. (1993). The mark of oppression? Racism and psychology reconsidered. In Lionel J Nicholas (ed.), *Psychology and oppression: critiques and proposals*, 52–87. Cambridge: Harvard University Press.

Foucault, M. (1965). *Madness and civilization*. New York: Pantheon.

Fox, M., Gibbs, M., and Auerbach, D. (1985). Age and gender dimensions of friendship. *Psychology of Women Quarterly*, 9: 489–502.

Fox, R. (2000). Grasping life: Five stories of will-filled men. In E. Norman (ed.), *Resiliency enhancement: Putting the strengths perspective into social work practice*, 83–101. New York: Columbia University Press.

Foy, D. W. (1992). *Treating PTSD: Cognitive behavioral strategies*. New York: Guilford.

Frankl, V. (1963). *Man's search for meaning: An introduction to logotherapy*. New York: Pocket Books.

———. (1967). *Psychotherapy and existentialism: Selected papers on logotherapy*. New York: Simon and Schuster.

Frederikse, M., Lu, A., Aylward, E., Barta, P., Sharma, T., and Pearlson, G. (2000). Sex differences in inferior parietal lobe volume in schizophrenia. *American Journal of Psychiatry*, 157, no. 3: 422–427.

Freedman, J., and Combs, G. (1996). *Narrative therapy: The social construction of preferred realities*. New York: Norton.

Fromm, E. (1961). *Marx's conception of man*. New York: Frederick Ungar.

Fuligni, A., and Zhang, W. (2004). Attitudes toward family obligation among adolescents in contemporary urban and rural China. *Child Development*, 7: 180–192.

Funk, R. E. (1994). *Stopping rape*. Philadelphia: New Society Publishers.

Furman, R. (2003a). Cognitive and existential theories in social work practice. *Social Work Forum*, 36: 59–68.

———. (2003b). Frameworks for understanding value discrepancies and ethical dilemmas in managed mental health for social work in the United States. *International Social Work*, 46, no. 1: 37–52.

———. (2004). Using poetry and narrative as qualitative data: Exploring a father's cancer through poetry. *Family, Systems and Health*, 22: 162–170.

———. (2008). Bringing the self into the academe: An antidote for alienated labor. Ms.

Furman, R., and Bender, K. (2003). The social problem of depression: A multi-theoretical analysis. *Journal of Sociology and Social Welfare*, 50, no. 3: 123–137.

Furman, R., and Collins, K. (2005). Culturally sensitive practices and crisis management: Social constructionism as an integrative model. *Journal of Police Crisis Negotiation*, 5, no. 2: 47–57.

Furman, R., Collins, K., and Swanson, J. (2003). Social work practice innovations: Helping clients understand, explore, and develop their friendships. *Advances in Social Work*, 42, no. 2: 116–129.

Furman, R., Downey, E. P., and Jackson, R. L. (2004). Exploring the ethics of treatments for depression: The ethics of care perspective. *Smith College Studies in Social Work*, 74, no. 3: 125–138.

Furman, R., Jackson, R. L., Downey, E. P., and Bender, K. (2002). Poetry therapy as a tool for strengths based practice. *Advances in Social Work*, 3, no. 2: 146–157.

Furman, R., Jackson, R. L., Downey, E. P., and Seiz, R. (2004). Using the biopsychosocial approach to resolve student dilemmas in field placements. *Journal of Teaching in Social Work*, 24, no. 1/2: 129–139.

Furman, R., Langer, C. L., and Anderson, D. K. (2006). The poet/practitioner: A new paradigm for the profession. *Journal of Sociology and Social Welfare*, 33, no. 3: 29–50.

Furman, R., and Negi, N. J. (2007). Social work practice with transnational Latino populations. *International Social Work*, 50, no. 1: 107–112.

Furman, R., Negi, N. J., Schatz, M. C. S and Jones, S. (2008). Transnational social work: Using a wrap-around model. *Global Networks: A Journal of Transnational Affairs*, 8, no. 4: 496–503.

Furman, R., Shears, J., and Badinelli, M. (2007). Mexican men and their fathers: Data re-representation through the research poem. *Journal of Poetry Therapy*, 20, no. 3: 141–151.

Gable, S. L., and Haidt, J. (2005). What (and why) is positive psychology. *Review of General Psychology*, 9, no. 2: 103–110.

Gable, S. L., Reis, H. T., and Elliot, A. (2000). Behavioral activation and inhibition in everyday life. *Journal of Personality and Social Psychology*, 78, no. 6: 1135–1149.

Gamezy, N., and Masten, A. S. (1986). Stress, competence and resilience: Common frontiers for therapist and psychopathologist. *Behavior Therapy*, 57, no. 2: 159–174.

Garland, D. (1985). *Punishment and welfare:* Aldershot, U.K.: Gower.

Geer, F. C. (1983). Marine-machine to poet of the rocks, poetry therapy as a bridge to inner reality: Some exploratory observations, *The Arts in Psychotherapy*, 10: 9–14.

Geertz, C. (1973). *The interpretation of cultures: Selected essays.* New York: Basic Books.

Genovese, E. D., and E. Fox-Genovese (1983). *Fruits of merchant capital: Slavery and bourgeois property in the rise and expansion of capitalism.* London: Oxford University Press.

Gergen, K. J., and Kaye, J. (1992). Beyond narrative in the negotiation of therapeutic meaning. In S. McNamee and K. J. Gergen (eds.), *Therapy as social construction*, 166–185. Newbury Park, Calif.: Sage.

Gibelman, M. (2003). *Navigating human service organizations.* Chicago: Lyceum.

Gibelman, M., and Furman, R. (2008). *Navigating human service organizations: Essential information for thriving and surviving in agencies.* (2nd ed.) Chicago: Lyceum.

Gil, D. (1990). *Unraveling social policy.* Rochester, Vt.: Schenkman.

Gilbert, N., and Terrell, P. (1998). *Dimensions of social welfare policy.* Boston: Allyn and Bacon.

Gilligan, P., and Furness, S. (2006). The role of religion and spirituality in social work practice. Views and experiences of social workers and students. *British Journal of Social Work,* 46, no. 4: 617–637.

Gilmore, D. (1990). *Manhood in the making: Cultural concepts of masculinity.* New Haven: Yale University Press.

Ginsberg, L. (ed.). (1998). *Social work in rural communities.* New York: Council on Social Work Education.

Glicken, M. D. (2004). *Using the strengths perspective in social work practice: A positive approach for the helping professions.* Boston: Pearson Education.

Gold, S. N., and Heffner, C. L. (1998). Sexual addiction: Many conceptions, minimal data. *Clinical Psychology,* 18, no. 3: 367–381.

Goldberg, H. (1976). *The hazards of being male: Surviving the myth of masculine privilege.* New York: New American Library.

Goldenberg, H., and Goldenberg, I. (2002). *Counseling today's families.* (4th ed.) Pacific Grove, Calif.:: Brooks/Cole.

Goldstein, H. (1981). *Social learning and change: A cognitive approach to human services.* Columbia: University of South Carolina Press.

———. (1984). *Creative change: A cognitive-humanistic approach to social work practice.* New York: Methuen.

———. (1990a). The limits and art of understanding in social work practice. *Families in Society,* 80, no. 4: 385–395.

———. (1990b). Strength or pathology: Ethical and rhetorical contrasts in approaches to practice. *Families in Society,* 71, no. 2: 267–275.

Goldstein, M. (1987). Poetry: A tool to induce reminiscing and creativity with geriatrics. *Journal of Social Psychiatry,* 7, no. 3: 117–121.

Golomb, M., Fava, M., Abraham, M., and Rosenbaum, J. F. (1995). Gender differences in personality disorders. *American Journal of Psychiatry,* 152, no. 4: 579–583.

Gomez Alcaraz, F. H., and Garcia Suarez, C. I. (2006). Masculinity and violence in Colombia: Deconstructing the conventional way of becoming a man. In I. Bannon and M. C. Correia (eds.), *The other half of gender,* 93–110. Washington, D.C.: World Bank.

Gonzalez, R. (ed.). (1996). *Muy macho: Latino men confront their manhood.* New York: Anchor.

Goodman, A. (2006). Addiction: Definition and implications. *Addictions*, 85, no. 11: 1403–1408.

Goodwin, D. W., and Guze, S. B. (1996). *Psychiatric diagnosis*. New York: Oxford University Press.

Gordon, W. E. (1965). Knowledge and value: Their distinction and relationship in clarifying social work practice. *Social Work*, 10, no. 3: 32–39.

Gray, J. (1992). *Men are from Mars, women are from Venus*. New York: Harper Collins.

Greaves, G. (1974). Toward an existential theory of drug-dependence. *Journal of Nervous and Mental Diseases*, 159, no. 3: 263–274.

Green, R. J. (2004). Risk and resilience in lesbian and gay couples: Comment on Solomon, Rothblum, and Balsam. *Journal of Family Psychology*, 18, no. 2: 290–292.

Greene, R. R. (2007). *Social work practice: A risk and resiliency perspective*. Belmont, Calif.: Brooks/Cole.

Greenstein, D., Lerch, J., Shaw, P., Clasen, L., Giedd, J., Gochman, P., Rapoport, J., and Gogtay, N. (2006). Childhood onset schizophrenia: Cortical brain abnormalities as young adults. *Journal of Child Psychology and Psychiatry*, 47, no. 10: 1003–1012.

Greig, A., Kimmel, M., and Lang, J. (2000) *Men, masculinities and development: Broadening our work towards gender equality*. Gender in Development Monograph Series no. 10. New York: United Nations Development Program.

Greim, J. L. (1992). *Adult/youth relationships pilot project*. Philadelphia: Public/Private Ventures.

Grob, G. N. (1994). *The mad among us*. New York: Free Press.

Groth, N. A, and Birnbaum, B. A. (1979). *Men who rape: The psychology of the offender*. New York: Plenum.

Guerriero, I. C. Z, Ayeres, J. R., and Hearst, N. (2002). Masculinity and vulnerability to HIV among heterosexual men in São Paulo, Brazil. *Journal of Public Health*, 36, no. 4, supplement: 50–60.

Gullo, J. M. (1977). Rational emotive therapy with hospitalized psychotics. In J. L. Wolfe and E. Brand (eds.), *Twenty years of rational emotive therapy*, 241–245. New York: Institute for Rational Living.

Gutman, M. (1996). *The meaning of macho. Being a man in Mexico City*. Berkeley: University of California Press.

Haaga, D. A., and Davison, G. C. (1989). Outcome studies of rational emotive therapy. In M. E. Bernard and Diguiseppe, R. (eds.), *Inside rational emotive therapy: A critical appraisal of the theory and therapy of Albert Ellis*, 156–197. New York: Academic Press.

Hafen, B. Q., Karren, K. J., Frandsen, K. J., and Smith, N. L. (1996). *Mind/body health*. Boston: Allyn and Bacon.

Hamberger, K. (1997). Cognitive behavioral treatment of men who batter their partners. *Cognitive Behavioral Practice*, 4, no. 1: 147–169.

Hardin, M. (2002). Altering masculinities: The Spanish conquest and the evolution of the Latin American Machismo. *International Journal of Sexual and Gender Studies*, 7, no. 1: 1–22.

Hare-Martin, R. T. (1987). The problem of gender in family therapy. *Family Process*, 26, no. 1: 15–27.

Harper, K., and Lantz, J. (1996). *Cross-cultural practice: Social work with diverse populations*. Chicago: Lyceum.

Harper Chelf, J., Deshler, A.M.B., Hillman S., and Durazo-Aruzu, R. (2000). Storytelling: A strategy for living and coping with cancer. *Cancer Nursing*, 23: 1–5.

Harris, J. L. (1998). Reminiscence: A culturally and developmentally appropriate language intervention for older adults. *American Journal of Speech-Language Pathology*, 6, no. 3: 19–26.

Harrower, M. (1972). *The therapy of poetry*. Springfield, Ill.: Charles C. Thomas.

Harry Benjamin International Gender Dysphoria Association (2001). Standards of care for gender identity disorders. (6th ed.). http://wpath.org/Documents2/socv6 .pdf.

Hart, S. D., and Hare, R. D. (1996). Psychopathy and antisocial personality disorder. *Current Opinion in Psychiatry*, 9, no. 2: 129–132.

Hartup, W. W. (1979). Peer relations and growth of social competence. In M. W. Kent and J. E. Rolf (eds.), *Primary prevention of psychopathology*, vol. 3. Lebanon: University Press of New England.

———. (1983). Peer relations. In P. H. Mussen (ed.), *Handbook of child psychology*, vol. 4. (4th ed.) New York: Wiley.

———. (1989). Social relationships and their developmental significance. *American Psychologist*, 44: 120–126.

Harvey, A., Watkins, E., Mansell, W., and Shafran, R. (2004). *Cognitive behavioural processes across psychological disorders: A transdiagnostic approach to research and treatment*. Oxford: Oxford University Press.

Harway, M., and Hansen, M. (1993). Therapist perceptions of family violence. In M. Hansen and H. Harway (eds.), *Battering and family therapy: A feminist perspective*, 42–53. Newbury Park, Calif.: Sage.

Head, D. M., Portnoy, S., and Woods, R. T. (1990). The impact of reminiscence groups in two different settings. *International Journal of Geriatric Psychiatry*, 5, no. 5: 295–302.

Head, J. (2004). *Understanding and overcoming depression in black men*. New York: Random House.

Healy, L. M. (2001). *International social work*. New York: Oxford University Press.

Heath, M. (2003). Soft-boiled masculinity: Renegotiating gender and racial identities in the Promise Keepers movement. *Gender and Society*, 17, no. 3: 423–444.

Hedtke, L., and Winslade, J. (2004/2005). The use of the subjunctive of re-remembering conversations with those who are grieving. *Omega*, 50, no. 3: 197–215.

Henderson, H. (1995). *Paradigms in progress.* San Francisco: Barrett-Koehler.

Henning, K., Jones, A. R., and Holdford, R. (2005). "I didn't do it, but if I did I had a good reason": Minimization, denial, and attributions of blame among male and female domestic violence offenders. *Journal of Family Violence*, 20, no. 3: 131–139.

Higbee, J. N. (1997). RET in dealing with alcohol dependent persons. In J. L. Wolfe and E. Brand (eds.), *Twenty years of rational emotive therapy*, 231–233. New York: Institute for Rational Living.

Hillman, J., and Stricker, G. (2001). A call for psychotherapy integration in work with older patients. *Journal of Psychotherapy Integration*, 12, no. 4: 395–405.

Hirose, S. (2001). Effective treatment of aggression and impulsivity in antisocial personality disorder with risperidone. *Psychiatry and Clinical Neurosciences*, 55: 161–162.

Hoff, R. A., and Rosenheck, R. A. (2000). Cross-system use among psychiatric patients: Data from the Department of Veteran Affairs. *Journal of Behavioral Health Services and Research*, 27, no. 1: 98–106.

Hogan, B. A. (1999). Narrative therapy in rehabilitation after brain injury: A case study. *NeuroRebhabilitation*, 13: 21–25.

Holder, H., Longabaugh, R., Miller, W. R., Robois, A. V. (1991). The cost effectiveness of treatment for alcoholism: A first approximation. *Journal of Studies on Alcohol*, 53, no. 2: 293–302.

Holma, J., and Aaltoonen, J. (1995). The self-narrative and acute psychosis. *Contemporary Family Therapy*, 17: 307–363.

———. (1997). The sense of agency and the search for narrative in acute psychosis. *Contemporary Family Therapy*, 19: 463–477.

Holt, D. B., and Thompson, C. J. (2004). Man-of-action heroes: The pursuit of heroic masculinity in everyday consumption. *Journal of Consumer Research*, 31, no. 3: 425–440.

Hooper, C. (2001). *Manly states: Masculinities, international relations, and gender politics.* New York: Columbia University Press.

Hooyman, N., and Kiyak, H. (2002). *Social gerontology.* Boston: Allyn and Bacon.

Hopps, J. G. (1988). Deja-vu or new view. *Social Work*, 33, no. 4: 291–292.

Hovarth, A. T. (2000). Smart recovery: Addiction recovery support from a cognitive-behavioralperspective. *Journal of Rational-Emotive and Cognitive-Behavioral Therapy*, 18, no. 3: 181–191.

Horwitz, A., and Scheid, T. (1999). *A handbook for the study of mental health: Social contexts, theories, and systems.* New York: Cambridge University Press.

Huerta, E. E. (2003). Cancer statistics for Hispanics, 2003: Good news, bad news and the need for a health system paradigm change. *CA Cancer Journal for Clinicians,* 53, no. 4: 205–207.

Hughes, M. (2003). Talking about sexual identity with older men. *Australian Social Work,* 56, no. 3: 258–266.

Humphreys, K. (1999). Professional interventions that facilitate 12-step self-help group involvement. *Alcohol Research and Health,* 23, no. 2: 93–98.

Hunter, A. G., & Davis, J. E. (1994). Hidden voices of black men: The meaning, structure and complexity of manhood. *Journal of Black Studies,* 25, no. 1: 20–40.

Hutchison, E. D. (1991). *Dimensions of human behavior: Person and environment.* Thousand Oaks, Calif.: Pine Forge.

Hutchison, E. D., and Charlesworth, L.W. (1998). Human behavior in the social environment: The role of gender expansion of practice knowledge. In J. Figueira-Mc-Donough, F. E. Netting, and A. Nichols-Casebolt (eds.), *The role of gender in practiced knowledge: Claming half the human experience,* 41–80. New York. Garland.

Hutter, H. (2001). On friendship. *Contemporary Sociology,* 30, no. 6: 579–581.

Ingham, M. (1985). *Men: The male myth exposed.* London: Century.

Inlander, C. B. (1998). *Men's health and wellness encyclopedia.* New York: Macmillan.

International Federation of Social Workers. (2004). Ethics in social work: Statement of principles. http://www.ifsw.org/en/p38000324.html.

Isay, R. A. (2006). *Commitment and healing: Gay men and the need for romantic love.* Hoboken, N.J.: Wiley.

Itzin, C. (1992). *Pornography: Women, violence and civil liberties.* New York: Oxford University Press.

———. (2006). *Tackling the health and mental health of domestic and sexual violence and abuse.* London: United Kingdom Department of Health.

Ivey, A. E., and Ivey, M. B. (2007). *Intentional interviewing and counseling.* Belmont, Calif.: Brooks/Cole.

Jackson, P., Crang, P., and Dwyer, C. (2004). *Transnational spaces.* New York: Routledge.

Jackson, R. L. (2001). *The clubhouse model: Empowering applications of theory to generalist practice.* Belmont, Calif.: Brooks/Cole.

Jackson, S., Feder, L., Forde, D. R., Davis, R. C., Maxwell, C. D., and Taylor, B. G. 2003. *Batterer intervention programs: Where do we go from here?* Special report. Washington, D.C.: Office of Justice Programs, National Institute of Justice, U.S. Department of Justice.

Jacobs, E. (1992). *Creative counseling: An illustrated guide.* Lutz, Fla.: Psychological Assessment Resources.

————. (1994). *Impact therapy.* Lutz, Fla.: Psychological Assessment Resources.

Jacobson, L., LaLonde, R., and Sullivan, D. (1993). *The cost of worker dislocation.* Kalamazoo, Mich.: W. E. Upjohn Institute for Employment Research.

James, D. J., and Glaze, L. E. (2006). Mental health problems of prison and jail inmates. Bureau of Justice Statistics Special Report. Washington, D.C.: United States Department of Justice.

James, R. K., and Gilliland, B. E. (2004). *Crisis intervention strategies.* (5th ed.) Pacific Grove, Calif.: Brooks Cole.

Joe, J. R. (2001). Out of harmony: Health problems and young Native American men. *Journal of American College Health,* 49: 237–242.

Jones, A. (2002). *The national nursing home survey: 1999 Summary.* National Health Statistics. *Vital Health Statistics* 13, no. 152. http://www.cdc.gov/nchs/data/series/sr_13/sr13_152.pdf.

Jones, T. (2008). Clinical diagnosis and awareness of hypogonadism. *Journal of Men's Health,* 5, supplement: 26–34.

Jones, W. K. (2004). Men's health as a public health issue. *Journal of Men's Health and Gender,* 1, no. 2/3: 147–149.

Joukhador, J., Maccallum, F., and Blaszczynski, A. (2003). Differences in cognitive distortions between problem and social gamblers. *Psychological Reports,* 92, no. 3: 1203–1214.

Jourard, S. (1968). *Disclosing man to himself.* New York: Van Nostrand Reinhold.

Juster, F. T., and Stafford, F. (eds.) (1985). *Time, good and well-being.* Ann Arbor: Institute for Social Research.

Kaelber, C. T., Moul, D. E. and Farmer, M. E. (1995). Epidemiology of depression. In E. E. Beckham and W. R. Leber (eds.), *Handbook of depression,* 125–146. New York: Guilford Press.

Kaplan, H., and Sadock, B. J. (1998). *Synopsis of psychiatry.* Baltimore: Williams and Wilkins.

Kaplan, L., and Girard, J. (1994). *Strengthening high-risk families: A handbook for practitioners.* New York: Lexington.

Karger, H. J., and Stoesz, D. (1998). *American social welfare policy: A pluralistic approach.* (3rd ed.) New York: Longman.

Kastoryano, R. (2000.) Settlement, transnational communities and citizenship. *International Social Science Journal,* 52, no. 165: 307–312.

Kearney, M., and Beserra, B. (2004). Introduction to special issue: Migration and identities: A class-based approach. *Latin American Perspectives,* 31, no. 5: 3–14.

Keen, S. (1991). *Fire in the belly: On being a man.* New York: Bantam.

Kelley, P. (2007). Full days, together. *Charlotte Observer,* October 7, A1, A6.

Kessler R. C., Chiu, W. T., Demler, O., Walters E. E. (2005). Prevalence, severity, and comorbidity of twelve-month DSM-IV disorders in the National Comorbidity Survey Replication (NCS-R). *Archives of General Psychiatry*, 62, no. 6: 617–627.

Kessler, R. C., and Cleary, P. D. (1980). Social class and psychological distress. *American Sociological Review*, 45, no. 4: 463–478.

Kierkegaard, S. (1954). *Fear and trembling and the sickness unto death.* Garden City, N.Y.: Doubleday.

Kim, D. Y. (1999). Beyond co-ethnic solidarity: Mexican and Ecuadorian employment in Korean-owned businesses in New York City. *Ethnic and Racial Studies*, 22, no. 4: 581–605.

Kim, Y. M., Kols, A., Mwarogo, P., and Awasum, D. (2000). Differences in counseling men and women: Family planning in Kenya. *Patient Education and Counseling*, 39, no. 1: 37–47.

Kimmel, M. S. (1996). *Manhood in America: A cultural history.* New York: Free Press.

King, D. W., King, L. A., Foy, D. W., Keane, T. M., and Fairbank, J. A. (1999). Posttraumatic stress disorder in a national sample of female and male Vietnam veterans: Risk factors, war-zone stressors, and resiliency-recovery variables. *Journal of Abnormal Psychology*, 108, no. 1: 164–170.

King, L., Hicks, J., Krull, J., and Del Gaiso, A. (2006). Positive affect and the experience of meaning in life. *Journal of Personality and Social Psychology*, 90, no. 1: 179–196.

King, M., and Woollett, E. (1997). Sexually assaulted males: 115 men consulting a counseling service. *Archives of Sexual Behavior*, 26, no. 6: 579–588.

Kingdon, D., Rathod, S., Weiden, P., and Turkington, D. (2008). Cognitive therapy of schizophrenia. *Journal of Psychiatric Practice*, 14, no. 1: 55–57.

Kirst-Ashman, K. K., and Hull, Grafton, H. (2006) *Generalist practice with organizations and communities.* (3rd ed.) Belmont, Calif.: Thomson Brooks/Cole.

Kisthardt, W. E. (2002). The strengths perspective in interpersonal helping: Purpose, principles and functions. In D. Saleebey (ed.), *The strengths perspective in social work*, 163–185. Boston: Allyn and Bacon.

Knaus, W. (1998). *SMART Recovery: A sensible primer.* (3rd ed.) Longmeadow, Mass.: William Knaus.

Kobasa, S. C. (1979). Stressful life events, personality, and health: An inquiry into hardiness. *Journal of Personality and Social Psychology*, 37, no. 1: 1–11.

Koob, G. F., Rocio, M., Carrera, A., Gold, L. H., Heyser, C. J., Maldonado-Irizarry, C., Markou, A., Parsons, L. H., Roberts, A. J., Schulteis, G., Stinus, L., Walker, J. R., Weissenborn, R., and Weiss, F. (1998). Substance dependence as a compulsive behavior. *Journal of Psychopharmacology*, 12, no. 1: 39–48.

Kosberg, J. I. (2002). Heterosexual males: A group forgotten by the profession of social work. *Journal of Sociology and Social Welfare*, 29, no. 3: 50–70.

———. (2005). Meeting the needs of older men: Challenges for those in the helping professions. *Journal of Sociology and Social Welfare*, 32: 9–31.

Kosberg, J. I., and Kaye, L. W. (eds.). (1997). *Elderly men: Special problems and professional responsibilities*. New York: Springer.

Kosberg, J. I., and Mangum, W. P. (2002). The invisibility of older men in gerontology. *Gerontology and Geriatrics Education*, 22, no. 4: 27–41.

Kosten, T. R., and O'Conner, P. G. (2003). Management of drug and alcohol withdrawal. The *New England Journal of Medicine*, 348, no. 18: 1786–1798.

Kotler, P., and Wingard, D. L. (1989). The effect of occupation, marital and parental roles on mortality: The Alameda County Study. *American Journal of Public Health*, 79, no. 5: 607–612.

Kraut, R., Kiesler, S., Boneva, B., Cummings, J., Helgeson, V., and Crawford, A. (2002). Internet paradox revisited. *Journal of Social Issues*, 58, no. 1: 49–74.

Kraut, R., Patterson, M., Lundmark, V., Kiesler, S., Mukopadhyah, T., and Scherlis, A. (1998). Internet paradox: A social technology that reduces social involvement and psychological well-being? *American Psychologist*, 53, no. 9:1017–1031.

Krech, P. R. (2002). Envisioning a health future: A re-becoming of Native American men. *Journal of Sociology and Social Welfare*, 29, no. 1: 77–95.

Kreuger, L. W. (1997). The end of social work. *Journal of Social Work Education*, 33, no. 1: 19–27.

Krill, D. (1969). Existential physiotherapy and the problem of anomie. *Social Work*, April: 137–152.

———. (1978). *Existential social work*. New York: Free Press.

———. (1986). Existential social work. In F. J. Turner (ed.), *Social work treatment*, (181–218). New York: Free Press.

Kruger, D. (2006). New record for U.S. life expectancy. *Human Nature*, 17, no. 1: 74–97.

Kulka, R. A., Schlenger, W. E., Fairbank, J. A., Hough, R. L., Jordan, B. K., Marmar, C. R., and Weiss, D. S. (1988). *Report of findings from the National Vietnam veterans readjustment study*. Research Triangle Park, N.C.: Research Triangle Institute.

Kurdek, L. A. (2004). Are gay and lesbian cohabitating couples really different from heterosexual couples? *Journal of Marriage and Family*, 66: 880–900.

Lacey, H. B., and Roberts, R. (1991). Sexual assault on men. *International Journal of STD and AIDS*, 2, no. 4: 258–260.

Ladd, G. T., and Petry, N. M. (2002). Gender differences among pathological gamblers seeking treatment. *Experimental and Clinical Psychopharmacology*, 10, no. 3: 302–309.

Laidlaw, K., Thompson, L., Gallagher-Thompson, D., and Dick-Siskin, L. (2003). *Cognitive behaviour therapy with older people.* West Sussex, UK: Wiley.

Lam, D. H., Watkins, E. R., Hayward, P., Bright, J., Wright, K, Kerr, N., Parr-Davis, G., and Sham, P. (2003). *Archives of General Psychiatry,* 60, no. 2: 145–152.

Lamb, M. E. (1997). *The role of the father in child development.* (3rd ed.) New York: Wiley.

Lang, F., and Carstensen, L. (1994). Close emotional relationships in late life: Further support for proactive aging in the social domain. *Psychology and Aging,* 9, no. 2: 315–324.

Lang, S. (1998). *Men as women, women as men: Changing gender in Native American cultures.* Austin: University of Texas Press.

Langlois, J. A. , Rutland-Brown W., and Thomas, K. E (2006). *Traumatic brain injury in the United States: Emergency department visits, hospitalizations, and deaths.* Atlanta: Centers for Disease Control and Prevention, National Center for Injury Prevention and Control.

Lau, A. (1986). Family therapy across cultures. In J. L. Cox (ed.), *Transcultural family psychiatry,* 73–97. London: Croom Helm Pearson.

Lazur, R. F., and Majors, R. (1995). Men of color: Ethnocultural variations of male gender role strain. In R. F. Levant and W. S. Pollack (eds.), *A new psychology of men,* 337–358. New York: Basic Books.

Leedy, J. (1987). Poetry therapy for drug abusers. *The Journal of Social Psychiatry,* 7, no. 2: 106–108.

Leininger, M. M. (1987). Transcultural caring: A different way to help people. In P. Pedersen (ed.), *Handbook of cross-cultural counseling and therapy,* 107–115. New York: Praeger.

Lerner, A. (1981). Poetry Therapy. In R. Corsini (ed.), *Handbook of innovative psychotherapies,* 131–152. New York: Wiley.

Levine, M. P., and Troiden, R. R. (1988). The myth of sexual compulsivity. *Journal of Search Research,* 25, no. 3: 347–363.

Levinson, D. L. (1978). *The seasons of a man's life.* New York: Knopf.

Levy, B. R., Slade, M. D., Kunkel, S., and Kasl, S. V. (2002). Longevity increased by positive self-perceptions of aging, *Journal of Personality and Social Psychology,* 83, no. 2: 261–170.

Linden, G. W. (2003). Friendship. *Journal of Individual Psychology,* 59, no. 2: 156–166.

Link, R. J., Ramanathan, C. S., and Asamoah, Y. (1999). Understanding the human condition and human behavior in a global era. In C. S. Ramanathan and R. J. Link (eds.) *All our futures: Principles and resources for social work practice in a global era,* 237–251. Pacific Grove, Calif.: Brooks/Cole.

Long, D. D., Tice, C. J., and Morrison, J.D. (2006). *Macro social work practice: A strengths perspective.* Belmont, Calif.: Thomson Brooks/Cole.

Lovallo, W. R. (2005). *Stress and Health: Biological and psychological interactions.* (2nd ed.) Thousand Oaks, Calif.: Sage.

Love, A. S., and Love, R. J. (2006). Measurement suitability of the Center for Epidemiological Studies depression scale among older black men. *International Journal of Men's Health,* 5, no. 2: 173–189.

Lundberg, U., and Frankenhaeuser, M. (1999). Stress and workload of men and women in high-ranking positions. *Journal of Occupational Health Psychology,* 4, no. 2: 142–151.

Luther, S., and Zigler, E. (1991). Vulnerability and competence: A review of research on resiliency in childhood. *American Journal of Orthopsychiatry,* 61, no. 1: 7–22.

Lyons, P., Wodarski, J. S., and Feit, M. D. (1998). Human behavior theory: Emerging trends and issues. *Journal of Human Behavior in the Social Environment,* 1, no. 1: 1–21.

Lysaker, P. H., Lancaster, R. S., and Lysaker, J. T. (2003). Narrative transformation as an outcome in psychotherapy of schizophrenia. *Psychology and Psychotherapy: Theory, Research and Practice,* 76: 285–299.

Mahalik, J. R., and Cournoyer, J. R. (2000). Identifying gender role conflict messages that distinguish mildly depressed men from nondepressed men. *Psychology of Men and Masculinities,* 1, no. 2: 109–115.

Mahalik, J. R., Good, G. E., and Englar-Carlson, M. (2003). Masculinity scripts, presenting concerns, and help seeking: Implications for practice and training. *Professional Psychology: Research and Practice,* 34, no. 2: 123–131.

Mahalik, J. R., Lagan, H. D., and Morrison, J. A. (2006). Health behaviors and masculinity in Kenyan and U.S. male college students. *Psychology of Men and Masculinity,* 7, no. 4: 191–202.

Mahalik, J. R., and Morrison, J. A. (2006). A cognitive therapy approach to increase father involvement by changing restrictive masculine schemas. *Cognitive and Behavioral Practice,* 13: 62–70.

Mahoney, M. J. (1974). *Cognition and behavior modification.* Cambridge, Mass.: Ballinger.

———. (1991). *Human change processes: The scientific foundations of psychotherapy.* New York: Basic Books.

Maluccio, A. N. (1981). *Promoting competence in clients.* New York: Free Press.

Mansfield, H. C. (2006). *Manliness.* New Haven: Yale University Press.

Markesbery, W., Schmitt, F., and Kryscio, R. (2007). Prevention of Alzheimer's disease by vitamin E and selenium: Ongoing clinical trial. http://clinicaltrials.gov/show/NCT00040378.

Martin, J. A., Sparacino, L. R., and Belenky (eds.). (1996). *The Gulf War and mental health: A comprehensive guide.* Westport, Conn.: Praeger.

Mayo Clinic. (2004). Male depression: Don't ignore the symptoms. *MSN Fitness and Health.* November 16. http://health.msn.com/centers/depression/articlepage .aspx?cp-documentid=100100328.

———. (2006). Heart disease: Coronary artery disease. http://www.mayoclinic.com/ health/coronary-artery-disease/DS00064/DSECTION=4.

Mayo-Smith, M. F. (1997). Pharmacological management of alcohol withdrawal. *Journal of the American Medical Association,* 298, no. 2: 144–151.

Mazza, N. (1999). *Poetry therapy: Interface of the arts and psychology.* Boca Raton, Fla.: CRC Press.

McCafferty, R. L., McCafferty, E., and McCafferty, M. A. (1992). Stress and suicide in police officers: Paradigm of occupational stress. *Southern Medical Journal,* 85, no. 2: 233–245.

McCloskey, K., and Grigsby, N. (2005). The ubiquitous clinical problem of adult intimate partner violence: The need for routine assessment. *Professional Psychology: Research and Practice,* 36, no. 3: 264–175.

McCracy, B. S., and Miller, W. R. (eds.). (1993). *Alcoholics Anonymous. Opportunities and alternatives.* New Brunswick, N.J.: Rutgers Center for Alcohol Studies.

McCullers, C. (1940). *The heart is a lonely hunter.* New York: Houghton Mifflin.

McElvaine, R. S. (1993). *The Great Depression: America, 1929–1941.* New York: Times Books.

McKay, J. R., Rutherford, M. J., Cacciola, J. S., Kabasakalian-McKay, R., and Alterman, A. I. (1996). Gender differences in the relapse experiences of cocaine patients. *Journal of Nervous and Mental Disease,* 184, no. 10: 616–622.

McLean, J. (2003). Men as minority: Men employed in statutory social care work. *Journal of Social Work,* 3, no. 1: 45–69.

Mechanic, D. (1969). *Mental health and social policy.* Engelwood Cliffs, N.J.: Prentice-Hall.

Meichenbaum, D. C. (1977). *Cognitive behavioral modification.* New York: Plenum.

———. (1985). *Stress-inoculation training.* New York: Pergamon.

Men Against Sexual Violence (2008). *Men against sexual violence.* http://www .menagainstsexualviolence.org/.

Mezey, G., and King, M. (1987). Male victims of sexual assault. *Medicine, Science and the Law* 27, no. 2: 122–124.

Michaelis, D. (1983). *The best of friends: Profiles in extraordinary friendships.* New York: William Morrow.

Miklowitz, (2008). *Bipolar disorder: A family-focused treatment approach.* (2nd ed.) New York: Guilford Press.

Miller, L. (1995). Tough guys: Psychotherapeutic strategies with law enforcement and emergency services personnel. *Psychotherapy*, 32, no. 4: 592–600.

Miller, P. H. (1993). *Theories of developmental psychology*. (3rd ed.) New York: W. H. Freeman.

Minuchin, S., and Fishman, H. C. (2004). *Family therapy techniques*. Cambridge: Harvard University Press.

Mirowsky, J., and Ross, C. E. (1989). *Social causes of psychological distress*. New York: Aldine de Gruyter.

Missouri State Highway Patrol (2000). Gangs fact sheet. Jefferson City, Mo. http://www.mshp.dps.missouri.gov/MSHPWeb/Publications/Brochures/SHP-543.pdf.

Moberg, M. (1997). *Myths of ethnicity and national: Immigration, work and identity in the Belize banana industry*. Knoxville: University of Tennessee Press.

Moeller, F. G., and Dougherty, D. M. (2001). Antisocial personality disorder, alcohol, and aggression. *Alcohol Research and Health*, 25, no. 1: 5–11.

Mohr, D.C., Likosky, W. Bertagnolli, A., Goodkin, D. E., Wende, J. V. D., Dwyer, P., and Dick, L. (2000). Telephone-administered cognitive-behavioral therapy for the treatment of depressive symptoms in multiple sclerosis. *Journal of Consulting and Clinical Psychology*, 68, no. 2: 356–361.

Momper, S. L., and Jackson, A. P. (2007). Maternal gambling, parenting, and child behavioral functioning in Native American families. *Social Work Research*, 31, no. 4: 209.

Monson, C. M., Schnurr, P. P., Resick, P. A., Friedman, M. J., Young-Xu, Y., and Stevens, S. P. (2006). Cognitive processing therapy for veterans with military-related Posttraumatic stress disorder. *Journal of Consulting and Clinical Psychology*, 74, no. 5: 989–907.

Montorsi, F., Briganti, A., Salonia, F., Deho, G., Zanni, A., Cestari, G., Guazzoni, P., Rigatti, P., and Stief, C. (2003). The aging male and erectile dysfunction. *BJU International*, 92, no. 5: 516–520.

Mooney, T. F. (1998). Cognitive behavior therapy for men. In W. S. Pollack and R. F. Levant (eds.), *New psychotherapy for men*, 57–82. New York: Wiley.

Moore, R., and Gillette, D. (1990). *King, warrior, magician, lover: Rediscovering the archetypes of the mature masculine*. New York: HarperCollins.

Moos, R. H., Nichol, A. C., and Moos, B. S. (2002). Global assessment of functioning ratings and the allocation and outcomes of mental health services. *Psychiatric Services*, 53: 730–737.

Morgan, A. 2000. What is narrative therapy? An easy to read introduction. Dulwich Centre, http://www.dulwichcentre.com.au/alicearticle.html.

Moscicki, E. K. (2001). Epidemiology of completed and attempted suicide: Toward a framework for prevention. *Clinical Neuroscience Research*, 1, no. 3: 210–223.

Mukamal, K. L., Chiuve, S. E., and Rimm, E. B. (2006). Alcohol consumptions and risk for coronary heart disease in men with healthy lifestyles. *Archives of Internal Medicine*, 166, no. 19: 2145–1250.

Mullan, H. (1992). Existential therapists and their group therapy practices. *International Journal of Group Psychotherapy*, 42, no. 4: 453–458.

Munch, R. (2004). Introduction to special issue: Globalization and labor flexibility: The Latin American case(s). *Latin American Perspectives*, 31, no. 4: 3–20.

Naiman, L. (1998). Creativity and meaning of work. *Perspectives on Business and Global Change*. http://www.creativityatwork.com/articlesContent/meaning.htm.

Nangeroni, N., and Mackenzie, G. O. (2002). [Gender Talk, Web Radio.] Interview with Harry Brod. August 5. Gender Education and Media. http://www.archive.org/details/gt371

National Association of Social Workers. (1999). *Code of ethics.* Washington, D.C.: NASW.

———. (2004). *NASW standards for palliative and end of life care.* Washington, D.C.: NASW.

National Center for Posttraumatic Stress Disorder (2006). A guide for families of military members. http://www.ncptsd.va.gov/ncmain/ncdocs/manuals/GuideforFamilies.pdf.

National Center for Post-Traumatic Stress Disorder and Walter Reed Army Medical Center. (2004). *Iraq war clinician guide.* (2nd ed.) Washington, D.C.: Department of Veterans Affairs.

National Center for Victims of Crime (2008). Male rape. http://www.ncvc.org/ncvc/main.aspx?dbName=DocumentViewer&DocumentID=32361.

National Heart, Lung, and Blood Institute. 2008. What is coronary artery disease? *Diseases and Conditions Index.* http://www.nhlbi.nih.gov/health/dci/Diseases/Cad/CAD_WhatIs.html.

National Institute of Mental Health. (2003). Real men/real depression. NIH Publication No. 03-5300. http://www.nimh.nih.gov/health/publications/real-men-real-depression.pdf.

———. (2005). Men and depression. NIH Publication no. 05-4972. Bethesda, Md.: NIMH.

———. (2007a). Anxiety disorders. NIH Publication no. 06-3879. Bethesda, Md.:: Department of Health and Human Services.

———. (2007b). Schizophrenia. http://www.nimh.nih.gov/healthinformation/schizophreniamenu.cfm.

National Institute of Mental Health Genetics Workgroup. (1998). *Genetics and mental disorders.* NIH Publication no. 98-4268. Rockville, Md.: NIMH.

National Institute of Neurological Disorders and Stroke. (2007). NINDS Alzheimer's disorder information page. http://www.ninds.nih.gov/disorders/alzheimersdisease/alzheimersdisease.htm.

National Institute on Aging. (2007). General information. http://www.nia.nih.gov/Alzheimers/AlzheimersInformation/GeneralInfo/.

National Library of Medicine. (2009). Many veterans need mental health care. http://www.nlm.nih.gov/medlineplus/news/fullstory_86993.html

National Organization for Men Against Sexism (2007). Statement of principles. http://www.nomas.org/principles.

Nelson, L. A., Rhoades, D. A., Noonan, C., Manson, S. M., and the AI-SUPERPFP Team. (2007). Traumatic brain injury and mental health among American Indian populations. *Journal of Head Trauma Rehabilitation*, 22, no. 2: 105–112.

Nghe, L. T., Mahalik, J. R., and Lowe, S. M (2003). Influences on Vietnamese men: Examining traditional gender roles, the refugee experience, acculturation, and racism in the United States. *Journal of Multicultural Counseling*, 31, no. 4: 245–261.

Nichols, M., and Schwartz, R. (1995). *Family therapy.* (3rd ed.) Boston: Allyn and Bacon.

Norman, E. (2000). Introduction: The strength perspective and resiliency enhancement—A natural partnership. In E. Norman (ed.), *Resiliency enhancement: Putting the strengths perspective into social work practice*, 1–18. New York: Columbia University Press.

Nunn, L. M. (2005). Measuring up as men: Hegemonic masculinity's foothold in school structures. Paper presented at the annual meeting of the American Sociological Association, Philadelphia.http://www.allacademic.com/meta/p19012_index.html.

Nylund, D., and Nylund, D. A. (2003). Narrative therapy as a counter-hegemonic practice. *Men and Masculinities*, 5, no. 4: 386–394.

O'Connell, R. (1989). *Of arms and men: A history of war, weapons and aggression.* New York: Oxford University Press.

Oei, T. P. S., and Jackson, P. R. (1982). Social skills and cognitive behavioral approaches to the treatment of problem thinking. *Journal of Studies on Alcohol*, 43, no. 4: 532–547.

Office of Community-oriented Policing Services. U,.S. Department of Justice. (2008). Gangs. *Community Policing Topics.* http://www.cops.usdoj.gov/Default.asp?Item=1593.

Office of the Attorney General. State of California. (1999). *Report on arrest for domestic violence in California, 1998.* Crime Justice Statistics Report. Sacramento.

Oliffe, J. (2005). Constructions of masculinity following prostatectomy-induced impotence. *Social Science and Medicine*, 60, no. 10: 2249–2259.

Olivardia, R. (2001). Mirror, mirror on the wall, who's the largest of them all? The features and phenomenology of muscle dysmorphia. *Harvard Review of Psychiatry*, 9, no. 4: 254–259.

Ollman, B. (1971). *Alienation.* New York: Cambridge University Press.

Ontario Ministry of Health and Long Term Care. 2005. *Intensive case management service standards for mental health services and supports*. Ontario: Ontario Ministry of Health and Long Term Care.

Osheron, S. (1992). *Wrestling with love: How men struggle with intimacy with women, children, parents and each other*. New York: Fawcett Columbine.

Padilla, A. M., Ruiz, R. A., and Alvarez, R. (1989). Community mental health services for the Spanish speaking/surname populations. In D. R. Atkinson, G. Morten, and D. W. Sue (eds.), *Counseling American minorities: A cross-cultural perspective*, 167–198. Dubuque, Ia.: Wm. C. Brown.

Palkovitz, R. (2002). *Improved fathering and men's development*. Mahwah, N.J.: Lawrence Erlbaum.

Park, D., and Schwarz, N. (eds.) (2000). *Cognitive aging: A primer*. Philadelphia: Psychology Press.

Parton, N. (2000). Some thoughts on the relationship between theory and practice in and for social work. *British Journal of Social Work*, 30, no. 3: 449–463.

Pausch, R. (2007). http://www.cs.cmu.edu/~pausch.

Payne, M. (1991). *Modern social work theory: A critical introduction*. Chicago: Lyceum.

———. (2000). *Narrative therapy: An introduction for counsellors*. London: Sage.

Payne, S. (2006). *The health of men and women*. Cambridge: Polity.

Peplau, L. A., and Fingerhunt, A. W. (2007). The close relationships of lesbians and gay men. *Annual Review of Psychology*, 58: 405–424.

Perlman, H. H. (1979). *Relationship: The heart of helping people*. Chicago: University of Chicago Press.

Phillips, D. (2006). Masculinity, male development, gender, and identity: Modern and post modern meanings. *Issues in Mental Health Nursing*, 27, no. 4: 403–423.

Pierre, M. R., Mahalik, J. R., and Woodland, M. H. (2002) .The effects of racism, African self-consciousness and psychological functioning on Black masculinity: A historical and social adaptation framework. *Journal of African American Men*, 6, no. 2: 19–40.

Pine Street Inn (2008). Pine Street Inn: Helping people. http://www.pinestreetinn.org.

Pinquart, M., and Sorensen, S. (2005). Ethnic differences in stressors, resources, and psychological outcomes of family caregiving: A meta-analysis. *Gerontologist*, 45, no. 1: 90–106.

Piven, F. F., and Cloward, R. A. (1993). *Regulating the Poor*. New York: Vintage.

Pleck, J. H. (1981). *The myth of masculinity*. Cambridge: MIT Press.

Pleck, J. H., Lamb, M. E., and Levine, J. A. (1986). Epilog: Facilitating future change in men's family roles. *Marriage and Family Review*, 9, no. 3/4: 11–16.

Poa, E. (2006). Trapped in transition: The complex young adult patient. *Bulletin of the Menninger Clinic*, 70, no. 1: 29–52.

Pollack, W. S., and Levant, R. F. (1998). Introduction: Treating men in the 21st century. In W. S. Pollack and R. F. Levant (eds.), *New psychotherapy for men*, 1–10. New York: Wiley.

Pope, H. G., Jr., Olivardia, R., Gruber, A., and Borowiecki, J. (1999). Evolving ideals of male body image as seen through action toys. *International Journal of Eating Disorders*, 26, no. 1: 65–72.

Popple, P. R., and Leighninger, L. (2004). *Social work, social welfare, and American society.* Boston: Allyn and Bacon.

Postman, N. (1992). Technopoly: The surrender of culture to technology. New York: Random House.

Potts, A. (2000). The essence of the hard-on. Hegemonic masculinity and the cultural construction of erectile dysfunction. *Men and Masculinities*, 3, no. 1: 85–103.

Powell, J. L., and Owen, T. (2007). Theorizing masculinity in modernity. *Sincronia* (Summer). http://sincronia.cucsh.udg.mx/powell07.htm.

Prigoff, A. (2000). *Economics for social workers: Social outcomes of economic globalization with strategies for community action.* Belmont, Calif.: Brooks/Cole.

Pringle, K. (1995). *Men, masculinities, and social welfare.* London: University College Press.

Pucci, A. R. (2005). Evidence-based counseling and psychotherapy. National Association of Cognitive-Behavioral Therapists Online Headquarters. http://www.nacbt .org/evidenced-based-therapy.htm.

RAINN (2007). Rape, Abuse, and Incest National Network. http://www.rainn.org/.

Rank, O. (1945). *Will therapy and truth and reality.* New York: Knopf.

Rapp, C., and Goscha, R. J. (eds.) (2006). *The strengths model: Case management with people with psychiatric disabilities.* (2nd ed.) New York: Oxford University Press.

Rapp, C.A., and Wintersteen, R. (1989). The strengths model of case management: Results from twelve demonstrations. *Psychosocial Rehabilitation Journal*, 13, no. 1: 23–32.

Rasheed, J. M., and Rasheed, M. N. (1999). *Social work practice with African American men.* Thousand Oaks, Calif.: Sage.

Real, T. (1998). *I don't want to talk about it: Overcoming the secret legacy of male depression.* New York: Simon and Schuster.

Redina, I., and Dickerschied, J. D. (1976). Father involvement with first-born infants. *Family Coordinator*, 25, no. 2: 373–379.

Reis, H. T., and Gable, S. L. (2003). Toward a positive psychology of relationships. In C. L. Keys and J. Haidt (eds.), *Flourishing: The positive person and the good life*, 129–159). Washington, D.C.: American Psychological Association.

Richert, A. J. (2002).The self in narrative therapy: Thoughts from a humanistic/existential perspective. *Journal of Psychotherapy Integration*, 12, no. 1: 77–104.

Rifkin, J. (1994). *The end of work: The decline of the global labor force and the dawn of the post-market era.* New York : G. P. Putnam's Sons.

Robertson, J., and Fitzgerald, L. F. (1992). Overcoming the masculine mystique: Preferences for alternative forms of assistance among men who avoid counseling. *Journal of Counseling Psychology*, 39, no. 2: 240–246.

Rochlen, A. B., McKelley, R. A., and Pituch, K. A. (2006). A preliminary examination of the "Real Men. Real Depression" Campaign. *Psychology of Men and Masculinity*, 1, no. 1: 1–13.

Roff, M. (1963). Childhood social interactions and young adulthood psychosis. *Journal of Clinical Psychology*, 19: 152–157.

Rogers, C. R. (1961). *On becoming a person.* Boston: Houghton Mifflin.

Roman, P. M. and Blum. 1997. *National treatment center study summary report: Public Treatment Centers.* Athens: Institute for Behavior Research, University of Georgia.

Rosenheck, R., Frisman, L., and Sindelar, J. (1995). Disability compensation and work among veterans with psychiatric and non-psychiatric impairments. *Psychiatric Services*, 46, no. 4: 359–365.

Roter, D. L., and Hall, J. A. (1997). *Doctors talking with patients/patients talking with doctors: Improving communication in medical visits.* Westport, Conn.: Auburn House.

Roth, A., and Fonagy, P. (1996). Alcohol dependency and abuse. In A. Roth and P. Fonagy (eds.), *What words for whom? A crucial review of psychotherapy research*, 216–233. New York: Guilford.

Rowan, J. (1997). Healing the male psyche: Therapy as initiation. London: Routledge.

Rowland, R. (1996). *Politics of intimacy. Heterosexuality, love and power.* Melbourne. Spinifex Press.

Rudolph, J. M., Stamm B .H., and Stamm, H. E. (1997). Compassion fatigue A concern for mental health policy, providers, and administration. Poster at the 13th Annual Meeting of the International Society for Traumatic Stress Studies, Montreal.

Russell, D.E.H., and Bolen, R. M. (2000). *The epidemic of rape and child sexual abuse in the United States.* Thousand Oaks, Calif.: Sage.

Safran, J. D., and Greenberg, L. S. (1991). *Emotion, psychotherapy and change.* New York: Guilford.

Saleebey, D. (1994). Culture, theory, and narrative: The intersection of meanings in practice. *Social Work*, 9, no. 4: 352–359.

Saleebey, D. (2002). *The strengths perspective in social work.* Boston: Allyn and Bacon

Sandage, S. T., and Hill, P. C. (2001). The virtue of positive psychology: The rapprochement and challenge of an affirmative postmodern perspective. *Journal of the Theory of Social Behavior*, 31, no. 3: 241–260.

Sartre, J. P. (1965). *Essays in existentialism.* Secaucus, N.J.: Carol Publishing Group.

Scarce, M. (1997). *Male on male rape: The hidden toll of stigma and shame.* New York: Plenum.

Schachter-Shalomi, Z., and Miller, R. (2001). Elderhood and spirituality: Reflections and discussion guide from age-ing to sage-ing. Religious Education Action Clearinghouse. http://archive.uua.org/re/reach/fall01/adult/elderhood_and_spirituality.html.

Schneider, B. (1990). *Organizational climate and culture.* San Francisco: Jossey-Bass.

Schore, J. R., and Schore, A. N. (2008). Modern attachment theory: The central role of affect regulation in development and treatment. *Clinical Social Work Journal,* 36, no. 1: 9–20.

Schriver, J. M. (2001). *Human behavior and the social environment: Shifting paradigms in essential knowledge for social work practice.* (3rd. ed.) Needham Heights, Mass.: Allyn and Bacon.

Schrock, D. P., and Padavic, I. (2007). Negotiating hegemonic masculinity in a batter intervention program. *Gender and Society,* 21, no. 5: 625–649.

Seidler, V. J. (1989). *Rediscovering masculinity: Reason, language and sexuality.* London: Routledge.

———. (1997). *Man enough: Embodying masculinities.* London: Sage.

Seidman, S. (ed.). (1996). *Queer theory/sociology.* Cambridge, Mass.: Blackwell.

Seidman, Stuart N., Roose, S. P., Menza, M. A., Shabsigh, R., and Rosen, R. C. (2001). Treatment of erectile dysfunction in men with depressive symptoms. *American Journal of Psychiatry,* 158, no. 4: 1623–1630.

Shay, J. J., and Maltas, C. P. (1998). Reluctant men in couple therapy: Corralling the Marlboro man. In W. S. Pollack and R. F. Levant (eds.), *New psychotherapy for men,* 97–126. New York: Wiley.

Shears, J. (2007). Understanding differences in fathering activities across race and ethnicity. *Early Childhood Research,* 5, no. 3: 245–261.

Shears, J., Furman, R., and Negi, N. J. (2008). The perception of Mexican-American men as fathers. *Advances in Social Work,* 8, no. 2: 228–352.

Shears, J., and Robinson, J. (2005). Fathering attitudes and practices: Influences on children's development. *Child Care in Practice,* 11: 63–79.

Shears, J., Summers J., Boller, K., and Barclay-McLaughlin, G. (2006). Exploring fathering roles in low-income families: The influence of intergenerational transmission. *Families in Society,* 87, no. 2: 259–268.

Sheehy, G. (1999). *Understanding men's passages: Discovering the new map of men's lives.* New York: Ballantine.

Shye, D., Mullooly, J. P., Freeborn, D. K., and Pope, C. R. (1995). Gender differences in the relationship between social network support and mortality: A longitudinal study of an elderly cohort. *Social Science and Medicine*, 41, no. 7: 935–947.

Silverberg, R. A. (1986). *Psychotherapy for men: Transcending the masculine mystique.* Springfield, Ill.: C. Thomas.

Simon, G. B. (2002). *The Harvard Medical School guide to men's health.* New York: Free Press.

Singha, R., and House, M. (1998). Nationalism, colonialism and the politics of masculinity. *Studies in History*, 14, no. 1.

Sinsheimer, R. (1969). The existential casework relationship. *Social Casework*, 50, no. 2: 67–73.

The Slanted Screen. (2006). Directed by J. Adachi. San Francisco: Center for Asian American Media.

Snarey, J. (1993). *How fathers care for the next generation: A four-decade study.* Cambridge: Harvard University Press.

Snyder, C. R., and Lopez, S. J. (2002). *Handbook of positive psychology.* Oxford: Oxford University Press.

Social Security Administration. (2008). What is the maximum Social Security retirement benefit? Find an answer to your question. http://ssa-custhelp.ssa.gov.

Solomon, S. E., Rothblum, E. E., and Balsam, K. F. (2004). Pioneers in partnership: Lesbian and gay male couples in civil unions compared with those not in civil unions and married heterosexual siblings. *Journal of Family Psychology*, 18, no. 2: 275–286.

Sommers, C. H. (2000). *The war against boys: How misguided feminism is harming our young men.* New York: Simon and Schuster.

Spanier, D. (1994). *Inside the gambler's mind.* Reno: University of Nevada Press.

Spearing, M. (2007). *Bipolar disorder.* (NIH publication number: NIH 5124). Bethesda, Md: National Institute of Mental Heath, U.S. Department of Health and Human Services.

Spector, A. Z. (2006). Fatherhood and depression: A review of risks, effects, and clinical application. *Issues in Mental Health Nursing*, 27, no. 8: 175–186.

Speedy, J. (2005). Failing to come to terms with things: A multi-storied conversation about poststructuralist ideas and narrative practices in response to some of life's failures. *Counselling and Psychotherapy Research*, 5, no. 1: 65–73.

Spitzer, R. L. (1981). The diagnostic status of homosexuality in DSM-III: A reformulation of the issues. *American Journal of Psychiatry*, 138: 210–215.

Spitzer, R. L., Yanovski, S., Wadden, T., Wing, R., Marcus, M. D., Stunkard, A., Devlin, M., Mitchell, J., Hasin, D., and Horne, R. L. (1993). Bing eating disorder: Its future validation in a multisite study. *International Journal of Eating Disorders*, 13, no. 2: 137–153.

Staudinger, U. M. (2001). Life reflection: A social-cognitive analysis of life review. *Review of General Psychology*, 5, no. 2: 148–160.

Steadman, H. J., Davidson, S., and Brown, C. (2001). Mental health courts: Their promise and unanswered questions. *Psychiatric Services*, 52, no. 4: 457–458.

Stephens, C., and Ahern, M. (2001). *Worker and community health impact related to mining relations internationally: A rapid review of the literature*. London: World Business Council for Sustainable Development.

Stinnett, N., and DeFrain, J. (1985). *Secrets of strong families*. Boston: Little Brown.

Stoesz, D., Guzzetta, C., and Lusk, M. (1999). *International development*. Boston: Allyn and Bacon.

Storey, A. E., Walsh, C. J., Quinton, R. L., and Wynne-Edwards, R. E. (2000). Hormonal correlates of paternal responsiveness in new and expectant fathers. *Evolution and Human Behavior*, 21: 79–95.

Straus, M. A. (2005). Women's violence towards men is a serious social problem. In D. R. Loseke, R. J. Gelles and M. M. Cavanaugh, eds., *Current controversies on family violence*, 55–78. Thousand Oaks, Calif.: Sage.

Straus, M. A., and Gelles, R. J. (1986). Societal change and change in family violence from 1975 to 1985 as revealed by two national surveys. *Journal of Marriage and Family*, 45, no. 3: 465–479.

Striker, G., and Hillman, J. L. (1996). Attitudes toward older adults: The perceived value of grandparents as a social role. *Journal of Adult Development*, 3, no. 2: 71–79.

Strumpfer, D. J. W. (2006). The strengths perspective: Fortigenesis in adult life. *Social Indicators Research*, 77, no. 1: 11–36.

Struttman, T. W, and Marsh, S. M. (2004). Work-related pilot fatalities in agriculture. United States, 1992–2001. *Morbidity and Mortality Weekly Report* (April 23): 12–16.

Swaine, R. L., and Baird, V. (1977). An existentially based approach to teaching social work. *Journal of Education for Social Work*, 13, no. 3: 99–106.

Tadaka, E., and Kanagawa, K. (2007). Effects of reminiscence group in elderly people with Alzheimer disease and vascular dementia in a community setting. *Geriatrics and Gerontology International*, 7, no. 2: 167–173.

Taft, C. T., Pless, A. P., Stalans, L. J., Koenen, K. C., King, L. A., and King, D. W. (2005). Risk factors for partner violence among a national sample of combat veterans. *Journal of Consulting and Clinical Psychology*, 73, no. 1: 151–159.

Tanielian, T., and Jaycox, L. (2008). *Invisible wounds of war*. Santa Monica, Calif.: Rand Corporation.

Tate, J. (1967). *The lost pilot*. New Haven: Yale University Press.

Taylor, B. A., and Behnke, A. (2005). Fathering across the border: Latino fathers in Mexico and the U.S. *Fathering: A Journal of Theory, Research, & Practice about Men as Fathers*, 3, no. 2: 99–120.

Telford, L. (1996). Selves in bunkers. In C. Cheng (ed.), *Masculinities in organizations*,73–95. London: Sage.

Thompson, K. (1982). What men really want: A New Age interview with Robert Bly. *New Age* (May): 30–37, 50–51.

Timberlake, E. M., Farber, M. Z., and Sabatino, C. A. (2002). *The generalist method of social work practice*. Boston: Allyn and Bacon.

Titmuss, R. M. (1959). *Essays on "The welfare state."* New Haven: Yale University Press.

Tjaden, P. and N. Thoennes. (1998). Prevalence, incidence, and consequences of violence against women: Findings from the National Violence Against Women Survey. *Research in Brief.* Washington, D.C.: Office of Justice Programs, National Institute of Justice. http://www.ncjrs.gov/pdffiles/172837.pdf.

———. (2000). Extent, nature, and consequences of intimate partner violence: Findings from the National Violence Against Women Survey. Publication NCJ 181867. Washington, D.C.: Office of Justice Programs, National Institute of Justice. http://www.ncjrs.gov/pdffiles1/nij/181867.pdf.

Tolman, R. M., and Bennett, L. W. (1990). A review of quantitative research on men who batter. *Journal of Interpersonal Violence*, 5, no. 1: 87–118.

Torgersen, S., Kringlen, E., Cramer, V. (2001). The prevalence of personality disorders in a community sample. *Archives of General Psychiatry,* 58, no. 6: 590–596.

Tower, P., Birchwood, M., Meaden, A., Byrne, S., and Ross, K. (2004). Cognitive therapy for command hallucinations: Randomized control trial. *British Journal of Psychiatry*, 184: 312–320.

Trotten, M. (2000). *Guys, grants and girlfriend abuse.* Ontario: Broadview Press.

Trujillo, J. (2004). An existential phenomenology of crack cocaine. *Janus Head*, 7, no. 1: 167–181.

Tubman, J. G., Montgomery, M. J., and Wagner, E. F. (2001). Letter writing as a tool to increase client motivation to change: Application to an inpatient crisis unit. *Journal of Mental Health Counseling*, 23, no. 4: 295–311.

Turnbull, J. E. (1991). Depression. In A. Gitterman (ed.), *Handbook of social work practice with vulnerable populations*, 165–204. New York: Columbia University Press.

Turner, F. J. (1986). *Social work treatment.* New York: Free Press.

———. (2005). *Social work diagnosis in contemporary practice.* New York: Oxford University Press.

Uggen, C., and Blackstone, A. (2004). Sexual harassment as a gendered expression of power. *American Sociological Review*, 69, no. 1: 64–92.

United Nations Conference on Trade and Development. (2002). *World investment report*. New York: United Nations.

United States Army Medical Department. (2007). Combat stress control. http://www.armymedicine.army.mil/about/tl/factscombatstresscontrol.html.

U.S. Census Bureau. (2006). *Hispanic Heritage Month 2005: September 15–October 15*. http://www.census.gov/Press Release/www/releases/archives/facts_for_features_special_editions/005338.html.

United States Department of Health and Human Services. (2006a). Healthy people 2010: An overview. http://www.healthypeople.gov.

———. (2006b). Men's health: Violence prevention. http://*Womenshealth.gov*.www.4woman.gov/mens/violence/.

United States Department of Justice. (2003). 2002 National crime victimization statistics. http://www.ojp.usdoj.gov/abstract/cvus/index.htm.

United States Department of Veterans Affairs. (2002). *A guide to Gulf War veterans' health*. Washington, D.C.: U.S. Department of Veterans Affairs.

———. (2003a). Gulf War veterans' illnesses: Questions and answers. Washington, D.C.: U.S. Department of Veterans Affairs.

———. (2003b). Agent Orange: Information for veterans who served in Vietnam. Washington, D.C.: Environmental Agents Service, Department of Veterans Affairs.

———. (2006). Miami VA Healthcare System. http://www1.va.gov/visn8/miami/clinical/socialwork.asp.

———. (2007a). History VA social work. http://www.socialwork.va.gov/about.asp.

———. (2007b). Social work in the Department of Veterans Affairs. http://www.socialwork.va.gov/about.asp

———. (2008). Miami VA health care system: Social work. http://www.miami.va.gov/services/socialwork.asp

———. (n.d.) War-zone related stress reactions: What families need to know. Factsheet. National Center for Posttraumatic Stress Disorder. http://www.ncptsd.va.gov/ncmain/ncdocs/fact_shts/war_families.html?opm=1&rr=rr125&srt=d&echorr=true.

Updegrave, W. (2006). Why men don't know jack about retirement. *CNNMoney.com*, June 26. http://money.cnn.com/magazines/moneymag/moneymag_archive/2006/07/01/8380769/index.htm.

Valliant, G. E., DiRago, A. C., and Mukamal, K. (2006). National history of male psychological health, 15: Retirement satisfaction. *American Journal of Psychiatry*, 163, no. 4: 682–688.

Van Deurzen-Smith, E. (1997). *Everyday mysteries: Existential dimensions of psychology*. London: Routledge.

Van Ness, D. W., and Strong, K. H. (2006). *Restoring justice: An introduction to restorative justice* (3rd ed.) Cincinnati: Anderson.

Van Soest, D. (1997). *The global crisis of violence: Common problems, universal causes, shared solutions.* Washington, D.C.: NASW Press.

Vig, E. K., and Pearlman, R. A. (2003). Quality of life while dying: A qualitative study of terminally ill older men. *Journal of the American Geriatrics Society*, 51, no. 1: 1595–1601.

Walby, S. (1997). *Gender transformations.* London: Routledge.

Walen, S. R., DiGiuseppe, R., and Dryden, W. (1992). *A practitioner's guide to Rational-Emotive Therapy.* (2nd ed.) New York: Oxford University Press.

Warren, J. (ed.). (1992). *Homophobia: How we all pay the price.* Boston: Beacon.

Weaver, H. N. (1999). Indigenous people and the social work profession: Defining culturally competent services. *Social Work*, 44, no. 3: 217–225.

Weick, A., Rapp, C. A., Sullivan, W. P., and Kishardt, W. E. (1989). A strengths perspective for social work practice. *Social Work*, 89: 350–454.

Weiss, D. (1975). *Existential human relations.* Montreal: Dawson College Press.

Werner, E. E. (1990). High risk children in young adulthood: A longitudinal study from birth to 32 years. *American Journal of Orthopsychiatry*, 59, no. 1: 72–81.

Werner, H. D. (1982). *Cognitive therapy: A humanistic approach.* New York: Free Press.

———. (1986). Cognitive therapy. In F. Turner (ed.), *Social work treatment: Interlocking theoretical approaches*, 91–130 (3rd. ed.) New York: Free Press.

Wetherell, M., and Edley, N. (1999). Negotiating hegemonic masculinity: Positions and psycho-discursive practices. *Feminism and Psychology*, 9, no. 3: 335–356.

White, M. (1997). *Narratives of therapists' lives.* Adelaide, Australia: DCP.

———. (2002). Addressing personal failure. *International Journal of Narrative Therapy and Community Work*, 3, no. 1: 33–77.

White, M., and Epston, D. (1990). *Narrative means to therapeutic ends.* New York: Norton.

Willett, W.C. (2005). *Eat, drink, and be healthy: The Harvard Medical School guide to healthy eating.* New York: Free Press.

Williams, D. M., Raynor, H. A., and Ciccolo, J. T. (2008) *American Journal of Lifestyle Medicine*, 2, no. 3: 250–259.

Williams, L. F. (1988). Frameworks for introducing racial and ethnic minority content into the curriculum. In C. Jacobs and D. D. Bowles (eds.), *Ethnicity & Race: Critical concepts in social work.* Washington, D.C.: National Association of Social Workers.

Williamson, O. (2000). Our elders speak: A word of welcome. *Wellbriety*, 1, no. 1: 12.

Willis, K. (2005). Latin American urban masculinities. In B. van Hoven and K. Horschelmann (eds.), *Spaces of masculinities*, 97–108. New York: Routledge.

Willis, R. J. (1994). *Transcendence in relationship: Existentialism and psychotherapy.* Norwood, N.J.: Ablex.

Wills, F., and Saunders. D. (2003). *Cognitive therapy: Transforming the image.* Thousand Oaks, Calif.: Sage.

Winnett, R. A., and Neale, M. (1980). Results of an experimental study on flextime and family life. *Monthly Labor Review*, 103, no. 11: 29–32.

Wise, R. A. (1996). Neurobiology of addiction. *Current Opinion in Neurobiology*, 6, no. 2: 243–251.

Wolfe, J. (2000). Assessment and treatment of compulsive sex/love behavior. *Journal of Rational-Emotive and Cognitive Behavior Therapy*, 18, no. 4: 235–246.

Wolin, S., and Wolin, S. (1993). *The resilient self.* New York: Villard.

World Health Organization (2002). Gender and mental health. http://www.who.int/gender/other_health/en/genderMH.pdf.

World Health Organization (2007, May 2-3). Expert meeting on the primary prevention of intimate partner violence and sexual violence: Meeting report. Department of Violence and Injury Prevention and Disability and Department of Gender, Women and Health Geneva, Switzerland. http://www.who.int/violence_injury_prevention/violence/activities/who_ipv_sv_prevention_meeting_report.pdf.

Yalom, I. D. (1980). *Existential psychotherapy.* New York: Harper/Collins.

———. (1995). *The theory and practice of group psychotherapy.* (3rd. ed.) New York: Basic Books.

———. (2002). *The gift of therapy.* New York: HarperCollins.

Yamauchi, K., Ono, Y., Baba, K., and Ikegami, N. (2001). The actual process of rating the global assessment of functioning scale. *Comprehensive Psychiatry*, 42, no. 5: 403–409.

Zastrow, C., and Ashman-Kirst, K. (1997) *Understanding human behavior and the social environment.* Chicago: Nelson-Hall.

Zimmerman, T. S., Holm, K. E., Daniels, K. C., and Haddock, S. A. (2002). Barriers and bridges to intimacy and mutuality. *Contemporary Family Therapy*, 24, no. 2: 289–311.

Zinn, H. (2005). *A people's history of the United States: 1492–Present.* New York: Harper Collins.

Zuniga, M. E. (1992). Using metaphors in therapy: Dichos and Latino clients. *Social Work*, 37, no. 1: 55–60.

Zwerdling, D. (2007). Army dismissals for mental health, conduct rise. Transcript of radio broadcast, *All Things Considered*, November 15. http://www.armymedicine.army.mil/about/tl/factscombatstresscontrol.htm.

Index